KV-326-274

# Regional Actors in Multilateral Negotiations

# ECPR Press

The ECPR Press is published by the European Consortium for Political Research in partnership with Rowman & Littlefield International. It publishes original research from leading political scientists and the best among early career researchers in the discipline. Its scope extends to all fields of political science, international relations and political thought, without restriction in either approach or regional focus. It is also open to interdisciplinary work with a predominant political dimension.

## ECPR Press Editors

### Editors

**Peter Kennealy** is Deputy Director of the European University Institute library in Florence, Italy.

**Alexandra Segerberg** is Associate Professor at the University of Stockholm, Sweden.

### Associate Editors

**Ian O'Flynn** is Senior Lecturer in Political Theory at Newcastle University, UK.

**Laura Sudulich** is Senior Lecturer in Politics and International Relations at the University of Kent, UK. She is also affiliated to Cevipol (Centre d'Étude de la vie Politique) at the Université libre de Bruxelles.

# Regional Actors in Multilateral Negotiations

## Active and Successful?

Diana Panke, Anke Wiedemann
and Stefan Lang

ecpr PRESS

ROWMAN &
LITTLEFIELD
INTERNATIONAL

London • New York

Published by Rowman & Littlefield International Ltd
Unit A, Whitacre Mews, 26–34 Stannary Street, London SE11 4AB
www.rowmaninternational.com

Rowman & Littlefield International Ltd. is an affiliate of Rowman & Littlefield
4501 Forbes Boulevard, Suite 200, Lanham, Maryland 20706, USA
With additional offices in Boulder, New York, Toronto (Canada), and Plymouth (UK)
www.rowman.com

Selection and editorial matter © Diana Panke, Anke Wiedemann, and Stefan Lang 2018

Copyright in individual chapters is held by the respective chapter authors.

*All rights reserved*. No part of this book may be reproduced in any form or by any
electronic or mechanical means, including information storage and retrieval systems,
without written permission from the publisher, except by a reviewer who may quote
passages in a review.

**British Library Cataloguing-in-Publication Data Is Available**
A catalogue record for this book is available from the British Library

ISBN:    HB 978-1-7866-0669-3

**Library of Congress Cataloging-in-Publication Data Is Available**
ISBN 978-1-78660-669-3 (cloth : alk. paper)
ISBN 978-1-78660-670-9 (electronic)

∞™ The paper used in this publication meets the minimum requirements of American
National Standard for Information Sciences – Permanence of Paper for Printed Library
Materials, ANSI/NISO Z39.48–1992.

Printed in the United States of America

# Contents

# List of Tables and Figures

## TABLES

**FIGURES**

# Preface

The project leading to this book started with two observations. First, the number of regional organisations and regional groups, as well as the number of international organisations, increased tremendously over the past decades. Second, the policy areas covered by these institutions have been broadened considerably as well. This has created a situation in which states are members of regional as well as international organisations at the same time, and the policy issues dealt with in regional and international organisations often overlap as well. Despite this trend, we know little about whether these interlinkages matter and whether they have created a window of opportunity for regional actors in international negotiations. Even in instances in which regional organisations and groups have no formal access to international negotiations themselves, their member states can act on their behalf. How prevalent are regional positions in international negotiations and to which extent have the current international negotiations become regionalised? Are all states equally inclined to express regional, rather than national, positions in IO negotiations? Are some regional organisations and groups more vocal in international negotiations than others? Does the activity of regional organisations and regional groups change not only the dynamics but also the outcomes of international negotiations? How and under what conditions can regional actors leave an imprint on an international norm?

This book summarises the findings of our project 'Nested Games. Regional Organisations in International Organisations'. We are grateful to the German Research Council (PA 1257/3–1), which funded our research and has allowed us to provide insights to the previous questions. Apart from this financial support, our project would not have been possible without the support of numerous people. We are grateful to the interviewees, who devoted their time and shared their insights with us. We would also like to express our thanks to Ikram Ali, Elliott Bourgeault, Matthias Edelmann, Marina Ermes, Paulina Grimm, Alena Hahn, Laura Kemper, Thomas Krebs, Eva Link, Laura Maghetiu, Paul Meiners, Anna Lena Mohrmann, Laura Lepsy, Frederike Oschinsky, Stephanie Pollhammer, Leonardo Rey, Martin Scharf and Fedor Unterlöhner for helping with literature and document research, transcribing interviews, supporting the generation of the dataset, as well as formatting and proofreading this book. For the administration of the project and budgetary oversight, we would like to thank Sabine Rose, Jasmin Wegner and Simone Ahrens.

We have presented our work at various workshops and conferences and have benefited from the discussions. For constructive comments, criticisms and support, we would like to thank Spyros Blavoukos, Tanja Börzel, Dimitris Bourantonis, Russ Burgos, Nicolas Burmester, Tom Delreux, Edith Drieskens, Sarah Eckstein, Tina Freyburg, Julia Gray, Toni Haastrup, Yoram Haftel, Axel Heck, Ingo Henneberg, Michael Jankowski, Anja Jetschke, Elisabeth Johansson-Nogues, Robert Kissack, Pascal König, Katie Laatikainen, Tobias Lenz, Sebastian Mayer, Detlef Nolte, Andrea Ribeiro Hoffmann, Karen Smith, Sören Stapel, Anna Starkmann, Jonathan R. Strand, Jale Tosun, Britta Weiffen, Oliver Westerwinter and Jan Wouters.

Diana Panke, Stefan Lang and Anke Wiedemann
July 2017

# List of Abbreviations

| | |
|---|---|
| ACP | African, Caribbean and Pacific States |
| AFR | WHO African Region group |
| AFRICA | FAO African Regional group |
| ALBA | Bolivarian Alliance for the Peoples of Our America |
| AMR | WHO Region of the Americas |
| ASEAN | Association of Southeast Asian Nations |
| ATT | Arms Trade Treaty |
| AU | African Union |
| BAG | Buenos Aires Group |
| BIC | Bayesian Information Criterion |
| C4 | Cotton 4 |
| CACEEC | WIPO Caucasian Central Asian and Eastern European Countries |
| CANWFZ | Central Asian Nuclear Weapon Free Zone |
| CARICOM | Caribbean Community |
| CBD | Convention on Biological Diversity |
| CD | Conference on Disarmament |
| CEBS | Central European and Baltic States |
| CELAC | Community of Latin American and Caribbean States |
| CIS | Commonwealth of Independent States |
| CoP | Conference of the Parties |
| DIC | Deviance Information Criterion |
| DV | Dependent Variable |
| EAC | East African Community |
| ECOSOC | United Nations Economic and Social Council |
| ECOWAS | Economic Community of West African States |

| | |
|---|---|
| EFTA | European Free Trade Association |
| EMLG | Expanded Multilevel Governance |
| EMR | WHO Eastern Mediterranean Region group |
| ERG | FAO European Regional Group |
| EU | European Union |
| EUR | WHO European Region |
| FAO | Food and Agriculture Organization |
| FAO NEG | FAO Near Eastern Group |
| GCC | Gulf Cooperation Council |
| GDP | Gross Domestic Product |
| GRULAC | Latin America and Caribbean Group |
| HRC | Human Rights Council |
| IAEA | International Atomic Energy Agency |
| IBRD Africa 1 | IBRD African Group 1 |
| IBRD Africa 2 | IBRD African Group 2 |
| IBRD African Govs | IBRD African Governors |
| IBRD Arab Govs | IBRD Arab Governors |
| IBRD/IMF | International Bank for Reconstruction and Development/International Monetary Fund |
| ICC | Intra-Class Correlation |
| ICCAT | International Commission for the Conservation of Atlantic Tunas |
| ICN1 | First International Conference on Nutrition |
| ICN2 | Second International Conference on Nutrition |
| ICRW | International Convention for the Regulation of Whaling |
| IGAD | Intergovernmental Authority on Development |
| II | International Institution |
| ILO | International Labour Organisation |
| IOM | International Organization for Migration |
| IOWS | Indian Ocean Sanctuary |
| IR | International Relations |
| IRR | Incidence Rate Ratio |
| ITTO | International Tropical Timber Organization |
| IWC SAGC | IWC South American Group of Countries |
| IWC | International Whaling Commission |
| JWG | Joint Working Group |
| MCMC | Markov Chains Monte Carlo |
| MERCOSUR | Mercado Comun del Sur |
| MFA | Ministry of Foreign Affairs |
| MLG | Multilevel Governance |
| MMMC | Multiple Membership-Multiple Classification |

| NASCO | North Atlantic Salmon Conservation Organization |
|---|---|
| NB8 | Nordic-Baltic Eight |
| NC | Nordic Council |
| NEEA | FAO Near East Regional Group |
| NGO | Non-Governmental Organisation |
| NOAM | FAO North America Group |
| NPANs | National Plans of Action for Nutrition |
| OEWG | Open-Ended Working Group |
| OPCW | Organisation for the Prohibition of Chemical Weapons |
| P5 | Permanent 5 |
| PIF | Pacific Islands Forum |
| PrepCom | Preparatory Committee |
| PSIDS | Pacific Small Island Developing States |
| RIO-clause | Regional Integration Organisation-clause |
| RO | Regional Organisation |
| SAARC | South Asian Association for Regional Cooperation |
| SADC | Southern African Development Community |
| SALWS | Small Arms and Light Weapons |
| SAWS | South Atlantic Whale Sanctuary |
| SC | United Nations Security Council |
| SCO | Shanghai Cooperation Organisation |
| SEAR | WHO South-East Asia Region |
| SICA | Central American Integration System |
| SOWS | Southern Ocean Whale Sanctuary |
| SWP | FAO Southwest Pacific Group |
| UN | United Nations |
| UNAG | UN African Group |
| UNASPAG | UN Asian and Pacific Group |
| UNASUR | Union of South American Nations |
| UNCLOS | United Nations Convention of the Law of the Sea |
| UNCTAD | United Nations Conference on Trade and Development |
| UNEEG | UN Eastern European Group |
| UNEP | United Nations Environmental Programme |
| UNESCO | United Nations Educational, Scientific and Cultural Organisation |
| UNFCCC | United Nations Framework Convention on Climate Change |
| UNGA | United Nations General Assembly |
| UNGA C1 | United Nations General Assembly First Committee |
| UNGA C2 | United Nations General Assembly Second Committee |
| UNGA C3 | United Nations General Assembly Third Committee |
| UNGA C4 | United Nations General Assembly Fourth Committee |
| UNHCR | United Nations High Commissioner for Refugees |

| | |
|---|---|
| UNGRULAC | UN Group of Latin American Countries |
| UNWEOG | UN Western European and Others Group |
| USD | US Dollar |
| VPC | Variance Partitioning Coefficient |
| WGI | World Governance Indicators |
| WHO | World Health Organization |
| WHO AR | WHO African Region |
| WHO EMR | WHO Eastern Mediterranean Region |
| WHO SEAR | WHO South East Asian Region |
| WIPO | World Intellectual Property Organization |
| WPIEI | Council of the Working Party on International Environmental Issues |
| WPR | WHO Western Pacific Region group |
| WTO | World Trade Organization |
| WWII | World War II |
| ZPCAS | South Atlantic Zone of Peace and Cooperation |

# Chapter 1

# Introduction

Today, states cooperate in hundreds of international intergovernmental organisations and regimes (IOs) in a very wide range of policy areas (Union of International Associations 2005/2006: 2966). A similar observation is in order regarding regional organisations and groups (ROs): there are hardly any parts of the world left in which cooperation between states is not institutionalised on a regional basis. The policies covered in IOs and ROs increasingly overlap (e.g. Börzel 2012, Götz and Haggrén 2008). While regional integration mainly started off as cooperation in the economic realm, ROs became increasingly active beyond their borders in the past decades. In addition, there is a considerable overlap in the membership of states in regional organisations and groups as well as in IOs today. Accordingly, we observe that not only states but also ROs are becoming active in IOs (Panke 2013b). Prominent examples include the League of Arab States' (LAS) request vis-à-vis the Security Council to send a peacekeeping mission into Syria in spring 2012, the Association of South East Asian Nations' (ASEAN) role in pushing the membership of Laos in the World Trade Organization (WTO) in 2012 or the European Union's (EU) failed attempt to obtain full member representation rights in the United Nations General Assembly in 2010 and its achievement in attaining enhanced participation rights in 2011. Besides such anecdotal evidence, we do not know much about whether and to which extent regional actor activity has led to a regionalisation of both the dynamics of today's international negotiations and international negotiation outcomes. We also do not know which factors drive such a regionalisation and whether it takes place evenly across policy areas (e.g. economy and trade, environment, security) and IO negotiation arenas. Filling this gap in our knowledge is important, as a regionalisation of international negotiations implies that international negotiations are no longer purely state–state interactions since regional positions are voiced and that active ROs can leave regional imprints on international norms and rules. Both can have significant implications for the effectiveness and legitimacy of governance beyond the nation-state more generally. Moreover, a regionalisation of today's international negotiations suggests that modifications of states' classical foreign policy approaches are called for, as they need to take into consideration that ROs have turned into essential actors on the international scene.

Despite the timeliness and relevance of the issue and although there is much talk about the regionalisation of world politics and of international relations (e.g. Acharya 2007, Katzenstein 1996, Pentland 1975), as of yet there is no comprehensive comparative study available on the phenomenon of how and to which extent regional actors alter dynamics and outcomes of international negotiations. To shed light on this blind spot, the book addresses the following research questions:

- Are some ROs more active than others and, if so, how can observed patterns be explained?
- Can ROs exert influence over international norms although they are not usually full members of IOs, and, if so, under what conditions are regional actors successful?

In answering these questions, the book provides a systematic analysis of how strongly today's international negotiation dynamics and outcomes are regionalised. More precisely, it describes and explains differences between more than sixty ROs across a high number of IOs regarding regional actor activity (first dependent variable) and regional actor success in international negotiations (second dependent variable).

The book takes stock of today's regionalisation of international negotiations. It shows that ROs are indeed active in a broad variety of different international negotiations either directly through RO delegates or indirectly through member states that negotiate on behalf of their regional group. On average, regional positions are voiced in nearly 12 per cent of the negotiation contributions. Thus, today every twelfth time a position is articulated in a multilateral negotiation on the international level, it is not national but regional in character. Interestingly, some regional actors are more vocal in international negotiations than others, and some IOs are more conducive to RO activity than others. For example, members of the Gulf Cooperation Council (GCC), the Association of South East Asian Nations (ASEAN) or the Caribbean Community (CARICOM) voice regional positions about twice as often as members of Mercado Comun del Sur (MERCOSUR) or the African Union (AU). Likewise, IOs such as the International Labour Organisation (ILO), the United Nations Conference on Trade and Development

(UNCTAD) or the International Commission for the Conservation of Atlantic Tunas (ICCAT) are more prone to regional actor participation during negotiations than the United Nations Educational, Scientific and Cultural Organisation (UNESCO), the Conference on Disarmament (CD) or the International Whaling Commission (IWC), as the former feature a considerably higher share of regional positions voiced (average 20 per cent of all speeches made are regional in character) than the latter (average 2 per cent of regional negotiation contributions). Drawing on multilevel governance approaches and applying mixed methods, the book demonstrates that ROs are most active if group coordination works well and RO members are able and willing to act on behalf of their group. Moreover, IOs feature a stronger regionalisation of negotiations if they are large in size so that states bundle positions into groups rather than individual interests, and if the issues covered in the international negotiations are closely linked to core RO themes.

The book also casts light on the extent to which today's international negotiation outcomes are regionalised. Thus it examines how and under which conditions the activity of ROs in international negotiations can lead to success. It shows that some regional actors are more successful in influencing negotiation dynamics and outcomes than others, most notably CARICOM and the Economic Community of West African States (ECOWAS) in the negotiations on the Arms Trade Treaty (ATT) or the Buenos Aires Group (BAG) in the negotiations on a whale sanctuary in the South Atlantic within the IWC, while others, such as the ASEAN in the IWC negotiations or the GCC and the Organisation of American States (OAS) in the ATT case, are not very effective either in lobbying outside states to support a specific regional position or in directly shaping international norms according to their own regional preferences. Apart from differences in the rate of success between ROs, IOs also differ in the extent to which regional interests translate into changes in international norms. Most open to RO influence are the Food and Agriculture Organization (FAO) and the World Trade Organization (WTO), while the Security Council (SC) or the UNESCO is least open in this respect. The book uses a multilevel governance approach and applies mixed methods, showing that the observed variation in RO success is best explained by the issue saliency of the international negotiation theme for ROs, internal burden-sharing and their internal homogeneity as well as the variety and effectiveness of negotiation strategies being used.

Studying how ROs act in IOs is important not only because it impacts dynamics and outcomes of international negotiations, but also because the actions of ROs can bring about a regionalisation of international relations. First, RO participation changes the nature of international negotiations by turning the orientation from classical state–state interaction into interactions between regional actors in which often regional instead of national positions are voiced. Moreover, vocal regional actors reduce the number of different positions at the IO negotiation table, which can speed up and render international negotiations more effective. Second, the regionalisation of international negotiations also affects voting patterns as well as the content of international norms. Individual states lose shaping power, while actors speaking on behalf of a regional organisation, such as the AU or the GCC, or a regional group, such as the United Nations Group of Latin American Countries (GRULAC), gain leverage. Accordingly, in such constellations, international norms tend to reflect the interests of those regional actors that are well organised, able to develop common positions and act in concert in international arenas in which multilateral negotiations take place. Third, this regionalisation has implications for the legitimacy of international negotiation dynamics and outcomes. On the one hand, regional organisations de facto exert influence, although they usually lack formal voting rights. On the other hand, even the biggest states, such as the United States, China or Russia, could lose considerable influence on the international level if they act on their own and do not increase their leverage through joining and operating in regional groups or in approaching and negotiating with ROs they are not members of.

## 1.1 THE ARGUMENT AND MAJOR FINDINGS

Globalisation is by no means a new phenomenon, as cross-border interactions have brought about complex economic, societal and political interdependencies over centuries (Baylis et al. 2011, Keohane 1984, 1989). Yet in the past 100 years changes in transportation technologies and communication have created a new intensity of interactions and interdependencies across borders (Keohane 2001, Krasner 1991). Thus, it does not come as much of a surprise that not only the number of IOs, but also the number of ROs, has increased tremendously since the end of World War II (WWII) (e.g. Hooghe and Marks 2014). Today there are hardly any parts of the world in which cooperation between states is not institutionalised on a regional basis. While regional integration mainly started off as cooperation in the economic realm, the external policy component has become increasingly important in the past decades. Accordingly, the policies covered in IOs and ROs increasingly overlap. Simultaneously, states are often members of regional and international organisations. Thus, we observe that not only states but also regional actors are becoming active in international negotiations (Panke 2013b). Prominent examples include the EU in international environmental or trade negotiations. Despite the importance of the issue the literature overwhelmingly focuses on the EU, and no one has yet comparatively studied the role of today's more than sixty ROs in a broad variety of prominent IOs. To shed light on this blind spot, the book *Regional Actors in Multilateral Negotiations* studies the interplay between states, regional and international organisations. It provides a systematic analysis of how active and how influential ROs are in international negotiations. More precisely, it describes and explains differences between regional actors and across international negotiation arenas in regard to RO activity (DV1) and RO success (DV2).

The book examines the following research questions:

- Are some regional actors more vocal in international negotiations than others, and, if so, how can the observed variation be explained?
- The book also examines under which conditions RO activity translates into influence over international negotiation dynamics and outcomes and asks: Are some regional actors more successful than others in international negotiations, and, if so, why?

In answering these research questions, we fill gaps in several strands of state-of-the-art research on the external actorness of regional organisations, comparative regionalism and international cooperation (c.f. below).

In order to answer these questions, the book adopts an explanatory research design. It is theory-guided, methodologically stringent and empirical in character. Theoretically, it develops an extended multilevel governance approach and develops hypotheses on RO activity (DV1) and RO success (DV2). These hypotheses are empirically tested on the basis of mixed methods. In a first step, we use quantitative methods in order to explain variation in RO activity across institutional contexts and policy areas. In a second step, we adopt qualitative methods in order to account for varying success of ROs in influencing international negotiation outcomes.

### 1.1.1 Theory: Expanded multilevel governance systems

Multilevel governance approaches (MLG) analytically account for the dispersion of decision-making authority across multiple layers of government (Hooghe and Marks 2001). They capture how policies are formulated and implemented on the basis of cross-level coordination, which often takes place via negotiations between actors from different levels of a multilevel system (c.f. Benz 2007, Börzel 2010, Scharpf 1997b, Zürn 2012). Prominent examples of MLG systems are federal states or regional organisations such as the EU. The political systems traditionally studied using MLG approaches are two-tier systems, which are typically comprised of either the state and federal levels, or the state and regional levels. Apart from the two-level MLG systems, there are also three-level systems comprised of, for example, a state, a regional and an international level. Such systems constitute extended multilevel governance systems (EMLGs) if there is some sort of power delegation from the state or regional to the international level and if there is some sort of division of labour between the levels (Zürn 2012). In EMLG systems, three layers of governance are of importance, namely the state level, the regional level and the international level (c.f. chapter 2). The state level is crucial for the development and adjustment of national positions in relation to draft international norms that have been put on the IO's negotiation agenda (domestic position formation). Based on national positions, states that are also members of a regional organisation or regional group can engage in coordinating common regional positions (RO-level negotiations) or directly participate in IO negotiations, voicing national positions. In cases where member states of regional organisations or regional groups have developed a common regional position, they or the representative of a regional organisation or regional group can act on behalf of the RO in international negotiations (IO-level negotiations). This might increase the leverage of RO members and might translate into more influence over the content of international norms.

The three-level negotiation framework captures the process of position formation and adjustment between regional actor member states, which is central to RO activity in international negotiations and crucial for the prospects of regional actors to successfully changing international negotiation dynamics and outcomes.

Since not all regional groups and organisations have speaking rights in all IOs, RO activity is not confined to RO representatives voicing a regional position during multilateral negotiations on the international level. In instances where regional actors have no formal roles in IOs, the member states of regional groups and organisations can (and often do; see chapter 3) speak on behalf of their respective group and voice regional positions instead of national ones. Accordingly, the hypotheses related to the member state level capture how state capacities and incentives influence whether they effectively coordinate a common regional group position with the other RO members so that they can speak on behalf of their regional organisation or group in international negotiations and possibly also influence negotiation dynamics and outcomes.

Usually, MLG approaches assume that states as actors know their position before negotiating with other states (c.f. König et al. 2012, Moravcsik 1993). Yet, this is not automatically the case for ROs in international negotiations (Panke 2013c). In order to be active in IOs, it is essential that RO members have a coordinated joint regional position in the first place. Accordingly, on the regional level, a set of hypotheses focus on how an RO's institutional rules and capacities influence its members' chances of developing common regional positions in relation to the items on the IO agenda, which is a precondition for being active and successful in international negotiations.

Institutional rules regulate who has access to negotiation arenas and how the decision-making competencies are distributed. This is essential for both negotiation dynamics and outcomes (Grande 2000, König et al. 2010, Scharpf 1988, Tsebelis 2002, Tsebelis and Garrett 1997). Accordingly, on the level of IOs, the hypotheses explicate how the formal rules influence ROs' prospects of directly (delegates of regional organisations or regional groups) or indirectly (member states on behalf of their ROs) voicing regional positions in IO negotiations and how and under what conditions this affects the prospects for regional actor success.

## 1.1.2 Mapping and analysis of RO negotiation activity (DV1)

In a first empirical step, the book presents insights into the patterns of negotiation activity of states and ROs in a sample of 512 international negotiations, in a broad range of policy areas (e.g. economy and trade, labour and social policies, environment, security and disarmament, human rights). To get a balanced sample of international negotiations we covered a broad spectrum of policy areas and systematically vary IO membership size and IO openness to ROs (no formal status, formal observer status, formal voting rights). Thus, we ended up with a sample of twenty-seven international organisations. On this basis, we selected 4 negotiations per year and per IO in a time period beginning in 2008 and ending in 2012, covering a total of 512 negotiations (c.f. chapter 3, annex table A3.1). The database is comprehensive. It entails not only 203 states and state-like actors (e.g. Taiwan, Holy See), but also all of today's more than sixty regional organisations as well as all other regional groups and coalitions (e.g. the UN's African Group [UNAG] or the BAG) that were active in at least 1 of the 512 negotiations studied in the book. On average, every 11.94th position voiced in international negotiations is regional in character.

There is interesting variation in regional actor activity. For instance, regional positions are twelve times more frequently articulated in the ILO (23.88 per cent of all statements) than in the UNESCO (1.96 per cent). Moreover, not all ROs are equally active. The respective members voiced positions of their regional groups to different extents. For example, of all statements made by EU member states, 33.43 per cent were made on behalf of the EU, while GCC members spoke for their RO 26.38 per cent of the time and members of the UNAG spoke for 19.81 per cent of possible opportunities. Moreover, the inclination of states to speak on behalf of their regional group or organisation varies as well. Some states exclusively express national interests, such as Rwanda, the Fijis or Armenia, while others articulate regional positions much more frequently, such as Denmark (61.62 per cent), Uganda (56.48 per cent) or Zimbabwe (32.82 per cent). These patterns are puzzling, not in the least since all states benefit from leveraging up in international negotiations through referring to collective positions, yet the extent to which they do so varies considerably. The variation of RO activity between IOs is counterintuitive as well, as it is not the case that IOs in which ROs can obtain voting rights (e.g. WTO, ITTO or UNFCCC) feature systematically the strongest regionalisation of negotiations.

Which ROs are most active in multilateral negotiations and why? In which IOs do we observe the strongest RO activity and why? In order to account for the observed variation and comprehensively examine the EMLG hypotheses, the book combines multilevel regression analysis with narrative evidence from more than 240 semi-structured interviews with national diplomats and RO members. This reveals that the extent to which international negotiations are regionalised varies, which can be explained by a combination of member state-, regional- and international-level variables.

With respect to the national level, the book argues that national positions vis-à-vis a draft international rule or norm or draft rule on the IO agenda do not naturally exist, but need to be formulated in the domestic realm and subsequently passed on to the national diplomat responsible for negotiating in the IO. The more administrative capacities states possess, the swifter the development of national positions for a broad range of issues on the IO negotiation agenda and the more actively the national diplomats can participate in RO coordination meetings and IO negotiations. Vice versa, states with capacity shortages are less likely to actively participate in group coordination meetings and in international negotiations. The book also shows that the extent to which a state's political culture is democratic has a positive effect on the chances of RO members to compromise on regional positions during RO coordination meetings, which, in turn, is a prerequisite for ROs to become active on the IO level.

With respect to the regional level, the book shows that RO institutional rules, such as membership rules, matter. The number of RO member states can increase the activity level of regional actors in international negotiations. The larger a regional actor is, the greater the chances are that at least one of them articulates the regional position. Also, the broader the scope of policy competencies of an RO, the more often past RO policies can serve as focal points rendering regional coordination and the construction of a common negotiation position easier. This, in turn, increases the likelihood that regional positions are voiced in international negotiations. Another RO-level property that affects RO member states' chances of successfully developing a common regional position that can subsequently be voiced on the IO level is the level of capacity devoted to facilitating state–state coordination meetings at the location of IO negotiations. ROs with many offices at the locations of IO headquarters are better able to develop and update common positions among their member states, which increases the prospects of RO activity in international negotiations.

The international level also accounts for variation in the extent to which international negotiations are regionalised. The size of IOs has important implications for how negotiations are conducted in practice. With a large membership of fifty or even more member states, negotiations would be extremely time-consuming if each member state voiced its national position and participated actively during the course of deliberations in IO institutions. Instead of making a tour de table, states aggregate national positions in groups and voice national positions only if they deviate or are incompatible with an RO position or in instances where RO members have not developed a regional position at all. Thus, larger IOs are more conducive to the regionalisation of international negotiations. In addition, the book illustrates that ROs are more active in IOs, when the latter grants them formal access to the negotiations.

State, regional and international levels are interlinked, which places state actors in a position where they could engage in forum-shopping and choose the level where they would like to deal with a specific item (Hooghe and Marks 2001, Kellow 2012). In nested negotiations within EMLG systems, states that are members of both the IO and ROs can choose between acting on their own or working through an RO for each item under negotiation in IOs. Accordingly, incentive structures of states matter for the prevalence of regional positions in IOs. For instance, states are more motivated to act on behalf of a specific RO and voice regional instead of national positions, when they serve as chairmen for this RO. Moreover, if an RO has a formal status in an IO, it is more vocal in this specific arena.

### 1.1.3 Analysis of RO negotiation success (DV2)

Which regional actors are most successful and why? The book illustrates that ROs vary in their ability to leave regional imprints on international norms. ROs are most successful in shaping international negotiation dynamics and the content of international negotiation outcomes according to how well their internal coordination works, how actively they participate in the negotiations on the basis of common regional positions and how effectively negotiation strategies are used on the basis of combined leverage and expertise of the RO member states. In addition, regional actors are more successful the more RO member states refrain from voicing deviating individual positions. Accordingly, regional actors are most influential if they do not only actively voice their positions, but also if their members possess economic leverage, vote-based leverage or expertise. The success of regional actors also varies across international negotiation contexts. According to our theoretical framework,

IOs should be most prone to regional actor success the more member states IOs have, and the more encompassing the formal rights that regional actors can obtain are in an IO.

We examine three qualitative case studies on the basis of the EMLG hypotheses about negotiation success and follow a structure-focused comparison design in order to select the negotiation arenas. Accordingly, the case selection systematically varies with respect to two core variables on the IO level (strength of formal RO status in IO and IO size), whilst keeping important alternative explanations constant across the cases (e.g. concerning RO and member state properties). A least likely instance for RO success is the IWC, as it is not very large in size and does not grant many ROs strong formal status. By contrast, the FAO is a negotiation arena in which RO success is most likely. It has many members and, regional actors have formal roles, and ROs can even apply for full membership. In between the ATT case, as this negotiation arena is large in size, while the formal roles of ROs are limited to observers. In each of the three contexts, one recent negotiation on an international norm was selected. The case studies use primary document analysis as well as more than 200 semi-structured interviews with RO members, state diplomats and representatives of IOs as well as civil society actors in order to trace the processes of how and under what conditions regional actor activity translates into the successful shaping of international negotiation dynamics and outcomes.

The negotiations on the South Atlantic Whale Sanctuary (SAWS) that took place in the IWC are a least likely case for RO success. The IWC is an IO made up of eighty-eight member states and responsible for the conservation of whales and the management of whaling. ROs may gain observer status and thereby 'will have speaking rights during Plenary sessions and sessions of Commission subsidiary groups and Committees to which they are admitted to' (International Whaling Commission 2014c, Art. C.3), but so far only the EU is a registered observer. The IWC's main task is to review and revise the measures laid down in the Convention's Schedule, which governs the conduct of whaling. Measures are, for example, the creation of a sanctuary, and set limits on the numbers and size of whales which may be hunted. The case study examines the 2011, 2012 and 2014 negotiations on the creation of a whale sanctuary in the South Atlantic Ocean, in which commercial whaling is prohibited. There were two important regional actors in the IWC negotiations, the EU and the BAG, a regional coalition founded by Argentina, Brazil, Chile, Mexico, Costa Rica, Peru and Panama. In both cases, the member states engaged in coordination meetings in order to develop common positions that were then presented as group positions rather than an individual state's preference in the IWC negotiation arena. While the BAG was strongly united, the internal homogeneity of the EU was more limited due to the often deviating position of Denmark, which was sympathetic to whaling due to the fact that it represents Greenland in the IWC. As a consequence, the BAG negotiated with full energy and was actively driving the international negotiations, while the EU operated on the basis of its minimal agreed position and applied only a limited array of negotiation strategies. Other ROs, such as Shanghai Cooperation Organisation (SCO), MERCOSUR or South African Development Community (SADC), were not active in the SAWS negotiations as their members did not coordinate to develop a common position. The case study illustrates that regional group activity is an essential prerequisite for RO success, but by no means in itself sufficient. Most important, ROs are successful in changing negotiation dynamics if they manage to talk third-party states into supporting their own position. To this end, the BAG and, to a more limited extent, also the EU engaged in lobbying and persuasion-based strategies on the basis of their respective regional positions. In order to be substantively successful and leave a regional imprint on an international negotiation outcome, regional actors must be able to alter norms in line with their own positions or prevent deviating changes. The BAG was the main driving force behind the SAWS proposal and had managed to change the language of the SAWS proposal in line with its preferences in 2011, 2012 and 2014. In 2011 and 2012, the BAG explicated that the SAWS area would not include national waters (Brazil being the only exception), and in 2014 the BAG strengthened the SAWS proposal substantively, as it strove to forbid no longer commercial whaling only, but all forms of whaling (including for scientific purposes) within the SAWS area. The EU had no interest in proposing text changes of their own or including additional elements, but agreed with the BAG on all points. Although the EU and especially the BAG were active, the SAWS norm was not passed in the 2012 and 2014 voting, respectively, since the required threshold of supporters was not reached. Thus, neither regional group was ultimately substantively successful. In short, the SAWS negotiations in the IWC constitute a least likely case for the regionalisation of international negotiations. Nevertheless, even in this arena international negotiations are regionalised to some extent, as there is RO activity and as ROs are able to successfully alter negotiation dynamics and the norm proposals, but failed to ultimately get them passed.

Compared to the SAWS case, regional actors were more active and also more successful in the ATT case. The negotiations started and ended in the UNGA and were held in the negotiation regime consisting of four Preparatory Committees and two Conferences of the Parties in between. The negotiation arenas are characterised by a high number of member states (193), while ROs can only be registered as observers. The ATT is part of the global efforts to reduce the illicit arms trade and as it establishes common standards for the international trade of conventional weapons. In the negotiations of an ATT, which lasted from 2010 to 2013, the CARICOM and ECOWAS, followed by the EU, were the most vocal regional actors. The members of African ROs, most notably ECOWAS and CARICOM, placed great emphasis on regulating the (illicit) trade of small arms and light weapons and redirected their administrative and political resources towards group coordination. This was effective and led to the formulation of regional positions that the respective RO member states articulated and pushed during the ATT negotiations in the Preparatory Committee (PrepCom) and during the Conference of the Parties (CoP) itself. Other ROs which were hardly active, such as Pacific Islands Forum (PIF) or SCO, had internal problems of coordination, not in the least due to the heterogeneity of member state interests combined with limited issue saliency. These hindrances resulted in the failure to swiftly develop and update common regional positions that could have been articulated during the ongoing international negotiations. Not every regional position voiced in the more than three years of negotiations was effectively influential on negotiation dynamics and outcomes. For example, the EU was not very successful with respect to the status of ROs in the ATT as signatories or with respect to the question of whether the ATT should also cover re-export, technical assistance, leases, gifts and loans related to conventional weapons, which was in part due to the fact that the EU member states could not agree on what the best approach would be. Other ROs were more successful. For instance, CARICOM was one of the strongest supporters for the inclusion of ammunition in the Treaty. They achieved the mentioning of bullets and other forms of ammunition in the Treaty by extensively using a broad array of argumentative and lobbying strategies. These strategies worked due to the expertise that backed up the arguments and the resources the regional actor invested in bilateral lobbying in New York as well as in various capitals. The fact that ECOWAS sided with CARICOM and also started to lobby for the inclusion of ammunition further helped to get the point across. Other instances in which ROs were successful include CARICOM's and PIF's negotiation efforts to promote capacity-sensitive solutions for states affected by transit or transshipment. Taken together, the ATT negotiations were highly regionalised, and regional actors induced significant changes in the negotiation outcome, although none of the ROs had formal voting rights.

The Food and Agricultural Organization (FAO) is a most likely arena for RO success. It comprises 194 member states and ROs can apply for full membership or can register as observers. Apart from the EU as a member organisation with speaking and voting rights, the FAO has between ten and sixteen regional group observers, the activity of which are varying over FAO committees and over time. In general, observers can speak up if invited by the Chairperson. The FAO's major task relates to agricultural and food-related issues, and the negotiations under scrutiny in the case study focus on the 'Rome Declaration on Nutrition' of 2014. The 2014 Rome Declaration seeks to fight malnutrition, foster food security and increase international cooperation to these ends. Between March and November 2014 representatives from more than 170 countries, as well as representatives of civil society organisations and the private sector, participated in the working groups and the subsequent second International Conference on Nutrition (ICN2) in the FAO Headquarter in Rome. The negotiations were conducted under FAO rules and express a joint effort of the FAO and the World Health Organization (WHO). In November 2014 the member states adopted the Rome Declaration on Nutrition by acclamation. With this declaration the member states obliged themselves to work towards eradicating hunger, preventing all forms of malnutrition worldwide as well as enhancing sustainable food systems. The case study examines the negotiations leading to the Rome Declaration on Nutrition and sheds light on which ROs were active and whether and how regional group activity translated into success. This reveals that especially the EU, the North America group (NOAM), GRULAC and African regional groups have been active throughout the negotiations, and often opposed one another. One of the conflicts focused on trade issues. On the one end of the spectrum, the GRULAC and the African group both placed a strong emphasis on mentioning the negative effects of trade distorting measures (e.g. subsidies), which was opposed by the EU. The former actors could not talk enough states into supporting their position, while the EU succeeded with its preference. Another point of discussion was the 'decade of nutrition'. GRULAC, with the support of the AFRICA group, pushed for a 'decade of nutrition', which the EU opposed as it wanted to avoid additional budgetary expenses. After extensive negotiation efforts, the actors compromised in agreeing to promote the decade of action on nutrition within existing structures and available resources. Hence, although the EU is a highly successful regional actor overall, it needed to compromise on a series of questions as well.

Thus the qualitative part of the book illustrates that the regional actor success first requires that their member states swiftly develop national positions on the basis of which their diplomats can engage in group coordination meetings. Only when the member states are united and formulate a common regional position, an RO member state or an RO delegate can voice it in international negotiations. The more strongly the regional position reflects a minimal compromise, the less motivated are RO members to invest their own resources into using a broad array of negotiation strategies on behalf of the group in international negotiations and the more limited the persuasive and bargaining force of the regional actor vis-à-vis third-party states. In addition, a large size of IOs, as well as formal access opportunities of ROs in IOs, are conducive to the chances that regional positions are successfully articulated in international negotiations. Yet, formal structures alone are not sufficient for RO success. Regional actors need to adopt negotiation strategies for which they possess the associated resources in order to have a chance in talking others into supporting the regional position. For example, argumentative persuasion-based strategies do not work without a high level of technical, scientific and legal expertise, with which ROs are equipped to varying extents. Lobbying strategies are not effective if ROs lack personnel resources to approach third-party states in various venues and through multiple channels, which provides richer and larger ROs with an advantage. Bargaining-based strategies require bargaining-leverage, such as being pivotal on the basis of votes, which allows for a series of tied-hand strategies by ROs, or economic power to offer side-payments or package deals to pull third-party states to one's side. All these strategies work better the more they are fine-tuned to the issue at the international negotiation table. Accordingly, ROs that meet frequently during ongoing negotiations in order to update and adjust regional positions and negotiation strategies are in a much better position to negotiate successfully in IOs, which is easier to achieve for ROs with high levels of capacities. Hence, ROs that place great emphasis on an international norm and at the same time able to turn into norm-entrepreneurs have good chances to leave regional imprints on international norms.

### 1.1.4 Core findings

In sum, the book shows that today's international negotiations are regionalised to a considerable extent, as more than one in ten speeches express regional interests. However, the phenomenon of the regionalisation of international politics is nuanced and not equally prevalent across all contexts and actors. It is not the case that ROs are equally active throughout each and every international institution. Large IOs attract more RO activity than smaller ones, especially if many ROs devote capacities to negotiations and if they have a large membership which is able and willing to express regional positions. This reveals that the extent of regionalisation of negotiation dynamics varies on the international level over negotiation arenas for several reasons. IOs that attract the most RO activity are large in membership size because states have greater incentives to aggregate their positions into regional ones and articulate them in order to speed up multilateral negotiations. Also, compared to IOs in which regional actors have no formal status at all, in IOs where a high number of ROs enjoy observer status, the chances increase that these actors become vocal. However, policy match can compensate for lacking formal access; whenever international negotiations touch on issues of high importance for a regional actor, the chances increase that member states voice regional positions so that we observe regionalised international negotiations.

On the regional level, the book shows that the larger an RO is and the more resources it devotes to the development of regional positions for the multilateral negotiations in IOs, the greater the probability for a regionalisation of international negotiations dynamics. Having a high number of member states increases the chances that at least one of the states will articulate a regional position. In addition, the more often an RO has offices at IO headquarter locations, and the better the regional actor is equipped, the more professionalised the negotiation approach of a regional actor is. The book further evidences that although the United Nations regional groups were not founded to coordinate voting behaviour in the first place but for administrative and procedural purposes within the UN system, by now their negotiation activity is also visible even in IOs not affiliated with the UN.

On the member state level, the observation that some states are more vocal for their ROs than others is due to administrative capacity differences between states and differences in their political culture, which ultimately influences their incentives to speak up on behalf of an RO. States that can swiftly develop national positions for a broad range of issues on the IO agenda can more actively participate in RO coordination meetings and are subsequently better able to become active in the IO and articulate the regional position. Diplomats familiar with the democratic culture of working in context with multiple points of view are oriented towards compromising and are therefore more inclined to support a regional position and speak up on behalf of ROs. Moreover, the book demonstrates that especially middle-sized states use their ROs to leverage up in international negotiations, while larger states can afford to negotiate on their own and while the smallest states would benefit from leveraging up through ROs in IOs, but lack the capacities to do so.

Activity and success are interlinked, and the extent to which international negotiation outcomes are regionalised varies as well. For regional actors to be successful in influencing dynamics and outcomes of international negotiations, it is essential that their respective member states swiftly develop national positions on the basis of which their diplomats can engage in group coordination meetings, most often taking place in the city of the IO headquarters. Only when the RO manages to formulate a regional position, it can be articulated in the IO by its members or, if the RO itself has speaking rights, by RO delegates directly. Since RO member states can negotiate on behalf of their regional group irrespective of the formal status of the regional actor in the IO, the formal access of ROs to IOs is not a necessary precondition for regional actorness in international negotiations. Activity is important for success, but active ROs are not automatically successful. Regional actors are most successful in shaping international negotiation dynamics and also the content of international norms in international negotiations the more effective the strategies used. Argumentative strategies are most effective if regional actors and their member states can rely on a high level of technical, scientific and legal expertise in regard to the issue on the negotiation table. Informal

lobbying strategies work best if the regional actors do not experience shortages in resources to approach third-party states in various venues and through
multiple channels. Bargaining strategies, such as no-vote threats, require bargaining leverage in order to be effective. To this end, RO members need to
be strongly united and not send mixed messages in international negotiations,
and they need to be pivotal on the basis of the distribution of votes in the IO.

Thus, the regionalisation of international negotiation dynamics and outcomes is a widespread and prevalent phenomenon in today's international
relations. Regional actors leave imprints on international norms and rules
and do so irrespective of their formal role in an IO. While the institutional
design of IOs is important, it does not determine the prospects of regional
actor success, as regional- and state-level factors are also of high importance
for both the ability of regional actors to develop and voice regional positions
in international negotiations and the ability of regional actors to negotiate
effectively.

## 1.2 THE STATE OF THE ART AND GAPS

The book makes distinctive contributions to four strands of research, namely
international relations, the EU as external actor, comparative regionalism and
multilevel governance.

### 1.2.1 Contributions to international relations

In addition to tackling questions of war and peace (Morgenthau 1948, Waltz
1979), international relations (IR) research of the past also focused on cooperation and discord (Axelrod 1984, Keohane 1984, Keohane and Nye 1989).
Today, the focus is not so much on whether there can be cooperation under
anarchy (Axelrod and Keohane 1986, Oye 1986), but rather on institutional
arenas for cooperation as well as the dynamics and outcomes of multilateral
negotiations (Crump and Zartman 2003, Kremenyuk 1991, Plantey 2007).
Not in the least because international negotiations are central for cooperation
beyond the nation-state, the study of the former is often state-centric in character, examining the role of state power (Berton et al. 1999, Druckman 1997,
Habeeb 1988, Powell 1999, Zartman and Rubin 2009), size (Drahos 2003,
Panke 2010, 2012e), state capacities (Panke 2013c) or the choice of strategies (Dür and Mateo 2010, Habeeb 1988, Pruitt 1991) for their ability to exert
influence and shape the nature and content of international norms. In addition to states as actors, scholars also study the role of NGOs or transnational
actors in international negotiations (Martens 2007, Peterson 1992, Risse
2001, Tallberg et al. 2013, Weiss and Gordenker 1996), examining their

access, activities and impact. Thus, the state-centric approach that dominated the discipline of IR has been supplemented by examining the role of different non-state actors such as NGOs, multinational companies, lobby groups and organised interests in international affairs. Despite the spread of regional integration after WWII, the role of ROs in international negotiations has not yet been systematically studied. This is surprising, as ROs have observer status in many other IOs, such as ASEAN, AU, CARICOM, ECOWAS, EFTA or SADC in the ILO, and are even full members in some (e.g. the EU in the WTO or the FAO). Even if an RO has no formal status in an IO at all (e.g. Blavoukos and Bourantonis 2010, Gehring et al. 2013), states that are members of both an RO and an IO can voice regional positions on behalf of the regional group or organisation (Panke 2013c). To shed light on this aspect of the regionalisation of international relations, this book systematically explores regional actors in IOs. How do they engage in international, multilateral negotiations, and how and under what conditions are ROs successful in influencing negotiation dynamics or in shaping the content of international norms as negotiation outcomes?

### 1.2.2 Contributions to research on the EU as external actor

The most prominent example of regional integration is the European Union (EU), which is the most integrated RO with the broadest scope (Börzel 2006). Regional integration research started off as a study of the processes and scope of conditions for regional integration to emerge and prosper (Haas 1970, Nye 1968, Schmitter 1970). The second wave of academic engagement examined the politics, policies and polity of various regional organisations, focusing on the impact of regional integration on its members and vice versa (Cowles et al. 2001, Featherstone and Radaelli 2003, Goetz and Hix 2000). In the third wave, researchers started to situate regional integration within the global context, analysing how regional groups and organisations are influenced by international developments as well as international and transnational actors (Amin and Thrift 1994, Verdier and Breen 2001). Less research has been done, however, on the role of the various regional organisations as players in global governance. There is one prominent exception, namely the study of the EU as an external actor, which illustrates that ROs are not necessarily passive on the international level. For example, scholarship highlights how actively the EU engages with states in its vicinity, either through pre-accession conditionality (Böhmelt and Freyburg 2013, Grabbe 2006, Schimmelfennig et al. 2003) or its neighbourhood policy (Freyburg et al. 2009, Kelley 2006, Lavenex 2008, Smith 2005). Over time the toolkit has been broadened, but it is still contested whether the EU has become more effective as a result (Bosse and Korosteleva-Polglase 2009, Lavenex and Schimmelfennig 2011). In addition, there are studies on how the EU seeks to export its model of governance, its core values and its liberal market approach beyond its borders (Börzel and Hackenesch 2013, Börzel and Risse 2012a, Damro 2012, Farrell 2009, Hettne and Soderbaum 2005, Jetschke and Murray 2012, Lenz 2012, Sedelmeier 2012). Other works examine the external activities of the EU in a broader context, assessing how the EU shapes the outcomes of individual multilateral negotiations to varying extents (e.g. Baroncelli 2011, Dee 2015, Delreux 2009b, 2011, Oberthür 1999, Smith 2006, Tsoukalis 2011, Zimmermann 2007) or how it acts in a range of different IOs (Blavoukos and Bourantonis 2011a, Delreux et al. 2012, Græger and Gaugevik 2011, Joergensen et al. 2011, Smith 2006, 2010, Smith 2013a, b). The finding that these studies have in common is that homogeneity among the EU member states' preferences is essential for the ability of the EU to speak with one voice in international negotiations (e.g. Dee 2012, Joergensen et al. 2011, Kissack 2011, Oberthür 2011, Shahin 2011, Simmons and DiSilvestro 2014, Smith 2013a). Yet, there is dissent on whether internal coherency is a necessary or sufficient condition for the EU's prospects to become influential in IOs (e.g. Gehring 2013, Groenleer and Schaik 2007, Panke 2013b, 2014b, Smith 2006, 2010, van Schaik and Schunz 2012, Wunderlich 2012, Xiarchogiannopoulou and Tsarouhas 2014). This difference in assessment of the coherency variable is not too surprising, as these studies are difficult to compare and do not add up to a precise picture of the influence of the EU. Some of them focus on goal achievements of the EU in different IOs in general, while others examine the negotiation of individual norms (e.g. Delreux 2012, Hivonnet 2012). In addition, the definition and measurement of performance, effectiveness or influence as prominent key concepts in the literature vary, and studies focus too often on different aspects. Moreover, there are no studies that systematically gather data on the activities of a broad range of different regional actors in different IOs, cover a wide range of policy areas, and systematically explain observed variation. This book closes these gaps. It examines the activity and success of ROs from all parts of the world in the most prominent IOs across different policy areas (security, economy/trade/finance, environment, human rights, labour/social and education/health). It puts the EU as an external actor into a comparative context and provides insights into questions such as: Is the EU an actor sui generis that is more vocal and engaged in negotiations than all other ROs, such as in the negotiations that take place in the UNGA, the FAO or the WTO? Compared to the EU, how active are other ROs?

### 1.2.3 Contributions to comparative regionalism

The book also contributes to comparative regionalism research, which has evolved over the past decades. Students of regional integration and regional cooperation have very often focused their attention on Europe, more specifically on the European Communities, and later on the European Union. Over time, this led to an EU bias in regard to theoretical and empirical insights gathered in regard to dynamics and outcomes of regional integration, which has been criticised by new regionalism approaches (Baccini and Dür 2011, Bowles 1997, Breslin and Higgott 2003, Chandra 2004, Gómez-Mera 2008, Keating 1998, MacLeod 2001, Söderbaum and Sbragia 2010, Söderbaum and Shaw 2003, Telò 2001, Warleigh and Rosamond 2010). This strand of research has increased the general scholarly awareness that cooperation in ROs is not confined to Europe but takes place all over the globe (Börzel and Risse 2016, Fawcett 2004, Fawcett and Hurrell 1995). In fact, today there are more than sixty ROs all over the globe (Panke and Stapel 2016). Comparative regionalism studies different regional actors in relation to one another and seeks to compare the dynamics and outcomes of various regional integration projects (e.g. Basu 2012, Kissack 2010). Scholars also started to analyse how ROs interact with one another, for example how policy ideas or institutional blueprints are diffused or 'travel' from one RO to another one (Börzel and Risse 2012a, b, Jetschke and Murray 2012, Lenz 2012, Sanchez Bajo 1999). Students of comparative regionalism have also turned towards studying the phenomenon of overlapping regionalism. Overlapping regionalism emerges if states become members of more than one RO, thereby creating overlaps between ROs not only in regard to membership but often also in regard to policy mandates. Despite the comparative turn in regionalism studies which led to studies on the evolution of regional integration in different geographical parts of the globe, the analysis of various integration outcomes and the examination of interactions between ROs, we still know very little about how the different ROs from all over the globe engage in international relations. More specifically, questions such as which ROs are most active in international negotiations, under which conditions ROs turn their attention to international arenas and participate in governance beyond their territorial borders, and why some ROs are more vocal in IOs than others have not yet been explored. Which state-, regional- and international-level features are conducive to RO activity in international negotiations? Which ROs are most likely to turn activity into success and shape outcomes of international negotiations? This book puts all of today's ROs into a comparative perspective and studies the regionalisation of international negotiation dynamics and outcomes, thus making a novel contribution to comparative regionalism research.

### 1.2.4 Contributions to multilevel governance research

Multilevel governance approaches mainly focus on federal states or regional organisations, most prominently the EU, but the approach has not yet been used to study the activity and influence of ROs in international negotiations within IOs. At their core, MLG approaches analytically capture the fact that decision-making authority is dispersed across multiple layers of government in many political systems (Hooghe and Marks 2001). Accordingly, they capture how policies are formulated on the basis of cross-level coordination, which often takes place via negotiations between actors from different levels of a multilevel system (c.f. Benz 2007, Börzel 2010, Scharpf 1997b). The nested negotiations examined in this book are instances of MLG in which the three layers of governance – the state level, the regional level and the international level – are of importance. Accordingly, in order to capture the dynamics and outcomes of nested negotiations, the book draws on and adds to multilevel governance approaches. It theorises how state, regional, international and policy properties influence the prospects of ROs to participate actively in IO negotiations (DV1) as well as the chances that ROs are successful in these negotiations (DV2). The nested negotiations framework builds on the neo-institutionalist insight that institutions structure but do not determine actor-behaviour (e.g. March and Olsen 1984, Peters 1999, Scharpf 1997a). Moreover, it is based on a broader conception of strategic rationality than orthodox rational-choice approaches since it assumes that actors are strategic and rational in character but have identities and follow norms that are embedded in institutions as well (Scharpf 2000). Based on this micro-foundation, the theoretical model specifies hypotheses on the role of IO properties, RO properties, member state properties and policy characteristics on the participation of ROs (RO activity, DV1) and on the prospects of regional actors to influence negotiation dynamics and outcomes (RO success, DV2). In doing so, the book provides an expanded multilevel governance approach, which captures the linkages between the state, the regional and the international levels.

## 1.3 CHAPTER OUTLINE

Do regional actors vary in their international negotiation activity and how can variation be explained? Under what conditions does RO activity translate into success in international negotiations? These two research questions are systematically addressed in eight chapters. Taken together, the book provides important and novel insights into the extent to which international negotiations are currently regionalised. It also sheds light on whether the regionalisation is spread evenly across IOs as well as policy areas, or whether there are certain IOs in which the regionalisation of international negotiation dynamics and outcomes is particularly well advanced. On this basis, it provides insights into the driving forces and ends with a reflection on the implications of today's regionalisation for the effectiveness and legitimacy of governance beyond the nation-state more generally.

Chapter 1 provides an introduction. Although the number of IOs and ROs has risen since the end of WWII and state membership, as well as policy scopes of ROs and IOs, increasingly overlap little is known about the effects of this development. The first chapter argues that it is important to close the research gap in regard to the active and effective participation of regional actors in international negotiations, as such participation brings about a regionalisation of international negotiations. This in turn not only alters the dynamics of international negotiations but also has important implications for the effectiveness and legitimacy of governance beyond the nation-state.

Chapter 2 presents the theoretical framework. Drawing on multilevel governance, liberal theory and negotiation literature, the book develops an EMLG approach which accommodates the interconnectedness between three levels. It theorises how and under what conditions member-state-, regional- and international-level variables as well as policy field–specific characteristics impact RO activity and success in IO negotiations.

Chapter 3 presents empirical insights into regional actor activity in international negotiations. It maps the extent to which today's international negotiations are already regionalised and sheds light on important empirical puzzles. At the state level, it is striking that the propensity to which states negotiate on behalf of a regional group or organisation varies tremendously. Since all states might be able to leverage up in international negotiations if they refer to an RO instead of framing a position as a purely national one, it begs explanation why not all states make use of their regional affiliations. On the regional level, there is considerable variation as well, as regional actors differ in their vocality. For example, the GCC or ASEAN are more active than the Arab League or the SCO, although the pairs are relatively similar with regard to institutional set-up. On the international level, IOs vary in the extent to which they attract the articulation of regional voices. In this respect it is, for example, puzzling that the WTO, which covers a policy area which is also covered by many ROs and is formally open to ROs as observers and potentially also members (as the EU case illustrates), has less strongly regionalised negotiations than UNCTAD or the ILO, both of which delimit the formal roles of ROs much more and feature a less pronounced policy field match with respect to ROs.

Chapter 4 empirically examines the theoretical expectations concerning regional actor activity. Due to the semi-hierarchical structure of the data advanced multilevel methods are utilised. In addition, the chapter draws on semi-structured interviews with RO members in order to complement the quantitative insights with narrative evidence. This provides insights into the larger pattern and the underlying causal mechanisms. The chapter shows how member state-, regional- and international-level variables interact and sheds light on the elements which are the most decisive for the extent to which today's international negotiation dynamics are regionalised.

Chapters 5, 6 and 7 present three in-depth case studies: the negotiations on the Arms Trade Treaty, the South Atlantic Whale Sanctuary and the Rome Declaration on Nutrition. The cases are selected to allow for structure-focused comparisons between the negotiations in the ATT, the IWC and the FAO negotiation arenas. The studies apply process-tracing and combine content analysis of a wide array of different primary sources with triangulated, semi-structured interviews with more than 240 state, RO and IO representatives as well as civil society actors. The chapters illustrate how member state-, regional- and international-level variables impact negotiation success of regional actors in international negotiations and shed light on the elements which are the most decisive for the extent to which today's international negotiation outcomes are regionalised.

The concluding chapter summarises the major findings. It takes stock of today's regionalisation of international negotiation dynamics and international negotiation outcomes and discusses important implications. It ends with outlining avenues for future research.

*Chapter 2*

# Theory – Accounting for RO activity and RO success in international negotiations

The book sheds light on the role of regional actors in multilateral negotiations, which is important due to the increase in both regional and international organisations and the accompanying overlap of state membership and policy areas in those institutions. To this end, it investigates the conditions under which member states of ROs develop common positions on the basis of which they can speak with one voice in international negotiations. How can it be explained that some RO positions are voiced in international negotiations more often and why are some IOs more prone to RO activity than others? Does RO activity vary across policy areas and why? Second, it analyses the nexus between active participation and success in negotiations. Are some ROs more effective in international negotiations than others and, if so, why? Are ROs more successful in some IOs or policy areas than others? In order to develop new insights into the role that ROs play beyond their home turf and to systematically answer these questions, the book will subsequently explain variation in the active participation of ROs in IOs (*dependent variable 1*) and the success of ROs in international negotiations (*dependent variable 2*).

This chapter draws on the rich literature on multilevel governance (MLG)[1] and advances a three-level negotiations framework[2] which captures the roles of states and of ROs in the dynamics and outcomes of negotiations within IOs. Thus, international negotiations are 'nested interactions' and characterised by complex linkages between various levels (Putnam 1988, Tsebelis 1990). Figure 2.1 illustrates that the three relevant levels in expanded multilevel governance (EMLG) systems are member states, ROs and international institutions. These levels are connected through upward arrows (engagement in higher-level negotiations on the basis of their own positions) and downward arrows (feedback from higher-level negotiations and possible position adjustment in response). The three-level EMLG framework captures the

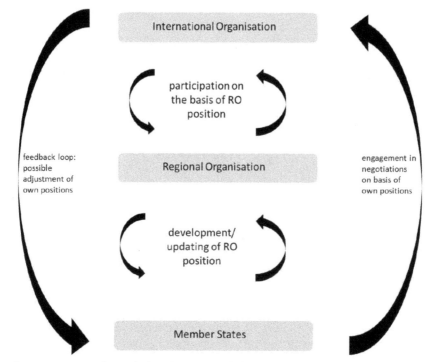

**Figure 2.1.   Nested negotiations in an expanded multilevel governance system**

process of position formation and adjustment between RO member states, which is central to RO activity in international negotiations and the prospects for ROs in successfully influencing international norms.

## 2.1 REGIONAL ACTORS IN IOs – DEFINITIONS

Since the end of WWII, a regionalisation of state cooperation has taken place, as the increase of numbers of regional organisations (ROs) illustrates. By now, there is a multitude of different ROs all around the globe, broadly defined as instances of state–state cooperation, in which collaboration between member states is institutionalised at least to some extent (e.g. definition of membership, common purpose/mission, regular meetings of members) and in which membership is based on geographic considerations.

The regional actors under scrutiny in this book encompasses supranational and intergovernmental regional organisations in which cooperation between at least three states takes place on the basis of geographic considerations, usually covers more than market creating policies and is formally institutionalised. Based on this definition, as of 2012, there were more than sixty supranational and intergovernmental regional organisations across the globe (Panke and

Stapel 2016) which differ in size, scope, depth, age and geographical location. Examples include the Andean Community of Nations (ANDEAN), Arab League, Association of South East Asian Nations (ASEAN), African Union (AU), Caribbean Community, Council of Europe (CoE), Economic Community of West African States (ECOWAS), European Free Trade Association (EFTA), EU, GCC, Mercado Comun del Sur (MERCOSUR), North American Free Trade Association (NAFTA), Organisation of American States (OAS), Pacific Islands Forum (PIF), South Asian Association for Regional Cooperation (SAARC), Southern African Development Community (SADC), Shanghai Cooperation Organisation (SCO), Central American Integration System (SICA) and the Union of South American Nations (UNASUR).

Furthermore, ROs, as studied in this book, also encompasses UN regional groups, which are forms of state–state coordination and cooperation that is institutionalised within IOs, permanent rather than ad hoc in character, and based on geographic considerations. Within IOs belonging to the UN umbrella[3] and also in some non-UN IOs[4] there are five regional groups. These are the Latin American and Caribbean Group (GRULAC), the Eastern European Group, the Asia-Pacific Group, the African Group and the Western European and Others Group (WEOG). Some other IOs, such as the FAO or the WHO, also have regional groups, such as the WHO African group or the FAO's Near East regional group.

Finally, our concept of ROs also includes groups of states from the same region which work together on a non–ad hoc basis (e.g. in more than just one or two instances) in an IO to further advance common regional interests during international negotiations. An example for such a regional group would be the Buenos Aires Group (BAG).

Not only the number of ROs, but also the number of international organisations (IOs), has increased considerably in the past sixty years. IOs are negotiation arenas in which states come together in order to develop international norms. An IO's institutional design transfers at least some power (at least temporarily) from the state level to the international level (see section 2.2). On the basis of this broad IO definition, the book covers international governmental organisations and international regimes, such as the ILO, the World Health Organization, the WTO or UNESCO.

## 2.2 REGIONAL ACTIVITY IN INTERNATIONAL NEGOTIATIONS AND MULTILEVEL GOVERNANCE SYSTEMS – THE STATE OF THE ART

Studies on the activity of regional actors in international negotiations focus mainly on two elements: access and formal standing of regional actors in IOs as well as the ability of ROs to negotiate as a unitary actor.

In regard to RO access, IOs differ in their institutional designs. Some are very open to ROs and provide access to international negotiations by registering ROs as observers upon their request (e.g. the UNGA, the FAO), while others have no such provisions in place. Moreover, there are also exceptional instances in which IOs allow ROs to become full members under certain conditions (e.g. the EU in the FAO, UNFCCC, WTO, ITTO). Shifting the perspective, studies on the EU as an external actor has noted that formal status is important (Debaere et al. 2014, Drieskens 2010, Gehring et al. 2013, Wetzel 2011, Wouters et al. 2012a). In instances in which the EU has formal access to and standing in IOs, third-party states are more inclined to recognise and accept the EU as an actor and partner in the international negotiation concerned (Blavoukos and Bourantonis 2011c, Panke 2013b). However, in itself, formal roles, such as being an observer, do not automatically lead to EU activity and EU success in international negotiations, as contextual variables such as the EU's action capability, the distribution of preferences of other actors, decision-making rules and other variables related to the institutional design of the international negotiation arena can also be of importance (Debaere et al. 2014, Gehring et al. 2013, Panke 2013b, van Schaik 2011).

Without having a regional position, ROs cannot actively engage in international negotiations either through their delegates or through their member states (Panke 2013b, 2014b). Since the RO member states remain sovereign in regard to their foreign policy behaviour in IOs, it is crucial that the states get together and coordinate a common group position prior to the international negotiations (Joergensen et al. 2011, Smith 2006, van Schaik and Schunz 2012). These regional coordination meetings can also fail if states cannot compromise on a common position, the probability of which increases with increasing veto points (Mo 1995, Tsebelis 2002). A factor often stressed in studies on EU actorness in international arenas is the internal coherence or homogeneity amongst member state preferences. If member states' positions are similar and converge, the EU (and its member states) can speak with one voice in international negotiations (Baroncelli 2011, Dee 2012, 2015, Delreux 2009b, Jin and Hosli 2013, Kissack 2010, 2011, Simmons and DiSilvestro 2014, van Schaik 2013). In contrast, if member states disagree and the differences in positions cannot be remedied in EU coordination meetings in Brussels and at the location of the IO headquarter, the EU is most likely not going to turn into a unitary actor during the international negotiations concerned (Blavoukos and Bourantonis 2011d, da Conceição-Heldt and Meunier 2014, Panke 2013b, 2014b, Smith 2013b). Preference homogeneity is important for internal cohesiveness,[5] but – again – not the only variable determining the international level behaviour of the EU. In addition, policy areas matter, as the internal coherence concerning items on the international negotiation agenda can be achieved the easier for policies in which the EU's competencies are broad and subject to supranational centralisation compared to policy areas in which the EU's competencies are very limited (or even exclusively in the member state realm) (Kissack 2011, Panke and Haubrich Seco 2017, Wessel 2011, Young 2011).

In short, state-of-the-art approaches have provided important insights into the external actorness of the EU, most notably that formal access to and standing in IOs is important as it positively contributes to the EU as being recognised as an actor by third-party states (Debaere et al. 2014, Gehring et al. 2013, Panke 2013b, van Schaik 2011). Moreover, studies have demonstrated that the EU tends to only speak with one voice when the member states' positions are relatively homogenous (Kissack 2011). The state of the art focuses extensively on the EU, but largely omits all other ROs. Nevertheless, it provides a very good starting point to theorise and comparatively empirically examine RO activity in a broad variety of different IOs. This book builds on the state-of-the-art insights, but considerably broadens the theoretical framework in utilising an EMLG approach on the basis of which it develops a set of hypotheses on the member state level, the regional level, the international level as well as in regard to the policy dimension. In addition, this book also extends the research designs often used in studying EU actorness in international negotiations in order to overcome limitations that arise from an EU bias, the lack of comparative analysis of different ROs and the lack of a systematic study of additional explanatory variables across a broad variety of different negotiation contexts.

MLG approaches analytically account for the dispersion of decision-making authority across multiple layers of government (Hooghe and Marks 2001). They capture how policies are formulated and implemented on the basis of cross-level coordination, which often takes place via negotiations between actors from different levels of a multilevel system (c.f. Benz 2007, Börzel 2010, Scharpf 1997b, Zürn 2012).

Prominent examples of MLG systems are federal states[6] or regional organisations, such as the EU.[7] The political systems traditionally studied on the basis of MLG approaches are two-layer systems typically comprised of either the state and federal levels or the state and regional levels. In addition to the two-level MLG systems, there are also three-level systems comprised of a state, regional and international levels. Such systems constitute EMLG if there is some power delegation from the state or regional to the international levels and if there is some sort of division of labour between the levels (Zürn 2012). International institutions meet the first criterion – the delegation of power to the international level – if they encompass at least one of these elements: majority voting, shadow of majority rule, agenda setting by secretariats or other non-state actors, compliance monitoring by non-state actors, implementation review by actors belonging to international institutions or other non-state actors, own IO (or institutional linkages to) adjudication systems or international courts, as well as formally or de facto binding norms and decisions. A division of labour is present if norms are formulated and passed on to the international level but implemented and applied on the regional or the state level.

In EMLG systems, three layers of governance are of importance, namely the state level, the regional level and the international level (see figure 2.1). The state level is crucial for the development and adjustment of national positions in relation to draft international norms that have been put on the negotiation agenda of an international institution (domestic position formation). On the basis of national positions, states that are also members of an RO can engage in coordinating common regional positions (regional-level negotiations) or they can directly participate in international negotiations and voice national positions. In cases where RO member states have developed a common regional position, they or RO representatives can act on behalf of the RO in international negotiations (international-level negotiations). This might increase the leverage of RO members and might translate into more success concerning international norm negotiations. During ongoing regional- and international-level negotiations, the respective lower level (state or RO) might be required to respond to developing negotiation dynamics on the respective higher level (RO or IO) with adjusted positions or strategy reconfigurations. Thus, EMLG systems are conducive to parallel negotiations on multiple levels of governance which are interlinked.

In order to capture the dynamics and outcomes of nested negotiations, the subsequent sections draw on and add to multilevel governance approaches. Section 2.2 theorises how state, RO, IO and policy properties influence the prospects for ROs in participating actively in international negotiations (DV1), whereas section 2.3 focuses on the nexus between activity and success, as it theorises how and under what conditions regional actors are expected to be successful in international negotiations (DV2).

The nested negotiations framework builds on the neo-institutionalist insight that institutions structure but do not determine actor behaviour (e.g. March and Olsen 1984, Peters 1999, Scharpf 1997a). Moreover, it is based on a broader conception of strategic-rationality than orthodox rational-choice approaches since it assumes that actors are strategic and rational in character but have identities and follow norms that are embedded in institutions as well (Scharpf 2000). On the basis of this micro-foundation, this chapter develops hypotheses on the role of *member-state* properties, *RO* properties and *IO* properties as well as *policy* properties on the active participation of RO representatives of member states in international negotiations and on the prospects of regional actors being successful in changing dynamics and outcomes of international negotiations (for an overview of hypotheses c.f. figure 2.2 and tables 2.1 and 2.2).

*Member states* usually have access to and decision-making competencies in IOs and ROs. Thus, they can negotiate on the IO level on their own, or they can coordinate with other RO members first in order to increase their collective weight in international negotiations. Accordingly, the member state level of the theoretical framework captures the ability and willingness of states to participate in the development and articulation of an RO position in international negotiations (DV1, section 2.2) or to invest their own negotiation resources on behalf of the RO to successfully influence IO negotiation dynamics and outcomes (DV2, section 2.3).

At the *level of ROs*, the book theorises how regional actor properties impact the development and subsequent articulation of regional positions in IOs and how ROs' negotiation approaches to influence the dynamics and outcomes in IO negotiations. Section 2.2.1 hypothesises how RO size, RO policy scope, as well as other RO properties affect the chances of developing joint regional positions for international negotiations, which are key for the ability of ROs to speak with one voice in international negotiations (DV1).[8] In IOs, ROs are often observers, whereas the full membership of ROs in IOs is limited. Nevertheless, even in situations where ROs have neither a voice nor a vote themselves, member states have incentives to negotiate on behalf of an RO in international negotiations instead of acting alone (Meunier 2000, Smith 2006).[9] Hence, section 2.3 develops hypotheses on the different strategies that RO can use in IO negotiations[10] and respective scope conditions for their effectiveness, which are important to successfully align international norms with their own regional positions (DV2).

On the *IO level*, the subsequent sections draw on institutional design approaches (Goodin 1995, Koremons et al. 2001, Panke 2016, Pierson 2000) and theorise how IO properties (e.g. IO size, IO decision-making rules) impact the extent to which ROs actively participate in international negotiations (DV1, activity). It also studies how institutional design properties of IOs, such as the openness of IOs for ROs (Gehring 2013, Orsini 2014), influence the prospects of ROs being effective in maximising support for their position, as well as in shaping the content of international norms (DV2, success).

Finally, the focus is on *policy* properties as they can also impact the propensity of RO activity and RO success in international negotiations. For instance, whenever the policy area to which international negotiations relate is close to the core competencies of an RO, the latter might be better able and more strongly incentivised to turn into and active and successful actor in IOs.

## 2.2.1 Theorising RO activity

This section systematically develops theoretical expectations on how member-state level properties, properties of ROs and IOs, as well as policy-related variables are conducive or delimiting to the active participation of ROs in international negotiations (for an overview of hypotheses, see table 2.1).

**Table 2.1. Overview of hypotheses on RO activity (DV1)**

| | |
|---|---|
| *H1: Member State Properties* | |
| H1a administrative capacities | The more administrative capacities they possess, the more often states voice RO positions in international negotiations. |
| H1b democratic socialisation | The more democratic states are, the more often they voice RO positions in international negotiations. |
| H1c power | The less powerful states are, the more often states voice RO positions in international negotiations. |
| H1d support for regional cooperation | The more strongly states support regional cooperation, the more often states voice RO positions in international negotiations. |
| *H2: RO properties* | |
| H2a RO size | The larger an RO, the more often its positions are articulated in international negotiations. |
| H2b RO policy scope | The broader an RO's policy scope, the more often its positions are articulated in international negotiations. |
| H2c RO offices at IO HQs | The more often an RO has an office at the location of IO headquarters, the more often its positions are articulated in international negotiations. |
| *H3: IO properties* | |
| H3a IO size | The more member states an IO has, the more prevalent are regional positions in international negotiations. |
| H3b IO decision making | When IO rules and norms are created by majority decisions, regional positions are more prevalent in international negotiations. |
| *H4: Policy properties* | |
| H4 Trade policies | If an international negotiation covers trade themes, ROs are more active. |
| *Hc: Cross-level effects* | |
| Hca RO homogeneity | The greater the homogeneity amongst RO member states, the more often the positions of the respective RO are articulated in international negotiations. |
| Hcb RO chair position | When states hold the position of being an RO chair, they are more often voicing the positions of that specific RO in international negotiations. |

| H1: Member State Properties | |
| --- | --- |
| Hcc RO–IO policy match | The more the policy scopes of an RO and an IO overlap, the more active the RO is in the respective IO. |
| Hcd formal status of RO in IO | When an RO has a formal status in an IO, its positions are articulated more often in the respective IO. |
| Hce RO resource allocation at IO | If an RO has an office at the location of an IO headquarter, its positions are more often articulated during international negotiations in the respective IO. |

Since not all ROs have speaking rights in all IOs, RO activity is not confined to RO representatives voicing a group position during multilateral negotiations on the IO level. RO member states can and often do speak on behalf of their respective group and voice regional positions instead of national ones in international negotiation arenas (c.f. chapter 3).

Not all ROs have formal access to all IOs. Yet, regional actor activity is not confined to RO representatives voicing a regional position during multilateral negotiations on the international level. Even in instances where ROs have no formal roles in IOs, its member states can speak on behalf of their respective group and voice regional positions in international negotiations. Accordingly, the hypotheses relating to the **member state level** capture how ability and incentives affect whether states are able and willing to speak on behalf of an RO in international negotiation arenas (DV1). While multilevel governance approaches usually assume that actors know what they want when they start negotiating with their peers (which might be influenced by sub-level constituencies, c.f. König et al. 2012, Moravcsik 1993) and thus have positions (e.g. Benz et al. 1992, Knodt 2000, von Krause 2008), this is not automatically the case for ROs in international negotiations (Panke 2013c). In order to be active in IO negotiations, it is essential that RO members have a common regional position in the first place. Hypotheses 1a and 1b focus on the ability of RO members to engage in group coordination and develop a common regional position and how this impacts the propensity of the states to voice regional positions in international negotiations.

National positions vis-à-vis a draft norm on the IO agenda do not naturally exist. Instead, they need to be developed. To this end, it is usually the ministries of foreign affairs or special government offices often supported by the respective line ministries who analyse the factual, normative and legal status quo and the induced positive or negative changes by the proposed draft international norm, and on this basis, they formulate national positions (Panke 2013a). This requires capacities in member states' ministries of foreign affairs (Panke 2013c). The more *administrative capacities* a state possesses, the swifter the development of national positions and the more national positions can be developed in total, which increases the chances for a national diplomat to be able to participate in RO coordination meetings and in international negotiations actively. Compared to states with capacity shortages, in which the ministries back home are slow in developing national positions and interacting with their diplomats, capacity-rich states have not only greater chances to actively shape regional positions in group coordination meetings, but also to actively voice the regional position in subsequent IO negotiations. Vice versa, states with capacity shortages are not only less likely to take an active part in group coordination meetings, but also to become active in international negotiations in general and are less likely to speak on behalf of the RO in international negotiations in particular. Thus, according to *hypothesis 1a,* states voice RO positions more often the more administrative capacities they possess.

The *extent to which a state's political culture is democratic* might have a positive effect on the chances of RO member states to develop common group positions during regional coordination meetings, which, in turn, is a prerequisite for ROs to become active on the international level. Diplomats from consolidated democracies are used to working in environments with multiple political points of view (Alderson 2001, Lewis 2005). Due to their experiences from the political system back home, they became socialised into a democratic culture of making compromises. On this basis, *hypothesis 1b* expects that the more democratic RO member states are, the easier it will be to compromise on a regional group position, and the more frequently member states will voice regional positions. If a greater number of state actors have learnt to cope with competing, pluralistic points of view in the domestic arena and engage in compromise-oriented behaviour on the regional level, it allows ROs to develop regional positions that can be voiced by RO member states in international negotiations and increases the activity level of states acting on behalf of ROs.

In federal multilevel systems, governance takes place on the state and the federal levels, while governance in regional organisations takes place on the state and the RO levels. These levels are interlinked, so it can place some actors in a position where they could engage in forum-shopping and choose the level where they would like to deal with a specific item (Hooghe and Marks 2001, Kellow 2012). This is similar to nested negotiations within EMLG systems. States that are members of both the IO and an RO can choose between acting on their own or working through the RO when negotiating in IOs. Hence, apart from the *ability* of RO members to work effectively on the development of a common regional position (H1a and b), *incentives* of states to subsequently voice regional positions in international negotiations are also of importance (H1c and d).

According to theories of cooperation, the power of states impacts their international behaviour (Alter and Meunier 2009, Axelrod 1984, Drezner 2009). Compared to poorer states, wealthier countries often have better alternatives for unilateral action and are therefore are less vulnerable than poorer ones (Axelrod 1984, Panke 2012a, e, Zartman and Rubin 2009). Moreover, poorer states cannot use their financial means for bargaining or side-payments to similar extents in international negotiations as wealthier states are able to (Habeeb 1988, Langan and Scott 2014, Moravcsik 1998, Pruitt 1991, Zartman and Rubin 2009). Thus, poorer states have more incentives to act through regional groups in international negotiation, while wealthier countries are less in need of ROs to leverage up since wealthier states are in a good position to act on their own. Hence, *hypothesis 1c* expects that the poorer states are, the stronger incentives they have to leverage up in international negotiations and the greater is the extent to which they voice regional positions. Vice versa, richer states are better able to negotiate on their own in international negotiations and have therefore only limited incentives to voice regional positions.

States that place a high value on regional cooperation are likely to join not only one but several ROs in their geographical region (Breslin et al. 2013, Fawcett and Hurrell 1995, Gamble and Payne 1996, Panke and Stapel 2016, Weiffen et al. 2013). Thus, an incentive for RO member states to speak on behalf of their group in IOs is linked to the *support for regional cooperation*. The stronger a state values regional cooperation, the greater its incentives to act in concert with the other RO members in international negotiations and speak up for their RO. In addition, the more ROs a state has joined, the greater the likelihood that at least one regional position is close to the national stance (Panke et al. 2017). This, in turn, increases the incentives of the respective state to voice the regional position in the IO. In contrast, if a country has only joined one RO, it is less often likely that the regional position is very close to the national position and the state in question will have less often incentives to articulate the RO position in the international negotiation arena. Hence, *hypothesis 1d* expects that the more strongly a state supports regional integration, the greater the likelihood is that it voices regional positions in international negotiations.

On the **RO level,** hypotheses focus on opportunity structures (H2a), the ability of ROs to become active based on the likelihood that the RO develops a regional position (H2b) as well as their incentives to articulate regional positions in IOs (H2c).

The institutional rules of ROs specify which states can become members (Jacoby 2004, Kydd 2001, Lewis 2001). The *number of RO member states* can increase the likelihood that positions of the ROs are articulated in IOs. The larger an RO is, the more opportunities exist that at least one state becomes active on behalf of the RO. This is due to the fact that at least one member state regards it as beneficial to voice a regional position and thereby leverage up in international negotiations increases, the larger a regional actor is. Thus, *hypothesis 2a* expects that an increase in RO size positively influences the number of RO positions articulated in IO negotiations.

Many ROs were initially founded to foster cooperation between states in geographical proximity in the economic policy area (Fawcett and Hurrell 1995, Gamble and Payne 1996, Keating and Loughlin 1997, Mansfield and Milner 1999, Mattli 1999). Over time, many of them have considerably increased their scope of policy competencies and cover now a broad variety of different policy fields (Jacobson 1979, Maoz 2011, Nye 1965, Panke and Stapel 2016, Schmitter 1970). In general, the broader the policy scope of an RO is, the greater the chances that the RO member states can recur to regional policies and norms as focal points when coordinating a common regional position for an issue on an IO negotiation agenda and, therefore, also the chances that a position of the RO is articulated in the IO. Thus according to *hypothesis 2b,* the broader the policy scope of an RO, the greater the likelihood that its positions are voiced in international negotiations.

Hypotheses 2a and b stress the importance of the ability of ROs to become active, while hypothesis 2c focuses on the incentives of ROs to become active. Not all ROs have the same interest in investing resources into the establishment of a common office at the cities in which IOs are located (e.g. Executive Office of the Secretary-General 2010). Investing in setting up an RO office abroad signifies that the RO seeks to act as a group in the IO located in the respective city (Huber and McCarty 2004, Panke 2013b). Thus, the RO in question should have stronger incentives to become active in international negotiations when they have an office at the location in which the international negotiation takes place; ROs should be more vocal in the respective international negotiations. Accordingly, *hypothesis 2c* expects that the more often an RO has *offices at the location of IO headquarters*, the greater the prospects of RO activity in IO negotiations.

The set-up of institutional design has an effect on actor behaviour within institutions (Goodin 1995, Koremons et al. 2001, Panke 2016, Pierson 2000). Institutional rules regulate who has access to negotiation arenas and how the decision-making competencies are distributed, which is essential for both negotiation dynamics and outcomes (Grande 2000, König et al. 2010, Scharpf 1988, Tsebelis 2002, Tsebelis and Garrett 1997). Accordingly, on the level of IOs, the hypotheses specify how the formal rules influence the prospects of ROs to directly (RO delegates) or indirectly (member states on behalf of ROs) voice regional positions in international negotiations.

*Hypothesis 3a* focuses on *IO size*. Depending on the institutional openness for new member states in IO founding treaties (Panke 2016), IOs can be large or small in size. For example, the North Atlantic Salmon Conservation Organization (NASCO) is the smallest IO in our dataset, as it comprises only six member states, and is preceded by the International Tropical Timber Organization (ITTO) with forty member states. By contrast, the United Nations Framework Convention on Climate Change (UNFCCC) and the United Nations Conference on Trade and Development (UNCTAD) are much bigger with 195 and 194 member states, respectively. The size of IOs could have important implications for how negotiations are conducted in practice (Berton et al. 1999, Kremenyuk 1991, Plantey 2007). With a large membership of 100 or even more member states, negotiations would be extremely time-consuming if each state voiced its national position and participated actively during the course of deliberations in IO institutions. Instead of making a tour de table, states could aggregate national positions in groups and voice national positions only in exceptional instances. This would especially increase the effectiveness of international negotiations in IOs with a large state membership. Thus, H3a expects that the more member states an IO has, the greater the activity level of ROs in international negotiations.

IOs also differ with respect to their formal decision-making rules, which can range from majority-voting to passing international norms and rules on the basis of consensus (Alvarez 2005, Hurd 2011, Martin and Simmons 2001). *Hypothesis 3b* focuses on the IO decision-making rules and their impact on the prospects for RO activity in international negotiations. If decisions are formally made by majority voting, every vote counts for the passing of international rules and norms in an IO. Thus, operating through ROs has advantages for RO members as ROs allow accumulating votes and punching above a single states' formal weight. Hence, compared to consensus IOs, majority-voting IOs should feature a higher-level or regionalised negotiations since the extent to which regional positions are voiced is greater.

MLG approaches often argue that the ability of actors to engage in collective action and effectively develop policies varies across policy fields.[11] Accordingly, the final set of hypotheses captures the **policy field properties** that might affect the ability of RO members to act in concert and voice regional positions. *Hypothesis 4a* takes into consideration that most ROs have started with regional integration in the trade area, increasing in scope over time (Mattli 1999, Nye 1965). Thus, it expects that when an international negotiation deals with trade themes, ROs will be more active because they are usually most strongly integrated into this sector, resulting in a higher likelihood that the RO members already share a common position.

In nested negotiations within EMLG systems, state, regional and international levels are interlinked. This places states as well as regional actors in a position where they could engage in forum-shopping and choose the level and arena where they would like to deal with a specific item, respectively (Hooghe and Marks 2001, Kellow 2012). Accordingly, in addition to the single-level hypotheses, we also shed light on **cross-level effects**. We examine the interrelatedness of state and RO properties (Hca and cb) and cross-level effects of RO and IO properties (Hcc, cd and ce).

Since RO member states need to agree on a common position first, before such a position can be voiced in international negotiations (e.g. Blavoukos and Bourantonis 2011a, da Conceição-Heldt and Meunier 2014, Dee 2015, Delreux 2013, Drieskens and Schaik 2014, Panke 2013b, Smith 2006), the level of an RO's internal homogeneity of member states is important. The more heterogeneous the member states of an RO are, the more difficult its internal coordination meetings and the less likely it is that a regional position is developed. This, in turn, reduces the chances that the position of the RO is voiced in international negotiations. *Hypothesis ca* expects that increasing homogeneity amongst the member states of an RO increases the likelihood that its regional positions are voiced in international negotiations.

Another incentive for states to voice regional positions in international negotiations is linked to their *formal roles in ROs*. RO members usually take turns in serving as chairs (Quaglia and Moxon-Browne 2006, Schalk et al. 2007, Tallberg 2003, Warntjen 2008). One important task of chairmen is to organise and lead group coordination meetings (Blavoukos et al. 2006), in which the member states formulate regional positions with respect to the issues on the international negotiation arena. With the role of being a chair comes not only the duty to convene and chair group meetings, but also an incentive to represent the group externally and articulate the regional position in international negotiations. Accordingly, *hypothesis cb* states: States are more likely to speak on behalf of an RO in international negotiations, if they hold the office of a chair in this RO.

Apart from shedding light on the nexus between states and ROs, one can also examine cross-level interactions between ROs and IOs. The first nexus of interest is the policy match between RO and IO. Not all ROs cover the same policy areas (Panke and Stapel 2016), and IOs vary in this respect as well (c.f. chapter 3). Focal point approaches emphasise the importance of commonalities between potentially diverse actors for decisions about courses of action (Binmore and Samuelson 2006, Binmore et al. 1993, Mehta et al. 1994). The less the policy scope covered in an RO and an IO match, the less likely it is that the RO member states can recur to prior agreements or already existing common policies when developing a regional position on the issue at stake in the IO negotiation arena in regional coordination meetings. This, in turn, reduces the effectiveness of regional coordination amongst the member states and can lead to situations in which they fail to develop a common regional position at all or in time for the international negotiations, both of which reduces the likelihood that regional positions are articulated in the IO. In contrast, the more the policy scopes of an RO and an IO overlap, the more active the RO is in the respective IO. This is because it is increasingly likely that RO member states already share a common policy approach that they can (directly or in a modified version) articulate in the international negotiations in form of a common regional position. Hence *hypothesis cc* expects that regional positions of ROs are voiced increasingly in international negotiations, the stronger the policy overlap between the RO and the IO at stake.

The *formal status of ROs* in IOs ranges from full membership, over observer status to no formal role at all (Blavoukos and Bourantonis 2010, Gehring 2013, Wetzel 2011). Since registering as observer or member in an IO is time- and resource-intensive for the ROs concerned, only ROs that have strong incentive to also use their formal access right subsequently are likely to apply for a formal status in an IO. Hence, whenever regional actors have access to international negotiation arenas (as either observers or members), they should have incentives to use this as an opportunity to voice regional positions either directly or through their members. Hence, *hypothesis cd* states: The regional positions of ROs with formal status in IOs should be voiced more often than the positions of ROs without formal status.

Finally, another regional-level property that might affect RO member states' behaviour in IOs relates to the resource allocation of ROs for specific IOs. Capacities play an important part for collective action in multilevel settings (Chayes and Handler-Chayes 1995, Panke 2013a, c, Panke et al. 2015). Thus, the chances of successfully developing a common regional position that is subsequently voiced on the IO level is influenced by the capacity devoted to facilitating state–state coordination meetings at the location of IO negotiations. ROs with headquarters at the location of an IO are better resourced and therefore better able to develop and update common positions among the RO member states, which increases the prospects of regional activity in these specific IO negotiations. Hence, *hypothesis ce* expects that if an RO has an office at the location of an IO headquarter, its positions are more often articulated during international negotiations in the respective IO.

### 2.2.2 Measuring RO activity

The first dependent variable under examination in this book is the prevalence of regional positions voiced in international negotiations. Unlike success over international norms (DV2),[12] the active participation of ROs in multilateral negotiations in IOs is not as often in the limelight of research (e.g. Burmester and Jankowski 2014).[13] This is not in the least due to the challenges of inter-subjectively assessing active participation of a broad variety of actors across a

broad variety of institutional contexts in a great number of international negotiations. In principle, active participation in negotiations can be measured in
three different ways: case studies and interviews, surveys or on the basis of
document analysis.

Case studies can reconstruct the activities of participants and obtain
information on how often each actor speaks up in order to further their
own positions in formal negotiation arenas, such as committees and plenary
assemblies, as well as in informal settings, such as coffee breaks, lunches,
receptions, external workshops or conferences, or bilateral contacts between
embassies and diplomats (Panke 2013c). This approach relies on semi-
structured interviews asking negotiation participants about their perceptions
and recollections of who said what, when and where. In order to avoid biases
of subjective recollections and individual actor perceptions, it is essential
that activity information is triangulated. This requires a high number of
interviews, especially if the international negotiations concerned have a large
number of actors. Case studies have the advantage of including all types of
negotiation arenas, both formal and informal. However, this endeavour is
highly time-intensive, as it requires a large number of interviews with different negotiation participants in order to triangulate the data on activity and
avoid carrying over the subjective biases of individual actors. Thus, case
studies can provide in-depth insights into negotiation activity, but they can do
so only for a very limited number of negotiations and only if the diplomats in
question are willing to give interviews.

The second option for obtaining data on the negotiation activity of many
actors across many negotiations in different IOs is to conduct a survey (Panke
2010, 2011b). Similar to semi-structured interviews, surveys are based on
structured questions asking for actors' recollections concerning active participation. Unlike interviews, surveys usually do not rely on open questions
but rather on categorical answer options (sometimes in the form of a Likert
scale, sometimes a 10-point scale) or continuous scales (asking respondents
to insert values on a defined range). Not relying on open answers makes
survey responses more easily comparable and more easily quantifiable than
interview-based case studies.[14] However, while interviews can ask for the
respondent's recollections of their own and third-party activity, surveys need
to focus on the assessment of an actor's own active participation. This is due
to the practical reasons, as a survey asking each respondent to rate the activity level of each IO member separately would be too time-consuming for any
actor to actually complete – especially for IOs with more than 20 or even
100 member states. As a consequence of relying on the self-assessments of
actors, surveys are at risk of suffering from 'positive answer biases' from the
respondents, who could have the tendency to evaluate their own performance
in a more positive light. Nevertheless, if all actors were subject to more or less

the same positive self-bias in the survey, the relative differences in the activity levels of actors would still be accurate, albeit at an overall higher activity rate.[15] Compared to case studies, surveys can provide activity data on a larger number of negotiations and across a larger number of actors. This requires high response rates from a representative sample of IO member states, without which the sample would risk being biased, which severely reduces the quality of the data.

The third option is to collect activity information on the basis of content analysis of official and publicly accessible written or oral records of negotiations in IOs. In a content analysis of minutes or reports, the number of times each actor voices a position can be counted in order to measure active participation in a negotiation. This allows for obtaining activity data for a broad range of different actors across a large number of negotiations. Thus, content analysis can avoid subjective biases due to positive self-attribution, biases based on limited triangulation, or biases due to a limited number of negotiations studied (case selection). There is a further advantage for the content analysis-based measurement of RO activity. Interviews rely on the correct recollection of diplomats in specific negotiations and surveys rely on the correct self-assessment of diplomats either across specific negotiations or, on average, in a specified period of time. Thus, the quality of interview and survey data might be best the more recent the negotiation(s) under scrutiny is, while false or incomplete memories are more likely to produce biases if more time has passed since the completion of the negotiation under scrutiny. Content analysis is, by contrast, time invariant and is not at risk of poorer quality of activity information with greater time lags between the issue of interest and the point of time at which the data is gathered. However, content analysis has two downsides. First, it is only possible to analyse IOs in which officially available minutes or reports are sufficiently detailed to count the number of times different actors speak up. Second, content analysis only captures negotiation activity in official negotiation arenas, depending on the IO in question's main legislative bodies, while it cannot capture how active states are in informal negotiation arenas, such as coffee breaks, receptions or informal bilateral contacts.

On the basis of these considerations, the book combines content analysis of official documents and interviews with comparative case studies. For the quantitative part in which a large-N dataset without subjective biases concerning activity perceptions is needed, it mainly uses content analysis of official IO records of negotiations in order to measure the activity of state and regional actors across a wide range of international negotiations (for the quantitative case selection, c.f. chapter 3). For the qualitative part, the book not only relies on content analysis but also supplements this information with triangulated interviews (c.f. chapter 5). As such, the case studies obtain information on activity in formal (Conferences of the Parties [CoP], plenary assemblies, committees, as well as preparatory meetings) and informal arenas (e.g. coffee breaks, lunches, receptions, external workshops or conferences, bilateral contact of embassies outside IO arenas).

The content analysis uses, depending on the IO's reporting system and institutional structure, officially available reports, minutes or press releases on the negotiations in the IO's main legislative arena (usually the assembly and respective committees). On this basis, it codes all speeches in relation to a specific negotiation and detects how often states voice their own positions as well as the frequency with which states speak on behalf of their RO, as well as how often an RO representative (e.g. the European Commission) directly voices a group position. In instances where ROs have no speaking rights themselves, states can articulate the positions of their ROs. Therefore, activity is operationalised on the speech-act level. For example, if a state representative declares in a speech that he or she is speaking 'on behalf of the RO', that 'the RO agrees to/disagrees with/objects/supports/ proposes/recommends etc.', the intervention is counted as RO activity, whereas the absence of a reference to the regional position or preference is counted as voicing national positions (state activity) (c.f. chapter 3). Thus, the content analysis captures not only the number of interventions of each actor and the content of the intervention, but also the share of total statements in which RO representatives or RO member states speak on behalf of the RO (= voicing RO group positions). This is important since it permits controlling for the number of RO members who are also IO members and the extent to which the states participate in international negotiations (c.f. chapter 3).

The qualitative case studies also rely on a content analysis of the officially available documents. However, since the latter captures activity in formal negotiation arenas, the case studies also use triangulated interviews. This also allows for gathering information on the activities of state and RO members in informal settings, such as coffee breaks, receptions or workshops (for more details, c.f. Chapter 5).

## 2.3 RO SUCCESS IN INTERNATIONAL NEGOTIATIONS – THE STATE OF THE ART

The second dependent variable with importance for the regionalisation of international negotiations is RO success. ROs can be successful in influencing negotiation dynamics (e.g. by talking third-party actors into supporting the regional position) as well as in influencing outcomes of international negotiations (e.g. by altering the international norm or rule on the IO negotiation table).

There is a rich body of literature on RO success, which again predominantly studies the EU. However, definitions and measurements of performance, effectiveness or influence as prominent key concepts used in the literature on RO success vary almost from author to author, rendering the development of a bigger picture concerning EU success in international negotiations somewhat difficult. Also, some scholars focus on goal attainment of the EU in different IOs in general (Græger and Gaugevik 2011, Kelemen 2001), while others are more specific and analyse the negotiation of individual norms (e.g. Delreux 2012, Hivonnet 2012, Joergensen et al. 2011, Oberthür 1999).

It is striking that the EU's ability to successfully influence negotiation dynamics and/or negotiation outcomes varies; sometimes it is considerable, but rather limited in other instances. For example, the EU is regarded as not being an effective external actor in the UNSC (Blavoukos and Bourantonis 2011c), the WHO (van Schaik 2011), the NATO (Græger and Gaugevik 2011) or the NPT negotiations (Dee 2015), but performs well in WTO-related negotiations (Dür and Zimmerman 2007, Kelemen 2001, Nicolaidis and Meunier 1999), and in the negotiations of the International Criminal Court (Groenleer and Schaik 2007). However, there is no clear-cut policy pattern. Even within the same policy field, the EU's performance is subject to variation. For example, while it was effective in the negotiations of the Kyoto Protocol (Groenleer and Schaik 2007), other environmental negotiations did not go that well, as the UNFCCC negotiations illustrate (Oberthür 2011). Similarly, the EU's influence is limited in the Human Rights Council (Smith 2010, 2013b), but high in regard to the UNGA resolution on the human rights situation in Myanmar (Panke 2013c, 2014a). Moreover, within one institutional context, the success of the EU can vary as well. For example, in UNGA negotiations on the African descent resolution and the 2011 resolution on the elimination of racism the EU was successful, but failed to influence the text of the international norm in the case of the resolution on the Convention on the Prohibition of the Use of Nuclear Weapons (Panke 2013b, 2014b).[16] Finally, even in regard to one and the same item in a constant international negotiation arena, the EU's success can vary over time, as the Telecommunication Union negotiations (van Schaik 2011) and the negotiations on the UNGA resolution on the elimination of racism illustrate (Panke 2013c, 2014b).

The variation in the EU's performance as the external actor is attributed to a variety of different variables. Some scholars flag that limited EU coherence and the inability to act as a unitary actor in IO negotiations render the EU less effective externally (Delreux 2009b, 2013, Groenleer and Schaik 2007), while others point out that limited homogeneity and speaking with several voices can increase the EU's prospects of being successful (Macaj and Nicolaïdis 2014). Moreover, depending on the policy area at stake, the EU's power and capacities vary, which might impact its ability to turn into an important player in international negotiations (da Conceição-Heldt 2014, Joergensen et al. 2011, Panke 2014a, 2015). Some studies stress that success in international negotiations is contingent upon the distribution of preferences and power among third-party states present in the international negotiation arena as well as upon the procedural decision-making rules laid out by the IO itself (Panke 2014b).

While these studies provide empirically rich insights into the EU's prospects to successfully alter negotiation dynamics and/or outcomes, their findings are difficult to generalise to regional actors in international negotiations in general, not in the least due to the EU bias in the empirical focus and the selected analytical and theoretical toolbox used for the analysis, but also because they look at different conceptual aspects of success and talk in some instances at cross purposes.

To remedy the first shortcoming, this book utilises an EMLG approach in order to develop hypotheses on RO success relating to the state, regional and international levels as well as policy dimension, and adopts a comparative approach to study the observable implications in regard to a broad set of ROs across a representative sample of international negotiations in different policy areas (next section). Thus, this book systematically examines the success (or failure) of a broad range of different ROs in different international negotiation arenas, covering a wide range of policy areas and systematically explaining observed variation.

In order to avoid the pitfall of conceptual ambivalence in regard to the second dependent variable, RO success, we distinguish between influence and success. The concept of 'influence' generally seeks to capture how much an actor has been able to shape the outcome of a negotiation in line with their own preferences (Keohane 1967, Tallberg 2000). Since influence exclusively relates to the outcome of negotiations whilst neglecting negotiation dynamics, this book focuses on success. In this respect, we distinguish between a procedural and a substantive component of success. The procedural aspect focuses on negotiation dynamics, and the substantive one on negotiation outcomes.

Thus, success encompasses the ability of an actor to actively increase support for its own position amongst third-party actors during negotiations (procedural success), to change the content of a negotiation outcome in line with its own positions (substantive success). Both dimensions have reactive and proactive components. Proactive success is present if an actor manages to talk additional states into supporting its position (procedural success), or if the actor manages to alter the text of the passed norm or rule in line with its position (substantive success). In contrast, reactive success focuses on

**Table 2.2.   Dimensionality of success**

| | *Procedural Success* | *Substantive Success* |
|---|---|---|
| Proactive | Talking third-party states into fully supporting one's position or into shifting their position gradually to one's own position | Achieving text changes in the norm in line with own position or (if the actor is also the norm sponsor) managing to pass the norm unaltered |
| Reactive | Reacting to lobbying of others and preventing third-party states from shifting their positions away from own position | Preventing third-party states from changing the text of a norm away from one's own position |

preventing others with opposing positions from being effective in doing the same. Accordingly, reactive procedural success is characterised by the ability of an actor to prevent a third-party actor from successfully changing the position of other states. Reactive substantive success encompasses to prevent third-party states or other ROs from changing the language of the norm under negotiation against one's preferences.

### 2.3.1 Theorising RO success

This section presents hypotheses on how the properties of IOs, of ROs and of member states, as well as of policy-related variables affect the prospects of ROs of being successful in international negotiations in EMLG systems (for an overview of hypotheses, see table 2.3). Success is conceptualised as the ability of an actor to actively increase support for its position amongst third-party actors (procedural success), or to change the content of a negotiation outcome in line with its own positions (substantive success) (see table 2.3). ROs can be successful directly through RO representatives that use RO speaking rights in order to further regional positions or indirectly through RO member states who apply negotiation strategies on behalf of their regional groups in order to shape the international norm in line with regional positions.

In order to capture the prospects of ROs to be successful in IO negotiations, it is essential to shed light on the **state level**. Member states are likely to play an important part on how successful an RO is in international negotiations (Habeeb 1988, Panke 2013c, Zartman and Rubin 2009). Yet, international negotiations are complex, work-intensive and time-consuming (Panke 2013c, Plantey 2007, Stein 1989, Zartman and Rubin 2009). Thus, the more complex the issue under negotiation is, and the more articles and paragraphs are on the IO negotiation agenda, the greater the capacity demands. Yet, the time and resources an individual actor can devote to negotiate for an RO in an IO are not endless. Thus, when the RO member states coordinate their actions

**Table 2.3. Hypotheses on RO success (DV2)**

| | |
|---|---|
| *H5: Member State Properties* | |
| H5a burden-sharing | The more extensively RO members use burden-sharing, the more successful the respective RO is international negotiations. |
| H5b national positions | An increase in heterogeneity amongst member states decreases the prospects of the respective RO to be successful in international negotiations. |
| *H6: RO properties* | |
| H6a Active participation of ROs | The more active an RO is, the greater its chances for influencing international norms. |
| H6b Bargaining | ROs are increasingly successful in international negotiations, when they use bargaining strategies whilst possessing bargaining leverage. |
| H6c Arguing | ROs are increasingly successful in international negotiations, when they use argumentative strategies whilst providing sound reasons. |
| H6d Lock-in | ROs are increasingly successful in international negotiations, when they can link the contested item to already agreed language from other sources. |
| H6e Lobbying | The more capacities ROs have, the greater the RO's prospects of exerting success through informal lobbying in international negotiations. |
| H6f Coalition-building | The more capacities ROs have to reach out to other groups in the IO, the greater the RO's prospects of exerting success in international negotiations via coalition-building. |
| *H7: IO properties* | |
| H7a Openness for ROs | The more ROs possess important formal competencies in IO decision-making processes, the RO's success in international negotiations increases. |
| H7b IO size | The larger IO are, the greater the importance of ROs for effective negotiations and the more successful they become. |
| H7c Decision making in IO – voting | If decisions are taken by vote in an IO, an RO's prospects of success in international negotiations increase the more members it has. |
| *H8: Policy properties* | |
| H8 issue salience | ROs are more successful, the higher they regard the saliency of the issue on the international negotiation agenda. |

concerning how and when to negotiate on its behalf instead of exclusively placing the burden to speak for the RO on a single actor, the chances for an RO to successfully influence negotiation dynamics and outcomes increase. Accordingly, *hypothesis 5a* expects that ROs are increasingly successful, if their member states engage in burden-sharing.

National positions play a key role in international negotiation dynamics and outcomes (Moravcsik 1991, Panke 2013a). Hence, a second member state factor that is likely to impact the prospects of regional actors to be successful in IOs is the diversity of national positions of the RO members. The more diverse state positions are, the more likely it is that they can at best agree on a minimalist regional position. Moreover, the more diverse RO member states positions concerning the issue on the IO negotiation table are, the less likely it is that they act in concert with respect to the regional minimal position during the entire international negotiation process. Yet, when individual states add nuances to the regional position voiced in international negotiation arenas, it showcases the presence of RO internal dissent for elements beyond the minimal position. A lack of internal homogeneity amongst the member states is negative for ROs as it renders RO negotiation strategies less effective. For instance, a bargaining threat with a collective no-vote loses effectiveness, when third-party states know that not all RO members would indeed vote this way. Similarly, an argumentative strategy that seeks to persuade third parties from the advantages of the RO position loses its convincing powers when it becomes clear that not even all of the RO members are themselves persuaded by the own reasons provided. Thus, *hypothesis 5b* states: An increase in heterogeneity amongst member states decreases the prospects of the respective RO to be successful in international negotiations.

Based on insights from two-level game theory and negotiation approaches more generally (Dür and Mateo 2010, Moravcsik 1998, Müller 2004, Pruitt 1991, Thomson 2011, Zartman and Rubin 2009), a set of **regional-level** hypotheses captures how RO properties affect their chances of being successful in international negotiations (DV2).

In negotiations, activity is key to success (Panke 2011a, 2014c). Hence, according to *hypothesis 6a*, ROs are more successful in international negotiations the more actively they participate. This general expectation is further specified by hypotheses on specific negotiation strategies.

*Hypothesis 6b* focuses on bargaining strategies, which focus on costs and benefits and are threat- or offer-based, and include flagging the possibility of no-votes, blockades or tied hands, demanding concessions or offering compromises (Bailer 2004, Busch 2003, da Conceição-Heldt 2014, Drahos 2003, Evans et al. 1993, Fearon 1998, Jönsson and Tallberg 1998, Mo 1995). The more bargaining leverage the members of an RO possess, the greater the RO's prospects of being successful in international negotiations when using bargaining-based strategies (*hypothesis 6b*). Bargaining power is contextual in nature, and sources of leverage can vary from context to context. For example, bargaining leverage can include an economic or financial power to offer concessions or side-payments, voting power, the power to prevent outcomes or the power to end cooperation and pursue own interests in an alternative venue or unilaterally.

Next, to bargaining, argumentative strategies are very prominent in international negotiations (Deitelhoff and Müller 2005, Elster 1992, Holzinger 2004, Johnstone 2003, Kleine and Risse 2005, Panke 2009, Risse 2000). At their core, argumentative strategies link positions to reasons in order to persuade third parties from the quality of one's position (Panke 2009, Risse 2000). Reasons can be related to technical, scientific, political, legal or normative insights, and the better the reasons fit to frames and prior ideas of third-party actors, the more persuasive the argumentative strategy becomes (Panke 2009). Vice versa, if there are competing policy frames, the power of argumentative strategies is more limited. Hence *hypothesis 6c* expects that regional actors are increasingly successful in international negotiations, when they use argumentative strategies that link regional position to sound reasons.

Another strategy that regional actors can use in order to influence dynamics and outcomes of international negotiations is the recurrence to other legal sources. Linking an issue to the IO negotiation table that is contested to pre-agreed language can help to overcome opposition (Cass 2005, Meerts 2005, Morin and Gold 2010, Panke 2015). In general, there are two pathways of how the strategy works: one related to bargaining-dynamics and one to argumentative dynamics. According to the bargaining pathway, such linkages allow to entrap opponents. Opponents cannot continue to disagree concerning the issue currently under discussion, since they would face reputation costs arising from violating their earlier commitments (Panke 2015). According to the argumentative pathway, linking a contested issue to pre-agreed international norms and rules creates focal points, which makes persuasion easier, as all actors have a common yardstick to evaluate the quality of communicated reasons (Panke 2009). Thus, ROs are increasingly successful in international negotiations, when they can link the contested item to already agreed-on language from other sources (*hypothesis 6d*).

A prominent informal strategy, which is not usually applied in the negotiation arena as such but used on a bilateral basis, is lobbying (Hojnacki and Kimball 1999, Panke 2012c). In lobbying, one actor approaches another one in an informal setting, in order to talk this actor into support, based either on arguments or on bargaining offers or threats. Lobbying is highly resource-intensive as it requires diplomatic staff and time as well as a higher level of technical, legal and political knowledge or bargaining leverage. Hence, *hypothesis 6e* expects that the more capacities ROs have, the greater the RO's prospects of exerting success through informal lobbying in international negotiations.

Especially in contexts with several states, another prominent strategy is to informally build an ad hoc coalition with other actors and thereby increase the number of actors making similar claims and pushing for similar outcomes (Coleman 1970, Panke 2010). Such strategies are increasingly likely to impact outcomes of negotiations, the greater the number of actors belonging to the formed coalition becomes. Yet, forming a coalition can be resource-intensive, so that especially well-equipped actors are likely to take the lead (Panke 2010). According to *hypothesis 6f*, the more capacities regional actors have to reach out to other groups in the IO, the greater the RO's prospects of exerting success in international negotiations via coalition-building.

On the **IO level**, institutional design is important not only for negotiation dynamics, but also for the prospects of different actors in being successful in shaping international norms (Goodin 1995, Koremons et al. 2001, Panke 2013c). IO treaties define not only how decisions should be made, but define also membership as well as the formal status of ROs in the negotiation arenas.

In many IOs, ROs can apply to become registered observers with formal access to international negotiations (Blavoukos and Bourantonis 2010, Gehring et al. 2013, Wetzel 2011), while full membership rights in which regional actors have voted on their own are very restricted and are so far only granted to the EU in few IOs, such as the WTO, the FAO or the ITTO. Whenever an IO has granted a high number of ROs competencies and the more far-reaching these competencies are, the more likely it is that regional actors are accepted by all IO member states as legitimate actors. Moreover, when regional actors have formal access to international negotiations, RO delegations have a chance of speaking directly for the RO. Both elements increase the chances of ROs to successfully participate in IO negotiation processes. Accordingly, *hypothesis 7a* expects that the RO's success in international negotiations increases, the more open IO decision-making processes are formally for ROs.

The number of member states of an IO has consequences for the effectiveness of negotiations (Albin and Druckman 2014, Panke 2012d, Scanzoni and Godwin 1990). The more actors possess speaking and voting rights; the lengthier negotiations do potentially become. One means to reduce the time of negotiations and speed up the creation of international norms and rules is to bundle individual positions into group positions and negotiate on this basis. Thus, an increase in IO size creates a window of opportunity for RO success with respect to influencing dynamics and outcomes of international negotiations. Hence, *hypothesis 7b* expects that the larger IOs in regard to the number of members, the greater the importance of ROs for the effectiveness of international negotiations and the more successful they become in international negotiations.

IO treaties also regulate how decisions are formally made (Alvarez 2005, Hurd 2011, Martin and Simmons 2001) and one of these regulations specify whether IO policies are passed by majority vote or consensus rule. *Hypothesis*

*7c* specifies how the formal IO decision-making modes might impact regional actor success. In IOs with some form of majority decisions, be it simple or qualified majorities, the number of votes matters. This should give ROs de facto a greater leverage over negotiation outcomes. Hence, if decisions are made by a vote in an IO, an RO's prospects of negotiation success increases the more members it has. If IO decisions are made by consensus, however, each state has the potential to block an outcome. Hence, in consensus IOs, regional actors should be less successful than in IOs that are based on a majority principle.

In regard to **policy properties**, the salience of items under negotiation in an IO is important, as it motivates the actors to invest their ultimately scarce resources into specific issues under negotiation rather than other ones (Bourantonis 2015, Panke 2013c, Ringquist et al. 2003, Segal 2000, Thomson and Stokman 2006). Accordingly, RO members should have greater incentives to invest their resources when they regard the saliency of the issue under negotiation in an IO as high for their RO. *Hypothesis 8* expects that the higher the saliency of the issue at stake for an RO, the more successful it is in international negotiations.

## 2.3.2 Measuring RO success

The concept of 'success' is difficult to measure, and the literature features three prominent alternatives (Dür 2008, Panke 2013c).

The first option to operationalise (substantive) success and influence and gather large-N data on these variables is to focus on the extent of the overlap between an actor's initial position and the final negotiation outcome (Thomson et al. 2003, 2006). In order to use the overlap between initial preferences and outcome as a proxy for (substantive) success or influence, it is essential to code both the distribution of initial preferences and the outcome on a scale. To this end, large-N studies have relied on expert interviews in order to reduce the complexity of the issue at stake, detect the most important dimensions of conflict and decide on the endpoints of each continuous or categorical dimension (Thomson 2011, Thomson et al. 2006). On this basis, either experts or negotiation participants are asked to place the actors' initial positions in the policy space and locate the final outcome. Although it is very time- and resource-intensive, this approach has the merit of potentially providing large-N data which is triangulated and therefore not strongly biased by individual actors' perceptions. However, this approach has two downsides. First, instead of reflecting the complexity of the issue and the negotiations, it reduces the number of cleavages at stake and gives them equal weight, although different actors might place emphasis on the various aspects of a norm under negotiation. Second, deducing influence or substantial success from an overlap between initial positions and final policy outcomes, while treating the negotiation process itself as a black box, can bring about incorrect interpretation. Most importantly, it could be the case that an actor remained passive or was freeriding on the negotiation efforts of others, so that the extent of overlap between initial positions and the outcome is either coincidental or not due to the active participation and the active usage of negotiation strategies of the actor at stake (Panke 2012b, 2013c). Both of these cases are *not* regarded as instances of 'substantive success' in this book, as they do not capture how much an actor *has been able to shape* the outcome of a negotiation in line with his or her own preferences. Success, as defined in this book, is an active concept that requires the participation of an actor in international negotiations.[17]

Second, large-N data on influence and success can be gathered from surveys (e.g. Panke 2010). Unlike the large-N dimensionality coding, surveys do not have to reduce the complexity of the issue into a small number of items at stake (dimensions of conflict) and they do not need to rate the relative weight of the different dimensions at stake, which is important because different actors might place salience on different aspects of the norm under negotiation. Similar to the large-N dimensionality coding, a survey needs to abstract from reality in order to measure success as a categorical or continuous variable. Surveys do this by specifying answer options, which brings about the possibility of subjective biases of respondents. Moreover, while a survey has the advantage of obtaining data across a broad range of actors and issues, it relies heavily on self-assessment and is therefore prone to positive biases (c.f. section 2.2.1).

Third, procedural as well as substantial success can be measured in case studies (Panke 2010) which use official documents, other primary as well as secondary sources, and semi-structured triangulated interviews in order to reconstruct the initial distribution of positions, as well as the negotiation dynamics and outcomes. While case studies only allow for capturing a small number of specific negotiations, they are well suited to trace how often and how effectively each actor uses which negotiation strategy and how this translates into changing the positions of third-party actors (procedural success) as well as the negotiation outcome in line (substantial success) with one's own positions. Due to triangulating sources and interviews instead of only relying on self or on third-party assessment, case studies can trace the negotiation process in great detail without being prone to the biases of an individual actor and without being forced to abstract from reality and limit the analysis to one or two dimensions or conflicts only (c.f. section 2.2.1).

To circumvent the problems associated with the two large-N measurement options, this book chooses process-tracing case studies in the qualitative section. Case studies permit measuring the different dimensions of the success of ROs in a series of selected negotiations and empirically examine the corresponding hypotheses in order to account for variation in the ability of ROs to shape international norms in line with group positions (c.f. chapter 4). In order to measure how successful different ROs are, the case study uses primary sources and triangulated semi-structured interviews. In a first step, the case studies analyse the draft norm as put on the negotiation agenda as well as the final outcomes and identify the cleavages at stake on the basis of negotiation protocols and interviews. In a second step, the case studies reconstruct the initial positions of states and regional groups, reconstruct how the different actors used negotiation strategies in order to promote their state or group positions and analyse how effective each of these activities was in obtaining support of third-party actors (procedural success), in changing the content of the passed international norms or rules in line with own positions (articles, paragraphs, sentences, words) (substantive success) on the basis of a series of triangulated interviews and official documents.

A regional actor is considered to be procedurally successful if its representative or a member state voiced regional positions and used negotiation strategies that were effective in talking formerly indifferent or opposing third-party actors into supporting the RO's position concerning a norm or rule under negotiation (proactive procedural success). If an RO counteracts the lobbying of outsiders to reduce the number of third-party supporters of a regional position, it is procedurally successful as well (reactive procedural success). Similarly, if an RO manages to obtain all promoted text changes for an international norm or if it is able to push through a draft norm that the group has tabled without substantial changes, it would be deemed substantively successful. If an RO is not active at all or is actively using negotiation strategies, but they fail to be effective so that the RO does not induce language changes in the international norm or rule, it is regarded as not substantially successful.

## 2.4 NESTED NEGOTIATIONS: EXPECTATIONS OF RO ACTIVITY AND RO SUCCESS IN INTERNATIONAL NEGOTIATIONS

In EMLG systems, governance takes place on different levels. Due to an increase in ROs and IOs and an overlap between member states and policy areas covered, multilateral negotiations within IOs resemble EMLGs. Accordingly, this chapter has developed hypotheses located at the member state, the RO and the IO as well as the policy levels in order to account for RO activity (DV1) and RO success (DV2) in international level negotiations.

Which regional actors are expected to be most active in multilateral negotiations? In which IOs should most RO activity be? In which policy areas are ROs expected to be the most engaged?

Based on the EMLG hypotheses, ROs are expected to participate more actively in international negotiations the larger they are and the broader their policy scope. In addition, ROs should be more vocal in IOs, the more democratic, the smaller and the more effective their member states are, the more offices at IO headquarters a regional actor has, and if they have registered as observers or members in IOs. Thus, not all ROs should be equally active. For instance, the European Union should be more active than the African Union. This is because the EU's member states have more administrative capacities and are more strongly oriented towards making compromises, which should render the coordination of member states to develop a group position easier in the EU than the AU. In addition, the EU also has more central coordination resources available at the locations of many IO headquarters.

The level of RO activity is also expected to vary between negotiation contexts. Regional positions should be voiced more often the larger IOs are, the greater the number of ROs with formal speaking rights (observers or members), and if IOs pass rules and norms by majority vote. For instance, the International Whaling Commission (IWC) or the Security Council (SC) should feature low levels of RO activity as ROs have very limited or no formal competencies and because the IOs are small (eighty-nine and fifteen member states). By contrast, ROs should be more active in the Human Rights Council (HRC) or the Economic and Social Council (ECOSOC), which allow for more ROs to have speaking rights but are also small (forty-seven and fifty-four member states, respectively). ROs should be very active in IOs, such as the World Intellectual Property Organization (WIPO), the International Labour Organisation (ILO) or the United Nations General Assembly (UNGA), which grants a high number of ROs observer status and are of large size (185, 185, 193).

Based on the EMLG framework (c.f. figure 2.2), we would also expect policy variation. Since ROs mainly began as enterprises of trade integration, it is most likely that RO member states have already agreed on many trade issues. Thus, ROs should be most active when international negotiations touch upon trade issues or in IOs that deal with trade themes, such as the WTO, because the chances that RO members already share a common position and so can speak with one voice increases. The latter is less likely in IOs dealing with issues that are not at the traditional 'core' of RO policies, such as the IWC or WHO.

Which ROs should be most successful? In which IOs can regional actors be expected to be successful? In which policy areas should RO activity translate the most into RO success?

If the hypotheses on RO success were supported empirically, ROs should be most successful in international negotiations the more actively they

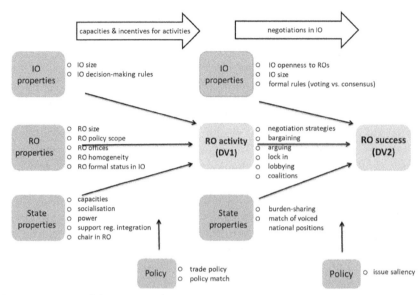

**Figure 2.2.   RO activity (DV1) and RO success (DV2)**

participate, the larger they are in size, and the greater the internal homogeneity. In addition, ROs should be increasingly successful if the RO members divide the negotiation work amongst themselves rather than just delegating it to a single regional actor and the more effective the negotiation strategies used. The latter requires manpower as well as economic leverage, vote-based leverage or legal, technical, political and normative expertise. Ceteris paribus, large ROs such as the AU should be more successful than small ROs such as UNASUR. Also, an RO with a considerable manpower and argumentative resources as well as economic bargaining leverage, such as the EU, should be more successful in altering the dynamics and outcomes of international negotiations than less well-resourced ROs such as SADC or EAC.

The success of ROs is also expected to vary across IOs. IOs are most prone to the regionalisation of negotiation outcomes; the larger IOs are, the more ROs they grant far-reaching rights and if they operate on the basis of majority rule. Thus, IOs such as the WTO or the United Nations Framework Convention on Climate Change (UNFCCC) or the Food and Agriculture Organization (FAO) should feature a higher level of RO success than the United Nations Environmental Programme (UNEP) or the Conference on Disarmament (CD), as the latter is not only smaller in terms of member states but also do not grant far-reaching competencies to ROs.

In terms of policy characteristics, saliency is likely to be of great importance, since ultimately all negotiation resources of ROs are limited. Thus,

ROs should be especially successful when the issue on the IO negotiation table is of great importance to them.

The subsequent chapters conduct a comprehensive empirical analysis of all hypotheses (see figure 2.2). In order to obtain insights into the bigger pattern as well as into underlying causal mechanisms, the project adopts a multiple-methods approach. Chapters 3 and 4 present the quantitative analysis of RO activity in international negotiations, while chapters 5, 6 and 7 present the qualitative case studies and the analysis of RO negotiation success.

On the basis of the cross-RO, cross-IO comparative examination of RO activity and success, the following chapters provide novel insights into the effects of ROs on multilateral negotiation dynamics and on outcomes of international negotiations. In doing so, the book sheds light on the current regionalisation of international politics (Katzenstein 1996, Rosenau and Czempiel 1992, Young 1999).

*Part I*

# ACTIVITY OF REGIONAL ACTORS

In order to examine the activity of regional actors in international negotiations (DV1), the next chapter introduces the dataset and maps the empirical puzzles (chapter 3), while chapter 4 examines the plausibility of the EMLG hypotheses on negotiation activity.

Chapter 3 illustrates that today's international negotiations are regionalised to a considerable extent. Yet, not all ROs are equally vocal on the international level, and not all states contribute to the regionalisation of international negotiation dynamics to equal extents. Furthermore, some IOs and some policy areas attract more regional actor participation in international negotiations than others.

Chapter 4 first addresses the empirical puzzles outlined with focused multilevel analysis, and uses more than 200 semi-structured interviews with diplomats from states and ROs as narrative evidence for the mechanisms underlying the EMLG hypotheses located on the state, the regional, the international and the policy dimensions. In a second step, the chapter conducts a comprehensive multilevel analysis, taking all levels into consideration. This allows examining both the share of explained variation at each level and the multilevel hypotheses on cross-level effects.

*Chapter 3*

# Mapping regional actor activity

This chapter presents the large-N dataset on regional actor activity in international negotiations (DV1). To his end, we first describe the rationale underlying the construction of the dataset and the coding of the negotiations (3.2). The section provides a mapping of regional actor activity in international negotiations, examining the state-level (3.3.1), the regional level (3.3.2), the international level (3.3.3) as well as policy clusters (3.3.4). On this basis, this chapter identifies the most interesting empirical puzzles that are addressed in greater detail in the next chapter (chapter 4).

The phenomenon of interest in this chapter is the activity of RO actors in international negotiations (DV1). The active participation of ROs in multilateral negotiations in IOs as such is seldom the focus of research,[1] although – as this chapter shows – today's international negotiations are regionalised to a considerable extent. International negotiations are traditionally based on state–state interactions, and regional actors have only limited formal rights in the form of being official observers. Nevertheless, we show that nearly 12 per cent of all speeches made in international negotiations do express regional positions.

Based on the methodical considerations laid out in chapter 2, we measure regional actor negotiation activity through a content analysis of official documents covering international negotiations. In combination with the in-depth-case studies (c.f. chapters 5–7) the method mix yields robust and reliable results.

## 3.1 THE CONSTRUCTION OF THE DATASET

This book examines a novel and encompassing dataset on the extent to which current international negotiations are regionalised. To this end, we put together a representative large-N database that comprehensively captures the dependent variable 'regional actor negotiation activity' by counting the instances in which regional positions are voiced in international negotiations. To this end, we made choices with respect to the selection of IOs, the time-frame, specific negotiations and the actors included.

The starting point for the construction of the dataset was the selection of international organisations. Since we are interested in mapping the negotiation activity of regional actors, we only included IOs that provided access to negotiation protocols and reports detailed enough to carry information on who spoke and if the speech made in the international negotiation was national in character or conveyed a regional position (more details later in this chapter). IOs follow very different publication policies with respect to the negotiation reports and documents as well as the content and style. There are IOs which do not provide public access to negotiation protocols and related documents at all. Others publish negotiation protocols and reports of negotiations, but only aggregated summaries or results of sessions. These are not suitable for the analysis of regional actor negotiation activity within an IO if they do not identify acting parties and the content of the negotiation (carrying a national or a regional position).[2] Hence, we selected IOs that provided the necessary access to suitable documents (protocols, verbatim records, minutes and detailed press releases) and in which negotiations take place regularly or at least at intervals frequent enough to obtain a sufficiently large number of observations with respect to individual negotiations (see below). Applying these criteria, we arrived at a sample of twenty-seven IOs, which cover a broad array of different policy areas (c.f. table 3.1).

After identifying the IOs that provide suitable documents, the follow-up decisions concerned the time frame and the frequency of meetings, as well as the selection of specific negotiations. We decided to use a five-year time frame from 2008 to 2012 in order to obtain a snapshot of the extent to which international negotiations are currently regionalised. Altogether we map 512 negotiations which take place in the twenty-seven IOs' major legislative arenas (e.g. CoPs, assemblies, member state committees)[3] and which cover issues typical for the respective IO (for a list of the negotiations, c.f. table A3.1 in the appendix).

With respect to the selection of state and regional actors, we did not make any limiting choices. Instead of only examining the speeches of some states or some regional actors, we included all states that were member of an IO in a given year as well as all regional actors that were active, either directly through their delegates (e.g. the European Commission) or indirectly through member states speaking on their behalf in international negotiations. Thus, the dataset is comprehensive in nature, including information on negotiation activity of 204 states and state-like actors (e.g. Cook Islands, Greenland

**Table 3.1. List of IOs and associated policy fields**

| Policy Area | | | Negotiation Arena |
|---|---|---|---|
| Security | 1 | ATT | Arms Trade Treaty |
| | 2 | CD | Conference on Disarmament |
| | 3 | OPCW | Organisation for the Prohibition of Chemical Weapons |
| | 4 | SC | Security Council |
| | 5 | UNGA C1 | United Nations General Assembly, Disarmament and International Security |
| Trade/finance | 6 | IAEA | International Atomic Energy Agency |
| | 7 | IBRD/IMF | International Bank for Reconstruction and Development |
| | 8 | ITTO | International Tropical Timber Organization |
| | 9 | NASCO | North Atlantic Salmon Conservation Organization |
| | 10 | UNCTAD | United Nations Conference on Trade and Development |
| | 11 | UNGA C2 | United Nations General Assembly, Economic and Financial Issues |
| | 12 | WTO | World Trade Organization |
| Labour/social | 13 | ECOSOC | Economic and Social Council |
| | 14 | ILO | International Labour Organisation |
| | 15 | UNGA C3 | United Nations General Assembly, Social, Humanitarian & Cultural Issues |
| Environment | 16 | ICCAT | International Commission for the Conservation of Atlantic Tuna |
| | 17 | IWC | International Whaling Commission |
| | 18 | UNEP | United Nations Environmental Programme |
| | 19 | UNFCCC | United Nations Framework Convention on Climate Change |
| Human rights | 20 | HRC | Human Rights Council |
| | 21 | IOM | International Organization for Migration |
| | 22 | UNHCR | United Nations High Commissioner for Refugees |
| Education/ health | 23 | FAO | Food and Agricultural Organization |
| | 24 | UNESCO | United Nations Educational, Scientific and Cultural Organisation |
| | 25 | WHO | World Health Organization |
| | 26 | WIPO | World Intellectual Property Organization |
| Broad | 27 | UNGA C4 | United Nations General Assembly, Special Political and Decolonization |

or the Holy See, which hold different statuses of autonomy) as well as all active regional actors. The dataset encompasses all active regional organisations (e.g. the EU, CARICOM and ECOWAS) and all active regional groups (e.g. the UN African Group or the BAG). Regional organisations are institutionalised forms of state cooperation, in which at least three states from the same geographically defined region cooperate in a variety of policy areas on a regular basis and develop common rules and norms on the basis of decision-making procedures. By contrast, regional groups also have membership criteria on the basis of geographic proximity, but are less strongly institutionalised, often formed either ad hoc for international negotiations (e.g. the BAG) or are have been created to operate only in one specific negotiation arena. They usually only cover specific issues or perform only formal functions within the IO (e.g. the UN African Group in the UNGA) and do not pass common rules and norms.

### 3.1.1 Coding of negotiations

The selected negotiation reports and protocols were hand-coded on the basis of a mapping guide. In the mapping guide, strict rules were formulated to formalise the decisions about which statements were coded as national or regional and which organisations, coalitions and groups were included in the mapping. This ensures that the data collection is systematic and consistent, resulting in intersubjectively traceable data (Mayring 2007). Coding includes voiced national positions of states, as well as statements by states on behalf of regional actors and regional actor representatives themselves. Therefore, activity is operationalised on the level of statements. For example, if a state representative declares that he/she is speaking 'on behalf of' an RO, that 'the RO agrees to/disagrees with/ objects/supports/proposes/recommends' and so on the speech is counted as voicing an RO position, while the absence of a reference to the regional position or preference is counted as voicing national positions (state activity). For example, the following statement was counted for the UN African Group:

> MIKE JAMU (<u>Malawi</u>), speaking on behalf of the African Group, said the continent had enormous potential in many respects, but its growth had recently slowed due to multiple crises. If development partners continued to provide support, existing gaps could be bridged and growth ensured. (UNGA Sixty-fifth General Assembly, Second Committee, 5 October 2010)

Alternatively, RO delegates themselves participate in negotiations in international organisations and negotiate directly for their respective organisations, like in the following example:

> CARICOM delegations wish to iterate as we have done time and again, that the members of our Community are not producers of small arms and light weapons nor are we large scale importers of such weapons. (CARICOM statement to the 2nd Meeting of the Preparatory Committee for the United Nations Conference on an Arms Trade Treaty, 28 February–3 March 2011)

An example for a national statement voiced in UNEP is:

> The representative of Norway said that his Government had contributed to enhancing the participation of developing countries in the international environmental governance process to date and would look favourably on any request from the secretariat to provide similar support in the future. (Committee of Permanent Representatives to the United Nations Environment Programme, 111th meeting, Nairobi, 15 June 2010)

Thus, the content analysis captures not only the number of interventions of each actor and the content of the intervention (regional or national position), but also the share that RO representatives or member states speak on behalf of the regional actor (= voicing regional group positions). This is important because it controls for the number of RO members who are also IO members and the extent to which the states participate in international negotiations. The data on regional activity in international negotiations (DV1) extracted from the documents went through multiple stages of control and correction to ensure adequate quality. We designed and implemented several strategies to trace and correct mapping mistakes, such as mathematical operations, random checks of coded negotiations and random samplings. Despite the fact that we designed a detailed mapping guide, the documents coded were text documents, and therefore, there was still room for interpretation, reading errors and other random mistakes, for example, caused by declining concentration in a coding session. To account for the human factor in the mapping, some parts of the mapping were double coded to test for intercoder reliability. To quantify intercoder reliability, we applied Krippendorff's $\alpha$, a measure of agreement among coders and the reliability of data generation processes, ranging from 0 to 1 as the best value (Hayes and Krippendorff 2007, Krippendorff 2011a, b). This test yielded Krippendorff's $\alpha = 0.996$, indicating that the mapping guide achieved its purpose and coding errors were minimised to a large extent.

## 3.2 MAPPING PATTERN OF NEGOTIATION ACTIVITY OF REGIONAL ACTORS (DV1)

By coding the speeches of 512 international negotiations in the twenty-seven IOs between 2008 and 2012, we create a novel and encompassing dataset. This dataset includes information on the number of times the positions of 204 states and autonomous territories as well as the more than fifty-one different active regional actors were articulated in international negotiations. In total, the mapping includes 74,484 observations of all state and regional actors present in the international negotiations. While in most cases the IOs provide participation lists for each negotiation, in 117 instances there was no explicit information on participation. In those negotiations, all member states viable for participation (as a member of the organisation or member of the negotiation arena) are treated as present. Of the nearly 75,000 data points, 62,215 are zero observations, resulting from the fact that a state was present, but remained silent during the negotiation. In 83.53 per cent of occasions that states had the possibility to speak up in the 512 negotiations, they did not take the opportunity. In 12,269 observations (16.47 per cent) in which a state or regional actor took the floor, a total number of 20,522 statements were made.[4] Of those, 18,072 are exclusively national positions voiced by states on their own behalf, while 2,450 positions were voiced by states for ROs or by RO delegates themselves. Overall, the regional statements amount to 11.94 per cent of all positions voiced in the negotiations.[5] Thus, in today's international multilateral negotiations regional positions are brought to the table in nearly 12 per cent of occasions. For the regression models in chapter 4 we aggregated negotiation activity within each IO on a yearly basis, in order to avoid inflated variances.

The remainder of this section maps the prevalence of regional positions on the state, the regional and the international levels as well as with respect to policy clusters, and outlines the pattern of interest and empirical puzzles.

### 3.2.1 State level

States in international negotiations can either speak for themselves or on behalf of a regional group of which they are a member. This section maps the frequency with which states articulate the positions of their ROs. Table 3.3 and figure 3.1 illustrate that there is considerable variation in the propensity to which states are inclined to voice regional interests.

Figure 3.1 depicts the number of times each state voiced regional positions. The centre of the respective circles is placed on the countries' capitals, while the size of the bubbles is determined by the number of times each state spoke up for a regional actor in the 512 international negotiations under scrutiny in this book. The most striking observation is the near-absence of regional statements in North America as well as the high prevalence of state negotiation activity on behalf of regional actors in Europe and Africa. A glance at the total number of statements on behalf of regional actors shows that Denmark, South Africa and Sweden were most active with 175, 129 and 118 regional positions voiced, respectively. The United States negotiated on behalf of a regional actor they are a member of in two instances, Russia twice and China once. Many states were not acting on behalf of regional actors at all. For example, states such as Uzbekistan, Luxembourg and the Federated States of Micronesia have not once spoken for a regional actor.

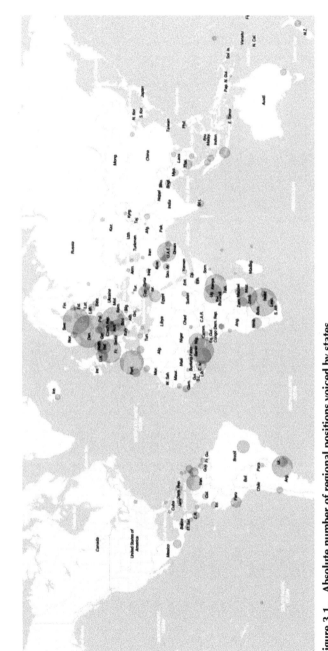

**Figure 3.1.** Absolute number of regional positions voiced by states

Table 3.2. Percentage of regional positions voiced by states – the empirical pattern

| State | National and Regional Statements | Regional Statements | %RO Statements | State | National and Regional Statements | Regional Statements | %RO Statements | State | National and Regional Statements | Regional Statements | %RO Statements | State | National and Regional Statements | Regional Statements | %RO Statements |
|---|---|---|---|---|---|---|---|---|---|---|---|---|---|---|---|
| DK | 284 | 175 | 61.62 | AU | 523 | 7 | 1.34 | ML | 38 | 2 | 5.26 | CF | 8 | 0 | 0.00 |
| ZA | 393 | 129 | 32.82 | QA | 54 | 6 | 11.11 | NI | 40 | 2 | 5.00 | CH | 274 | 0 | 0.00 |
| SE | 234 | 118 | 50.43 | PL | 58 | 6 | 10.34 | TD | 42 | 2 | 4.76 | CK | 2 | 0 | 0.00 |
| BJ | 141 | 103 | 73.05 | AT | 120 | 6 | 5.00 | GR | 45 | 2 | 4.44 | CV | 9 | 0 | 0.00 |
| ES | 229 | 96 | 41.92 | CO | 148 | 6 | 4.05 | AO | 50 | 2 | 4.00 | CW | 1 | 0 | 0.00 |
| HU | 131 | 95 | 72.52 | MA | 210 | 6 | 2.86 | HR | 50 | 2 | 4.00 | DP | 66 | 0 | 0.00 |
| FR | 466 | 92 | 19.74 | PK | 248 | 6 | 2.42 | AZ | 52 | 2 | 3.85 | ER | 19 | 0 | 0.00 |
| KE | 211 | 83 | 39.34 | BD | 285 | 6 | 2.11 | GT | 59 | 2 | 3.39 | FJ | 24 | 0 | 0.00 |
| AR | 497 | 75 | 15.09 | GY | 13 | 5 | 38.46 | SV | 64 | 2 | 3.13 | FM | 15 | 0 | 0.00 |
| ZW | 148 | 69 | 46.62 | KH | 23 | 5 | 21.74 | UA | 71 | 2 | 2.82 | FO | 1 | 0 | 0.00 |
| AE | 126 | 63 | 50.00 | TL | 23 | 5 | 21.74 | TZ | 73 | 2 | 2.74 | GL | 2 | 0 | 0.00 |
| UG | 108 | 61 | 56.48 | OM | 30 | 5 | 16.67 | BY | 96 | 2 | 2.08 | GM | 14 | 0 | 0.00 |
| CZ | 110 | 50 | 45.45 | MZ | 40 | 5 | 12.50 | IT | 111 | 2 | 1.80 | GN | 27 | 0 | 0.00 |
| SI | 74 | 44 | 59.46 | MM | 44 | 5 | 11.36 | CU | 218 | 2 | 0.92 | GW | 7 | 0 | 0.00 |
| NG | 216 | 44 | 20.37 | CD | 45 | 5 | 11.11 | IR | 322 | 2 | 0.62 | HK | 9 | 0 | 0.00 |
| GH | 116 | 42 | 36.21 | IS | 48 | 5 | 10.42 | RU | 329 | 2 | 0.61 | Holy See | 29 | 0 | 0.00 |
| VE | 315 | 40 | 12.70 | BH | 52 | 5 | 9.62 | US | 912 | 2 | 0.22 | IL | 122 | 0 | 0.00 |
| BE | 113 | 29 | 25.66 | FI | 68 | 5 | 7.35 | DM | 6 | 1 | 16.67 | IN | 405 | 0 | 0.00 |
| BR | 715 | 28 | 3.92 | SD | 89 | 5 | 5.62 | LV | 11 | 1 | 9.09 | JO | 48 | 0 | 0.00 |
| EG | 292 | 23 | 7.88 | LB | 116 | 5 | 4.31 | TO | 11 | 1 | 9.09 | KI | 4 | 0 | 0.00 |
| GB | 389 | 23 | 5.91 | SR | 15 | 4 | 26.67 | VC | 11 | 1 | 9.09 | KN | 18 | 0 | 0.00 |
| CY | 35 | 21 | 60.00 | MR | 23 | 4 | 17.39 | KM | 12 | 1 | 8.33 | KR | 238 | 0 | 0.00 |
| PE | 117 | 19 | 16.24 | SZ | 24 | 4 | 16.67 | SC | 13 | 1 | 7.69 | LA | 21 | 0 | 0.00 |
| ID | 295 | 19 | 6.44 | MU | 31 | 4 | 12.90 | SO | 13 | 1 | 7.69 | LC | 29 | 0 | 0.00 |
| CI | 78 | 17 | 21.79 | CG | 36 | 4 | 11.11 | GD | 18 | 1 | 5.56 | LI | 17 | 0 | 0.00 |

| Code | Total | n | % | Code | Total | n | % | Code | Total | n | % | Code | Total | n | % |
|---|---|---|---|---|---|---|---|---|---|---|---|---|---|---|---|
| NL | 173 | 16 | 9.25 | SP | 51 | 4 | 7.84 | ME | 19 | 1 | 5.26 | LR | 21 | 0 | 0.00 |
| ZM | 77 | 15 | 19.48 | VN | 56 | 4 | 7.14 | DJ | 21 | 1 | 4.76 | LU | 24 | 0 | 0.00 |
| MW | 43 | 14 | 32.56 | YE | 59 | 4 | 6.78 | MG | 23 | 1 | 4.35 | MC | 22 | 0 | 0.00 |
| TT | 141 | 14 | 9.93 | CM | 68 | 4 | 5.88 | HN | 26 | 1 | 3.85 | MD | 24 | 0 | 0.00 |
| TH | 158 | 14 | 8.86 | ET | 75 | 4 | 5.33 | AM | 31 | 1 | 3.23 | MH | 7 | 0 | 0.00 |
| UY | 222 | 14 | 6.31 | SY | 115 | 4 | 3.48 | NE | 32 | 1 | 3.13 | MK | 11 | 0 | 0.00 |
| MX | 312 | 12 | 3.85 | TN | 118 | 4 | 3.39 | PN | 32 | 1 | 3.13 | MN | 42 | 0 | 0.00 |
| PT | 74 | 11 | 14.86 | CN | 370 | 4 | 1.08 | GA | 35 | 1 | 2.86 | MV | 35 | 0 | 0.00 |
| KW | 78 | 10 | 12.82 | NR | 4 | 3 | 75.00 | PG | 39 | 1 | 2.56 | NU | 4 | 0 | 0.00 |
| DZ | 301 | 9 | 2.99 | BZ | 15 | 3 | 20.00 | SK | 41 | 1 | 2.44 | PW | 7 | 0 | 0.00 |
| LT | 28 | 8 | 28.57 | HT | 23 | 3 | 13.04 | AF | 49 | 1 | 2.04 | RO | 41 | 0 | 0.00 |
| LS | 44 | 8 | 18.18 | PY | 40 | 3 | 7.50 | NP | 64 | 1 | 1.56 | RW | 22 | 0 | 0.00 |
| BB | 56 | 8 | 14.29 | KZ | 50 | 3 | 6.00 | IE | 77 | 1 | 1.30 | SB | 9 | 0 | 0.00 |
| JM | 61 | 8 | 13.11 | BF | 54 | 3 | 5.56 | LY | 98 | 1 | 1.02 | SM | 7 | 0 | 0.00 |
| DO | 84 | 8 | 9.52 | PA | 62 | 3 | 4.84 | PH | 208 | 1 | 0.48 | SS | 8 | 0 | 0.00 |
| CR | 113 | 8 | 7.08 | IQ | 112 | 3 | 2.68 | TR | 216 | 1 | 0.46 | ST | 2 | 0 | 0.00 |
| SN | 113 | 8 | 7.08 | GQ | 11 | 2 | 18.18 | JP | 450 | 1 | 0.22 | TG | 39 | 0 | 0.00 |
| CL | 217 | 8 | 3.69 | AG | 13 | 2 | 15.38 | CA | 550 | 1 | 0.18 | TJ | 12 | 0 | 0.00 |
| DE | 219 | 8 | 3.65 | BT | 15 | 2 | 13.33 | AD | 2 | 0 | 0.00 | TM | 5 | 0 | 0.00 |
| SG | 65 | 7 | 10.77 | BS | 23 | 2 | 8.70 | AL | 19 | 0 | 0.00 | TV | 5 | 0 | 0.00 |
| SA | 82 | 7 | 8.54 | EE | 24 | 2 | 8.33 | AN | 1 | 0 | 0.00 | TW | 22 | 0 | 0.00 |
| LK | 112 | 7 | 6.25 | KG | 25 | 2 | 8.00 | BA | 21 | 0 | 0.00 | UZ | 9 | 0 | 0.00 |
| MY | 158 | 7 | 4.43 | GE | 28 | 2 | 7.14 | BI | 18 | 0 | 0.00 | VG | 1 | 0 | 0.00 |
| EC | 168 | 7 | 4.17 | MT | 30 | 2 | 6.67 | BN | 10 | 0 | 0.00 | VU | 5 | 0 | 0.00 |
| NZ | 231 | 7 | 3.03 | BG | 33 | 2 | 6.06 | BO | 98 | 0 | 0.00 | WS | 22 | 0 | 0.00 |
| NO | 315 | 7 | 2.22 | SL | 33 | 2 | 6.06 | BW | 31 | 0 | 0.00 | | | | |

Yet, examining the absolute number of regional positions voiced by states entails a bias, since not every country is a member of each of the twenty-seven IOs for the period under investigation. For example, the UNSC consists of five permanent and ten non-permanent members, which are elected for a two-year term. Consequently, states that are elected for UNSC membership in 2008 have to drop their membership in 2010. While countries like the United States, Russia or China are members of most IOs and, thus, have the opportunity to make statements in a large share of the 512 negotiations (US 502, RU 497, CN 478), the Democratic People's Republic of Korea, South Sudan or Andorra are member of fewer IOs and had access to only 268 (DP), 242 (SS) and 264 (AD) negotiations, respectively. In order to avoid bias in the cross-country variation of articulating regional positions, the following table controls for the number of times each state voiced national positions.

Table 3.2 controls for access to international negotiations as it features the number of times states voiced regional positions relative to national positions. In total, 20,517 negotiation statements were voiced in the 512 negotiations by the 204 states and autonomous territories in the IO-years under investigation, of which 2,446 expressed regional positions. On average, states spoke on behalf of regional actors in 11.92 per cent of all instances. Thus, roughly every tenth time a state was active in an international negotiation, it spoke on behalf of a regional actor. However, not all states are equally likely to express the positions of their regional groups or organisations. In relative terms, Nauru's contributions to multilateral negotiations in IOs were most strongly regionalised seeing as 75 per cent of the time it voiced regional positions, followed by Benin with 73.05 per cent RO positions. Hungary also made considerably more regional than national statements (the former accumulated to 72.52 per cent of its contributions). Slovenia, Zimbabwe and United Arab Emirates spoke on behalf of regional actors in about half of their contributions. On the lower end of the continuum are, for instance, El Salvador (3.13 per cent), Libya (1.02 per cent), Russia (0.61 per cent), Norway (2.22 per cent) and China with 1.08 per cent as well as fifty-eight states scoring 0 per cent for not having spoken on behalf of a regional actor at all (e.g. the Solomon Islands, Tonga, Taiwan).

## 3.2.2 Regional level

Like state activity, the prevalence of regional actor activity varies to a large extent. In table 3.3, the overall number of times RO member states, as well as the delegates of regional actors, articulated regional positions is listed. The total mean of statements per regional actor is 48.04, and the median is 7. Table 3.4 reveals that the absolute numbers of regional

**Table 3.3. Absolute number of regional statements per active RO**

| RO | Statements for/by ROs | RO | Statements for/by ROs |
|---|---|---|---|
| EU | 1052 | CELAC | 6 |
| UNAG | 655 | ACP | 6 |
| GRULAC | 207 | IBRD Arab Govs | 6 |
| GCC | 86 | RioGroup | 6 |
| ASEAN | 51 | FAO NEG | 4 |
| CARICOM | 47 | CCAEC | 3 |
| ASPAG | 46 | IBRD African Govs | 3 |
| Arab Group | 40 | PSIDS | 3 |
| MERCOSUR | 22 | CSTO | 2 |
| NC8 | 18 | IGAD | 2 |
| AU | 17 | BAG | 2 |
| SADC | 17 | IBRD Africa 2 | 2 |
| WHO AR | 17 | EFTA | 1 |
| LAS | 14 | OAS | 1 |
| SICA | 11 | SAARC | 1 |
| WHO EMR | 11 | SCO | 1 |
| NC | 10 | EAC | 1 |
| UNASUR | 9 | NATO | 1 |
| ALBA | 9 | OSCE | 1 |
| ECOWAS | 8 | CIS | 1 |
| EEG | 8 | WEOG | 1 |
| CEBS | 8 | WIPO Asian Group | 1 |
| WHO SEAR | 8 | C4 | 1 |
| PIF | 7 | IWC SAGC | 1 |
| CoE | 7 | CANWFZ | 1 |
| IBRD Africa 1 | 7 | Total | 2450 |

positions voiced as well as the percentages vary tremendously. Given that there are more than sixty regional organisations and numerous regional groups (Panke and Stapel 2016), many of which are small and struggle with capacity shortages, it is remarkable that twenty-six regional organisations and twenty-five regional groups were vocal in the international negotiations. In this respect, the most active regional actor is the EU, with a total of 1,052 statements in the 512 negotiations. The RO with the second-highest number of statements recorded is the UNAG with 655 instances in which its position was articulated, followed by the GRULAC with 207 statements. On the other end of the spectrum, several regional actors feature relatively low levels of activity, such as the CIS, the SCO or the UNWEOG (one regional position voiced each).

The picture looks somewhat different when controlling for the vocality of the RO member states in the 512 international negotiations. Table 3.4

**Table 3.4.    Regional statements per RO relative to member state statements**

| RO | National Statements | Statements for ROs | Percentage of RO Activity | RO | National Statements | Statements for ROs | Percentage of RO Activity |
|---|---|---|---|---|---|---|---|
| EU | 2426 | 811 | 33.43 | WHO EMR | 2201 | 11 | 0.50 |
| GCC | 326 | 86 | 26.38 | WHO SEAR | 1616 | 8 | 0.50 |
| UNAG | 3216 | 637 | 19.81 | CACEEC | 692 | 3 | 0.43 |
| CARICOM | 390 | 40 | 10.26 | UNASUR | 2356 | 9 | 0.38 |
| GRULAC | 3665 | 195 | 5.32 | ALBA | 814 | 3 | 0.37 |
| ASEAN | 977 | 49 | 5.02 | IBRD Arab Govs | 1913 | 6 | 0.31 |
| NB8 | 691 | 18 | 2.60 | IBRD Africa 2 | 732 | 2 | 0.27 |
| SADC | 875 | 17 | 1.94 | IGAD | 389 | 1 | 0.26 |
| PSIDS | 171 | 3 | 1.75 | FAO NEG | 1650 | 4 | 0.24 |
| Arab Group | 1913 | 33 | 1.73 | RioGroup | 2637 | 6 | 0.23 |
| SICA | 358 | 6 | 1.68 | ACP | 3129 | 6 | 0.19 |
| CEBS | 557 | 8 | 1.44 | CELAC | 3665 | 6 | 0.16 |
| NC | 642 | 9 | 1.40 | EFTA | 642 | 1 | 0.16 |
| MERCO-SUR | 1629 | 22 | 1.35 | CIS | 690 | 1 | 0.14 |
| CANWFZ | 96 | 1 | 1.04 | ECOWAS | 717 | 1 | 0.14 |
| ASPAG | 4449 | 46 | 1.03 | IBRD African Govs | 2211 | 3 | 0.14 |
| PIF | 893 | 7 | 0.78 | SAARC | 1190 | 1 | 0.08 |
| IBRD Africa 1 | 949 | 7 | 0.74 | BAG | 2467 | 2 | 0.08 |
| WHO AR | 2436 | 17 | 0.70 | WEOG | 5203 | 1 | 0.02 |
| EEG | 1126 | 7 | 0.62 | WIPO Asian Group | n/a | 1 | n/a |
| C4 | 165 | 1 | 0.61 | IWC SAGC | n/a | 1 | n/a |

presents the share of statements made for the regional actor by their member states only (without statements of RO delegates themselves)[6] relative to the negotiation activity of the respective member states. Of the 2.426 positions voiced by member states of the EU, 33.43 per cent or 811 statements are made on behalf of the EU. The GCC, UNAG and CARICOM also receive much more attention from their member states than average (26.38 per cent, 19.81 per cent and 10.26 per cent, respectively). On the other end of the spectrum of active ROs are, for example, the SAARC, the BAG, and UNWEOG.

Members of SAARC and BAG voice positions for them in 0.08 per cent of statements, while UNWEOG receives the least attention: only 0.02 per cent of statements are on its behalf.

The GCC, while achieving the second-highest percentage (20.87 per cent) of statements with regional content, only ranks fourth in the field of absolute activity (eighty-six regional positions voiced by member states). Another RO that has a notable discrepancy between total and relative activity is UNASPAG. Ranking seventh in the absolute number of statements, its members voice the positions of UNASPAG in only 1.03 per cent of contributions.

At first glance, one might regard the RO activity as limited overall, since thirty-four of the fifty-one active regional actors voice positions ten times or less in the 512 negotiations. Moreover, in relative terms, many regional actors do not cross the 1 per cent threshold in terms of vocality (c.f. table 3.4). Yet, there is the phenomenon of overlapping and multiple memberships in regional actors. States are not only in one regional group or organisation, but have joined several regional actors over time. For example, Kenya is a member of eight of the active regional actors (and in addition in six regional organisations that were completely silent in the 512 negotiations), Ecuador is a member of seven active ROs (as well as in eight inactive ones), and Kiribati is in four active (and two inactive) ROs. Thus, in a given negotiation, it is unlikely that Kenya, Ecuador or Kiribati speaks on behalf of each of their regional actors. Our data shows that a country becomes active for only one of its ROs at a time if it voices a regional position at all. This is not surprising, but reflects a rational negotiation strategy. If a country were voicing different regional positions at the same time, it would be sending mixed messages to the other participants in international negotiations. Accordingly, countries pick and choose which regional organisations they will speak for in international negotiations or tend to have fixed preferences in this respect. For example, for the EU member states, the EU is the primary regional actor, and they hardly voice positions on behalf of UNWEOG, the CoE or the OSCE. Similarly, in Latin America, GRULAC has a dominant position as a coordination body, while MERCOSUR, SICA or ALBA shows a much lower level of activity.

In fact, for most of the macro regions of today, one regional actor seems to be predominant in IO negotiations. For Europe, this is the EU, for the Middle East it is the GCC, for Africa it is the UNAG, and for Asia is it is the ASEAN. In Latin America, there is not just one dominant regional actor that is vocal in international negotiations, as Latin American states often voice the positions of GRULAC, CARICOM and SICA.

### 3.2.3 IO level

Most interestingly, the prevalence of regional actor negotiation activity varies over international negotiation contexts. Table 3.5 sheds light on the number of times that regional positions are articulated by states as well as RO delegates directly across IOs. Of all recorded statements, 2,447 were made by or on behalf of regional actors. While the average participation of ROs in 512 negotiations within the twenty-seven IOs is 9.49 per cent, there is considerable variation across institutional contexts. The share of articulated regional positions ranges, for instance, from less than 1 per cent in the IAEA, followed by UNESCO with 1.96 per cent, to more than 50 per cent, such as the ILO with 23.88 per cent, and UNGA C2 with 24.38 per cent. In between are IOs such as the ITTO (9–51), UNHCR (5.57) or the FAO (3.66).[7] States and regional delegates (e.g. the European Commission) speak on behalf of

Table 3.5. Variation in the regionalisation of negotiations across IOs

| Negotiation Arena | Total Number of Speech Acts | Percentage of Regional Statements |
|---|---|---|
| UNGA C2 | 406 | 24.38 |
| ILO | 5,733 | 23.88 |
| UNCTAD | 331 | 21.75 |
| ICCAT | 365 | 20.27 |
| NASCO | 174 | 15.52 |
| UNEP | 198 | 12.12 |
| WHO | 632 | 11.23 |
| ATT | 398 | 10.80 |
| WTO | 388 | 10.57 |
| IBRD/IMF | 551 | 9.80 |
| ITTO | 164 | 9.15 |
| SC | 385 | 8.83 |
| UNGA C1 | 626 | 8.63 |
| UNFCCC | 835 | 8.62 |
| HRC | 651 | 7.99 |
| UNGA C3 | 734 | 7.49 |
| OPCW | 481 | 7.48 |
| WIPO | 1,115 | 6.73 |
| UNHCR | 637 | 5.97 |
| ECOSOC | 360 | 5.83 |
| IOM | 396 | 4.80 |
| UNGA C4 | 378 | 3.70 |
| FAO | 519 | 3.66 |
| CD | 1,697 | 2.24 |
| IWC | 459 | 2.18 |
| UNESCO | 764 | 1.96 |
| IAEA | 1,140 | 0.53 |

regional actors most often in the second committee of the UNGA. Between 2008 and 2012 the average number of regional statements in the twenty-seven different negotiation arenas was 90.63, with the ILO as an extreme outlier with 1,369 statements made on behalf of regional actors. The ILO is also the IO with by far the most overall statements expressing national interests (4,364), and the second-highest percentage of RO activities (23.88 per cent of all speeches in the ILO).

### 3.2.4 Policy clusters

The 512 negotiations in the dataset vary in scope and issues. While some negotiations can be clearly assigned to a policy field, others cover cross-cutting themes. For example, the negotiations on the Arms Trade Treaty cover aspects of security and trade at the same time. For every negotiation, the negotiation themes are coded and categorised in eleven distinct policy fields and one category for negotiations on internal and procedural negotiations, resulting in a total of twelve categories.[8]

Figure 3.2 breaks down the frequency of policy fields that are discussed and the number of policy themes touched upon in the negotiations per IO. The least frequent policy theme is education, with nine times in IOs like ECOSOC (once), ILO (two times), ITTO (once), UNESCO (four times) and UNHCR (once). On the other end of the spectrum, internal themes such as how a specific policy should be administered or overseen by an IO are most often discussed (156 instances) in conjunction with the substantive policy focus (e.g. on trade or environment).[9] The second most discussed policy theme is security (122 instances), followed by development and environmental policies (105 and 96 instances, respectively).

There is also variation when we look at the IO level. While some cover a wide array of themes, other IOs have a rather narrow focus on a comparably small number of policy fields. SC and UNGA C1 cover security in all twenty included negotiations. In the OPCW and the CD, security issues are also prevalent, being part of the negotiations in nineteen and eighteen instances, respectively. The IO with the narrowest policy focus is the UNGA C1. In the twenty negotiations, only security issues are discussed.

The policy themes attract regional statements to different extents (c.f. table 3.6). In absolute terms, ROs are least vocal when negotiations cover themes such as technology, trade or agriculture, and most vocal when negotiations cover social affairs themes, followed by developmental and health issues. Controlling for variation in the number of times the different policy themes occur in the 512 negotiations reveals that regional positions are voiced on average the most often in social affairs, health and education and the least often in environment security and agriculture as well as internal affairs.

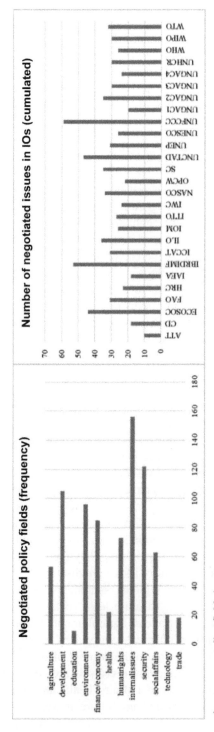

Figure 3.2.    Policy fields in IOs

Table 3.6.　**Average regional positions over policy themes**

| Policy Theme | Number of RO Positions | Number of Times Theme is Covered in Negotiations | RO Positions per Average Negotiation Covering Policy Theme |
|---|---|---|---|
| Agriculture | 110 | 42 | 2.62 |
| Development | 567 | 105 | 5.40 |
| Education | 155 | 9 | 17.22 |
| Environment | 168 | 96 | 1.75 |
| Finance | 276 | 85 | 3.25 |
| Health | 466 | 22 | 21.18 |
| Human rights | 425 | 73 | 5.82 |
| Internal | 409 | 156 | 2.62 |
| Security | 244 | 122 | 2.00 |
| Social affairs | 1,419 | 63 | 22.52 |
| Technology | 72 | 20 | 3.60 |
| Trade | 74 | 18 | 4.11 |

## 3.3  EMPIRICAL PUZZLES

The mapping of the prevalence of regional statements articulated in multilateral negotiations on the state, the regional and the international levels as well as with respect to policy clusters reveals several interesting empirical puzzles.

Formally, only a few regional actors have full membership status in IOs (including voting rights), such as the EU in the WTO, the ITTO and the FAO. ROs are most often observers, such as ASEAN, AU, CARICOM, ECOWAS, EFTA and SADC in the ILO. Even if regional actors have neither a formal voice nor a vote themselves in international negotiations (e.g. the Arab League in the SC, the WEOG and the African Group in the UN system), their member states can and do speak on behalf of their regional actors. As chapters 5–7 show, states often speak on behalf of regional actors in order to leverage international negotiations and increase the chances that they can influence international negotiation outcomes. Thus, voicing regional positions at the international negotiation table is often advantageous for state diplomats. But why do states differ in the extent that they speak on behalf of their regional group or organisation? For example, Nauru, as a small country, is inclined to act on behalf of ROs very often (75 per cent), whereas Luxembourg and Turkmenistan both do not speak up for a regional actor at all, even though these states do not differ much in size and would all benefit from leveraging their regional groups. Looking at the Nuclear Weapon States as a measure of Great Power, we also see substantive variation. France is most vocal with regard to regional positions (19.74 per cent) followed by the United Kingdom (5.91 per cent), the United States (0.22 per cent), Russia (0.61 per cent) and

China (1.08 per cent). Given that all of these countries are members of more than one regional organisation (Panke and Stapel 2016), it needs an explanation why some states are referencing ROs less often than others.

Zooming into the activity of regional actors, we see an interesting pattern. Despite the fact that most regional actors have no formal status in the 512 negotiations at all, a total number of fifty-one regional actors were voicing regional positions. In total that amounts to 2.097 regional statements made by states on behalf of an RO and 353 regional statements made by RO delegates directly. With respect to the number of regional statements, the most active regional actors are the EU (1,052) and the UNAG (655). In relative terms, EU, GCC and GRULAC positions are voiced most frequently; in 33.43 per cent of all instances in which an EU member state was active in the sampled negotiations, it expressed EU positions. GCC members spoke up in 26.38 per cent of occasions for their RO and members of UNAG voiced positions on its behalf in 19.81 per cent of negotiation contributions. As expected the EU stands out, which is in line with the rich body of scholarship that sheds light on the EU's activities in IOs (c.f. chapters 1 and 2). Yet, it is puzzling why regional actors with considerably lower levels of supranationality, such as UNAG, GRULAC and GCC, are also quite active in international negotiations. Moreover, since members of regional actors could benefit from negotiating as groups on the international level and leave regional imprints on international norms, it is puzzling why not all regional actors are active and try to exert influence. Finally, not every RO has registered itself as an observer in the IOs under scrutiny, which allows for such formal access to negotiations. Yet, the ones that have observer status have, by the very fact that the application and certification process is time and resource intensive, demonstrated that they have an interest in becoming active in the respective IO. Nevertheless, there is considerable variation in the prevalence of regional statements made by observer ROs. For example, the ANDEAN holds an observer status in the UNGA, but, as mentioned previously, always remains silent during observation. The ASEAN, however, also holding an observer status in the UNGA, is one of the more active regional actors.

Shifting the attention to the IO level, this chapter has demonstrated that IOs vary in the extent to which they attract regional actor activity. The share of regional speeches relative to the total ones ranges between 24.38 per cent and 0.53 per cent in the 512 negotiations. The most regionalised negotiations take place within the UNGA C2, the ILO and the UNCTAD, while negotiations in the IWC, UNESCO and the IAEA are the least regionalised. This is puzzling, first, since neither the top three nor the bottom three IOs provide regional actors with full membership right. Thus, regional groups and organisations are dependent on their member states' inclination to speak on their behalf. Yet, they seem to do so more often in some rather than other IOs. Second,

IOs and the negotiation's taking place under their umbrella are important as they allow states to develop and pass international rules and norms, thus contributing to the architecture of the international legal system. In such contexts, voicing one's position is an important (but not sufficient) step towards exerting influence over negotiation outcomes. Accordingly, it is puzzling why state and regional actors are more inclined to make regional statements in some rather than other IOs. Third, most of the IOs were founded in the early or mid-twentieth century, allowing enough time for state and regional actors to adapt to the specific negotiation contexts and act in concert in order to increase the chances of influencing negotiation outcomes in the period from 2008 to 2012. It is, furthermore, puzzling that even IOs operating in the same policy field attract a varying share of regional positions. For example, in the policy area of environment, the UNFCCC accumulates 8.62 per cent of regional actor statements while only 2.18 per cent of all contributions to negotiations in the IWC are regional in character. Also, the CD and the ATT are all security-related IOs but differ in the extent to which negotiations are regionalised (ATT 10.8 per cent, CD 2.24 per cent).

With respect to the policy dimension, it is remarkable that negotiations covering some policy themes are more strongly characterised by the prevalence of regional statements than other. The average number of regional statements per negotiation is 4.78. Yet, there is variation in the propensity of regional actor statements across policy themes. In relative terms, regional positions are voiced in an average negotiation the least often in environment security and agriculture as well as internal affairs themes and the most often when negotiations cover social affairs, health and education themes. It seems puzzling that social affairs negotiations are most strongly regionalised, which requires further investigations.

Why is it that some states speak on behalf of regional actors more often than others? Why are some regional actors more active in international negotiations than others? Why are negotiations in some IOs decisively more regionalised than negotiations in other IOs? Why are regional positions more prevalent in some policy themes rather than others? The subsequent chapter provides answers to these questions in comprehensively examining the EMLG hypotheses on RO activity (see chapter 2).

*Chapter 4*

# Analysis of regional actor activity

This chapter provides answers to the following questions: Why does regional actor activity vary in international negotiations, and why are some states more prone to speak for regional actors than others? In doing so, it sheds light on the factors accounting for the outlined empirical puzzles (c.f. chapter 3). To this end, chapter 4 empirically analyses the hypotheses on regional actor activity as developed in chapter 2. Section 4.1 discusses the methodology used for the empirical analysis. Section 4.2 presents the operationalisation of the independent variables. Subsequently, the EMLG hypotheses on regional actor activity in international negotiations are under scrutiny in sections 4.3 and 4.4, respectively. In order to comprehensively examine the empirical plausibility of the activity hypotheses (see chapter 2), we begin by focusing on each of the levels separately (section 4.3). Thus, the dependent variable is aggregated on different levels, and we zoom into state-specific, RO-specific, IO-specific variables and the policy dimension, respectively. We then complement these four focused studies with a comprehensive, multilevel analysis (section 4.4), to shed light on the complex interactions between actors and negotiation arenas in EMLG systems. This takes into account level-specific as well as cross-level effects in order to examine which factors influence states' propensity to speak on behalf of ROs.

## 4.1 METHODOLOGY

In order to analyse regional actor activity, we use quantitative methods. We supplement this analysis qualitatively. To this end, we use narrative evidence based on more than 200 semi-structured interviews with state diplomats and

RO representatives to shed additional light on underlying dynamics of international negotiations.

In the quantitative analyses, we aggregated the dependent variable in different ways to provide a comprehensive picture of the phenomena under research. In sections 4.3.1 (state-level) and 4.4 (comprehensive, multilevel analysis) the focus lies on states as actors in international negotiations. The DV is the number of times a state voices regional positions in a negotiation year. On the level of ROs (section 4.3.2), the DV captures the number of times ROs raise their voice in a negotiation year, irrespective of the way the statement is conveyed. This includes both states speaking on behalf of ROs and RO delegates, who take part in negotiations and voice regional positions directly. The state-level analysis, the RO-level analysis and the comprehensive, multilevel analysis are actor-centred in character, while the IO- and policy-focused analysis adopts an institution-based perspective. Thus, in sections 4.3.3 and 4.3.4, we examine the prevalence of regional positions in IOs and policy areas. Since the IO in question specifies the policy area covered in negotiations, the aggregation level is the negotiation arena in both instances. Therefore, the DV is the overall number of statements made by ROs directly or through their member states in a given arena for the IO level. The policy level is analysed by focusing on regional actor activity in the coded negotiations individually. The DV on the policy level is the number of negotiation contributions by or for ROs. Table 4.1 provides an overview of the number of observations on the different levels resulting from the aggregation of negotiations to IO-years, which we undertook in order to avoid inflated variances. On the state level, actors had a chance to make a total of 17,381 statements in the IO-years covered in the dataset. On the RO level, states or RO delegates took the opportunity to make a regional statement in 741 instances. On the IO level, we capture the negotiation activity of regional actors in the 27 contexts. Finally, on the policy level we did not aggregate to the IO-years, but keep all 512 individual negotiations, because the policies covered vary over Individual negotiations.

Independent of aggregation levels, all DV specifications are count variables. They are all discrete and positive, and the state and the policy levels show a high degree of overdispersion. This implies the use of Poisson, extra-Poisson or negative binomial regression models for analysis (Almasi et al. 2016, Hoef and Boveng 2007). Negative binomial and Poisson regression models are applied in the focused level analysis (see below), while in the comprehensive multilevel models extra-Poisson regression models are used (Hox and Roberts 2011, Leyland and Goldstein 2001).

The sample is a snapshot of five years. In order to adjust for the fact that states tend to negotiate path dependent from one year to the next (Hampton and Christensen 2014, Martin and Sunley 2006), we tested two approaches to model the time dimension: a cluster structure as well as year dummies

**Table 4.1. Levels of aggregation**

|              | N      | *Aggregation Level* |
|--------------|--------|---------------------|
| State level  | 17,381 | State               |
| RO level     | 741    | RO                  |
| IO level     | 27     | IO                  |
| Policy level | 512    | Negotiations        |

for each of the five years. The cluster structure shows consistently better model fit. Therefore, the time cluster constitutes the topmost level in most of the regression analyses. In addition, an exposure variable is included in the actor-centric models to model the differences in size between the IOs under scrutiny to mitigate the heterogeneity of negotiation arenas in terms of parties present at negotiations. Thus, the exposure variable is equivalent to weights attributed to observations.

In order to examine the hypotheses on regional activity in international negotiations, a two-step approach is used: Before fitting comprehensive multilevel models (section 4.4), the phenomenon is analysed on four distinct focused levels (section 4.3). Due to the different aggregation levels (c.f. table 4.1), various data distributions are observable in the single-level analyses. Because there is considerable overdispersion on the state level, negative binomial regressions are used. In addition, we assume that states (as well as ROs) tend to behave rather congruently in negotiation arenas from one year to the next. Therefore, on the state level, we fitted two-level negative binomial models. In contrast, on the RO and IO levels, overdispersion is a negligible phenomenon, allowing for the use of Poisson models. On the RO level, multilevel Poisson models yielded best results and showed best model fit. While level one accounts for the similarity of the ROs over different negotiation arenas, the time dimension is accounted for by year dummies. Due to the level of aggregation, standard Poisson models are applied on the IO level to perform the analysis. The policy-level analysis uses single-level negative binomial regression models, since this aggregation level shows considerable overdispersion. The time dimension is not included in the policy-level analysis since the individual negotiations are not consecutive but independent from each other. Therefore, there is no reason to assume that the year a negotiation took place influences negotiated policies.

For the complex multilevel analysis, frequentist logic approaches are not appropriate. While both linear and non-linear regression models are applied in many instances of multilevel modelling, they are still quite limited when data structures are more complex. One commonly known example for a strictly hierarchical data structure commonly applied in political science is citizens nested in countries (Raudenbush and Bryk 2010, Wenzelburger et al. 2014). When there are more complex structures, like multiple memberships

*Chapter 4*

or cross-classification, more sophisticated regression models are necessary. Suggestions for this are, for example, duplicating observations with multiple memberships or the use of 'superclusters'. Those approaches indeed provide a solution to the stated problems, but those solutions are rather coarse, and regression estimates and standard errors can be heavily biased if there is either a considerable share of problematic cases or the problematic cases follow a pattern (Chung and Beretvas 2012, Leckie 2013a, 2013b).

Exploring the data structure in the dataset on RO activity, there are two intertwined levels of complexity. First, there is a complex multiple membership structure of states in ROs. As already stated, states tend to become a member of more than one RO (c.f. figure 4.1). While there are indeed actors with one exclusive or even without any membership in ROs, there is not one single regional actor with exclusive state membership. For instance, focusing solely on state membership in active regional organisations and groups in our dataset, the number of regional actor memberships ranges from zero for states like Taiwan, Sint Maarten or Curacao, to up to eleven memberships in active regional organisations and groups for Djibouti and Sudan. Figure 4.1 contrasts the number of memberships states hold in vocal regional actors, and the number of ROs states speak on behalf of. Clearly, states that are only a member of one or two ROs are a minority. The mode is six memberships in ROs, while others hold up to eleven memberships. Silent membership of states in multiple ROs would be a negligible phenomenon if all but one of the ROs remained silent over the observed period of time. However, states are active for multiple ROs in temporal proximity. For example, Chile was active for six different ROs, and it is not the only case. It is a common

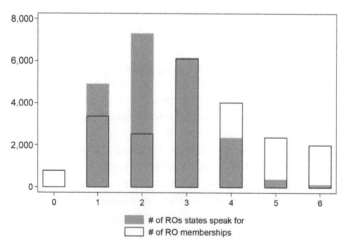

**Figure 4.1.** **Number of regional actor memberships and activity for ROs**

phenomenon for states to speak for more than one RO (c.f. figure 4.1). Hence, the data analysis needs to model the multiple membership structure, which can be accomplished through constrained hierarchical models with artificial superclusters (Leckie 2013a, Rasbash and Goldstein 1994). Unfortunately, this approach reaches its limits in terms of computational efficiency rather quickly. This is especially a problem when the dependent variable is a count variable (i.e. positive and discrete) as it is the case in our analysis.

The levels between states, ROs and IOs are not strictly hierarchical, but feature cross-classification (c.f. figure 4.2). While states are members in multiple ROs (multiple memberships specified by double arrows), they are simultaneously members of a number of IOs. At the same time, ROs themselves show activity in various IOs through their own delegates or those of their member states (MS). ROs are usually not limited to one negotiation arena, but tend to be active in multiple IOs. This results in a multilevel structure with limited nesting, cross-classification of states in ROs and IOs and multiple memberships on the state as well as the RO level.

Figure 4.3 illustrates the data structure, omitting level four, the time dimension. Level one, delineated in the centre in figure 4.3, is the state level: states which are members of one or more active ROs and, at the same time, members of more than one IO. On level two, featured topmost, states are clustered in fifty-one active ROs. Level three, on the bottom of figure 4.3, is composed of twenty-seven negotiation arenas, the IOs.

States are clearly nested in ROs (despite their multiple memberships) and in IOs, respectively. This, however, is not the case for ROs in IOs. As described in chapter 3, in most cases ROs do not hold a formal membership and, in many cases, not even an observer status in IOs. Nonetheless, there is the informal pathway for ROs to express their positions in international

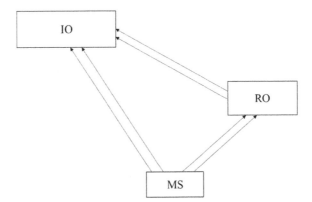

**Figure 4.2.   Classification diagram of multiple memberships and cross-classification**

negotiations: through their member states. But this hierarchical structure is not exclusive: states are members of multiple ROs and ROs are not restricted to be vocal in one specific IO. However, hierarchical structures do exist in institutionally predefined regional groups, for example in the UNGA, the IBRD or the FAO (c.f. chapter 7). Of the fifty-one vocal regional actors in the dataset, fourteen are IO-specific regional groups. The most common situation is that membership in an IO does not in any way restrict or compel membership in any RO.

Moreover, the IO level is much more interconnected than the RO level (c.f. figure 4.3). There are IOs with nearly universal membership, like the UNGA. By contrast, on the regional level, there are separate clusters without any connections to others, since membership in ROs is defined on the basis of geographical proximity. For example, there are no members of the AU in North America, while the UNGA has members all over the world. Other than in standard multilevel data structures, which necessitate hierarchical clustering of units, level two units are not at all hierarchically nested in level three units. Or, put in another way, there is no exclusive relationship between states and ROs, and there is no exclusivity between RO and IO memberships.

The regression analysis needs to account for cross-classification. This can be accomplished in frequentist approaches by using an artificial supercluster. An artificial supercluster contains all other lower-level clusters, for instance, a super-IO, uniting all other IOs in one virtual cluster (Browne et al. 2001, Rasbash and Browne 2008, Rasbash and Goldstein 1994). However, this comes with problems of computational efficiency similar to the supercluster for the multiple membership structure.

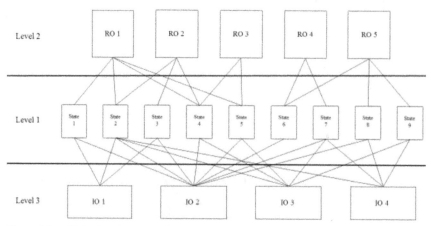

**Figure 4.3.  Data structure overview**

In addition, there are methodical reasons not to use artificial superclusters to analyse data combining cross-classification and multiple memberships (Beretvas 2011). Superclusters constitute an imaginary, overarching cluster, including all sub-units and thereby creating imaginary nesting. This brings about two problems: First, the hierarchy of superclusters results in the inherent prioritisation of either the multiple membership structure or the cross-classification. If for example, the cross-classification supercluster would be at level four (the 'first' artificial supercluster), this prioritises multiple membership structure over the cross-classification (and vice versa), causing a strong bias in estimation results and an overrepresentation of the multiple memberships structure over cross-classification. The second problem is that the allocation of variance on the different levels would become next to impossible, since the two superclusters, while non-existent in the initial dataset, would soak up much of the between-levels-variance, leading to a situation where seemingly explained variation cannot be clearly allocated to a level. In this situation, incidence rate ratios (IRRs) and estimates, as well as intraclass correlations (ICCs) and variance partitions coefficients (VPCs), would be severely corrupted. In sum, the multiple membership structure and cross-classification can be captured separately by standard frequentist statistics. However, the combination of both requires a more elaborate approach.

Considering the complex data structure that results from multiple memberships and cross-classification coinciding, and the difficulties resulting from the use of superclusters, Bayesian Markov Chains Monte Carlo (MCMC) modelling is the appropriate way for the comprehensive multilevel analyses (Browne et al. 2001). On the one hand, using Bayesian statistics allows drawing on prior information from the focused level analyses. On the other hand, as described previously, analysing the complex system of multiple memberships and semi-hierarchical relationships is intractable with frequentist statistics. Compared to frequentist statistic, Bayesian approaches are based on a different notion of inference (Draper 2008, Gelman et al. 2013, Jackman 2000, 2004, Western and Jackman 1994). In frequentist statistics, the starting point is a sample of an imaginary universe of cases. (1) describes that the observed data $y$ is matched using unknown parameters $\phi$, leading to inferences of the type

(1)  $y \sim f(y \,|\, \phi)$

While $\phi$ is treated as fixed, $\hat{\phi}$ is sample-dependent and may vary for other samples drawn from the universe of cases. (2) describes the likelihood function:

(2)  $L(\phi \,|\, y) \alpha f(y \,|\, \phi)$

And evaluates the plausibility of alternative $\hat{\phi}$, resulting from different samples (Tanner 1996). Bayesian inference, on the contrary, assumes $\hat{\phi}$ is a fixed value, which is conditional on the observed data $y$. $\phi$ is treated as random.

Instead of fitting a model with a presupposed distribution to a number of observations that are part of an imagined universe of cases, the available data is analysed starting at a presupposed or *prior* distribution to match the observed data resulting in a posterior distribution which is derived from the prior distribution and a model-specific, data-dependent likelihood (Jackman 2000, 2004). In (3) this is described in mathematical notation:

$$(3) \quad p(\phi \mid y) = \frac{p(y \mid \phi) p(\phi)}{p(\phi)}$$

results in (4)

$$(4) \quad p(\phi \mid y) \alpha p(\phi) L(\phi \mid y)$$

Two things become visible in (4): First, a posterior density is proportional to the product of the prior distribution and the likelihood function. Second, even when the priors are not very well chosen (i.e. the starting points are suboptimal) the likelihood function remains unaffected and yields valid results, while if the priors are well chosen, the results improve substantially (Western and Jackman 1994). In our case, MCMC modelling avoids the consequences of distorted clusters (Goldstein 1995, 1996, Rabe-Hesketh and Anders 2012). By modelling the cross-classification and the multiple membership in the data structure, MCMC models yield valid estimates and can shed light on the cross-level hypotheses outlined in chapter 2 (Browne 1998, Draper 2008, Gelman et al. 2013, Goldstein 2016, Tunaru 2002). The use of MCMC models has further implications. Fitting negative binomial models, equivalently to the focused models with reduced complexity, results in non-convergence in the complex multilevel analysis. The Poisson distribution is a special case of the negative binomial distribution and estimates between those models do not differ significantly, other than their respective standard errors. Accordingly, the Poisson distribution (5)

$$(5) \quad Var(y) = E(y) = \mu$$

is modified by a factor $\phi$, resulting in the extra-Poisson distribution (6)

$$(6) \quad Var(y) = \Phi E(y) = \Phi \mu$$

In the comprehensive multilevel analyses, extra-Poisson variance is modelled by a dispersion factor. This is possible because the dispersion is proportional and therefore can be modelled by a parameter in Poisson models (Rodríguez 1993).

The schematic equation for our Multiple Membership-Multiple Classification (MMMC) multilevel models reads

$$y_i \sim \text{Poisson}(\lambda_i)$$
$$(7)\quad \log(\lambda_i) = X_i\beta + Z_i^{(2)}u_{C_2(i)}^{(2)} + \sum_{j \in C_3(i)} w_{i,j}^{(3)}Z_i^{(3)}u_j^{(3)}$$
$$u_{C_2(i)}^{(2)} \sim N(0, \Sigma_{u(2)})\, u_j^{(3)} \sim N(0, \Sigma_{u(3)})$$

The first part of (4), $X_i\beta$, equals the intercept. $Z_i u_c$ represents the random part of the
model, while

$$(8)\quad \sum_{j \in C_3(i)} W_{i,j}^{(3)}Z_i^{(3)}u_j^{(3)}$$

describes the multiple membership structure. Cross-classification is captured by

$$(9)\quad u_{C_2(i)}^{(2)} \sim N(0, \Sigma_{u(2)}) \quad u_j^{(3)} \sim N(0, \Sigma_{u(3)})$$

Since MMMC models rely on prior information, standard extra-Poisson regression models with equivalent specifications of levels and variables were fitted to the data, but ignored multiple memberships and cross-classification.

Fitting variance component models without covariates provide information concerning the number of levels to be included in the comprehensive multilevel analysis. Table 4.1 features the results of the variance component model regressions. Using the deviance information criterion (DIC) as an indicator reveals that the three-level variance component models (*States in ROs* and *States in IOs*) do not fit the data as well as the four-level model. Thus, model four shows the best model fit, which validates the choice for the rather complex four-level MCMC models (Gelman et al. 2013).

Accordingly, as a baseline, the time cluster is included in all regression models, since states tend to behave path dependently in negotiations over the years (Hampton and Christensen 2014, Martin and Sunley 2006). Another preliminary consideration refers to the size of negotiation arenas. While some negotiation arenas include nearly all actors in the dataset (UNGA, for example, consists of 193 states + observers such as the Holy See, Palestine or the

**Table 4.2. Variance component models**

|  | *Model 1* | *Model 2* | *Model 3* | *Model 4* |
|---|---|---|---|---|
| RO level | 2.218*** |  |  | 1.947*** |
|  | (0.644) |  |  | (0.510) |
| IO level |  | 1.665** |  | 1.604** |
|  |  | (0.590) |  | (0.557) |
| Year level | 0.181 | 0.174 | 0.185 | 0.157 |
|  | (0.316) | (0.274) | (0.281) | (0.302) |
| Intercept | −4.071*** | −3.452*** | −2.196*** | −4.517*** |
|  | (0.433) | (0.287) | (0.172) | (0.584) |
| N | 17,381 | 17,381 | 17,381 | 17,381 |
| DIC | 18248.0 | 14986.9 | 20641.9 | 12777.5 |

Variance components and intercepts; standard errors in parentheses; DIC, Deviance Information Criterion; significance levels are: * $p < 0.05$, ** $p < 0.01$, *** $p < 0.001$.

EU), there are others which have limited membership. NASCO, for instance, consists only of six parties and one observer. Since negotiation arenas vary in size and since this has a huge impact on opportunities for RO activity, it is necessary to include this in the models (Rabe-Hesketh 2012). In order to account for the variation in size of negotiation arenas, the logarithm of the variable *number of participants* is used as an exposure variable. This avoids the deflation of estimates and the inflation of standard errors.

## 4.2 THE INDEPENDENT VARIABLES

The EMLG hypotheses on the active participation of regional actors in international negotiations distinguish between state, RO, IO and policy levels. In addition, we also specify cross-level hypotheses (c.f. chapter 2). This section discusses the operationalisation of the variables of interest. Descriptive statistics of all variables are given in annex (table A4.1).

To operationalise administrative capacities (H1a), we use the *government effectiveness* index drawn from the WGI-database (FAO 2013). It captures the efficiency of the policy cycle and quality of administration of countries and therefore is used as a proxy for the overall administrative capacity of a state's institutional system. The index can range from −2.5 to 2.5, which is nearly fully reflected in our sample that ranges from −2.45 to 2.43. Democratic socialisation (H1b) is measured using the *Polity4-index* (FAO 2014), ranging from −10 to +10, with the latter being the most democratic. The data covers the full range of the index. In order to measure the power of a state (H1c), we use GDP as a proxy, since it captures the potential of a state to formulate its own positions on a large number of issues as well as capacities to lobby for the positions. We use the GDP data from the WDI dataset (World Bank 2015). GDP data is made suitable for our analysis by converting it into billion USD. To account for the outliers and compensate the skewed distribution, we use a logged version of the variable. The range of *Log GDP (billion USD)* in our dataset is -2.94 to 7.39. Measurement of the *support for regional integration* (hypothesis 1d) is based on the number of memberships a state holds in the active regional organisations. The variable is based on our own research on the homepages of the respective regional organisations and of the MFAs of member states. The variable ranges from 0 to 6.

The *size of ROs* (H2a) is the number of states, which are members of a specific RO. The data was gathered from the homepages of the ROs, with the number of members ranging from 4 to 79. The *RO policy scope* (H2b) is the number of policy fields ROs cover. The data stems from the IO Yearbook as well as the respective RO homepages. This number ranges from 1 to 11, including agriculture, development, education, environment, finance/economy, health, human rights, technology, trade, security and social affairs. Information on the *number of RO coordination offices at IO headquarter locations* (H2c) has been acquired through the RO and IO websites as well as the UN Blue Book on Permanent Missions in New York (e.g. Executive Office of the Secretary-General 2010). It is a count variable ranging from 0 to 13.

On the IO level, the *size of IOs* (H3a) was operationalised by the number of member states and stems from the respective IO websites. The variable *IO size* ranges from 7 to 198. The *formal decision-making mode* in IO negotiations (H3b) is operationalised as a dummy variable, with 1 for majority voting and 0 for consensus decisions. The data stems from IO founding treaties and the IO rules of procedures and were obtained through their respective websites.

The policy fields (H4) covered in negotiations are clustered in twelve policy areas (agriculture, development, education, environment/ecology, finance/economy, health, human rights, internal issues, technology, trade, security, social affairs). The data stems from IO founding treaties and IO websites. The policy fields are coded as dummy variables indicating if a policy field is covered in a given negotiation.

Due to the multiple membership structure of the dataset (c.f. section 4.1), the regional-level variables need special treatment before they can be included in the comprehensive multilevel analysis. IVs in a multiple membership environment are weighted sums of the individual-level IV values. Initial values of variables are weighted according to the extent of the observed multiple membership, before aggregating them on the RO level to account for the differing membership patterns states show in the sampled data. For example, if a state is a member of one single RO, the IV value for this RO is used as the value. If a state is a member of five ROs, the IVs for the individual ROs are multiplied by 0.2 and added up to the resulting IV value. As a result,

ranges and values of variables at the RO level differ from the equivalent focus
level variables. The variable 'size of ROs' in the aggregated version ranges
from 21.29 to 56. RO policy scope ranges from 0 to 5.5. The variable *RO
coordination office at IO headquarter locations* ranges from 0 to 0.8 in the
comprehensive multilevel analysis.

The *homogeneity of ROs* (Hca) is operationalised by the aggregated devia-
tion of member states' average GDP per capita in a specific RO. The data
on GDP per capita was taken from the WDI dataset (World Bank 2015).
The variable ranges from 1097.931 to 28139.078, with more homogeneous
ROs achieving lower values. Data for the variable *Chair of RO* (Hcb) was
taken from homepages of ROs and is coded as a dummy variable: 1 for states
holding a chair in a given year and 0 otherwise. *RO–IO policy overlap* (Hcc)
captures the number of shared of policy overlaps between ROs and the issues
at stake in the negotiations. If an RO has no competencies in the issue area
at stake in the international negotiation, the variable has the value '0'. When
the negotiated issue covers multiple policy areas (e.g. trade and security as
in the case of the ATT), the max overlap value is defined by the number of
policies at stake in the negotiation. In the ATT example, this would be 2 if the
RO in question also has security and trade policy competencies. The actual
range of the variable is 0 to 7. The data is based on information from RO
and IO websites. Similarly, *formal status of an RO in an IO* (Hcd) captures
whether an RO holds any kind of formal status in a negotiation arena and the
data stems from RO and IO websites as well. Included varieties of formal
statuses are full membership, enhanced observer status, observer status or a
standing invitation to participate in negotiations. This variable ranges from 0
to 0.5, due to the aggregation of variables for the comprehensive multilevel
analysis. The independent variable of Hce is the presence/absence of an *RO
coordination office at the headquarter location of an IO*. The data was com-
piled based on information of RO and IO websites as well as the UN Blue
Book on Permanent Missions in New York. It is coded as a dummy variable,
taking '1' if there is a coordination office and '0' otherwise.

## 4.3 FOCUSED ANALYSIS

The focused analysis provides insights into the plausibility of the state, the
RO, the IO and the policy hypotheses by aggregating each of the four levels
separately. Accordingly, the levels feature different dependent variables (see
table 4.1) and focus on a level-specific set of hypotheses. The state level
examines the probability of each of the 205 state actors speaking on behalf
of ROs. The dependent variable on the regional level is the probability that
RO positions are voiced. On the IO and the policy levels, we study which

negotiation arenas and policy areas are conducive to the prevalence of regional positions. We supplement the quantitative analysis with narrative evidence from more than 200 semi-structured interviews with state diplomats and RO officials, conducted between 2010 and 2016.

### 4.3.1 The state level

As demonstrated in chapter 3, not all states take the floor equally often in international negotiations in order to speak on behalf of their ROs.

Table 4.3 illustrates that the dispersion parameter is consistently larger than twenty over all models. This considerable overdispersion implies that states' activities for ROs are strongly correlated. To put it in numbers: for a state that has voiced a regional position, the probability to speak up again for an RO increases by a factor of twenty, compared to a state that remained silent up to that point. Thus, the likelihood of states speaking on behalf of ROs early in a negotiation also increases the chance that they become active later on as well.

*Hypotheses 1a and b* are based on the notion that the ability of RO member states to formulate common regional positions is a precondition for being

**Table 4.3. Member-state-level regression results**

|  | Model 1 | Model 2 | Model 3 | Model 4 | Model 5 | Model 6 | Model 7 |
|---|---|---|---|---|---|---|---|
| Government effectiveness | 1.443*** (0.089) |  |  |  | 1.405*** (0.089) |  |  |
| Polity |  | 1.042** (0.014) |  |  | 1.013 (0.015) |  |  |
| GDP (billions, log) |  |  | 1.279*** (0.042) |  |  | 1.264*** (0.042) | 1.274*** (0.041) |
| Membership in ROs |  |  |  | 1.177** (0.055) | 1.147* (0.054) | 1.147* (0.056) | 1.165* (0.053) |
| Intercept | −8.512*** (0.111) | −8.703*** (0.129) | −8.966*** (0.139) | −9.061*** (0.214) | −8.950*** (0.211) | −9.434*** (0.223) | −9.445*** (0.223) |
| Dispersion | 20.491*** (0.081) | 20.532*** (0.081) | 20.369*** (0.080) | 20.532*** (0.081) | 20.512*** (0.081) | 20.389*** (0.080) | 20.369*** (0.080) |
| Level 1 variance | 2.318*** (0.299) | 2.380*** (0.305) | 2.237*** (0.290) | 2.375*** (0.305) | 2.252*** (0.294) | 2.145*** (0.284) | 2.157*** (0.284) |
| Level 2 variance | 0.000 (0.000) | 0.000 (0.000) | 0.000 (0.000) | 0.000 (0.000) | 0.000 (0.000) | 0.000 (0.000) | 0.000 (0.000) |
| N | 17,381 | 17,381 | 17,381 | 17,381 | 17,381 | 17,381 | 17,381 |
| BIC | 6502.5 | 6511.3 | 6484.9 | 6510.7 | 6505.9 | 6495.5 | 6486.5 |

Incidence rate ratios; standard errors in parentheses; BIC, Bayesian Information Criterion; significance levels are: $^* p < 0.05$, $^{**} p < 0.01$, $^{***} p < 0.001$.

able to act on behalf of the regional group in international negotiations.[1] Both hypotheses find empirical support.

*Hypothesis 1a* expects a positive relationship between a country's administrative capacities and the likelihood to articulate regional positions. Our findings presented in table 4.1 support H1a. Administrative capacities have a robustly positive effect on the probability that states voice regional positions and are therefore highly significant (models 1 and 5). Thus, a better-functioning government apparatus increases the probability that states will speak on behalf of ROs. If the government effectiveness indicator increases by one unit, the expected probability for a state to become active for an RO increases by 40.5 per cent to 44.3 per cent, depending on the model. This is supported by narrative evidence from interviews as well. States with ineffective government apparatuses cannot develop national positions for all issues on an IO negotiation table,[2] so that diplomats do not know their national position in time for the RO coordination meeting. As a consequence, they have very limited chances to influence regional positions during these meetings and are also often silent in international negotiations as such.[3]

In line with *hypothesis 1b,* democratic socialisation has a positive effect on the chances that RO members will formulate regional positions that the member states can subsequently articulate in international negotiations. Models 2 and 6 show that an increase in democracy scores robustly increases the chances that states articulate regional positions in international negotiations (H1b). While the bivariate analysis features significant findings, the significance gets lost in the model that controls for the other state-level variables (compare models 2 and 6). Interpreting the size of the effect of democratic socialisation in the significant model shows that if a state becomes more democratic by one point on the PolityIV-index, its probability to voice a regional position increases by 4.2 per cent. The propensity that democracy is favourable for the inclination of states to act on behalf of ROs is supported by qualitative interviews. The more democratic a country is, the more it is used to accommodating a multitude of positions and make political compromises, which increases their ability to successfully formulate regional positions.[4] Thus, the findings tend to support H1b.

Apart from being able to act in concert, the RO members need to also be motivated to voice the regional position in international negotiations. Hypotheses 1c and d capture how states' incentive structures impact their chances to act on behalf of an RO in IOs.

*Hypothesis 1c* expects that less powerful countries feature a smaller probability to articulate regional positions, as large states have incentives to negotiate on their own, while small states gain leverage from ROs in international negotiations. We tested H1c in various set-ups in order to accommodate the fact that the variable is highly skewed and not normally distributed. First, we included GDP in billions of dollar into the analysis, which featured a robustly negative, significant finding. This would have been in line with H1c. However, performing an outlier analysis shows that very high values of GDP are influential cases and must be controlled for by log transforming the power variable. Table 4.3 illustrates that this leads to a different picture, as the effect of power on regional positions voiced turns positive in the bivariate and the full models, respectively (models 3, 6, 7). At first glance, this seems to refute H1c. Yet, it also shows that the most powerful states are less inclined to operate through ROs in IO negotiations since controlling for them has a rather big effect on the directionality of how power plays out. H1c expects this. Figure 4.4 illustrates that the effect of power on regional actor activity is not linear. While states with very limited power show very low activity, states in the second and third quartiles become more active for ROs, and we see a sharp decline for the fourth quartile. Very powerful states behave differently from very poor states and the intermediate category.

Interview insights support the findings on the most and least powerful states. Especially very poor small states are selective when it comes to international negotiations and pursue only those issues on the international negotiation table that are of very high importance to them (Panke 2013a, c). As a consequence, diplomats of such countries do not actively participate in all international negotiations and instead often remain silent, unless the topic is of very high priority to them (c.f. Panke 2013a, c).[5] Yet, although they often

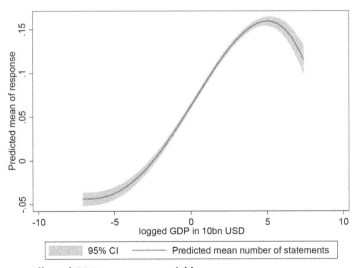

**Figure 4.4.   Effect of GDP on response variable**

lack capacities to act on behalf of regional actors in international negotiations, small states that have developed a position on an issue have incentives to leverage their influence in international negotiations through regional groups.[6] Vice versa, large states often prefer and are able to operate on their own in IOs, rather than through regional groups.[7]

Nevertheless, hypothesis 1c is rejected as there is no linear relationship between the power of states and the probability that they will act on behalf of ROs in IOs. Instead, the very weak and the very powerful states follow different logics. While the largest states have the incentives and the means to operate on their own, the smallest states have incentives to work through regional groups, but are unable to do so for all issues on the IO negotiation agenda.

In accordance with *hypothesis 1d*, models 4–7 show a positive and robust relationship between the extent to which states are in favour of regional cooperation and the number of times they articulate regional positions. The stronger states support the idea of regional cooperation, the more ROs they tend to join,[8] and the greater their incentives to support their RO on the international level. For instance, Benin, Denmark and Sweden all take the floor on behalf of their regional groups very often in international negotiations, and have joined seven, five and five ROs, respectively, while countries such as China or the United States have joined very few ROs (two and four, respectively) and only rarely speak on behalf of ROs (China four times, United States two times). On average, if a state joins one additional RO, the expected chances for this state to bring an RO position to the table increase by 14.7 per cent to 17.7 per cent, depending on the model.

### 4.3.2 The regional level

Regional positions do not just naturally exist, but need to be developed in RO coordination meetings. Only when the RO members agree on a regional position can it be voiced in international negotiations by RO members.

Regional positions are articulated only if the group members agree on what the common position is. For instance, diplomats reported that 'normally you go through a process of consultation with the various members of the group and whomever is chairing the group tries to bring forward an agreement, a consensus on whatever issue is being discussed' (interview#114, 04-08-11). Another diplomat elaborated on the same point: 'if we have a statement about a subject, there is no secretariat of the group that develops a statement and then speaks. If the group wants to speak and have meaning, not a single word will be spoken unless everyone in the group has endorsed it. So, for example, we have important meetings coming up and the chair's responsibility, and this changes every year, is that he would present a draft and circulate it to the group and wait for comment. After the comments come, he revises it accordingly, then passes it back as a final version. Once it is endorsed by each and all members, then the group will deliver a statement on behalf of the group' (interview#69, 22-03-11).[9]

In rare instances, however, it can happen that not all RO members are behind all parts of a group position on an issue on the international negotiation arena. Usually, such disagreement leads to situations in which the contested parts are not mentioned in the overall group position: 'That's the whole idea being a part of the regional group. You get your interest voiced from a regional platform, a wider platform than a national position. Most cases, you have countries speaking with one voice. Very rarely you have the regional coordinator or chairman speaking on issues that have not had the support of the group. In the cases where you have differences within members of the group, those issues do not get raised by chair coordinator, they are left out' (interview#61, 11-03-11). Similarly, a diplomat from the Global South explained: 'Most groups try to avoid splits in coordination, so a split rarely happens. Where it does happen, there is always an attempt to reconcile the group position by formulating a very broad agreement that can accommodate competing interests within the group. It is very infrequent that a group position would be announced on the floor and a member state would take the floor to basically disassociate from that group position. It does not happen very often at all. Normally, within group coordination, the group realises they cannot come to an agreement on a particular issue, they would remain silent. Or they would give a very, very general group position that can be agreed upon as non-controversial within the area of that controversial issue, and they would leave the controversial issues silent' (interview#96, 12-04-11).

Not all ROs are equally vocal in international negotiations (c.f. chapter 3). The vocality of the fifty-one active regional groups and organisations in the dataset ranges from 1 statement (e.g. EFTA, NATO or CIS) to 211 statements (EU) brought to the negotiation table by member states or RO delegates themselves. Hypotheses 2a–c focus on whether RO properties impact their chances to articulate regional positions in IOs.

The RO-level analysis supports *hypothesis 2a,* according to which larger ROs tend to be more active in international negotiations. The bivariate and multivariate models feature the expected positive relationship between IV and DV in a robust manner, but do not cross the threshold of significance (models 1 and 4, table 4.4). The tendency observed in the quantitative models is supplemented by narrative evidence. Diplomats report that irrespective of the formal status of an RO in an IO, RO member states can always use their

**Table 4.4.   RO-level regression results**

|                          | Model 1    | Model 2    | Model 3    | Model 4    | Model 5    |
|--------------------------|------------|------------|------------|------------|------------|
| RO size                  | 1.007      |            |            | 1.003      |            |
|                          | (0.006)    |            |            | (0.011)    |            |
| RO policy scope          |            | 1.016      |            | 1.014      | 1.012      |
|                          |            | (0.047)    |            | (0.047)    | (0.046)    |
| RO office at             |            |            | 1.029***   |            | 1.036***   |
| IO headquarters          |            |            | (0.008)    |            | (0.008)    |
| 2009                     | 1.324***   | 1.279*     | 1.293***   | 1.279*     | 1.22       |
|                          | (0.075)    | (0.102)    | (0.075)    | (0.102)    | (0.102)    |
| 2010                     | 1.496***   | 1.578***   | 1.43***    | 1.578***   | 1.436***   |
|                          | (0.073)    | (0.098)    | (0.074)    | (0.098)    | (0.101)    |
| 2011                     | 1.305***   | 1.692***   | 1.284**    | 1.692***   | 1.644***   |
|                          | (0.077)    | (0.099)    | (0.077)    | (0.099)    | (0.010)    |
| 2012                     | 1.527***   | 1.839***   | 1.528***   | 1.839***   | 1.863***   |
|                          | (0.074)    | (0.099)    | (0.074)    | (0.099)    | (0.099)    |
| Intercept                | −5.058***  | −5.078***  | −4.898***  | −5.117***  | −5.045***  |
|                          | (0.170)    | (0.344)    | (0.113)    | (0.371)    | (0.340)    |
| Dispersion               | 1.32***    | 1.399**    | 1.328***   | 1.402**    | 1.379**    |
|                          | (0.072)    | (0.119)    | (0.073)    | (0.120)    | (0.115)    |
| N                        | 739        | 409        | 741        | 409        | 409        |
| BIC                      | 6752.4     | 3867.6     | 6745.9     | 3873.6     | 3854.4     |

Incidence rate ratios; standard errors in parentheses; BIC, Bayesian Information Criterion; significance levels are: $^* p < 0.05$, $^{**} p < 0.01$, $^{***} p < 0.001$.

participation rights in order to speak on behalf of their RO.[10] Accordingly, the more member states a regional group has, the more national diplomats can take the floor and speak on behalf of the RO.[11] By contrast, small ROs have fewer opportunities to have their positions articulated, as the number of national diplomats that could potentially speak up for the group is smaller. In sum, H2a can be regarded as being plausible in tendency.

*Hypothesis 2b* addresses the role of the policy scopes of ROs. The variable 'RO policy scope' shows a positive and robust effect on the likelihood that ROs participate actively in international negotiations, but the findings are not significant (models 2, 4 and 5, table 4.4). Qualitative insights reinforce the positive tendency of the quantitative analysis. The more policy competencies an RO has, the more often its members can refer to past common policies, norms and rules as focal points,[12] which renders the development of regional positions easier and increases the likelihood that a position of the RO is voiced in international negotiations. An example for a negotiation in which an RO could use their former common policy as a starting point and negotiate internationally with one voice is the EU in the negotiations on the Arms Trade Treaty. In this respect, a diplomat reported: 'They agreed already on this regional, sort of, common policy on the arms trade anyway. So, I mean, they already have their existing very high standards, so you know we wanted to . . . the EU had a very valid concern on ensuring that, you know, the treaty didn't, sort of, undercut their already strong standards . . . it was about making sure again in a very kind of tricky area to sort of put down in the Treaty that that was at least consistent with their own policy' (interview#210, 29-07-15).[13] Considering both the quantitative and qualitative insights, H2b is supported in tendency.

*Hypothesis 2c* expects that having RO offices in many IO headquarter locations signals the RO's willingness to act as a group and positively impacts the chances for RO activity in international negotiations. The regression results reveal that the number of times ROs have coordination offices at IO headquarters does increase the likelihood for RO activity in international negotiations significantly (models 3 and 5, table 4.4). Similarly, diplomats highlight that incentives are important for RO activity in international negotiations (e.g. interviews#208, 20-05-15, #212, 28-10-15, #170, 22-07-14, #199, 24-02-15). Thus, we can reject the null hypothesis for H2c. Having RO offices in many of the IO headquarter locations has a positive effect on the ROs' likelihood to act as a group. One additional RO office increases the probability that regional positions of this group are voiced by 2.9 per cent and 3.6 per cent, respectively (models 3 and 5).

Looking at the year dummies, in some models, there is a tendency to increased RO activity over time. In models 1 and 3, in which all ROs are included, time has no robustly increasing effect on the likelihood that RO actors speak up for their group. Models 2, 4 and 5 do not include IO-specific regional actors like, for example, the UN regional groups or FAO regional groups, since the policy scope variable is not applicable for these groups. The models that exclude IO-specific regional groups show that compared to the reference year 2008, the probability for ROs to become active increases from one year to another consistently. Despite capturing a five-year snapshot with our negotiation data (c.f. chapter 3), we observe a slight tendency towards an increasing regionalisation of international negotiations.

### 4.3.3 The international level

IOs vary in the extent to which they attract RO activity. As chapter 3 illustrated, the greatest share of articulated regional positions is prevalent in the IOM, while negotiations are the least regionalised in the NASCO.

Table 4.3 sheds light on the plausibility of the hypotheses related to international negotiation arenas. First, according to *hypothesis 3a,* an increase in IO size is significantly and positively related to the number of regional positions voiced in the IO in a given year. Table 4.3 illustrates that the more members an IO has, the greater the probability that regional positions are prevalent in

**Table 4.5.  IO-level regression results**

|                | Model 1 | Model 2 | Model 3 |
|----------------|---------|---------|---------|
| IO size        | 1.009*  |         | 1.01*   |
|                | (0.004) |         | (0.004) |
| IO majority    |         | 2.028   | 2.243   |
|                |         | (0.604) | (0.618) |
| Intercept      | 3.063***| 3.882***| 2.321** |
|                | (0.326) | (0.138) | (0.785) |
| N              | 27      | 27      | 27      |
| BIC            | 5601.5  | 6151.0  | 5458.3  |

Incidence rate ratios; standard errors in parentheses; BIC, Bayesian Information Criterion; significance levels are: $p < 0.05$, $p < 0.01$, $p < 0.001$.

the negotiations. The findings are significant and robust in the bivariate and the multivariate models (models 1 and 3). With every single member state in an RO, the probability that an additional regional position will be voiced increases by up to 1 per cent (model 3, table 4.5). This is considerable, given the range of the variable and the fact that not every state speaks up in each negotiation. Diplomats also suggest that IO size is important for regional actor activity because international negotiations are time-consuming per se. Especially in instances in which the number of IO member states is high, negotiations would take very long, if each state negotiated on its own and made formal statements in a tour de table. In such constellations, aggregating state positions into group positions renders international negotiations much more effective.[14] Accordingly, large IOs exhibit a greater extent of regionalised negotiations.

Second and according to *hypothesis 3b*, if IOs formal decision making allows for majority voting, every vote counts and numbers matter for the passing of international rules and norms. While the directionality of the incidence rates is robustly positive as expected, the findings lack significance (model 2, table 4.3). In general, states have advantages when working through regional groups as the latter increase their chances to exert influence over IO policy outcomes (interviews #127, 29-11-11, #129, 29-11-11).[15] In IOs in which policies are passed on the basis of unanimity, a single no-vote can theoretically block decisions and states have much more limited gains from working through regional groups. However, interviewees did not corroborate this point. In practice, many international negotiations seek to obtain consensus between the state parties, even if formally decision making by voting is possible (for the UNGA c.f. Panke 2013c).[16] Thus, hypothesis 3b is not supported.

### 4.3.4 The policy dimension

Finally, regional actors are more vocal in some policy areas than others (c.f. chapter 3). To examine the policy-level hypothesis, we use negative binomial regressions with a series of dummy variables capturing the issues of the 512 coded negotiations.

Model 1 in table 4.6 illustrates that negotiations covering trade policy issues do not per se attract more RO activity than other policy issues. The outlier analysis reveals that the ILO and, to a lesser extent, the WHO are influential cases. Consequently, model 2 excludes the ILO from the analysis, while model 3 omits the ILO and the WHO. Excluding influential cases reveals that trade issues under negotiation increase the probability for RO activity. This effect is robust, and the effect size is higher than for any of the other policy issues, which is in line with *hypothesis*

**Table 4.6. Policy-level regression results**

|  | *Model 1* | *Model 2* | *Model 3* | *Model 4* | *Model 5* | *Model 6* |
|---|---|---|---|---|---|---|
| Agriculture | 1.137 | 1.315 | 1.315 | 1.124 | 1.230 | 1.234 |
|  | (0.261) | (0.201) | (0.204) | (0.259) | (0.198) | (0.201) |
| Development | 1.131 | 1.597** | 1.680*** | 1.119 | 1.492** | 1.575** |
|  | (0.177) | (0.144) | (0.146) | (0.174) | (0.139) | (0.141) |
| Education | 1.251 | 0.071* | 0.086* | 1.237 | 0.067* | 0.081* |
|  | (0.460) | (1.059) | (1.067) | (0.459) | (1.058) | (1.065) |
| Environment | 0.568** | 0.750 | 0.764 | 0.563** | 0.715* | 0.731* |
|  | (0.183) | (0.147) | (0.151) | (0.181) | (0.145) | (0.149) |
| Finance, economy | 1.149 | 1.399* | 1.413* | 1.142 | 1.383 | 1.392* |
|  | (0.186) | (0.146) | (0.149) | (0.185) | (0.146) | (0.149) |
| Health | 2.171* | 1.649 | 0.244 | 2.115* | 1.402 | 0.226 |
|  | (0.304) | (0.273) | (0.842) | (0.296) | (0.259) | (0.839) |
| Human rights | 0.986 | 1.445* | 1.514* | 0.965 | 1.287 | 1.350 |
|  | (0.193) | (0.166) | (0.167) | (0.183) | (0.154) | (0.155) |
| Internal issues | 1.059 | 1.288 | 1.283 |  |  |  |
|  | (0.160) | (0.133) | (0.135) |  |  |  |
| Technology | 1.551 | 1.636 | 1.829* | 1.548 | 1.6012 | 1.788* |
|  | (0.335) | (0.254) | (0.275) | (0.335) | (0.253) | (0.275) |
| Trade | 1.978* | 2.106** | 2.113** | 1.956* | 2.012** | 2.020** |
|  | (0.330) | (0.250) | (0.251) | (0.328) | (0.250) | (0.251) |
| Security | 0.790 | 1.123 | 1.192 | 0.766 | 0.977 | 1.040 |
|  | (0.189) | (0.154) | (0.156) | (0.169) | (0.135) | (0.138) |
| Social affairs | 8.029*** | 0.877 | 0.882 | 7.862*** | 0.855 | 0.861 |
|  | (0.199) | (0.180) | (0.181) | (0.190) | (0.180) | (0.181) |
| Intercept | 0.813*** | 0.410** | 0.353** | 0.851*** | 0.587*** | 0.525*** |
|  | (0.157) | (0.133) | (0.135) | (0.115) | (0.095) | (0.098) |
| Dispersion | 1.493*** | 0.753* | 0.764* | 1.493*** | 0.76* | 0.771* |
|  | (0.079) | (0.114) | (0.118) | (0.079) | (0.114) | (0.118) |
| N | 512 | 492 | 472 | 512 | 492 | 472 |
| BIC | 2359.0 | 1983.6 | 1878.1 | 2352.9 | 1981.1 | 1875.4 |

Incidence rate ratios; standard errors in parentheses; BIC, Bayesian Information Criterion; significance levels are: $^*p < 0.05$, $^{**}p < 0.01$, $^{***}p < 0.001$.

*4*. Interviews also support the notion that ROs are especially active concerning trade issues. Diplomats stress that regional positions can be developed more easily during regional group coordination meetings, when the member states had already covered the policy at stake in the past.[17] Since regional integration started in most cases in the trade realm,[18] the policy area covered by most ROs and advanced the furthest is trade. Thus, compared to other policy areas, regional positions are articulated most often when trade elements are discussed in international negotiations, as past RO policies serve as focal points so that it is easier for RO member states to develop regional positions in their respective group coordination meetings and subsequently articulate these positions in the international negotiation arena.

## 4.4 COMPREHENSIVE MULTILEVEL ANALYSIS

The cross-level hypotheses are empirically examined by a comprehensive multilevel analysis (c.f. section 4.1).

First, we investigate the multilevel structure. To this end, we study the components of variance over the three distinct levels and discuss variance partition coefficients (VPC). This provides insights into the explained variation allocated to the levels of the analysis and leads in a second step to the discussion of five cross-level hypotheses.

Table 4.7 shows coefficients and variance components for the comprehensive multilevel models. The estimated MMMC models assume a Poisson distribution. Therefore, they do not yield level 1 variances in the estimations. This is due to the assumptions of the Poisson distribution that the variance equals the mean, leading to:

$$R = \text{Variance-to-mean ratio} = \frac{\sigma^2}{\mu}$$

In Poisson models, one of the core assumptions is R=1. This is the prerequisite to calculate VPCs. Since in a Poisson environment VPCs depend on the independent variables, we use a latent variable approach to determine the VPC for all models (Browne et al. 2005, Snijders and Bosker 2012). Table 4.7 gives an overview of the VPCs for the variance components model discussed in section 4.1 (model 0, table 4.7) as well as the six models reported in the comprehensive multilevel analysis. Variance is partitioned into four components, corresponding to the levels: in model 0, the year level accounts for 3.3 per cent of the variance and 34.1 per cent is allocated at the IO level. The RO level holds the largest share with 41.4 per cent of the variance.

Table 4.7. **Variance partition coefficients**

|  | Model 0 | Model 1 | Model 2 | Model 3 | Model 4 | Model 5 | Model 6 |
|---|---|---|---|---|---|---|---|
| State | 0.212 | 0.206 | 0.214 | 0.214 | 0.211 | 0.202 | 0.200 |
| RO | 0.414 | 0.218 | 0.172 | 0.180 | 0.191 | 0.183 | 0.189 |
| IO | 0.341 | 0.537 | 0.563 | 0.562 | 0.552 | 0.569 | 0.556 |
| Year | 0.033 | 0.039 | 0.051 | 0.044 | 0.046 | 0.046 | 0.055 |

Differences between states account for 21.2 per cent of the variance, when no independent variables are included.

When including independent variables, one major shift in the variance components occurs. While the year level features a minor increase, ranging from 3.9 per cent to 5.5 per cent, the state level remains rather stationary, with a range from 20.0 per cent to 21.4 per cent (models 1 to 6, table 4.7). Major shifts are observed between RO and IO levels. While the explained variance in the IO level increases by about 20 per cent, the RO level loses nearly the same amount of observed variance.

Since the data is overdispersed, we include a parameter capturing the extra Poisson variance, quantifying the degree of overdispersion in the data (Rodríguez 1993). This allows modelling the overdispersion, rescaling standard errors and improving overall model fit. The parameters for all models are also reported in table 4.8.

All models in table 4.8 are kept parsimonious in order to avoid multicollinearity.

The comprehensive multilevel regressions back the focused analysis, which looked at four levels of aggregation in turn: the state, the regional, the IO and the policy levels (c.f. 4.3.1–4.3.4). In general, the comprehensive multilevel regressions support the findings of the various EMLG hypotheses from the focused analysis, whilst controlling for the nested structure and clusters in the data.[19]

Three of the state-level hypotheses are supported by the comprehensive multilevel analysis. Table 4.7 shows that an increase in administrative capacities (H1a; models 2, 4 and 5, table 4.8), an increase in democracy (H1b; model 3, table 4.8) and an increase in the support of regional integration (H1d; models 3–5, table 4.8) increase the probability that states voice regional positions and does so in a robust manner. For H1c, the multilevel analysis also does not support the expectation that power influences the chance that states voice regional positions, which is due to the non-linear relationship between power and the activity of states for their ROs (see section 4.3.1). Thus, all findings of the focused level analysis are in line with the findings of the comprehensive multilevel analysis.

Table 4.8. Comprehensive multilevel regressions

| | Model 1 | Model 2 | Model 3 | Model 4 | Model 5 | Model 6 |
|---|---|---|---|---|---|---|
| Government effectiveness | | 1.224** (0.064) | | 1.209** (0.065) | 1.211** (0.065) | |
| Polity | | | 1.022* (0.009) | | | 1.020* (0.010) |
| GDP (billions, log); fixed part | | 1.000* (0.000) | 1.000** (0.000) | 1.000** (0.000) | 1.000* (0.000) | 1.000** (0.000) |
| GDP (billions, log); random part | | 0.998*** (0.000) | 0.998*** (0.000) | 0.998*** (0.000) | 0.998*** (0.000) | 0.998*** (0.000) |
| Membership in ROs | | 1.368*** (0.066) | 1.367*** (0.067) | 1 342*** (0.068) | 1.340*** (0.067) | 1.334*** (0.069) |
| RO size | | | | 0.930* (0.029) | 0.932* (0.029) | 0.926** (0.030) |
| RO policy scope | | | | 1.002 (0.14) | 1.008 (0.134) | 1.023 (0.14) |
| IO size | | | | | 0.998 (0.006) | 0.997 (0.005) |
| IO majority | | | | | 0.506 (0.937) | 0.511 (0.932) |
| Homogeneity of ROs | 0.983 (0.016) | 1.022 (0.017) | 1.028 (0.016) | 1.025 (0.018) | 1.024 (0.018) | 1.031 (0.018) |
| RO chair position | 33.02*** (0.057) | 33.20*** (0.057) | 33.17*** (0.057) | 33.31*** (0.058) | 33.25*** (0.058) | 33.24*** (0.057) |
| RO policy overlap | 28.28*** (0.169) | 29.57*** (0.171) | 29.36*** (0.17) | 28.99*** (0.171) | 29.52*** (0.171) | 29.20*** (0.17) |
| Formal status of RO in IO | 6.973** (0.664) | 14.83*** (0.684) | 16.03*** (0.687) | 13.96*** (0.692) | 13.75*** (0.69) | 14 93*** (0.69) |
| RO office at IO headquarters | 1.237 (0.244) | 1.223 (0.241) | 1.193 (0.245) | 1.225 (0.241) | 1.225 (0.242) | 1.202 (0.244) |
| Intercept | −10.34*** (0.623) | −9.996*** (0.628) | −10.16*** (0.621) | −7.653*** (1.157) | −6.815*** (1.566) | −6.757*** (1.691) |
| Level 2 variance | 1.060** (0.332) | 0.806** (0.262) | 0.838** (0.277) | 0.903** (0.314) | 0.905** (0.308) | 0.947** (0.317) |
| Level 3 variance | 2.608** (0.879) | 2.634** (0.886) | 2.623** (0.882) | 2.612** (0.882) | 2.812** (1.017) | 2.784** (0.986) |
| Level 4 variance | 0.190 (0.325) | 0.241 (0.467) | 0.205 (0.422) | 0.220 (0.344) | 0.228 (0.420) | 0.277 (1.193) |
| Overdispersion | 14.16 | 11.49 | 12.89 | 11.06 | 9.981 | 10.75 |
| N | 17360 | 17360 | 17360 | 17360 | 17360 | 17360 |
| DIC | 7449.1 | 7362.8 | 7366.0 | 7355.9 | 7354.9 | 7358.1 |

Incidence rate ratios; standard errors in parentheses; DIC, Deviance Information Criterion; significance levels are: $p < 0.05$, $p < 0.01$, $p < 0.001$.

Concerning the regional-level hypotheses, model 4 illustrates that the single-level findings on the policy scope of an RO (H2b) is replicated in the multilevel analysis (model 4, table 4.8). The probability that states act on behalf of their RO increases, as the RO's scope of policy competencies broadens.

The picture looks different for H2a, which focuses on the size of ROs. The focused level analysis illustrated that an increase in RO size tends to increase the probability that the position of the respective RO is voiced in the IO. The complex multilevel analysis suggests that there is a different logic at play with respect to the probability that a specific RO member state becomes active. The effect is negative, which indicates that a specific state is decreasingly likely to speak on behalf of an RO, the larger the latter is. This can be interpreted as an empirical expression of burden-sharing behaviour, according to which RO members divide the work amongst them and take turns acting on behalf of the regional group (interview#59, 11-03-11).[20] In smaller ROs burden-sharing is more prevalent and it is more frequently the case that an individual state is called upon to speak on behalf of the RO (e.g. interviews #140, 01-12-11, #139, 01-12-11, #105, 19-07-11, #67, 17-03-11).[21] The same state is less often in a situation in which it needs to become active due to burden-sharing between the RO members, when the number of RO members is higher (e.g. interviews #202, 27-02-15, #155, 15-02-12, #143, 02-12-11, #110, 21-07-11). Thus, member state diplomats from large ROs often report that they are less active in international negotiations.[22]

Hypothesis 2c cannot be tested as such in the comprehensive multilevel analysis, due to the different mode of aggregation. Yet, it is still plausible, since the effect of having an RO office on the likelihood for this RO's activity is robustly positive (c.f. discussion on cross-level hypothesis; see below).

Similar to the RO size variable, the IO size variable also features different directions in the complex multilevel analysis compared to the focused level analysis. Table 4.7 shows that the effect is negative with respect to IO size (model 5). The larger an IO is, the more limited the probability that a specific state will voice a regional position. At first glance, this seems to contradict H3a. However, it is actually in line with H3a, since it also expects that large IOs attract less state activity in general in order to prevent overly long ineffective negotiations. Instead, states bundle their positions into groups in order to reduce the overall amount of speech acts in the international negotiation. If a regional group position is voiced by one of the RO member states, all other members of the same RO are expected to remain silent (see burden-sharing discussion previously). Thus, the multilevel analysis that features a negative sign supports the IO size hypothesis, since the chances that a state voices a regional position (or any position) decline with an increase in IO size.

The comprehensive multilevel regression models also feature a different sign for H3b on the effect of IO decision-making rules on RO activity (model

5, table 4.8). In the focused level analysis, regional positions have a higher probability to be articulated in majority voting IOs, but this effect is not significant and is not supported by qualitative interviews. The comprehensive multilevel analysis features a negative effect on majority voting and therefore also does not support H3b. Majority rule decreases the likelihood that an individual state speaks on behalf of an RO. Again, not every RO member speaks for the RO in question. Instead, burden-sharing takes place, and one of the RO members voices the regional position, while the other RO members remain silent. Thus, while the collective incentive of ROs to become active increases under majority voting, burden-sharing reduces the probability that a specific state speaks on behalf of the RO and, thus, brings about a negative effect in the comprehensive multilevel model.

The effect of RO trade competencies (H4) is not included in the comprehensive multilevel analysis. Similar to H2c, this is due to a different level of aggregation. Yet, hypothesis Hcc on the match of policy scopes between RO competencies and issues under negotiation supports the notion that the type of negotiated policies impacts the likelihood for RO activity in negotiations.

In addition to the featured-level hypotheses H1–H4, this section also examines cross-level hypotheses (Hca–ce). They shed light on how state activity on behalf of ROs is shaped by factors from two different levels (c.f. chapter 2).

Hca focuses on cross-level interactions between the state and the regional levels (models 1–5, table 4.8). It expects that the internal homogeneity in ROs is conducive to the successful development of regional positions in RO coordination meetings and thus increases the voice of the specific RO in international negotiations. The more homogenous ROs are internally, the more likely it is that states do not differ fundamentally concerning international negotiation issues and the easier it is to agree on a common regional position that can subsequently be articulated in the international negotiations. Yet, the quantitative analysis does not support *hypothesis ca*. It is not the case that an increase in RO internal homogeneity increases the probability of regional positions being voiced in international negotiations (model 1 features negative and models 2–6 positive effects, table 4.7). The qualitative evidence is also mixed and does not systematically support the plausibility of the hypothesis. On the one hand, interviewees point out that speaking with one voice is important for the prospect of the RO to be effective in the international negotiations as 'it is worse having a split up regional group, than not having any' (interview#101, 24-06-11) and that 'it is a general feeling among the group that unless we have coherency, unless we have a single voice we might be left out. So it is the whole group as such has a mind-set that we have to be more united' (interview#33, 21-12-10).[23] On the other hand, even in relatively homogenous regional groups, such as the EU, the heterogeneity of member states can be high with respect to certain issues: 'the thing is with this issue is the substance because among EU member states, quite frankly we have a very different historical legacy with regard to the issue of racism. And we come to the table with the different history, with a different set of baggage's, some of them with a post-colonial baggage, other not with that and I think to be honest I think that does inform approaches, and so maybe it shouldn't be as shocking, three-way splits as it might otherwise be' (interview#105 19-07-11, similar interviews#225, 06-05-16, #148, 06-12-11, #140, 01-12-11, #134, 30-11-11, #105, 19-07-11).[24]

The second state–RO cross-level hypothesis focuses on the chairmanship of ROs (*Hcb*). Models 1–5 illustrate that group chairs are robustly more likely to act on behalf of the RO. If a state serves as RO chair, the probability increases by a factor of more than thirty that it voices a regional position. This is in line with the theoretical expectation. Interviews also support this finding.[25] With their role as chairs in ROs comes not only an obligation to organise group meetings amongst the member states in advance of international negotiations in order to coordinate common regional positions.[26] States holding the chairmanship of an RO also have strong incentives to articulate regional positions afterwards in IOs and take the lead in negotiating on behalf of the regional group.[27]

The first RO–IO cross-level hypothesis (Hcc) expects that an increase in policy match between the RO and the IO in question positively impacts the likelihood that a regional position is articulated by a member state. This is in line with the complex multilevel analysis, which shows that the RO–IO policy match robustly increases the probability of RO vocality (models 1–5, table 4.8). When the match between the policy competencies of an RO and the issue under negotiation in the IO increases by one unit, the likelihood for positions of this RO being voiced in this specific international negotiation increases by a factor of about 24.96 to 29.57, depending on the model. Narrative evidence also supports the notion that the match between policy scopes of ROs and IOs is important because it influences the dynamics of group coordination and the prospects of RO positions being formulated and voiced. For instance, an interviewee reported that the 'position of the EU and its image and power is very dependent on our being able to show unity and having a new voice in external affairs issues so that should also happen in terms of multilateral representation. But the problem actually [*sic*] is that different international organisations have different responsibilities and some of these are within community competence, and some are mixed competence and some are still totally on the responsibility of the member states, so for instance, in OECD we're dealing with many, many issues that are not in the community competence' (interview#16, 25-11-10).[28]

According to second RO–IO cross-level hypothesis (Hcd), states are more likely to voice regional positions, when their RO has a formal status in the international negotiation arena in question. In line with this, the models feature a robustly positive finding (c.f. models 1–5, table 4.8). The effect of this variable is strong, as having a formal status increases the probability of regional positions being voiced by a factor ranging between 6.9 and 16.0. Although member states can and do speak for their ROs irrespective of the formal status, investing resources to get an RO accredited as an observer or formal IO member indicates the high importance RO members place on acting in concert.[29] In line with this, positions of ROs with membership rights in an IO, such as the EU in the FAO and the WTO, have a higher probability to become articulated in the international negotiation arena, also since RO delegates can speak directly for their RO (c.f. chapter 3).[30] Observer ROs usually do not have their own speaking rights in IOs, but depend on their member states to voice the regional positions.[31] The member states are more motivated to act on behalf of their RO, when the latter has an observer status, not only because of the sunk costs invested in getting this status as a group in the first place, but also because they expect to be recognised as legitimate collective actors in the respective IO arena.[32]

According to the final RO–IO cross-level hypothesis (Hce), states are more likely to voice regional positions in the international negotiations, for which their RO has opened a regional office at the IO negotiation location. As expected, models 1–5 illustrate that the effect is positive and robust. Having an office at the HQ location of an IO increases the likelihood for the RO to becoming active in the negotiations by 19.3–23.7 per cent, depending on the model. In line with the quantitative analysis, qualitative interviews also lend support to the hypothesis. Diplomats point out that group coordination meetings are time- and resource-intensive[33] and stressed that having a regional office that provides staff and administrative support is conducive to RO activity in the IO in questions. Staff and other administrative resources provided by RO offices at IO headquarter locations are helpful in supporting the group coordination meetings and help to facilitate the construction of a common position that the RO member states can subsequently voice in the respective IO.[34]

# Part II

# SUCCESS OF REGIONAL ACTORS

The second part of the book shifts its focus from regional actor activity (DV1) towards regional actor success (DV2). It examines how and under which conditions the active participation of ROs in international negotiations turns into success. Which ROs are best able to shape negotiation dynamics and outcomes? How do ROs talk third-party states into supporting their stance and how do they manage to ultimately influence international norms? When does the regionalisation of international negotiation dynamics lead to regional imprints on international norms?

In order to shed light on the nexus between regional actor activity and regional actor success, this part of the book presents qualitative case studies that apply process-tracing methodology in order to uncover the dynamics underlying regional actor success. The case studies are (1) the negotiations on the South Atlantic Whale Sanctuary (SAWS), (2) the negotiations of the Arms Trade Treaty (ATT) and (3) the negotiations of the Rome Declaration on Nutrition.

The negotiation arenas are selected on the basis of the IO-level hypotheses on negotiation success (c.f. chapter 2) and follow a structure-focused comparison (SFC) design. SFC case selection is based on independent variables (George and Bennett 2005) and allows for pairwise comparisons which systematically vary core IO-level variables.

We select three negotiation arenas that systematically vary with respect to two core variables on the IO level, the openness of IOs for ROs (H7a) and the size of IOs (H7b), whilst keeping important alternative explanations constant across the cases (e.g. concerning RO and member state properties). IOs should feature high levels of regionalisation of international negotiations, the more ROs possess important formal competencies in IOs decision-making processes (H7a) and the larger IOs are (H7b) (c.f. chapter 2). Accordingly, we select two cases in which the IOs are of equal size, but differ in the formal openness for ROs. In addition, we keep the formal openness of IOs for ROs constant and select a third case study, in which IO size differs considerably.

This leads to the following selection of negotiation arenas. First, we select the FAO and the ATT as they are equal in IO size (194 and 193 member states, respectively), but differ in the IO openness towards ROs. While ROs can obtain important formal competencies in the FAO, as they can become full members, ROs can only become observers in the ATT. The third negotiation arena that we select is the International Whaling Commission (IWC), which is small in size (eighty-eight member states), while its openness to ROs is limited as well. Similar to the ATT, ROs can only become observers but not full members of the IWC.

Hence, the IWC forms a least likely arena for RO success, since it is not very large in size and does not grant ROs full membership status. By contrast, the FAO is a most likely case for RO success. It is a large IO, and ROs can apply for full membership. The ATT constitutes the case for which we expect a medium level of regional actor success, since the negotiation arena is large in size, but limits the formal roles of ROs to observers. Comparing the negotiations on the Rome Declaration on Nutrition with the negotiations of the ATT allows isolating the role of the IO openness for ROs for the regionalisation of international negotiation outcomes. Comparing the ATT negotiations with the SAWS negotiations allows isolating the importance of IO size for the prospects of ROs to leave regional imprints on international norms.

In each of the three negotiation arenas, we select one recent negotiation on an international norm, which is typical for what the respective IO is doing and which is relatively recent to allow for interviews as methods of data generation. On this basis, we selected the SAWS negotiations for the IWC (2011–2014), the Treaty negotiation for the ATT (2009–2013) and the negotiations on the Rome Declaration of 2014 for the FAO. With respect to the state- and regional-level hypotheses (c.f. chapter 2), each case study features considerable in-case variation, as in each negotiation under scrutiny, a variety of actors became engaged in regard to numerous elements in the international norm under discussion. This in-case variation can also be captured with respect to the negotiation strategies applied and the issue saliency attached by the different actors, because we use process-tracing methodology. Furthermore, all case studies make use of primary document analysis of negotiation protocols, speeches, press releases and official homepages as well as semi-structured interviews with RO members, state diplomats and representatives of IOs as well as civil society actors. This allows studying how regional actor activity translates into the successful shaping of international negotiation dynamics and outcomes and allows systematically examining the hypotheses on regional actor negotiation success.

Chapter 5 presents the SAWS negotiations in the IWC, chapter 6 the ATT negotiations on the General Treaty and chapter 7 the negotiations on the Rome Declaration in the FAO.

*Chapter 5*

# Case Study 1: The negotiations of the South Atlantic Whale Sanctuary

This chapter studies the role of different regional actors in recent negotiations in the International Whaling Commission (IWC). It focuses on the 2011, 2012 and 2014 negotiations on the proposal establishing a South Atlantic Whale Sanctuary (SAWS). According to several environmental groups and anti-whaling countries, such as Latin American countries, the EU, South Africa or Australia, the creation of a sanctuary is necessary to protect whale stocks in the long run. Others do not share this environmental orientation,[1] but focus on economic aspects. Countries such as Japan, Iceland and others are opposed to the creation of a sanctuary, claiming that a zero-catch policy is not necessary for the conservation of whales (Busby and Holt 2012).[2]

The IWC is an intergovernmental organisation tasked with the conservation of whales and the management of whaling. It is set up under the International Convention for the Regulation of Whaling (ICRW), signed in 1946, which also established the founding document of the IWC (International Whaling Commission 1946). The preamble to the ICRW states that the contracting parties wish 'to establish a system of international regulation for the whale fisheries to ensure proper and effective conservation and development of whale stocks' (International Whaling Commission 1946). The IWC's main task is to review and revise the measures laid down in the Schedule to the ICRW. Measures are, for example, the creation of a sanctuary, set limits on the number and size of whales which may be hunted, prescribed open and closed seasons and areas for whaling, and the prohibition of the capture of suckling calves and female whales accompanied by calves. The compilation of catch reports and other statistical and biological records is also required (International Whaling Commission 2012d). In addition, the Commission coordinates and funds conservation work on many species of cetaceans and to establish Conservation Management Plans for key species and populations (International Whaling Commission 2012d).

Due to the formal status of regional actors in the IWC (no voting rights, only the EU has observer status) as well as the rather moderate size of the IWC (eighty-eight member states), regional actor success is least likely to occur in IWC negotiations. Analysing official documents and extensive interview material, the case study shows that only a few regional actors participate in the international negotiations (most notably, the EU and the Buenos Aires Group). The institutional set-up of the IWC with its eighty-eight member states is not large by comparison to IOs such as the UNGA or the FAO; nevertheless, diplomats reported that regional actors render IWC negotiations more effective, since regional groups reduce the overall number of positions and the complexity of multilateral negotiations (interview#175, 01-09-14).

## 5.1 THE IWC: MEMBERSHIP, GOVERNANCE AND DECISION-MAKING PROCEDURE

The IWC contains eighty-eight member states.[3] Membership in the IWC is open to any country that formally adheres to the 1946 ICRW.[4] When a state becomes a 'Contracting Government', it is eligible to vote.[5] The statute and the rules and procedures of the IWC specify the status of intergovernmental organisations: 'Any Government not a party to the ICRW or any intergovernmental organisation may be represented at meetings of the Commission by an observer or observers' (IWC 2012: 2). Thus, regional actors may gain formal observer status and thereby 'will have speaking rights during Plenary sessions and sessions of Commission subsidiary groups and Committees to which they are admitted to' (IWC 2014, Art. C.3). In the period under scrutiny, only the EU is registered as an 'Intergovernmental Organisation Observer' with the IWC. Formally, the EU Council presidency speaks on behalf of the EU, if this state happens also to be a member of the IWC.[6] Other ROs lack observer status and have therefore no formal speaking rights. Nevertheless, their member states can voice regional positions.

The main decision-making forum in the IWC is the Commission Meeting. In the Commission, each of the member states is represented by one Commissioner, who is assisted by experts and advisers (IWC 2012:1).[7] The Commission convenes annually and, since 2012, biannually, either in one of the member states, by invitation, or in the United Kingdom – the Secretariat's base. The task of the IWC's decision-making body is to regulate the management of whaling and the conservation of whales. To this end, the IWC can pass resolutions and amendments to the 1946 ICRW by simple majority for regulations and by a three-quarter majority for Schedule amendments, each time on the basis of a one-state, one-vote system.

On the basis of this institutional design, the IWC's decision-making procedure, in which each member state has equal weight, operates in the following manner: with regard to agenda-setting, a proposal on a Schedule amendment or a regulation can be introduced by any contracting government party of the IWC. On the basis of such a proposal, the various consultative committees can give their advice. Negotiations take place mainly in the Commission arena. At the end of the debate, a decision of the IWC can either be taken by consensus or by vote. 'Thereby the Commission shall make every effort to reach its decisions by consensus. If no agreement can be reached, each Commissioner has the right to vote at Plenary Meetings of the Commission' (IWC 2012: 3). There is a difference between regulations and Schedule amendments. The former can be passed by simple majority, while the latter require a three-quarter majority.[8] Ninety days after a new regulation has been passed it comes into effect for the member states.[9] New regulations are implemented through the national legislation of the member state.

### 5.1.1 The IWC and the establishment of sanctuaries

Several international treaties deal with the conservation and management of the sea. The most prominent ones are the United Nations Convention on the Law of the Sea (UNCLOS), which focuses on maritime matters in general, and the Convention on Biological Diversity (CBD), which provides an international framework for the conservation and sustainable development and use of biodiversity.[10] Compared to the UNCLOS and the CBD, the IWC is much more specialised, as it exclusively focuses on whaling.

A global anti-whaling movement began in the 1970s accompanied by a growing concern with the whaling industry and commercial whaling.[11] In the 1970s and 1980s many anti-whaling nations joined the IWC; in 1982 these countries succeeded in the establishment of a moratorium on commercial whaling, declaring a zero-catch policy to begin in 1986. This is often referred to as the commercial whaling moratorium, and it is still in place today (Greenpeace Essen 2011). It includes some exceptions, namely whaling for scientific research as well as aboriginal-subsistence whaling. As of 2015, a number of countries, including the United States, engage in aboriginal-subsistence whaling. Others, such as Japan, use the scientific-research exception embedded in the moratorium to carry on whaling. Japan, Norway and Iceland are the strongest proponents of lifting the commercial whaling ban (e.g. during the 2010 Annual Meeting of the IWC). Many conservationist countries are therefore in support of the creation of sanctuaries where commercial whaling would be forbidden.

Since 1946, the IWC regulates the conservation of whales as well as the management of commercial whaling. An instrument to achieve the environmental goal of conserving whales is to create a sanctuary. A sanctuary is a defined marine area where the hunting of whales is forbidden (Morgera 2004).[12] Accordingly, with the creation of each new sanctuary whaling is further delimited. Therefore, in sanctuaries, it is not necessary to engage in typical management activities concerning whaling, such as the introduction of quotas. Establishing sanctuaries is regulated by Article V (1) (c)[13] of the ICRW, which specifies that sanctuaries could be created through making Schedule amendments. Currently, there are two sanctuaries in place, both of which prohibit commercial whaling (see figure 5.1). The Indian Ocean Sanctuary (IOWS) was established in 1979 and covers the whole of the Indian Ocean south to 55°S. The second was adopted in 1994 and covers the waters of the Southern Ocean around Antarctica (Southern Ocean Whale Sanctuary – SOWS) (Morgera 2004).[14]

A proposal to also create a sanctuary in the South Atlantic Ocean, the South Atlantic Whale Sanctuary (SAWS), was first introduced by Brazil in 2001 and was subject to negotiations in 2011, 2012 and 2014. This case

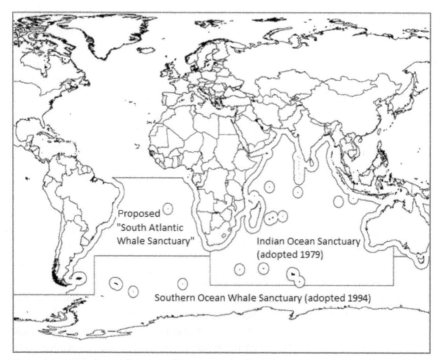

**Figure 5.1. Existing and proposed IWC sanctuaries**[17]

study examines the SAWS negotiations and sheds light on the role of regional actors in this process. The Brazilian proposal envisions a sanctuary that would cover the waters of the South Atlantic, extending to the Equator in the north, the Atlantic coast of South America in the west, the northern limit of the Southern Ocean Sanctuary in the south and the coast of Africa and the western boundary of the Indian Ocean Sanctuary in the east (see figure 5.1).[15] The SAWS would ban commercial whaling[16] and also promote non-lethal biological studies on whale population.

### 5.1.2 The SAWS proposal: Opponents and proponents

The IWC is de facto divided into two blocks: the conservationists who pursue environmental goals and those who support whale hunting and pursue economic goals (Embassy Tokio 2008, Xinhua General News Service 2008).[18] This division of member states (where almost equal numbers of pro- and anti-whaling nations exist) has led to a deadlock in the organisation (Hurd 2012). This also affects the approval or modification of IWC sanctuaries, which requires a three-quarter majority vote by the Commissioners: 'One group can't get a majority of 75% votes to take it forward and to get it approved, and that is where the deadlock is, because one group is trying to go for pro-whaling and the other group is trying to go for scientific sanctuaries.. . . It is basically the debate on conservation on one side versus sustainable, almost sustainable, but ethical grounds on the other side, you know, that is the debate' (interview#170, 22-07-14). Therefore, the IWC has been described as 'rather locked' and 'dysfunctional' (interview#174, 29-08-14).

A very controversial point in current IWC negotiations is the creation of a South Atlantic Whale Sanctuary (SAWS). The SAWS proposal is an amendment of the IWC Convention Schedule (Article 5), which implements the IWC's goals with regard to the utilisation and conservation of whale resources through designating sanctuaries.

The main proponents of the environmental goal (conservation of whales) are the Latin American member states of the IWC, who form the 'Buenos Aires Group' (BAG). Argentina, Brazil, Chile, Mexico, Costa Rica, Peru and Panama founded the BAG in Buenos Aires in 2005 (Bailey 2012).[19] Together with Colombia, the Dominican Republic, Ecuador and Uruguay, the BAG today comprises eleven members (Buenos Aires Group 2014b).[20] Within the IWC, these Latin American countries have become an active regional actor, which votes together on many topics (interview#187, 18-09-14). The BAG supports the non-lethal use of cetaceans and the creation of sanctuaries in general. It is also in favour of maintaining the moratorium, and furthermore proposed the creation of the SAWS, with Brazil leading the proposal (Buenos Aires Group 2008, 2011, 2012,

2014b). The EU also decided to support the creation of sanctuaries in general (interview#175, 01-09-14, EU Commission 2007). Proponents of the proposal argue that the creation of a sanctuary is necessary to protect the whale stocks as around 80 per cent of the world's whales go to the South Atlantic each summer to feed (Bellestri 2011, Hogarth 2008a). Moreover, the SAWS would support the people of the region who want to profit from whales in sustainable ways, such as whale watching (interview#189, 18-09-14).

In contrast, proponents of the economic goal (management of whaling) oppose the creation of SAWSs. These encompass whale hunting countries like Japan, Norway and Iceland, which belong to the 'sustainable-use-group' (interview#175, 29-08-14). This group is not regional in character, as it includes members from Asia, Northern Europe, Africa and the Caribbean, and forms an issue-specific coalition, which is led and dominated by Japan.

A proposal for the SAWS as a Schedule amendment to the ICRW was presented at several Commission Meetings starting in 2001 (International Whaling Commission 2012c: 3). At the 53rd Annual Meeting the proposal was submitted jointly by the governments of Argentina and Brazil[21] and has been presented several times since then. As table 5.1 illustrates, the proposal has always had more supporters than opponents. Although it received a growing number of votes in favour over time, it has so far failed to reach the three-quarters majority needed to pass the SAWS norm and thereby amend the Schedule to the IWC Convention. While the number of supporters has increased from nineteen to forty, the number of opponents grew in the mid-2000s and started to decline again from 2012 onwards.

Table 5.1.  Voting on the SAWS proposal[22]

| Year | Meeting | In Favour | Against | Abstentions |
|------|---------|-----------|---------|-------------|
| 2001 | IWC 53rd Annual Meeting in London, UK | 19 | 13 | 5 |
| 2002 | IWC 54th Annual Meeting in Shimonoseki, Japan | 23 | 18 | 4 |
| 2003 | IWC 55th Annual Meeting in Berlin, Germany | 24 | 19 | 3 |
| 2004 | IWC 56th Annual Meeting in Sorrento, Italy | 26 | 22 | 4 |
| 2005 | IWC 57th Annual Meeting in Ulsan, South Korea | 29 | 26 | 2 |
| 2006 | IWC 58th Annual Meeting in Frigate Bay, Saint Kitts and Nevis | No vote on the proposal | | |
| 2007 | IWC 59th Annual Meeting in Anchorage, Alaska | 39 | 29 | 3 |
| 2008 | IWC 60th Annual Meeting in Santiago, Chile | No vote on the proposal | | |
| 2009 | IWC 61st Annual Meeting in Madeira, Portugal | No vote on the proposal | | |
| 2010 | IWC 62nd Annual Meeting in Agadir, Morocco | No vote on the proposal | | |
| 2011 | IWC 63rd Annual Meeting in Saint Helier, Jersey | No vote on the proposal | | |
| 2012 | IWC 64th Annual Meeting in Panama City, Panama | 38 | 21 | 2 |
| 2014 | IWC 65th Biannual Meeting in Portoroz, Slovenia | 40 | 18 | 2 |

### 5.1.3 History of the SAWS proposal from 2001 to 2010

Brazil first made its intention to propose the creation of a SAWS public at the Commission Meeting in Oman in 1998. At the IWC52 Annual Meeting in 2000, a general discussion in favour and against sanctuary proposals took place (Busby and Holt 2012). Following this general debate, Brazil and Argentina (co-sponsor) tabled a proposal for a SAWS at the 53rd annual meeting of the IWC in 2001 in London.[23] The SAWS proposal would amend the Schedule of the IWC Convention:

In accordance with Article V(1)(c) of the Convention, commercial whaling, whether by pelagic operations or from land stations, is prohibited in a region designated as the South Atlantic Whale Sanctuary. This Sanctuary comprises the waters of the South Atlantic Ocean enclosed by the following line: starting from the Equator, then generally south following the eastern coastline of South America to the coast of Tierra del Fuego and, starting from a point situated at Lat 55°07,3'S Long 066°25,0'W; thence to the point Lat 55°11,0'S Long 066°04,7'W; thence to the point Lat 55°22,9'S Long 065°43,6'W; thence due South to Parallel 56°22,8'S; thence to the point Lat 56°22,8'S Long 067°16,0'W; thence due South, along the Cape Horn Meridian, to 60°S, where it reaches the boundary of the Southern Ocean Sanctuary; thence due east following the boundaries of this Sanctuary to the point where it reaches the boundary of the Indian Ocean Sanctuary at 40°S; thence due north following the boundary of this Sanctuary until it reaches the coast of South Africa; thence it follows the coastline of Africa to the west and north until it reaches the Equator; thence due west to the coast of Brazil, closing the perimeter at the starting point. This prohibition shall be reviewed twenty years after its initial adoption and at succeeding ten-year intervals, and could be revised at such times by the Commission. Nothing in this sub-paragraph shall prejudice the sovereign rights of coastal states according to, inter alia, the United Nations Convention on the Law of the Sea. (International Whaling Commission 2002)

Thus, the 2001 SAWS Schedule amendment did seek to establish a whale sanctuary in the South Atlantic, more precisely the international waters in this area as defined by the UNCLOS. In such a sanctuary, commercial whaling is prohibited. This includes whale hunting for nutritional purposes (meat), hunting whales to harvest their oil, and whaling for medical or cosmetic purposes (blubber).

In 2002, the proposal was again introduced by Brazil (co-sponsored by Argentina) and put to a vote, but the proposed Schedule amendment did not receive a three-quarter majority and was therefore not adopted (International Whaling Commission 2003: 35). Between 2001 and 2002, Brazil consulted other states on this matter, which resulted in Spain changing its voting behaviour to support the creation of a sanctuary in 2002. In 2003, 2004 and 2005

the proposal was again put on the IWC negotiation agenda by Brazil but failed
to be adopted in each instance (International Whaling Commission 2005). In
2006 Brazil decided not to put the proposal to a vote (Hogarth 2008b). In def-
erence to the 'Future of the IWC'[24] process launched in 2007, the proponents
of the SAWS proposal refrained from calling for a vote at the 2008–2010
Annual Meetings but continued to insist that the establishment of the SAWS
was essential to successfully agree on any eventually negotiated package.
With the failure of the 'Future of the IWC' negotiation process in 2010, the
proponents re-tabled the SAWS proposal at the 2011 Annual Meeting.

It is remarkable that the language of the SAWS proposal was not at all
changed until 2011. The first text change in 2011 (see below) was merely
symbolic in character (specifying that the scope of application would not
include national, but only international, waters as defined by UNCLOS).
In 2014, the proposed SAWS Schedule amendment was for the very first
time strengthened to prohibit whaling of any kind (including for scientific
purposes) .

## 5.2 ACTIVITY AND SUCCESS OF ROs IN THE SAWS NEGOTIATIONS IN THE YEARS 2011, 2012 AND 2014

### 5.2.1 The IWC 63rd Negotiations, 2011

In 2011 after a two-year break due to the 'IWC and the future' process,[25]
the SAWS Schedule amendment was reintroduced by Brazil and again co-
sponsored by Argentina (International Whaling Commission 2012a: 9.2.1).
The SAWS proposal submitted to the meeting was changed for the first time
since 2001 and contained one new sentence, to the effect that the proposed
Sanctuary would not, 'with the exception of Brazil . . . apply to waters under
the national jurisdiction of coastal states within the area described above,
unless those States notify the Secretariat to the contrary and this information is transmitted to the Contracting Governments' (International Whaling
Commission 2012a: 22). The text insertion in the 2011 amendment reflects
neither a strengthening nor a weakening of the proposal, but is symbolic in
character. The insertion draws attention to the fact that the national waters
of each country, as defined in the UNCLOS, are not automatically part of
the provisions described in the SAWS proposal. This was already the case
in the 2001 SAWS Schedule amendment, which also related to international
waters and not the national waters (within the coastal line as illustrated in
figure 5.1). To avoid misunderstandings, the sponsors stressed that the SAWS
would not apply to the national coastal waters – an element which might have
been a factor as to why some countries were not in line with the proposal. In

addition, Brazil flagged its strong commitment to the SAWS, as it empha-sised that Brazil would apply the SAWS in their national waters.[26]

In the IWC, as in other IOs, regional groups and organisations can help to structure international negotiations and possibly render them more effective, if few collective statements, rather than many individual national statements, are put forward.[27] Since a three-fourths majority of IWC member states is needed in order to pass the SAWS Schedule amendment, regional groups are possibly of importance as they combine a potentially large share of votes if their member states were united.

With respect to the SAWS negotiations, the BAG was the most vocal and influential regional actor. Argentina, Brazil, Chile, Mexico, Costa Rica, Peru, Panama Colombia, the Dominican Republic, Ecuador and Uruguay are mem-bers of the BAG. The BAG 'opposed to commercial and scientific whaling' (interview#168, 10-07-14).

From early on, the BAG member states frequently met to formulate com-mon positions and strategies for negotiating in the IWC (e.g. interview#178, 16-09-14).[28] This worked well since the member states were not hetero-geneous with respect to the SAWS issue. The BAG members all strongly oppose whale hunting and belong to the conservationist camp. Its member states also expect economic benefits from tourist whale watching.[29] More-over, although the BAG does not have an institutionalised chair or central coordinator, the strong reliance of the BAG members on outside expertise provided by scientists and NGOs compensates to some extent for the lack of central resources and helps the BAG formulate common argumentative nego-tiation approaches (interviews #171, 25-07-14, #189, 18-09-14). Thus, the BAG effectively coordinated its position, namely that they fully supported the SAWS proposal and were in favour of prohibiting any form of commer-cial whaling in the area designated as the new sanctuary, even including the national waters of Brazil,[30] on the basis of which it actively engaged in the international negotiations in the IWC arena in 2011 (as expected by H6a).

Brazil has taken on the role of the BAG's informal leader (interview#189, 18-09-14). Accordingly, it expresses BAG positions in written form before the IWC meetings and in oral form during the meetings. In addition, the members engaged in burden-sharing (H5a),[31] since each BAG member lob-bied third parties to which it had the closest diplomatic ties already (inter-view#178, 16-09-14) (H6e). On this basis, the BAG did try to influence on dynamics and outcomes of the IWC negotiation process through expertise-based arguments that were backed up by a wide array of scientists and policy experts (interview#168, 10-07-14). For example, BAG members argued that they are 'confident that the proposal had scientific merit, given that it focused on a region where cetacean populations were depleted by commercial whal-ing and are still in need of protection. It noted that whilst some species such as right and humpback whales are recovering; they remain at levels well below estimated initial stocks. Other species such as the blue and fin whales are in much worse shape and little is known about the distribution of surviving animals' (International Whaling Commission 2012a: 22). The BAC used close contacts to other IWC member states in order to explain how exactly a sanctuary would help the population of whales recover and to convey advice 'on how to strengthen the proposal' (interview#168, 10-07-14). Moreover, BAG members stressed that the SAWS would also bring economic benefits to coastal states as 'the development of non-lethal use of cetacean resources through whale watching in a coordinated manner would further benefit coastal communities in the region' (International Whaling Commission 2012a: 22). In line with hypothesis 6c, several of the approached coastal countries responded positively due to the fact that the BAG could refer to external scientific advice (interviews #171, 25-07-14, #189, 18-09-14). Yet, the argumentative strategy of the BAG did not work vis-à-vis those third parties with vested interests in whaling (interview#175, 01-09-14). Whale proponents challenged the validity of the arguments put forward by the BAG, since the goodness of fit between the BAG's environmental arguments and their own economic and tradition-based framings of the whaling issue was very low.[32]

In addition to argumentative strategies in the official negotiation arena, the BAG also engaged in third-party lobbying in informal settings (H6e) and managed to secure the support of other non-whaling states and (interview#193, 19-09-14). In this respect, the BAG was procedurally successful in the IWC negotiations. Had the SAWS been passed, the BAG would have been substantially successful in a proactive manner as well. The 2011 SAWS proposal entailed a change from the 2001 version, as the BAG sponsors now explicitly emphasised that the national waters within the costal line would *not* be subject to the SAWS area in general (with the exception of Brazil's coastal waters). Yet, while the BAG's proposed text modification was unaltered in the course 2011 negotiations, the norm was not passed.

The EU held internal coordination meetings in order to work towards a common EU position for the IWC negotiations (interview#169, 17-07-14). Similar to the BAG, the member states of the EU met frequently in preparation for the IWC negotiations as well as during the ongoing international negotiations (interviews #193, 19-09-14, #175, 01-09-14, #176, 15-09-14, #182, 17-09-14).[33] During the coordination sessions, the EU Commission as well as the Council Presidency invested time and personnel resources to chair the meetings and help the member states develop a joint position (H2c and d).[34] These meetings took place behind closed doors (interviews#188, 18-09-14, #175, 01-09-14).[35] Despite the homogeneity amongst member state positions on supporting the IWC in general (interview#193, 19-09-14), Denmark, which represented the interests of Greenland in the IWC, had deviating ideas,[36] and did not systematically subscribe to the conservationist goal.[37] After several rounds of difficult internal negotiations, a lowest common denominator compromise emerged: while the EU supported the draft SAWS Schedule amendment in general, it expressed its preference for a consensual, rather than a voted, norm – although the latter was much more difficult to achieve as it would have required universal support rather than a majority (International Whaling Commission 2012a: 9.2.2).

On the basis of the EU's minimalist common position, Poland as the EU's Council Presidency lobbied third-party actors in the attempt to achieve support for the EU's position (H6e).[38] However, although EU members agreed on burden-sharing (H5a),[39] not all member states acted in concert during the IWC negotiations. Spain, Portugal, Germany, the United Kingdom and Denmark each voiced national positions in addition to the EU position. On the one end of the spectrum was Denmark. Whale hunting has been a tradition in Greenland, which is why Denmark traditionally did not reject whaling as long as the populations were not endangered (interviews #187, 18-09-14, #175, 01-09-14). Denmark stressed that it opposes all drafts of an SAWS that do not lead to a 'real sanctuary' which fulfils 'defining requirements' in a *sufficient* manner (International Whaling Commission 2012a: 9.2.2). This, in effect, meant that as long as the implementation of a sanctuary norm cannot be guaranteed to be universally unproblematic, a 'real sanctuary' will not be achieved and Denmark would not support a SAWS proposal. By contrast, Spain regarded the 2011 proposal as an improvement compared to earlier versions, in particular as it took the concerns of non-member coastal states more seriously and would have supported the SAWS norm even if no unanimity can be reached in the IWC (International Whaling Commission 2012a: 9.2.2).[40] Thus, the EU members showcased that they were not all on the same page. The internal heterogeneity rendered the EU's Council Presidency's lobbying in informal arenas ineffective (H5b).[41]

The EU Council Presidency also applied bargaining strategies (H6b) assuming to have sufficient leverage as the EU regards itself as being 'more powerful by operating as a block' (interview#188, 18-09-14).[42] However, due to the noticeable heterogeneity amongst the EU member states, the collective bargaining efforts were not effective in increasing support for the SAWS norm (in line with H5b and H6b).

Some of the most pro-SAWS EU members tried to convince other countries using argumentative strategies (H6c), but were not successful in this respect since environmental claims did not resonate well with the economic framing adopted by many SAWS opponents (interview#188, 18-09-14, also #174, 28-08-14),[43] and since the EU's visible heterogeneity made evident that not even all EU members were persuaded by the environmentalist arguments themselves (H5b).

The BAG also approached the EU in order to form an ad hoc coalition, although 'communication is not always easy, to be honest' (interview#193, 19-09-14, similar interview#175, 01-09-14).[44] Together, the regional groups formed a large, non-institutionalised, coalition (H6f).[45] However, even as a coalition both regional groups lacked the votes to actually pass the SAWS norm and ultimately failed to conclude the negotiations by creating a new SAWS norm.

During the debate, several countries explicitly expressed their support for the SAWS proposal (International Whaling Commission 2012a: 9.2.2).[46] Colombia is a member of the UNASUR and the BAG, but did not speak on behalf of any of its regional groups. Nevertheless, it did not harm the BAG's collective negotiation approach as Columbia reiterated two arguments for the SAWS, which were also mentioned by Argentina and Brazil as the two sponsors: first, it allows the whale population to recover, and second, it enables the development of whale watching tourism (International Whaling Commission 2012a: 9.2.2).

Palau opposed the SAWS, as it also rejected the creation of a sanctuary in the South Pacific by denying that there is evidence that whales are 'threatened with extinction' (International Whaling Commission 2012a: 9.2.2). Saint Kitts and Nevis rejected the 2011 SAWS proposal because it regarded this text as unnecessary from an ecosystem perspective and as an illegitimate restriction on the right to use marine resources (International Whaling Commission 2012a: 9.2.2). Iceland, a country fiercely opposing the proposal, stated that 'there was no scientific basis or justification for such a Sanctuary' (International Whaling Commission 2012a: 9.2.2). The Russian Federation, backed by Cameroon, took an even stronger stance. It asked to *withdraw the proposal* with regard to the ongoing 'Future of the IWC' process (International Whaling Commission 2012a: 9.2.2). In the Russian line of reasoning, the SAWS proposal can only be part of a possible package-deal in order to end the deadlock situation, but cannot be decided separately. Switzerland also addressed the package deal issue, but was more moderate than Russia and simply 'asked that the item remain open' (International Whaling Commission 2012a: 9.2.2).

Japan was most strongly against the 2011 SAWS.[47] It referred to the support of twenty-one other states and stated that 'they were not willing to participate in a vote on the proposal because they considered that reverting to voting could be harmful to the constructive dialogue and atmosphere in the Commission that have been achieved in recent years' (International Whaling Commission 2012a: 9.2.2). With this negotiation move, Japan made it clear that it expects the sponsors to withdraw the whole proposal. This preference was also echoed by the members of the sustainable-use group: Cambodia, Cameroon, Côte d'Ivoire, the Gambia, Iceland, Norway, Nauru, Mongolia, Mauritania, Guinea-Bissau, Grenada, Kiribati, Morocco, Republic of Korea, Ghana, Palau, Togo, the Russian Federation, Tuvalu, Saint Kitts and Nevis, and Saint Lucia (International Whaling Commission 2012a: 9.2.2).[48] As summarised by a Commissioner, 'Japan and the what they call the "Sustainable Use Group" . . . have been the sole reason that it (the SAWS proposal) has not passed' (interview#168, 10-07-14). Japan actively and successfully employed bargaining-based negotiation strategies to maximise support for its own position: 'Japan, for instance, is the leader from the other part of the world. And it's pressing permanently with small islands in the Caribbean and small countries in Africa' (interview#178, 16-09-14). Thus, Japan managed to talk states into opposing the SAWS (these countries are often referred to as the sustainable-use group), although many of the countries that sided with Japan have little or no interest in the whaling industry (Fortin 2012). Since neither the EU nor the BAG were able to employ negotiation strategies to effectively counteract the Japanese endeavours (e.g. vote-buying, c.f. Jung 2010, Miller and Dolšak 2007, Petitjean Roget 2002, Strand 2012), both regional groups failed to be reactively successful in a procedural manner.

After the discussions, the Chair shared his observation that there was no consensus for the proposal (International Whaling Commission 2012a: 9.2.2). Nonetheless, Brazil and Argentina as sponsors wished to put it to a formal vote (International Whaling Commission 2012a: 9.2.2).[49] This escalated the entire situation; before the vote on the proposal could be conducted, the pro-whaling countries present, a group of twenty-two countries – led by Japan (except for the Russian Federation) – walked out of the meeting room in an attempt to bring the meeting below the three-quarters majority needed (International Whaling Commission 2012a: 9.2.2, interviews #170, 22-07-14, #187, 18-09-14). The rules of procedure and the Convention of the IWC were unclear with regard to which states count towards the quorum necessary to pass a resolution by vote as it was not clear whether the countries that just left the room are counted as present or absent. A commissioner recollected that 'we went back to the terms of references and the procedures of the IWC and it was not very clear' (interview#170, 22-07-14, similar interview#187, 18-09-14).[50] Thereupon, the Commission decided that it would be best if an intersessional group were established to interpret the Rules of Procedure regarding the quorum necessary for a decision to be taken. Therefore, the Commission postponed the discussion on the creation of a SAWS to the next IWC Annual Meeting in 2012 (International Whaling Commission 2012a:24).

## 5.2.2 The IWC 64th Negotiations, 2012

After the disruption of the IWC's 63rd meeting in 2011, the IWC members gathered in Panama City in July 2012 for the IWC's 64th Annual Meeting. The SAWS proposal was again put on the negotiation table by the sponsor Brazil and co-sponsored by Argentina, South Africa and Uruguay (International Whaling Commission 2013: 4.1.1). The 2012 SAWS schedule amendment was hardly changed. Compared to the 2011 version, one sentence that concerns the wording related to coastal waters under national jurisdiction was modified in the 2012 draft: the section 'With the exception of Brazil, this provision does not apply to waters under the national jurisdiction of coastal states within the area described above, unless those States notify the Secretariat to the contrary and this information is transmitted to the Contracting Governments' was amended by inserting the phrase 'according to its current delimitation or another that may be established in the future' between the two phrases 'under the national jurisdiction' and 'coastal states within the area' (International Whaling Commission 2013: 4.1.1). This insertion is a tribute to the ever-changing nature of international law, safeguarding the proposed mechanisms to possible future changes in the definition of national waters and contestations of the sanctuary's legitimacy that may accompany such changes. By including this qualification, the sponsors of the proposal wanted to emphasise that whenever there is a change in the definition of 'waters under the national jurisdiction' laid down in the UNCLOS, this definition will be predominant and the IWC has to comply. The insertion, however, does not alter the aim, procedures, scope and exceptions of the SAWS norm and is first and foremost of legal character. The text insertion moreover represents a symbolic concession to the opponents of the proposal and interprets the regulations already determined in the UNCLOS by explaining that the territorial waters of a state are not affected by the SAWS Schedule amendment and therefore refers directly to the objections of many African states bordering the planned sanctuary. As the text modification is only of symbolic nature and the negotiations were not highly politicised, not much attention was dedicated to the SAWS proposal discussion in 2012.

As in 2011, in 2012 the only two vocal regional actors were the BAG and the EU (interview#170, 22-07-2014). Again, the BAG member states swiftly synchronised their positions before the IWC64 meeting and again formulated a homogeneous common position in regard to the draft of the 2012 SAWS norm (interviews#171, 25-07-14, #189, 18-09-14). On the basis of its common position, the BAG engaged in lobbying third-party actors to supporting the proposal (interview#193, 19-09-14). Most importantly, in line with H6e, the BAG informally approached EU members and other pro-conservationist countries and succeeded in ensuring the continuing support for the proposal (interview#193, 19-09-14).[51] In order to persuade additional third-party states to support the 2012 SAWS norm, or at least convince them to gradually shift their position towards the norm, the members of the BAG strongly focused on African states: 'We did negotiations during the IWC plenary . . . in order to try to get them to make them abstain from voting against' (interview#196, 22-12-14). While this was not effective in all instances (interview#196, 22-12-14), some African countries shifted towards supporting the BAG's position. Thus, in 2012 the BAG was not only very active, but also procedurally successful in a proactive manner, as they achieved increasing support for their proposal (c.f. table 5.1).

Similar to 2011, the 2012 proposal text was altered by the BAG, but without either strengthening or weakening it in substance. Instead, the change of the SAWS proposal was mainly symbolic in character. The BAG members under the lead of Brazil were again the ones responsible for modifying one sentence of the SAWS norm in line with their own position. They inserted 'according to its current delimitation or another that may be established in the future' which modified the sentence to say, 'With the exception of Brazil, this provision does not apply to waters under the national jurisdiction, *according to its current delimitation or another that may be established in the future,* of coastal states within the area described above, unless those States notify the Secretariat to the contrary, and this information is transmitted to the Contracting Governments' [emphasis not in the original, added by the authors]. Thus, while the 2011 SAWS text would have constructed a SAWS area in international waters and would have excluded the national coastal waters at that time, the 2012 SAWS text proposal made explicit that all current and future areas under national jurisdiction will not be subject to the SAWS (with Brazil being the only exception).

During the 2012 IWC negotiations, the BAG kept its preferred formulation as opponents to the SAWS, such as Japan and Iceland, 'didn't try to change the proposal' with respect to the wording inserted by BAG members in 2012 (interview#196, 22-12-14). Instead, they preferred to have no SAWS at all and blocked the proposal from being adopted.

In the course of 2011, the Folketing had softened its traditional position towards whaling. Accordingly, the Danish delegation gradually shifted towards being less reserved concerning the conditions under which they could support the SAWS, which contributed to a greater homogeneity of EU member positions in 2012 compared to the preceding year. The 'EU certainly did coordinate' (interview#169, 17-07-14), and was effective in developing a common stance (interview#170, 22-07-14). Thus, in its 2012 opening statement the EU stated, 'The EU and its Member States are strongly committed to the protection of whales and acknowledge that an effective conservation and management regime can only be created through joint efforts and by initiatives that promote mutual trust and cooperation between IWC parties' (Cyprus on behalf of the European Union 2012). Also due to the greater homogeneity of EU member states' interests, in 2012 the EU coherently opposed commercial whaling, and supported the SAWS proposal more strongly (interview#168, 10-07-14). Consequently, unlike 2011, in the 2012 meeting, no other EU member state took the floor in the discussion on the SAWS Schedule amendment to express a distinct national position before the vote on the proposal (interview#170, 22-07-14).[52] In fact, only Cyprus, which had the EU Council Presidency at that time, spoke on behalf of the EU and was not amended or contradicted by any of the other EU members. The EU was much more strongly united and therefore able to leverage up and was – as expected by H5b – 'probably the most influential regional organisation at the IWC' (interview#168, 10-07-14).[53]

Since the EU's internal coordination worked very well in 2012 (interviews#175, 01-09-14, #170, 22-07-14), the EU members could use their combined bargaining leverage better than in 2011 in order to promote their own interests (H6b).[54] However, even though the EU is a huge regional bloc inside the IWC, the three-quarter threshold makes it difficult to pass a proposal: 'in blocking things they can do that, but to swing things in favor of a thing that is more difficult, because of the 75%' (interview#170, 22-07-14). Tied-hands strategies were possible: if the EU is united, it has 'control over a quarter of the votes' in the IWC (interview#168, 10-07-14); the EU 'can be quite powerful, you can dictate matters' because of 'quite a substantial amount of votes that they got' (interview#170, 22-07-14). As a consequence, a diplomat declared that 'you have to have the EU member states on board' in order to pass the SAWS Schedule amendment (interview#168, 10-07-14).[55] However, despite the EU speaking with one voice and being in a much better position to engage in collective bargaining in 2012 compared to 2011, there is no evidence that the EU was effective with its bargaining strategies. This is not too surprising, however since tied-hands strategies work especially well when the actor using them can fend off demands, but are not very effective to obtain concessions from norm opponents who have a blocking majority in the IWC.

Moreover, argumentative strategies of the EU did not work (H6e), as the environmental frame was incompatible to the cognitive and normative priors of the SAWS opponents. For example, Japan stated that 'there is no scientific justification for the sanctuary, and so it's against the Convention, which states that sanctuaries have to be established on the basis of scientific evidence. Also, this proposal is being proposed even though there is already a moratorium on commercial whaling. There is no commercial whaling conducted in the South Atlantic, so it's like building a roof upon a roof, and is unnecessary' (International Whaling Commission 2013: 8).[56]

Once the negotiations started in the IWC arena, the most vocal country was again the main sponsor of the SAWS proposal, Brazil. The Commissioner of Brazil emphasised the ecological advantages that come with the creation of a sanctuary in the South Atlantic Ocean and referred to breeding and calving areas for whales and the recovery of whale populations (International Whaling Commission 2013: 4.1.1). Furthermore, Brazil noted that this sanctuary would encourage ecotourism and whale-watching and thereby made economic arguments (International Whaling Commission 2013: 8).[57] Yet, the negotiations were controversial once more and, as in previous years, the countries were divided into two camps (interview#174, 29-08-14). The proponents of the Brazilian proposal flagged the importance of ecological values (India, Ecuador, Mexico and the United States),[58] as well as the importance of economic aspects in conjunction with ecological ones (Columbia and Australia)[59] (International Whaling Commission 2013: 4.1.2).

The opponents of the proposal brought up a variety of nuanced positions. Japan, as years before the strongest and most vocal opponent of the creation of a sanctuary in the South Atlantic, made two arguments why the creation of a sanctuary is not necessary: first as there is a moratorium currently in existence, and second, as 'the recovery of cetacean resources [is] already underway' (International Whaling Commission 2013: 4.1.2). In addition, it stated 'that the proposal did not contain specific or measurable objectives, and that it represented a shotgun approach to conservation whereby a large area would be protected with little rationale for boundary selection or establishment of management regimes' (International Whaling Commission 2013: 4.1.2). Together with Antigua and Barbuda, Japan made an expertise-based argument by expressing that the proposal did not get the support of the Scientific Committee, and all IWC decisions should be based upon science (International Whaling Commission 2013: 4.1.2). Moreover, Japan was effectively lobbying third-party states and made sure that the opposition against the SAWS remained strong in 2012. To this end, Japan also engaged in carrot-and-stick approaches (Miller and Dolšak 2007). In line with this, a delegate reported that countries close to Japan 'have some kind of an instruction on how to vote' (interview#175, 29-08-14, similar interview#168, 10-07-14). Thus, Japan succeeded in winning support for its position, while neither the BAG nor the EU could effectively use counter-strategies to minimise the countries referred to as sustainable-use group. Thus, both regional groups – the BAG and the EU – failed to be procedurally successful in a reactive manner.

Saint Kitts and Nevis argued that the legitimacy of the IWC was in question by stating that the organisation 'represented just under half the countries in the international community' and therefore is not the appropriate body to be concerned with the topics covered by the IWC as 'the entire international community and not just relatively small number of states' has to deal with it (International Whaling Commission 2013: 4.1.2).[60] Other countries firmly opposing the SAWS, most notably Iceland, pointed out the inconsistency of some supporting countries' positions by stating that they do not include their own national waters in the Sanctuary (International Whaling Commission 2013: 4.1.2). Furthermore, Iceland called attention to the fact that the supporters of the sanctuary are mostly countries on the western side of the Atlantic, while the sanctuary would affect countries on the eastern side, of whom many are against the proposal (International Whaling Commission 2013: 4.1.2). Antigua and Barbuda supported Iceland's argument and pointed out that 'peoples in coastal states whose livelihoods may be affected by the establishment of the Sanctuary' should be consulted in order to include their opinions in the SAWS proposal (International Whaling Commission 2013: 4.1.2). This procedure would lead to a deferment of the process and eventually to a reformulation of the proposal. Saint Kitts and Nevis took up the mentioned arguments regarding the legitimacy of the IWC by remarking that 'no other competent international organisations had supported the Sanctuary' (International Whaling Commission 2013: 4.1.2). Saint Kitts and Nevis and Norway also made statements concerning the countries affected by the SAWS: Saint Kitts and Nevis expressed concerns that the sanctuary could disadvantage developing countries with access to coasts and thereby indirectly accused countries supporting the SAWS proposal of not including the affected countries or paying attention to their needs (International Whaling Commission 2013: 4.1.2). Norway used the expertise-based argument against the proposal and pointed out that the establishment of the SAWS is not scientifically justified and therefore could not be backed by Norway (International Whaling Commission 2013: 4.1.2). Iceland challenged the significance of the sanctuary by indicating that there is no whaling taking place in the SAWS area and that the sanctuary does not offer any 'additional conservation benefits' (International Whaling Commission 2013: 4.1.2).

After the discussions, Brazil, as the sponsor-state, was asked by the Chair how to continue, and insisted on a vote on the proposal.[61] The EU and BAG votes together with the votes of the other supporters were not sufficient to pass the three-quarter threshold and pass the SAWS norm.[62] This is due to the negotiation activities of Japan. 'Japan and what they call the "Sustainable Use Group" are coherent and employed their collective voting power to block the proposal from being passed' (interview#168, 10-07-14). In addition, Japan engaged in bargaining-based strategies, using a broad array of concessions and package deals, and has in this respect often been suspected of being engaged in vote-buying (Beeson 2005b, Jung 2010, Petitjean Roget 2002).[63]

Denmark, Brazil and Norway took the floor after the vote. Although Denmark supported the sanctuary in the vote on the proposal, in line with the

EU position, they expressed, that a sanctuary needs to fulfil 'a number of defining requirements' which are backed up by the IWC Scientific Committee and the affected coastal states and might, if those conditions are not fulfilled, change its voting behaviour (International Whaling Commission 2013: 4.1.2).[64] Moreover, Denmark suggested that any new proposals for sanctuaries 'should contain provisions to regulate all human activities including, for example, fishing, sea transport, and oil drilling', and thereby favours a more comprehensive proposal (International Whaling Commission 2013: 4.1.2). Brazil voiced frustration at the voting result, but, at the same time, indicated that it wouldn't stop pushing for the proposal by articulating hopes for a new process. Norway touched on that aspect and suggested that in case the SAWS would be tabled again, it should be in the form of a new proposal and under the review of the Scientific Committee (International Whaling Commission 2013: 4.1.2).

### 5.2.3 The IWC 65th Negotiations, 2014

In 2012 the IWC decided to move to a biennial meeting schedule. Thus, the 65th meeting of the IWC took place in September 2014 in Portoroz, Slovenia. Once more the SAWS proposal was sponsored by Brazil, with Argentina, South Africa and Uruguay as co-sponsors, and, for the first time, also strongly supported by Gabon.[65] The 2014 schedule amendment contained a new intersection according to which 'whaling activities of any kind' would be prohibited in the designated area of the SAWS. While in previous versions the text stated that 'commercial whaling' would be prohibited, the 2014 amendment strengthened the SAWS proposal significantly, *as all forms of whaling, including whaling for scientific purposes, would be banned.* In contrast to the previous modifications of the SAWS draft, which was purely symbolic in character, Brazil and the BAG strengthened the text considerably for the first time in 2014. If the norm would be passed all whaling activities would be banned in the international waters to which the SAWS apply and countries, such as Japan or Iceland, that justify whale hunting with references to scientific purposes (International Whaling Commission 2015c, Rothwell 2010) would be prohibited from all whaling endeavours in the international waters. Moreover, Argentina, South Africa and Uruguay underlined their strong commitment to the amendment by including their national waters to the domain of the SAWS, as already done by Brazil in 2011. The strengthening of the norm provoked a heated debate in the IWC65 negotiations.

As in the preceding negotiations, the BAG and the EU were the only active regional groups on the 2014 negotiations.

The BAG was again able to operate on the basis of a common position (Buenos Aires Group 2014a, interview#189, 18-09-14) and was very active

in order to promote the now-strengthened SAWS norm. Brazil as the BAG
leader informally lobbied other states prior to tabling the proposal in order
to maximise the number of co-sponsors. A BAG member elaborated, 'Yes
we made negotiations in order to get the support of other states, for example,
that's what happened with Gabon . . . we tried to convince as much countries
as we could' (interview#196, 22-12-14). To this end, high-level negotiations
between the ministers of foreign affairs took place beforehand and during
the meeting in order to seek support for the SAWS proposal, 'mainly with
African countries' (interview#189, 18-09-14). Thereby representatives of the
BAG offered cooperation: 'We never impose anything, we say we are open
to a dialogue, an offer in this possibilities, to work together on research, on
developing whale watching or on capacity whaling in some issues in relation
with the conservation of whales and so' (interview#189, 08-09-14).[66]

During a conference in 2013 and a BAG-initiated workshop in Bahia,
Brazil, in March 2014, African countries were invited as well 'in order to
explain the proposal to them and to seek for their support to the proposal'
(interview#196, 22-12-14).[67] The BAG used these informal venues to lobby
for the SAWS (H6e) and succeeded as the SAWS 'proposal has been gaining increasing support of the members of the IWC plenary after plenary. In
this regard, we would also like to highlight and express our appreciation
to the Member States of the Zone of Peace and Cooperation of the South
Atlantic (that is to say, Argentina, Brazil, Uruguay, and the African countries
Angola, Benin, Cameroon, Cape Verde, Republic of the Congo, Democratic
Republic of the Congo, Ivory Coast, Equatorial Guinea, Gabon, Gambia,
Ghana, Guinea, Guinea-Bissau, Liberia, Namibia, Nigeria, São Tomé and
Príncipe, Senegal, Sierra Leone, South Africa and Togo), whose Ministers
of Foreign Affairs expressed their support to the proposal to create the South
Atlantic Whale Sanctuary' (Buenos Aires Group 2014a). In promoting the
SAWS draft, Brazil as the most active member of the BAG, once more made
the conservationist argument that a sanctuary would make an important
contribution to increasing the population of whales.[68] Furthermore, the diplomat emphasised that the sanctuary would benefit the coastal communities
(Compton-Antoine 2014). Brazil was committed to preparing a management
plan for the sanctuary and at the same time explained that sovereign rights of
the coastal states are not restricted in any sense and anticipated the concerns
of opponents by addressing the issue of food security and fear of economic
disadvantages in fishing for the coastal states. Under the lead of Brazil, the
BAG members convinced the Caribbean, Asian and European countries to
support the 2014 SAWS norm. Thereby, expertise-based arguments were
used to gain support (in line with H6c): 'Scientific arguments . . . those were
the main arguments we used to convince Gabon' (interview#196, 22-12-14).
In addition, the BAG tried to talk other states into support in alluding to

economic implications of the SAWS norm (H6c). To this end, representatives of the BAG linked the establishment of a sanctuary in the South Atlantic to an income rise for the coastal communities in the form of whale-watching activities, and therefore clearly stressed an economic aspect: 'To protect the whales or dolphins alike generate more income if you really make responsible whale watching, generate more income for the coastal community than just to kill. . . . This is basically the message' (interview#189, 18-09-14). Moreover, economic incentives and the link to tourism and whale-watching activities represent one of the main lines of argumentation in convincing other countries to support the SAWS proposal.[69]

These strategies together culminated in several positive vote-shifts by third-party countries, which is remarkable given that the 2014 SAWS norm was considerably strengthened compared to the version of 2012. A total of seven states changed their voting behaviour towards the BAG position: China, Nauru and Palau shifted from no to absent, while Croatia, Hungary, Slovakia and Oman changed from being absent to a yes vote. Hence the BAG had considerable procedural proactive success despite having made the SAWS norm more demanding in prohibiting any form of whaling instead of only prohibiting commercial whaling.

In 2014 the proposal text was strengthened in comparison to the 2012 version. Even though some countries preferred the weaker version, the BAG members adhered to its text (Governments of Argentina 2005). For the 2014 proposal, it was mainly Brazil and Argentina that introduced changes (interview#196, 22-12-14). However, they cooperated with other BAG states and EU members (H6g) who added comments and suggestions in order to strengthen the proposal (interview#195, 22-12-14).[70] The text of the SAWS schedule amendment was modified in line with the BAG position, but since the SAWS was ultimately not adopted by the IWC Parties, the BAG did not achieve substantive success.

The other regional actor that was active in the 2014 meeting was once more the EU. Its members met every day during the IWC65 in Slovenia, on some days up to three times, to coordinate a common position. Italy as the Council Presidency and the EU delegation invested a significant amount of coordination capacities. With these administrative, legal and scientific resources, and by using the 2012 EU position as a focal point (increasing the homogeneity of member state positions, H1a) the EU was able to effectively develop a common EU position in regard to the 2014 SAWS draft (in line with H2b, c, H1b) (interviews#175, 01-09-14, #193, 19-09-14). The European Commission became active and strengthened the homogeneity among its member states (H2b) (interview#193, 19-09-14). In 2014, the European Commission made sure that the common position was only voiced by the country that held the Council Presidency.[71] The Council Presidency was not only active

in the major formal negotiation arena of the IWC, but also engaged in lobbying in the informal settings (e.g. coffee breaks, lunches) (interview#193,
19-09-14). Due to the limited issue salience of the SAWS for the EU, it did
not regard itself as the lead negotiator on the SAWS norm but attributed
this role to the BAG.[72] Aside from informal lobbying (H6e), the EU also
employed only a few other strategies in the formal negotiation arena. Consequently, the EU remained less active than the BAG (H6a). For instance,
the EU used bargaining strategies as it was one of the biggest players in the
IWC due to accumulating twenty-five votes (interview#195, 22-12-14). An
EU diplomat explained that 'the EU will be quite clear about what it is supporting. And that in itself, from a negotiating point of view, can often help
others, if you're clear on how you're going to vote, others may be swayed to
vote in the same way as the EU or perhaps against the EU depending on the
general views' (interview#195, 22-12-14). Nevertheless, in discussions with
third-party states, individual EU member states 'obviously ask what positions
others were taking, and if they were opposed to something . . . we would, of
course, question more and see whether we get [to] apply any pressure' (inter-
view#195, 22-12-14). However, since the EU did not have a majority to pass
the SAWS norm by itself, its bargaining leverage was not sufficiently strong
to push third-party states into making compromises (H6b).

As in previous years, the EU and the BAG were in contact before and
during the negotiations in the IWC arena. Both supported the proposal and
strengthened each other's negotiation efforts (H6f). The EU, together with the
BAG, addressed 'concerns that others have raised with regards it's been weak
in parts' (interview#195, 22-12-14).[73] Thus, together they formed a large pro-
SAWS block in the IWC and managed to achieve a high level of support for
the 2014 norm, although the norm was strengthened for the very first time in
this particular year. In line with this, the EU claims that it 'had influence on
the text, adding comments . . . all with the intent to clarify or strengthening the
proposal, we did so at the scientific committee' (interview#195, 22-12-14).

In sum, had the SAWS been adopted by the IWC in 2014, the EU would
have achieved substantive proactive success. Given that the norm was not
passed, the EU ultimately failed to leave an imprint on an international negotiation outcome.

In addition to these regional groups, several individual countries took the
floor during the IWC65 SAWS negotiations. Many of the issues were already
on the table in the preceding 2011 and 2012 rounds of discussion on the SAWS
and were therefore no longer debated at length (interview#175, 01-09-14).
Many countries raised their voice and spoke either in favour[74] or against[75] the
proposal (Compton-Antoine 2014: 11). Gabon even declared its intent to co-
sponsor the proposal in the future.[76] Brazil and Uruguay referred to the Montevideo Declaration of 2013 (Seventh Ministerial Meeting of the Zone of Peace and

Cooperation of the South Atlantic 2013) through which all African and Latin American countries bordering the proposed sanctuary agreed to support the establishment of the SAWS (Compton-Antoine 2014: 11). With reference to the Montevideo declaration, Brazil and Uruguay wanted to counter arguments from the opposing side that not all countries involved in the process are included.[77] Nevertheless, once more the legitimacy of the proposal was questioned by Iceland as the countries of the eastern side are not included in the process. Also speaking against the Montevideo argument was Côte d'Ivoire emphasising that the appropriate body for dealing with the sanctuary is the IWC.

Countries rejecting the 2014 SAWS norm – among them Norway, Japan, Iceland and the Russian Federation – criticised the timing of the proposal and remarked that the Scientific Committee should first review the proposal before it can be discussed in the IWC plenum. In addition, Japan stressed that the sanctuary would not protect whales from actual threats such as 'ship strikes, oil exploration, or climate change' and thereby counteracts the aim of the proposed sanctuary and opposes the aims of the convention (International Whaling Commission 1946). Again, Japan actively approached other states in order to maximise the support for its own position, through alleged vote-buying (Strand 2012) and lobbying. Compared to the previous votes on the SAWS, Côte d'Ivoire and Guinea shifted from not present to no, while Morocco changed from abstaining to no. As in 2011 and 2012, Brazil and the BAG, as well as the EU, failed to prevent such shifts.

Japan proposed cooperation through a Memorandum of Understanding rather than pursuing the matter in the IWC as an amendment to the Schedule Convention. This would have led to a completely different norm, which would have been much weaker in a legal sense. The BAG managed to fend this proposal off, as it did not withdraw its SAWS proposal from the 2014 negotiation agenda.

Nevertheless, at the end of the IWC negotiations, it became obvious that there was again no consensus for the SAWS norm, which the sponsors had hoped to pass. Still, Brazil asked for a vote, which failed to reach the required three-quarter majority. In total thirty-eight states voted in favour of the proposal in 2012, and forty in 2014.[78]

Several countries raised their voices after the vote: Denmark voted for the SAWS proposal and stated, 'Future proposals should undergo review and recognise food security needs'. On the other hand, the Republic of Guinea, which opposed the SAWS, once more referred to a missing recommendation from the Scientific Committee and explained that the moratorium in existence makes the sanctuary redundant (Compton-Antoine 2014). Brazil and Monaco showed disappointment over the result, but Brazil also raised hopes for the proposal as the level of support increased and asked the Scientific Committee to complete the review of the proposal (Compton-Antoine 2014).

## 5.3 CONCLUSIONS

The SAWS negotiations are the least likely case for regional actor success since the number of regional groups with formal speaking rights is very limited (only the EU was a registered observer in 2011, 2012 and 2014) and since the IWC is a comparatively small IO. Nevertheless, there is the regional group activity and even some success in this case, since regional actors reduce the overall number of positions and the complexity of multi-lateral negotiations (interview#175, 01-09-14). It is striking that the BAG and the EU are the only two regional actors that were vocal in the SAWS negotiations in 2011, 2012 and 2014. The main sponsors of the proposal (Brazil, Argentina and Uruguay) could have evoked a regional organisation in order to improve their position in the IWC as well. For example, they are all member of the MERCOSUR or UNASUR, but have not made use of these memberships. A diplomat reported that 'it is impossible to work on whales inside the Mercosur' (interview#178, 16-09-14). It is not the case that internal coordination was attempted but failed, but rather that Brazil, Argentina and Uruguay formed an alternative regional coalition from early on, focusing not on the multiplicity of economic topics of the MERCOSUR, but more specifically on only one item: conservation of maritime resources (interview#178, 16-09-14). By contrast, 'The agenda is too big in Mercosur' (interview#178, 16-09-14).

Concerning the AU and SADC, a diplomat stressed that these regional organisations do not play a role: 'No, no, in the IWC that doesn't work that way' (interview#170, 22-07-14). Most SADC and AU members do not attend the IWC meetings, notable exceptions being, for example, Tanzania and South Africa (interview#170, 22-07-14, International Whaling Commission 2013: 4.1.2). As they only represent a small number of African States, 'There is not an African Voice' (interview#191, 18-09-14). Similarly, a representative of an Arab country explained that not enough member states of the Arab League are simultaneously members of the IWC to coordinate a common position and act upon it (interview#185, 17-09-14). Similarly, there were not enough ASEAN members present at the IWC in order to form a group position and whaling does not present one of the core issues of ASEAN (interview#192, 18-09-14). Likewise, countries located in the Caribbean or in the Pacific which are members of the IWC did not speak on behalf of the CARICOM or the PIF. A representative of a Pacific island state reported that 'there are not enough member states in the IWC from that region and that their interests in the organisation are shared by others, such as members of the sustainable-use-group'. Moreover, the diplomat explained, 'We have conflicting opinions inside the PIF on whaling. That's why we don't talk in the name of PIF' (interview#181, 17-09-14).

The IWC is an instance of an institutional context, which is least likely to have regional actor success, as its institutional design combines a moderate number of member states and weak formal roles of regional actors in the negotiation process. Accordingly, it is not too surprising that only two regional actors tried to exert influence over the South Atlantic Whale Sanctuary proposal during the negotiations that took place in the IWC in 2011, 2012 and 2014. The BAG and the EU, the two regional actors that were vocal in the negotiations, differ in two important respects with important implications for their prospects to be successful in the IWC.

First, the BAG is an IWC-specific regional group that was formed in order to voice the common positions with respect to whaling of its member states (Argentina, Brazil, Chile, Mexico, Costa Rica, Peru, Panama Colombia, the Dominican Republic, Ecuador and Uruguay). The EU is a cross-issue, regional organisation that is not specialised in whaling as such. Thus, the issue salience of whaling topics is much higher for the BAG than the EU, as it is their core policy area. The former is more active overall and also more constructive in tabling proposals which subsequently leads to better prospects for success in the IWC negotiations than the latter (in line with hypothesis 8).

Second, the internal homogeneity of member states preferences was much higher in the BAG, than the EU. While the BAG members not only preferred the establishment of a sanctuary for whales in the South Atlantic, they also had a common negotiation approach, proactively pushing the sanctuary proposal and making text changes. By contrast, the EU member states were less homogenous, due to Denmark's link to Greenland and their whaling approach, and operated on a minimal lowest common denominator basis, by only tentatively supporting the proposal. In the 2011 negotiations, the EU's limited internal homogeneity was particularly noticeable to third parties. Denmark and a few other states made formal statements in addition to the EU statement. In 2012 and 2014, the EU homogeneity increased somewhat as Denmark softened its whaling policies. Thus, the BAG was in a better position to exert influence over the whale sanctuary norm than the EU, as their argumentative negotiation strategies, as well as their bargaining endeavours, were not weakened by showing internal group dissent (H5b and H6b, H6c). In contrast, the EU's argumentative strategies to support the sanctuary proposal were less persuasive than they could have been, had Denmark not flagged that they only supported the sanctuaries under certain conditions (H5b and H6c). Collective bargaining was not effective under conditions of internal heterogeneity either (H5b and H6b). Yet, the effectiveness of EU negotiations increased in 2012 and 2014 once internal homogeneity increased and EU member states no longer made additional formal statements, which hinted at internal dissent.

In both regional groups, the member states had incentives to engage in burden-sharing during the negotiations. This is largely due to the fact that many of the BAG members had fewer resources (finances, staff in the line ministry at home, policy experts at hand, the number of diplomatic staff) than EU member states. As a result, burden-sharing was more strongly practised by the BAG than the EU (in line with H5a). This was reinforced by the fact that the internal homogeneity of preferences was much higher in the BAG than the EU (H5b).

In general, the BAG was more active and also somewhat more successful than the EU (H6a). With respect to the 2011 negotiations on a SAWS proposal that excluded coastal waters under national jurisdiction, the BAG proactively achieved procedural success, while the – at that point heterogeneous – EU fully failed to be successful. In 2012 both regional actors managed to increase support for the norm, but the BAG was not effective in pushing a text change, since the norm was not passed. In 2014 the SAWS proposal was strengthened, now prohibiting all forms of whaling instead of commercial whaling only, and both regional actors were very vocal in the negotiations in pushing for this substantive text change. The EU and especially the BAG succeeded in talking additional states into supporting the norm, but in the end, the majority threshold for formally passing the norm was not reached. Nevertheless, the very fact that even in the IWC regional actors played a role in the negotiations is indicative of a broader and more widespread regionalisation of international negotiations in other IOs as well.

Although the majority voting set-up of the IWC favours the clustering of votes in groups, bargaining strategies were not used extensively in the negotiations. The reasons for the infrequent bargaining exchanges is that the EU and the BAG were in weak bargaining positions as they did not represent a sufficient number of votes to pass the sanctuary norm by themselves and could not threaten other states accordingly. At the same time, they did not have much leeway to offer concessions in exchange for voting support, as the whaling sanctuary proposal was very specific and did not leave room for issue linkages itself. While the EU is larger in membership size than the BAG and should have had more bargaining leverage than the other group, the internal heterogeneity especially in 2011 worked against it and prevented bargaining from being effective (not in line with H6b). Also, tied-hands strategies did not work well in the IWC negotiations for both the BAG throughout the negotiations and the EU in 2012 and 2014 when its homogeneity was increased. The reason for the failure of this collective negotiation strategy is that it can be used to fend off concession demands from others, but cannot be used to obtain concessions from third parties to support a norm under negotiation when the latter is in a blocking minority.

Argumentative strategies were used throughout the negotiations, but in using them the BAG and the EU both faced the difficulty of persuading many third-party states that did not adopt the environmental framing of the whaling issue, but instead framed whaling as an economic activity that is culturally embedded in certain countries of the world. Thus, since two competing frames dominated the discussions in the IWC, the effectiveness of reason-giving strategies focusing on environmental claims was limited to those third-party states that were potentially sympathetic from the start. In 2014, the BAG adjusted its argumentative strategy. It increasingly used economic arguments (e.g. linked to increases of whale watching tourism in the sanctuary) and succeeded in obtaining voting support even from some formerly sceptical states (in line with H6c).

Only one of the two regional actors, the BAG, made references to pre-agreed language, linking the sanctuary proposal UNCLOS in order to flag that the IWC norm would not interfere with territorial waters of states. Yet, the strategy did not push opponents into support the norm, as they would not face reputational losses domestically if they nevertheless continued to oppose the sanctuary proposal (H6d).

The EU has more member states and, thus, more contact points for bilateral lobbying of third-party states than the BAG. On this basis, hypothesis 6e would have expected the EU to be more effective in lobbying for the sanctuary proposal than the BAG. However, the BAG compensated for its more limited lobbying capacities (due to its smaller membership size) by organising workshops that they could use as a platform for bilateral lobbying. Thus, while both groups effectively used lobbying strategies, the EU was not overall better in achieving negotiation success on this basis, due to its limited homogeneity in 2011 and due to the fact that the whaling issue was a much higher priority for the BAG than the EU.

Finally, linked to differences in the issue saliency between the EU and the BAG, it was the BAG who successfully approached the EU for coalition-building (H6f).

As a three-fourths majority is needed in order to pass the SAWS proposal, regional groups can become very important, since they combine a potentially large share of votes. If a regional group such as the EU is united, it has 'control over a quarter of the votes' in the IWC (interview#168, 10-07-14). As a result, regional actors 'can be quite powerful' (interview#170, 22-07-14). However, if heterogeneity amongst member states' positions persists, the coherency of the group is limited and hampers the effectiveness of negotiation strategies in the international negotiation arena. Yet, having a common regional position and high group coherence alone is not sufficient for regional actor success. The examples of the BAG and the EU in the IWC negotiations on a SAWS have illustrated that procedural success requires actors to be able

**Table 5.2.   Regional actor success in the SAWS negotiations**

| Year and Issue | Active ROs | Procedural Success – Proactive | Procedural Success – Reactive | Substantive Success – Proactive | Substantive Success – Reactive |
|---|---|---|---|---|---|
| 2011: exclusion of coastal waters under national jurisdiction | BAG | Yes | No | No, since norm not passed | No |
| | EU | No | No | No | No |
| 2012: exclusion of coastal waters under current and future national jurisdictions | BAG | Yes | No | No, since norm not passed | No |
| | EU | Yes | No | No | No |
| 2014: strengthening of norm: prohibition of all forms of whaling in SAWS (instead of commercial whaling only) | BAG | Yes | No | No, since norm not passed | Yes |
| | EU | Yes | No | No, since norm not passed | No |

to use negotiation strategies that either talk additional states into supporting one's position (proactive procedural success) or to prevent opponents from increasing support for their position (reactive procedural success). As table 5.2 shows, the BAG was procedurally successful in a proactive manner in all three years of negotiating the SAWS norm. By contrast, the EU's negotiation strategies were less effective at least partially due to its limited internal homogeneity in 2011. In regard to counteracting strategies of SAWS opponents in 2011, 2012 and 2014, neither the BAG nor the EU was effective, as Japan managed to talk additional states into rejecting the norm.

In order to be substantively successful and influence the content of international negotiation outcomes, regional actors must be able to alter international norms or rules in line with their own positions or prevent deviating changes. While the BAG managed to change the language of the SAWS proposal in line with their preferences in the years 2011, 2012 and 2014, the norm was not passed. In 2011 the BAG pushed the SAWS by stressing that its geographical scope would be within international waters and not the waters currently under national jurisdiction. In 2012 this was further explicated by emphasising that coastal waters are excluded – even if their scopes are changed in the future. Finally, in 2014 the BAG pushed for a substantively stronger norm that prohibits all forms of whaling in the SAWS instead of only prohibiting commercial whaling. The EU had no interest in changing the SAWS proposal fundamentally and did not develop its own initiatives, but agreed with the BAG on all major points in 2011, 2012 and 2014. Together these two regional actors were able to remedy the fact that the 2001–2012 SAWS norm had 'been weak in parts' (interview#195, 22-12-14), but since the SAWS was not passed, they did not achieve substantive success (see table 5.2). In 2014, Japan de facto proposed a new norm which was much weaker in a legal sense (Memorandum of Understanding) and which the BAG was able to fight off, with the BAG ultimately refraining from withdrawing the proposed SAWS Schedule amendment to the IWC Convention.

It is striking that even though the BAG was founded for only the IWC and only plays an active role in this arena without having a formal status in the IWC at all, this regional actor is in charge of the proposal text and leads the negotiation process. The BAG was in the driver's seat, but its negotiation endeavours were actively supported by the EU's negotiation strategies, in particular in 2012 and 2014. Although the EU and the BAG were both active in the SAWS negotiations, and in part also successful (see table 5.2), the SAWS norm was not passed in the 2012 and 2014 votes. This failure was due to the fact that the required three-fourths majority was not achieved.

*Chapter 6*

# Case Study 2: The negotiations on the Arms Trade Treaty

The Arms Trade Treaty (ATT) expresses the global efforts to reduce the illicit arms trade and to establish common standards for the international trade of conventional weapons by promoting accountability and transparency of state parties concerning the transfer of conventional arms. The Treaty is legally binding and obliges states that plan to authorise a transfer of conventional arms to another state first to undertake a rigorous risk assessment based on whether there is a substantial risk that those arms will be used to facilitate serious violations of human rights or humanitarian law (Callixtus 2013). The ATT is not an arms control treaty per se, and does not place restrictions on the types or quantities of arms that may be bought, sold or possessed by states. It also does not impact a state's domestic gun control laws or other firearm ownership policies (Bauer et al. 2014, Williams 2013).

Section 6.1.1 provides an overview of the processes leading to the ATT and introduces the negotiation arenas (6.1). On this basis, this case study examines whether and how regional actors influenced the ATT (6.2).

## 6.1 TOWARDS AN ARMS TRADE TREATY

### 6.1.1 History of the ATT

Armed conflicts around the globe resulted in between 37,175 and 60,260 battle-related deaths in 2012 (Themnér and Wallensteen 2013:1). The extent of this death toll is in large part due to a poorly controlled flow of weapons and ammunition around the world and the absence of a comprehensive, international, binding regulation in the trade in conventional arms.[1] For decades governments and civil society actors lobbied for an international treaty on arms trade in order to establish universal standards on international arms trade, including legal obligations on and clear guidelines about the transfer of arms across borders.[2] Existing national, regional and international rules have failed to create a comprehensive arms trading regime, which has resulted in inconsistencies and contradictions which also can be exploited by illicit arms trafficking. From early on, an important aim of an Arms Trade Treaty (ATT, hereafter also 'the Treaty') was to create an instrument to regulate the global arms market and to close major arms transfer loopholes in order to prevent weapons from reaching parties which violate human rights and/or humanitarian law.

The origins of the ATT can be traced back to the 1997. In this year Costa Rican President and Nobel Peace Prize laureate Óscar Arias invited a group of Nobel Peace Prize laureates – among them the Dalai Lama, José Ramos-Horta and representatives of human rights organisations – to develop an 'International Code of Conduct on Arms Transfer' (Mahmoud 2012).

Yet, it took more than a decade until the United Nations General Assembly (UNGA) adopted a resolution to start the negotiation process. The UNGA is the only organ of the UN in which all of today's sovereign states are represented and have equal weight (Panke 2013c): Each of the current 193 member states in the Assembly has one vote.[3] The resolution 64/48 from 2009 set up a Conference of the Parties (CoP) to be convened in 2012 in order 'to elaborate a legally-binding instrument on the highest possible common international standards for the transfer of conventional arms' (United Nations General Assembly 2009). Resolution 64/48 furthermore established four preparatory committees to be held in July 2010, February 2011, July 2011 and February 2012 to make 'recommendations to the Conference on the elements that would be needed to attain an effective and balanced legally binding instrument on the highest possible common international standards for the transfer of conventional arms' (United Nations General Assembly 2009).[4] The resolution also specified that the CoP would be convened in an 'open and transparent manner, on the basis of consensus, to achieve a strong and robust treaty' (United Nations General Assembly 2012c). In total, 151 states voted in favour, 20 abstained, and only Zimbabwe voted against the resolution.[5]

The ATT negotiations started and ended in the UNGA, but the better part of the negotiations took place in a special venue, namely in two diplomatic conferences, the Conference of the Parties (CoP) under the auspices of the United Nations (UN). Between July 2012 and March 2013, the ATT was negotiated in two CoPs. It was not possible to reach consensus at these meetings, which was required for the Treaty to be adopted. As a consequence, ATT supporters[6] moved the Treaty from the Conference of the Parties to the UNGA, where the ATT was adopted on 2 April 2013 via majority voting (United Nations Coverage and Press Releases 2013). On 24 December 2014, the Arms Trade Treaty entered into force.[7] Thus, for the very first time, there is now a multilateral treaty that regulates the international trade in conventional weapons and legally obligates states to ensure responsible and effective control of all types of international transfers of conventional arms and ammunition (Callixtus 2013).

### 6.1.2 The role of regional actors in the ATT negotiations

ROs are not full members of the UNGA and the ATT negotiation arenas and cannot cast votes. Yet, in obtaining observer status, ROs can gain formal access to the negotiations.

Many regional organisations have received a standing invitation to participate as observers in the UNGA. These are the African Union, Cooperation Council for the Arab States of the Gulf, Caribbean Community, Central American Integration System, Economic Community of West African States, European Union, League of Arab States, Organisation of Islamic Cooperation, Association of Caribbean States, Andean Community, Association of Southeast Asian Nations, Black Sea Economic Cooperation Organisation, Community of Sahelo-Saharan States, Council of Europe, Collective Security Treaty Organisation, East African Community, Economic Cooperation Organisation, Economic Community of Central African States, Eurasian Economic Community, GUUAM Organisation for Democracy and Economic Development, Intergovernmental Authority on Development, Latin American Integration Association, Organisation of American States, Organisation of Eastern Caribbean States, Organisation for Security and Cooperation in Europe, Pacific Islands Forum, South Asian Association for Regional Cooperation, Southern African Development Community, Shanghai Cooperation Organisation and Union of South American Nations (United Nations 2015). Since May 2011, the EU is the first and so far only RO which has an enhanced observer status at the UNGA. This includes the right to speak in debates among representatives of major groups.

All ROs with a standing invitation to be observers in the UNGA could also operate as observers in the PrepComs and the CoPs. Thus, they had access to all formal negotiation arenas, but had no formal votes (United Nations General Assembly 2012d; rule 59). The African Union, the European Union, ECOWAS, CARICOM, League of Arab States and the Pacific Island Forum were officially registered as observers in the ATT negotiations (United Nations General Assembly 2011a, 2012a, 2013c).

In addition to these regional organisations, there are also five UN-specific regional groups. GRULAC, UNAG, UNASPAG, UNEEG and UNWEOG. These groups have no formal roles in negotiations taking place under the auspices of the UN as such but were initially created for administrative purposes (e.g. rotating offices). Nevertheless, members of the UN groups can coordinate common position and voice them on behalf of these groups as well (c.f. chapter 3).

### 6.1.3 The ATT negotiation arenas

The negotiations of the ATT started and ended in the UNGA and lasted from 2009 to 2013 (c.f. figure 6.1).

The first PrepCom was convened at the UN Headquarters in New York City on July 2010. Three ROs attended, namely the African Union, ECOWAS and the EU, and 125 states were present as well (United Nations General Assembly 2010). During the first PrepCom, it became evident that a majority of countries supported the aim of creating an ATT. However, at that stage, it was not clear 'what precisely the Treaty will regulate and how far it will prevent illicit transfers or the diversion of conventional weapons as well as "illicit" transfers of weapons that are subsequently used for unlawful purposes' (ATT Legal bloggers 2010).[8]

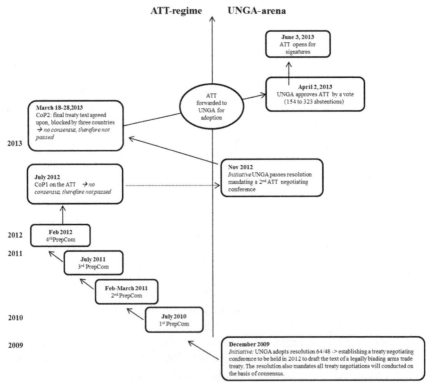

**Figure 6.1.  Timeline of the negotiation process**

The second PrepCom took place from February to March 2011 under the chairmanship of Ambassador Moritán. Apart from the UNGA member states, representatives of the League of Arab States, ECOWAS and the EU participated as well (United Nations General Assembly 2011a).

In July 2011, the third PrepCom was convened. A total of 132 countries as well as delegates from CARICOM, ECOWAS, EU and League of Arab States attended the meetings (United Nations General Assembly 2011b). The chair distributed the first complete draft version of a possible Treaty (Moritán 2011), which triggered intense discussions between India, Pakistan, Egypt as importers, and the United States as the major exporter of arms (ATT Legal Bloggers 2011).

The fourth PrepCom took place in February 2012. Representatives of four ROs attended the meetings: CARICOM, EU, League of Arab States and the Pacific Islands Forum Secretariat and a total of 129 UN member states participated (United Nations General Assembly 2012b). This PrepCom was supposed to exclusively deal with organisational and procedural matters regarding the upcoming CoP, such as the rules of procedure or the access of NGOs. However, several states and regional actors shifted into substantive discussions on what an ATT should look like. Nevertheless, in the end, the participants of the fourth PrepCom agreed on the Provisional Rules of Procedure for the CoP. The rules of procedure excluded voting on any matter of substance: 'The Conference shall take its decisions, and consider the text of the Treaty, by consensus, in accordance with General Assembly Resolution 64/48' (United Nations General Assembly 2012c, Rule 33). At the same meeting, the Committee adopted the (revised) draft report.

In July 2012, the first CoP was convened at the UN headquarters in New York. Despite the work already done during the four PrepComs, the ATT negotiations were still controversial. Even after four weeks of negotiations, the member states had not yet agreed on a draft treaty text. Several arms exporting countries such as the United States, Russia, Cuba, the Democratic People's Republic of Korea (DPRK), Russia and Venezuela requested additional time in order to find common ground and conclude the agreement (Callixtus 2013). Yet, a Treaty could be passed only by consensus of the UN member states. Since dissent prevailed in the CoP which was divided into 'more progressive, like-minded' states and the so-called sceptics (Geneva Academy 2013), no ATT was adopted in 2012.

On 7 November 2012, after the failure of CoP1 and back in the UNGA arena, the states passed resolution 67/234[9] deciding to convene a second United Nations Conference on the Arms Trade. CoP2 should finalise an ATT (United Nations General Assembly 2012e). Since the same rules as in CoP1 apply, any Treaty adopted by CoP2 would have to be consensual as well.

CoP2 took place in March 2013. At the last day of CoP2, it became clear that three states, namely Iran, the Democratic People's Republic of Korea and Syria, would not vote in favour of the Treaty and would, therefore, block consensus in the CoP. Therewith CoP2 also ended without adopting an ATT (Woolcott 2013).

However, since the ATT negotiation arena required consensus in order to pass an ATT, whereas the UNGA can pass international norms by a majority, over 100 treaty-supporting countries moved the draft text to the UNGA arena (c.f. figure 6.1). These countries co-sponsored a draft UNGA resolution calling for the adoption of the ATT (United Nations General Assembly 2013b). The UNGA member states approved the ATT by a vote 154 to 3 (with 23 abstentions) on 2 April 2013, only five days after the end of CoP2. Only Iran, North Korea and Syria voted against the Treaty.[10]

In line with Article 22§1, the Treaty required ratification by fifty UN signatories before it went into effect (United Nations General Assembly 2013a). On 24 December 2014 the Arms Trade Treaty entered into force.[11]

## 6.2 EMPIRICAL ANALYSIS: THE NEGOTIATION DYNAMICS IN THE ATT CASE

This section examines the roles of regional actors in the ATT negotiations that took place in the four PrepComs and the two CoPs between 2010 and 2013. How vocal were regional actors? Which negotiation strategies did they employ? How successful were ROs in shaping negotiation dynamics and negotiation outcomes?

Since the PrepComs and the CoPs are more open to ROs than the IWC, and since the ATT regime is also larger in membership size than the IWC, regional actors should have better prospects for success in the ATT than the IWC. The ATT case covered a considerably larger number of Articles than the IWC case (twenty-eight Articles and numerous subparagraphs in the ATT case versus a half-paged Schedule Amendment in the IWC case), and the number of different issues in which ROs became active is also much higher in the ATT negotiations.

The subsequent empirical analysis focuses on the most important issues in the ATT negotiations in which regional actors had stakes and in which the level of contestation between the actors was high. By contrast, we exclude those issues in which regional actors remained completely silent (e.g. Articles 17 and 18),[12] those in which ROs had no regional positions (Articles 20–28),[13] and those in which all actors more or less agreed on the substance of an issue from early on (e.g. brokering [Article 10][14] or enforcement [Article 14]).[15]

### 6.2.1 Preamble

The preamble of the ATT lays out the background and purpose of the Treaty as well as the general principles. The preamble underlines 'the need to prevent and eradicate the illicit trade in conventional arms and to prevent their diversion to the illicit market'. Moreover, the preamble explicitly emphasises the sovereign right of the states to 'regulate and control conventional arms exclusively within its territory' (United Nations General Assembly 2013d) and therewith makes clear that the ATT is a treaty which does not interfere in domestic issues.

One of the issues that the EU pushed as a regional position in the negotiations on the Preamble referred to the formal status of ROs as signatories to the ATT – the so called regional integration organisation (RIO) clause. The idea of upgrading the position of ROs in the ATT and allow the EU and other ROs to become formal parties to the Treaty goes back to a decision of the Council of the European Union in Brussels (interviews #211, 29-07-15, #212, 28-10-15). However, this idea only turned into a regional position that EU members pursued in international negotiations after all PrepCom sessions had ended. It was first voiced during the first CoP in July 2012 by the Head of the EU delegation.[16] Yet, the EU members did not engage in coordinated, burden-sharing activities, as the EU's position left leeway for how the individual member states would negotiate for the inclusion of the RIO clause (interview#211, 29-07-15). Thus, the EU did not extensively lobby a large number of third-party actors (Romanyshyn 2013). Moreover, the EU did not conduct compelling argumentative strategies, failing to provide good reasons why the status of ROs should be upgraded in the final ATT text. Thus, states that regarded security and arms trade issues as the prerogative for countries rather than ROs did not side with the EU (interviews #209, 17-07-15, #211, 29-07-15, Geneva Academy 2012). Together, the EU's prospects for negotiation success were limited, and its first attempts to promote the RIO clause failed (H5a, H6c, H6e).[17]

In the very final stages of negotiations on the preamble, the EU once more pushed for the inclusion of the RIO clause (interview#212, 28-10-15; European Union 2012b). This time, the EU emphasised a functional reason pointing out that the RIO clause would contribute to strengthening the role of ROs in the external security policy field in general. Moreover, it argues that the implementation of the ATT can be more effective when ROs play a role. Thus, the EU argued that it is beneficial for all parties when they 'take into account the specific responsibilities that some regional organisations have acquired or could acquire in regulating arms transfers in several regions of the world' (European Union 2012b). This argument found resonance in the East African Community (EAC) and the Economic Community of West African

States (ECOWAS) (interview#209, 17-07-15), and the EU achieved in this respect some success in talking third parties into supporting its regional position.

Thus, the EAC became active itself, stressing the 'increasing Peace and Security responsibility that these organisations continue to shoulder' (East African Community 2012). It engaged in argumentative strategies in order to support the EU's proposal. However, the EAC was not successful in winning the support of additional states for the RIO clause, many of which regarded peace and security matters as a prerogative for countries rather than a field in which ROs should be strengthened (interview#198, 24-02-15). Some powerful states were actively opposing the RIO clause, most notably the Chinese delegation which issued a no-vote threat should the RIO clause remain (interviews #209, 17-07-15, #211, 29-07-15, Geneva Academy 2012).

The formal status of ROs in the ATT came up only in 2012, when the negotiations were already well advanced, and the states were primarily concerned with questions of scope and substance of an ATT (interviews #211, 29-07-15, #212, 28-10-15). At this late point, neither the EU nor the EAC managed to change the text of the ATT to include the RIO clause. Accordingly, ROs did not obtain a formal status in the final version of the Treaty, which only refers to 'States Parties' (United Nations General Assembly 2013a).

### 6.2.2 Article 1: Object and purpose

The ATT has two objectives and three purposes. The objectives are (1) establishing high standards for the regulation of international trade in conventional arms and (2) preventing illicit conventional arms trade (Article 1, United Nations General Assembly 2013a). Both objectives serve the purpose of contributing to stability, peace and security internationally and regionally, to delimit human suffering and to make arms trade between states more transparent (Article 1, United Nations General Assembly 2013a).

The issue concerning Article 1, in which regional actors became active, was whether to *prevent* and/or to *combat* and/or to *eradicate* the illicit trade in conventional arms. Brazil, CARICOM and the African Group preferred a demanding version of the ATT's objective, including all three elements (African Group 2011, Brazil 2010, 2011a, Canada 2012, Grenada 2012, Kazakhstan 2013).[18] While the 2012 draft of the ATT included the three elements, the final Treaty did not mention the proactive element anymore: the combatting of the illicit trade in conventional weapons has been dropped from the list of objectives (United Nations General Assembly 2013a, Woolcott 2012). In this sense, the final Treaty was less demanding than the previous drafts. This change is due to the negotiation dynamics that took place in CoP1 and CoP2.

On the one side, CARICOM and PIF wanted to keep the proactive aim. The PIF emphasised that 'the Members of the Forum are committed to negotiating and concluding an Arms Trade Treaty (ATT) that will help *deter* and prevent illicit trafficking and proliferation of arms, including small arms and light weapons' (Pacific Islands Forum 2012; emphasis added by the authors). However, other than stating their regional position, the PIF did not use argumentative, bargaining or coalition strategies in order to maximise support for their position.

CARICOM also pushed for the ATT to 'include clauses to prevent, combat and eradicate the illicit transfer, production, and brokering of conventional weapons' (CARICOM 2012c). It argued that a broad objective is important for the ATT's effectiveness in combating the negative implications of illicit arms trade (H6c). A CARICOM member explained, 'The countries of CARICOM have suffered for way too long because of the illicit trade in Small Arms and Light Weapons and associated ammunition. The combination of porous borders and insufficient resources have resulted in increased levels of armed violence within the CARICOM region' (Grenada 2012, similar CARICOM 2012c). Yet, this argument did not resonate well amongst countries fearing that the ATT could legitimise interventions into countries' arms trade affairs, which many states objected to. In this respect, CSTO argued that 'in order to be effective, it [the ATT, insertion by the authors] should focus on specific goals and objectives arising from the key problems affecting the interests of all UN Member States. It remains of key importance for the 2012 UN Conference on the ATT to agree on its goals and objectives which are essential for determining its content. The main purpose of this mechanism, in our view, is to prevent the diversion of arms from legal trade to illicit traffic by strengthening or establishing, were not in place, national systems of governmental controls over arms transfers' (Collective Security Treaty Organization 2012). Similar to CSTO, several individual states emphasised that there is also legitimate arms trade and hesitated to opt for ATT wording that would be open to interpretation concerning third-party activity in combating illicit arms trade.[19] Thus, opponents with strong preferences, such as the United States, Ukraine, Tanzania, Vietnam, Russia, China and others did not give in (e.g. China 2012, Tanzania 2013, Ukraine 2013, USA 2013b, Vietnam 2013) and continued to insist that the ATT should not place too many, or too many new, responsibilities on the signature states (e.g. Russian Federation 2010b, Vietnam 2011).These countries pushed for a final ATT text that would not include proactive objectives (combatting illicit arms trade) as that would be too demanding for the states to achieve. Similarly, China, France, Russian Federation, United Kingdom and United States as the permanent five nuclear powers (P5) pointed out, 'Our objective remains the same: an ATT that is simple, short, and easy to implement, and at the same time sets the highest possible common standards by which states will regulate the international transfer of conventional arms. An effective ATT should not hinder the legitimate arms trade or the legitimate right to self-defense under the UN Charter. It should help curb the illicit trafficking in conventional weapons that undermines peace, security and prosperity' (Common position of P5 2013).[20]

In the end, the opponents of the proactive goal succeeded and the final ATT text does not mention 'combatting' illicit international conventional arms trade anymore as an objective of the ATT. While PIF and CARICOM failed to achieve substantive text changes in line with their preference, CSTO was more effective. Yet, It was not the only actor negotiating actively in order to prevent the ATT from including the combat of illicit arms trade.

### 6.2.3 Article 2: Scope

Article 2 defines the scope of the Treaty and describes the type of activities and items to be controlled by the ATT. As Article 1 specifies the objective of the ATT as regulating the trade of arms as well as eradicating the illicit trade of 'conventional arms', it was crucial that the states agree on a definition of which weapons and arms are to be considered 'conventional'. In the final version of Article 2§1, 'Conventional weapons' include: 'Battle tanks, armoured combat vehicles; large-calibre artillery systems; combat aircraft; attack helicopters; warships; missiles and missile launchers; and small arms and light weapons' (United Nations General Assembly 2013d). Article 2§2 specifies that for the arms listed in §1, the rules of the Treaty concerning 'international trade comprises export, import, transit, trans-shipment and brokering' (United Nations General Assembly 2013d: Article 2.2) apply. Thus, Article 2 specifies which arms are regulated by the Treaty and which ensuing Articles on arms trade, namely the rules on export, import, transit trans-shipment and brokering, all apply to the listed types of arms.

The negotiations on Article 2 in which regional actors played prominent roles focused on whether small arms and light weapons should also be part of the Treaty's scope (Issue 1), whether to adopt the 7+1+1 formula (Issue 2), whether the ATT scope should also include re-export, technical assistance, leases, gifts and loans related to conventional weapons (Issue 3) and whether transit control should be incorporated (Issue 4).

*Issue 1: Which weapons should be covered, inclusion
of small arms and light weapons*

Article 2 was highly contested throughout the negotiations (Geneva Academy 2012, interview#198, 24-02-15). The most controversial issue was which categories of weapons should be covered by the ATT. On the one hand, some actors would have preferred a narrow definition of conventional arms, focusing on battle tanks, for example, and excluding small arms and light weapons, such as Egypt or the United States (Egypt 2012, Geneva Academy 2013). Others opted for a broader definition of 'conventional weapons' which would encompass not only heavy arms but also small arms and light weapons, such as pistols, revolvers or rifles (Australia 2010b, Mexico 2010, Philippines 2010).

Members of CARICOM placed great importance on arms trade issues, engaged in regional group coordination before and during the ongoing ATT process,[21] and actively participated in the negotiations (H8, H6a).[22] For CARICOM small arms and light weapons and the illicit trade of these weapons constitute one of the main problems in the region so that the regional actor regarded a strong ATT as a remedy (interviews #199, 24-02-15, #208, 20-05-15). The two themes that had the highest saliency for CARICOM were the inclusion of small arms and light weapons under the Treaty's scope as well as the inclusion of ammunition (interviews #199, 24-02-15, #208, 20-05-2015, CARICOM 2010e, b, 2011c, f).

Due to their swift group coordination, CARICOM was frequently the first actor who tabled specific proposals on ATT text changes and could thereby benefit from a first mover advantage in negotiations (interview#208, 20-05-15). Already in the first PrepCom, Antigua and Barbuda acted on behalf of CARICOM and emphasised that the Treaty needs to be 'comprehensive in scope' and 'should make provision for all categories of weapons which are capable of being used in ways that can result in violations of the United Nations Charter, or, International Humanitarian Law' (CARICOM 2010a). Thus, initially, CARICOM did not explicitly request the wording 'small arms and light weapons' (SALWS) but based their argument for the ATT's ideal scope on another legal text. CARICOM engaged in linking strategies and referred to the 'UN Register of Conventional Arms' as the source that should define which weapons an ATT would cover. However, this first attempt to use pre-agreed language of international law as a means to entrap states that oppose a broad ATT scope was not effective (H6d). Referring to an external legal document for such an essential component of the ATT was regarded as a source of too much future legal uncertainty. This was because ATT members as such are not in absolute control over whether the legal reference source will be changed in the future and, if so, which types of weapons it will list. Thus, several states preferred to list the specific types of weapons that should be covered by an ATT explicitly (among them, for example, Bangladesh 2010, Norway 2010, Tanzania 2010). In addition, some ROs, most notably the EU, preferred listing specific types of weapons in order to define the ATT scope, instead of referencing an existing document (European Union 2010h).

While CARICOM was not successful with respect to linking the ATT scope to the UN Register of Conventional Arms in 2010, they managed to entrapp states in another respect later on (in line with H6d). CARICOM pointed to existing international law to establish that the Register of Conventional Arms – *with the date of the ATT entry into force* – should constitute the minimal definition of relevant weapons covered by the final ATT with respect to implementation (Article 5) and reporting in the 2011 negotiations (Article 13). Thus, the initial arguments against such a reference were no longer valid. As a consequence CARICOM succeeded (CARICOM 2011e).

Explicitly regulating small arms and light weapons in the ATT was also very much in the interest of ECOWAS. Already back in 2006, their members had passed a 'Convention on Small Arms and Light Weapons' (ECOWAS 2006).[23] This Convention served as focal point for the swift development of a regional group position in the ATT negotiations. ECOWAS members had a common position on trade with and proliferation of small arms and light weapons and effectively used two negotiation strategies, most notably coalition-building (H6f) and arguing (H6c), in order to push for the inclusion of small arms and light weapons in addition to the heavier conventional weapons (e.g. tanks, warships, armoured combat vehicles or combat aircraft) (ECOWAS 2010, 2012).[24] In addition, coalition-building ensured that the EU would not oppose an ATT that explicitly incorporated small arms and light weapons (e.g. compare European Union 2010d with European Union 2012a) instead of being based on a narrow definition of conventional weapons.

Moreover, ECOWAS and CARICOM successfully pushed their regional positions and talked additional states into supporting them based on making compelling arguments (H6c). ECOWAS 'was basically voicing the negative impact [of small arms and light weapons on African soil, insertion of the authors], putting at the front what we are facing, because at that time there had been very difficult crises on the continent where we know that small arms are the basic tools being used. It was difficult for us at the highest level, even at a technical level, to accept a treaty which does not control small arms and light weapons' (interview#209, 17-07-15).[25] Similarly, CARICOM pointed out that the majority of deaths are caused by small arms and light weapons and also evidence-based arguments related to economic costs and to other negative impacts on countries (CARICOM 2012c).[26]

### Issue 2: 7+1+1 formula

CARICOM not only proposed the addition of the words 'small arms' and 'light weapons' into Article 2, but suggested more detailed text changes broadening the scope of the Treaty (CARICOM 2011e). Thus, in the second PrepCom, CARICOM argued that a '7+1+1 formula' would be an ideal specific definition of the ATT's scope. The formula stated that SALWS and ammunition should be subject to the ATT irrespective of whether they are carried by battle tanks, armoured combat vehicles, large-calibre artillery systems, combat aircraft, attack helicopters, warships or missiles and missile launchers. CARICOM underlined the importance of a broad ATT scope by using a functionalist argument according to which a broad scope 'is the only way to meet the goal of achieving a comprehensive and effective ATT' (CARICOM 2011e). Apart from functionalist, legal and moral arguments related to the harm done by illicit arms to society at large (H6c), CARICOM members engaged in burden-sharing. They strategically lobbied potentially like-minded countries (H6e) in order to maximise support for the 7+1+1 formula (interview#208, 20-05-15). In addition, they also approached those powerful states, including Germany, the United States or Russia, that they regarded as more difficult to convince, largely due to their respective weapon industries (interview#208, 20-05-15). In order to talk such actors into supporting the 7+1+1 formula, CARICOM strategically 'worked together with civil society' (interview#208, 20-05-15), thereby creating potential reputation losses in case these countries would oppose a strong ATT. In addition, CARICOM gained support for the 7+1+1 formula from several African countries in the ECOWAS[27] (interview#15, 29-07-15),[28] which in turn had bargaining leverage over some opposing states, such as China.[29] Taken together, CARICOM was not only 'the most vocal regional organisation' (interview#211, 29-07-15), but its strategy mix also worked well.

The negotiation endeavours of CARICOM were reinforced by the East African Community (EAC), which in the course of the negotiations pointed out that it 'strongly supports the inclusion of Small Arms and Light Weapons and ammunitions in the future Arms Trade Treaty' (Burundi on behalf of the East African Community 2011). The EAC wishes 'to have a Treaty including the regulations of Trade on Small Arms and Light Weapons in all their aspects' (East African Community 2011). During CoP1 the EAC repeated its support for a comprehensive scope and arguing that SALWS (small arms and light weapons) represent the 'most potent threat to stability, security and development' (East African Community 2012).

Ultimately, CARICOM was supported by ECOWAS and EAC and achieved substantive success. In the final ATT text of 2013, the 7+1+1 formula was incorporated into Article 2 (scope) with the exception of ammunition (as one of the +1 elements), which was treated separately in Article 3 of the ATT (c.f. below).

*Issue 3: Re-export, technical assistance, leases, gifts and
loans related to conventional weapons*

The EU was vocal not only concerning what the ATT Preamble should look like, but also concerning Article 2 (European Union 2010h, 2011f). In a statement exclusively dedicated to the scope of the Treaty, the EU suggested the inclusion of export, import, re-export, transit, trans-shipment, brokering, transfer of technology, technical assistance, as well as leases, gifts and loans related to conventional weapons (European Union 2010h). Compared to this wish list, the final ATT text of 2013 is less encompassing, stating, 'For the purposes of this Treaty, the activities of the international trade comprise export, import, transit, trans-shipment and brokering, hereafter referred to as "transfer"' (Article 2.2). This indicates that the EU was not successful in all respects since the following elements were not part of the final version of Article 2 ATT: re-export, technical assistance, leases, gifts and loans related to conventional weapons.

The EU's limited success is not too surprising. First, its internal homogeneity was not very high (H5b). Some EU members favoured broad applicatory scopes, while others feared that the inclusion of too many elements into the ATT would be counterproductive, largely because the ATT members differ immensely with regard to their governance capacities, which would lead to an uneven implementation performance of ATT provisions (Depauw 2012).[30] In this situation, the EU operated on the basis of a lowest common denominator approach and made only few negotiation efforts (H6a). While the EU made scope proposals (European Union 2011f), it did not use a broad array of negotiation strategies to promote re-export, technical assistance, leases, gifts and loans related to conventional weapons and did not provide scientific, technical, functional, legal, moral or political reasons why these items should become part of the ATT (e.g. European Union 2010h).

*Issue 4: Transit controls*

CARICOM and PIF were also successful in opposing and preventing text changes of others which were not in line with their own positions. For example, Australia and Mexico proposed the inclusion of transit controls, according to which governments should check cross-border weapon trade in order to make sure that weapons and arms covered by the ATT are not traded in an illicit manner (Australia 2010b, Mexico 2010). However, transit controls would have required substantive government resources to be implemented on the ground. For this reason, 'CARICOM did not want to be transit controls written down as to what they have to do, if it's feasible, they would do it, but certainly didn't want the burden of doing this. And that was certainly the same for the Pacific Islands Forum. So those two, sort of, found an alliance and they played off each other, and they joined forces, and they said those things. So it wasn't just one region, they were all saying we can't have this, it was two regions plus a couple of others like Singapore saying, the transit, we just cannot do them' (interview#15, 29-07-15). The mixture of argumentative strategies, bargaining strategies and coalition-building (H6b, 6c, 6f) worked out for PIF and CARICOM. Transit controls were not included in Article 2 of the 2013 final text of the ATT as such, but moved into Article 9 on transit and trans-shipment. Even more importantly, Article 9 did not outline how exactly states should engage in transit control activities or which standards these controls should meet. Instead, Article 9 was formulated in a manner leaving it up to the individual ATT member state which measures to adopt in order to prevent illicit trade across one's own borders. Thus, CARICOM and PIF succeeded in avoiding a formulation in the ATT text which they would struggle to implement domestically due to limited government capacities (interview#15, 29-07-15).

### 6.2.4 Article 3: Ammunition

The topic 'ammunition' was on the negotiation table from early on (CARICOM 2011e) and was highly contested. Ammunition did not become part of the ATT's scope in Article 2§1 and the rules regulating the trade of arms as listed in Articles 2§2 do consequently not automatically apply to ammunition as well. Nevertheless, since ammunition was regarded as an essential element in the arms trade, the Parties regulated it in a specific Article. Thus, Article 3 calls for every state party to 'establish and maintain a *national control system* to regulate the export of ammunition/munitions fired, launched or delivered' (United Nations General Assembly 2013d: Article 3, emphasis added by the authors). Moreover, this should happen in compliance with the rules laid out in Article 6 (prohibitions) and Article 7 (export and export assessment).

Ammunition was discussed in two respects by regional actors. First, whether it should be part of the ATT scope and would, consequently, belong to Article 2. Second, it was contested that if ammunition is not part of Article 2, should it be featured in the ATT at all?

*Issue 1: Ammunition under Article 2*

CARICOM actively lobbied for the inclusion of ammunition in Article 2 of the ATT (interviews' #208, 20-05-15, #211, 29-07-15). In its famous 7+1+1 formula, ammunition was one of the +1s (United Nations Office for Disarmament Affairs 2013). Already during the first PrepCom meeting, CARICOM pointed out that ammunition should be covered by the ATT (e.g. CARICOM 2010a). To stress the urgency of this demand, Suriname as a member of

CARICOM explained that ammunition trade has an immense negative impact on his region, even though the region is not among the major importers or exporters of ammunition. Thus, ammunition is to blame for 'causing loss of life, increased criminality and violence, instability and the diversion of scarce resources away from developmental priorities' (CARICOM 2010c). This sentiment was iterated by like-minded actors. Most notably ECOWAS also regarded ammunition as highly important for the effective eradication of the negative effects of unregulated arms trade on the safety and health of their citizens (ECOWAS 2010, 2012).[31] During the second and third PrepComs, CARICOM continued to be very active and demanded that ammunition should be an integral part of the ATT's scope as well (CARICOM 2011d, 2011e). To this end, they engaged in arguing strategies (H6c). The CARI-COM representative pointed towards functional necessities and explained that an ATT would be effective only in ultimately reducing harm resulting from trade with arms and weapons, if ammunition were to be included into the Treaty's scope as well.[32] This claim was further substantiated by figures on causalities from firearms and light weapons in general.[33] During the CoP in 2012, CARICOM stressed that ammunition was of such high saliency for them, that they became active on the regional level (H8).[34] Moreover, they used a new framing to argumentatively push for the inclusion of ammunition into the ATT. Previously they discussed how ammunition and SALWS harm humans and endanger regional security and stability.[35] Now they added that it is putting additional economic and administrative strains on those states that are economically not well of.[36] Through its argumentative endeavours, CARICOM could increase the number of actors on its side. It obtained the support of the PIF[37] and the UN African Group also became increasingly concerned 'that ammunition was not going to be included within the scope of the ATT and the history there was, because ammunition is considered part of the parcel, it's a, it's a, you can argue that you make a mockery of the process if you only address the weapons and not the ammunition' (interview#201, 26-02-15). Nevertheless, CARICOM failed to persuade its opponents and did not succeed to push ammunition into Article 2 on the scope (compare Moritán 2011 with Woolcott 2012 and United Nations General Assembly 2013a). This was largely due to continuing opposition by Russia (Geneva Academy 2013, Russian Federation 2010b),[38] the EU,[39] and the United States which argued 'that exports of ammunition are too difficult to monitor under an ATT' (Depauw 2012).

*Issue 2: Ammunition in the Treaty at all?*

After it had become apparent that ammunition would not be part of the ATT scope Article, ECOWAS took the lead and engaged in lobbying and arguing strategies pushing for the inclusion of ammunition in the Treaty, without explicitly requiring it to be part of its scope definition (H6c, H6e). A diplomat explained, 'We didn't give up. Because what is small arms and light weapons without ammunitions? It's nonsense to say that ammunitions will not be included' (interview#209, 17-07-15). The diplomat further elaborated that 'every states parties at the negotiations beginning who were not in favour or who were very neutral as far as ammunitions were concerned progressively begun to understand that our logic was something that can't move' (interview#209, 17-07-15). In the end, ammunition got a prominent status in the ATT, not within Article 2, but by moving ammunition to a separate article. Thus, the final version of the ATT leaves loopholes for states, as they alone are responsible for designing their control and regulatory regimes with respect to the trade of ammunition.[40]

Nevertheless, the compromise to create Article 3 was regarded as a partial success by the two regional actors involved:[41] 'I think many people would acknowledge that in the end, well, the compromise reached was pretty good. It's pretty robust, if you actually look at, you know, where it's not quite as amply covered as weapons, but if you look at all the cross-references and what's latent, I think it was a pretty good deal. So that was why Africa was very outspoken on that. I think Nigeria was the key; I think they were certain, you know, because of its position as the host of ECOWAS' (interview#201, 26-02-15). In addition to ECOWAS, CARICOM could also claim partial substantial success: 'Another battle for us was to get ammunition included in the Treaty. We were able to get ammunition included, notwithstanding, in fact, that ammunition is not part of the scope, but it is mentioned in the Treaty. So I believe CARICOM was able to influence the Treaty very positively' (interview#208, 20-05-2015).[42]

### 6.2.5 Article 4: Parts and components

Article 4 deals with the export of parts and components of the conventional weapons that are covered by Article 2 (scope). The final version states: 'Each State Party shall establish and maintain a national control system to regulate the export of parts and components where the export is in a form that provides the capability to assemble the conventional arms covered under Article 2§1 and shall apply the provisions of Article 6 and Article 7 prior to authorizing the export of such parts and components' (United Nations General Assembly 2013d: Article 4).

Compared to the preceding Articles, the issue of how to deal with parts and components of the arms and weapons regulated under the ATT (Article 2§1) was less contested. The EU and CARICOM were the only two ROs to engage in the debate, in addition to several states (e.g. Australia 2011b, Canada 2011,

Colombia 2012, Denmark 2011a, Fiji 2013, Guyana 2012, Israel 2011b, Mexico 2011, South Africa 2012, Switzerland 2011, UK 2011).

CARICOM pushed for the incorporation of weapons' parts and components into the ATT into Article 2 (scope) (CARICOM 2012c, interview#208, 20-05-15). Arguing that conventional weapons must be considered 'in tandem' with parts and components of these weapons (CARICOM 2011e), it pointed out that they contribute to the negative impact of arms in general. However, CARICOM was not able to win sufficient support with its argument. While some countries supported it,[43] others, such as Iran and Vietnam, kept opposing the broadening of the ATT's scope in this manner (Iran 2012, Vietnam 2012). Thus, in addition, CARICOM reached out to the EU, which also wanted to include parts and components into the ATT scope (European Union 2011f, 2012b), and together they formed an ad hoc coalition, increasing their collective bargaining leverage.

Subsequently, compromise dynamics emerged,[44] in which the opponents and the two ROs agreed to deal with parts and components in a separate Article (interview ATT #14, 29-07-15). A diplomat explained it is 'a win that we could get ammunition and parts and components in there in a specific way, so it's clearly within the scope, but not necessarily the same as the actual scope of the Treaty' (interview#210, 29-07-15).[45] Similar to Article 3, in which ammunition has been separated from the ATT scope and placed under the national responsibility for regulation, parts and components were also moved into a separate Article (Art. 4), which puts the ATT member states in charge of setting up and designing their own regulatory systems for dealing with trade of parts and components of conventional weapons. Thus, the final version of the ATT was less demanding with respect to parts and components of conventional weapons than the scope inclusion of the issue would have been.

### 6.2.6 Article 5: General implementation

Article 5 deals with the implementation of the Treaty provisions and defines the responsibility of the state parties in this respect. In §2 this Article refers to the establishment of national control systems and §4 regulates that this information should be handed to the Secretariat in order to distribute them to all state parties. Article 5§3 states, 'Each State Party is encouraged to apply the provisions of this Treaty to the broadest range of conventional arms' (United Nations General Assembly 2013d: Article 5.3). Paragraphs 5 and 6 refer to the establishment of national authorities in order to have effective national control systems in place and national points of contact in order to exchange information 'on matters related to the implementation of this Treaty' (United Nations General Assembly 2013d: Article 5§5 and §6).

Although Article 5 explicates how states should implement the Treaty, some regional actors became active in the discussions on Article 5 as well. These concerned whether to opt for a central or a decentral database (Issue 1) and how to deal with the potential upgrading of national regulatory systems (Issue 2).

*Issue 1: Central or decentral database?*

In the first session of the PrepCom, the EU made a case for strong national implementation systems together with strong national oversight and control mechanisms, and used a variety of argumentative and lobbying strategies to promote its ideas. Initially, the EU clarified that implementation 'remains a national responsibility' and demanded clear provisions for the national implementation of the ATT as well as the introduction of control systems at the national level (European Union 2010c). Accordingly, the EU stressed that it is the obligation of state parties to implement the legal provisions and to set up an administrative structure to control all transactions of conventional arms. The EU suggested guidelines to facilitate the implementation of the Treaty at the national level, namely that the proposed national legal and administrative systems should include 'national legislative and administrative measures to control exports, imports, transits, etc; national provisions to prohibit, prosecute and penalize participation in illicit arms trade; record keeping and reporting, tracing of diverted weapons in order to determine loopholes and increase accountability; and the obligation to report on assessed transfers to a UN database'.

Opposing the EU's last point on a UN database, ECOWAS suggested the installation of 'databases or registers of arms to be established and maintained by member states' (ECOWAS 2010). The negotiations were controversial as some states were on the EU's side while others supported ECOWAS' position, and no side succeeded in winning sufficient support. The arguments exchanged were limited in numbers, and the actors talked at cross-purposes as neither the EU nor ECOWAS referred to technical or legal reasons explaining why their preferred approach was superior to the other one (e.g. ECOWAS 2010).

As arguing did not work (H6c), the EU adopted bargaining strategies (H6b) and tried to obtain support for its position by offering a side-payment as a compromise, namely implementation support for other states once the ATT was passed. An EU member stated: 'Once we get this ATT there will be many EU programs that help you implement it, there'll be lots of support for you . . . we've got a lot of experience putting these things in place, we can help you with the practical implementation. That was a lot of the sort of, carrot as it were, for the stick to support the approach, to support what we wanted to get out of there' (interview#211, 29-07-15).[46] However, making such offers was not effective either, as the sovereignty stakes were simply too high for these third parties, which placed great emphasis on handling implementation solely at the national level (e.g. Russian Federation 2010a).[47] In the end, the actors had to acknowledge that there was a stalemate with respect to the level of international involvement in ATT matters. The EU and its supporters favoured one central database hosted by an international body (e.g. a UN database), while ECOWAS and its supporters preferred decentralised national databases on arms trades.

Ultimately, neither the EU nor ECOWAS was entirely successful. States that placed a strong emphasis on their sovereignty (e.g. Russia or the United States) tended to object to the EU's proposal, while states that regarded transparency in approved arms trades as very important opposed the ECOWAS proposal. The result of the discussions about how to collect and publish information on assessed conventional weapon transfers by the ATT member states resulted in a compromise. Thus, the final ATT states: 'Each State Party, pursuant to its national laws, shall provide its national control list to the Secretariat, which shall make it available to other States Parties. States Parties are encouraged to make their control lists publicly available' (Article 5§4; United Nations General Assembly 2013a).

## Issue 2: Upgrading national regulatory systems?

Prior to the ATT, many states already had national regulatory rules in place for arms controls and trade-related matters. Yet, these systems varied widely in scope and depth. The African Group pointed out that this was a problem that needed to be addressed in the negotiations: 'The African Group wishes to reiterate its call for an equitable ATT – one which takes into account, specific regional dynamics in line with the principles of the UN Charter on the sovereign equality among nations and the right of every nation to legitimate self-defense. This is so in view of the fact that while many States, including majority of arms producing States, may have in place certain regulatory framework, there is no consensus yet on the exact' (African Group 2011).

The EU was also active in this regard. It suggested a solution: for countries that already have control systems in place, the 'ATT would imply the obligation to raise and improve, as needed, relevant legislative and administrative measures to match the common international standards' (European Union 2010e). This pragmatic argument was made in the formal negotiations as well as during informal lobbying and resonated well as it minimised the adaptation costs for affected states (H6c, H6e). Accordingly, several states also emphasised the importance of effective national control systems that adopt the regulatory standards as outlined in the ATT (Nicaragua 2012). Thus, none of the states opposed the inclusion of paragraphs on the role of national control systems for the ATT implementation in the end. In line with the EU's suggestion, the ATT Article 5§2 states that 'each State Party shall establish and maintain a national control system, including a national control list, in order to implement the provisions of this Treaty' and §5 explicates, 'Each State Party shall take measures necessary to implement the provisions of this Treaty and shall designate competent national authorities in order to have an effective and transparent national control system regulating the transfer of conventional arms covered under Article 2 (1) and of items covered under Article 3 and Article 4' (United Nations General Assembly 2013a).

Thus, in emphasising the strong and important role of national regulatory systems, the EU was successful. At the same time, the African Group's imprint is not clearly visible in the final ATT, as they did not constructively propose specific formulations of how to deal with the identified problem of a multitude of different national pre-existing regulatory systems.

### 6.2.7 Article 6: Prohibitions

This rather short Article represents one of the most important parts of the Treaty: it forbids the transfer of conventional weapons if the state party would thereby violate arms embargoes of the Security Council, other treaties, or even if a state is aware of the fact that those arms would be used to 'commit genocide, crimes against humanity, or certain war crimes' (Geneva Academy 2013).[48] Article 6§3 determines that state parties have to deny the authorisation of a proposed transfer if they have knowledge that the conventional arms would be used to 'commit genocide, crimes against humanity, or certain war crimes' (ATT Article 6§3).

Several regional actors took the floor concerning prohibitions in order to clarify the role of the states and in order to promote specific prohibitions.

*Issue 1: Role of states*

The African Group demanded that an ATT should require the explicit authorisation of all transfers of conventional weapons and SALWS by 'competent government authorities of the importing State, as well as a clear prohibition of transfers to unauthorised non-State actors' (African Group 2010). This was echoed by several delegates emphasising that states (as opposed to international actors or independent regulatory agencies) are responsible for the prohibition of conventional arms transfer (e.g. Australia 2011a, Egypt 2011a). Of the other ROs, PIF also strongly supported the notion of state responsibility and explained, 'Members of the Forum believe that all States involved in the transfer of arms have responsibilities to ensure that arms transfers are responsible and transparent. However, States' obligations should depend on their respective role in the transfer chain' (Pacific Islands Forum 2012). None of the other actors made counterarguments in the ATT negotiations, and the parties, therefore, agreed that it is the states that need to be responsible for prohibitions of the arms trade.

### Issue 2: Specific prohibitions

CARICOM advanced the debate further by pushing for the inclusion of 'objective and non-discriminatory criteria governing the transfer of conventional weapons. In this regard, CARICOM is of the view that state parties to the Treaty in assessing whether or not to transfer arms, should *not* permit such transfers if there is a risk that they would be in *violation of international human rights law; international humanitarian law; the Charter of the UN; and international or regional treaties* to which the State Party is bound. Transfers should also *not* be permitted if they are likely to be *diverted to assist in fueling transnational organised crime, armed conflict or armed violence*' (CARICOM 2012c, emphasis added by the authors). Largely because CARICOM's argument referred to already agreed-upon treaties, rules and norms, it resonated well with prior beliefs and normative commitments of third parties and locked them further into support. Most states were on the same page and agreed that conventional weapon transfers need to be prohibited for the reasons included in the final version of the ATT (e.g. Australia 2011a, Italy 2012, New Zealand 2010, Uruguay 2010).[49] While only a few others preferred a more precise language, but did not oppose the ATT's Article 6 as such due to the lock-in strategy used (H6d).[50] Hence, according to Article 6§1–3, transfers of conventional weapons are prohibited if they would violate Chapter VII of the UN Security Council, the Charter of the United Nations (in particular concerning arms embargoes), international obligations under international agreements relating to international transfer of, or illicit trafficking in, conventional arms, or, if transfers would facilitate committing genocide or crimes against humanity or war crimes, especially those that breach the 1949 Geneva Conventions.

While other actors were also pushing for the same inclusions into the article on what the ATT should prohibit, CARICOM contributed to silencing the opposition due to the references made to already agreed-upon treaties or institutions, such as the UN Charter, the 1949 Geneva Conventions or UN Security Council resolutions (H6d).

### 6.2.8 Article 7: Export and export assessment

While Article 6 specifies which conventional arms transfers are prohibited, Article 7 outlines the procedures and criteria that arms exporting states must follow if they want to sell arms to another state in instances where Article 6 does *not* already prohibit arms transfer. To this end, in the final version of the ATT, Article 7§1 specifies that the exporting state must undertake a risk assessment prior to an arms export that checks whether the arms export '(a) would contribute to or undermine peace and security; (b) could be used to: (i) commit or facilitate a serious violation of international humanitarian law; (ii) commit or facilitate a serious violation of international human rights law; (iii) commit or facilitate an act constituting an offence under international conventions or protocols relating to terrorism to which the exporting State is a Party; or (iv) commit or facilitate an act constituting an offence under international conventions or protocols relating to transnational organised crime to which the exporting State is a Party' (United Nations General Assembly 2013a: Article 7).

From early on, the UN members engaged in debates about which parameters states need to take into consideration, before authorising an arms export to another country (e.g. European Union 2011b). The parties agreed that it is necessary to specify in the ATT which criteria states need to check before allowing arms exports (ECOWAS 2010). The main points of contestations were which parameters should apply in the risk assessment, how specific the parameters need to be formulated and which consequences a negative risk assessment should have on the ability of a state to export arms. While ROs were active concerning the first issue, they remained silent regarding the other two.[51]

Regarding the first cleavage, ECOWAS was a proponent of clear-cut criteria. It suggested that states need to take into account:

Respect of States obligation under international law including obligations under the UN Charter, Security Council Resolutions such as those imposing arms embargoes and universally agreed principles of international humanitarian law . . ., the final user of the arms to prevent diversion and access of arms to non-authorized entities or groups, . . . the possible final use of the arms to prevent violations of IHL and human rights . . ., the consideration of the internal situation in the country of final destination to avoid a situation where arms transfer may aggravate existing tensions or help prolong armed conflicts . . ., and finally consideration of the regional peace and security situation in order to avert a situation where arms transfer may adversely affect regional security, endanger peace and contribute to regional instability. (ECOWAS 2010)

Many but not all of these highly specific provisions were taken up by other actors in the course of the negotiation process, largely because ECOWAS made compelling cause-effect-related arguments in their favour (Australia 2011a, CARICOM 2012a, Norway 2010).[52] Yet some states[53] and the Arab Group did not agree to the ECOWAS list. The Arab Group explained 'the criteria that have been proposed for the Treaty, the group is of the view that resorting to any specific *criteria as a basis for rejecting or accepting the transfer of arms and trade, must be based on conclusive indisputable decisions and resolutions adopted by relevant United Nations bodies dealing substantively with such criteria,* and should not be based on subjective criteria open to a wide range of variation and even dispute between countries in assessing the implementation of such criteria, and allowing room for arms-producing and exporting States to translate and interpret, according to their independent national perspectives, the extent to which other countries respect these criteria, in such a way that will definitely not compatible to the stated aim of the proposed treaty' (Arab Group 2011a, emphasis added by the authors). Thus, compared to the ECOWAS proposal on export-related risk assessment, the Arab Group preferred less-demanding export rules.

The two sides needed to agree on a common text since an ATT without rules on how to authorise exports of conventional arms would have been meaningless. Accordingly, compromise dynamics evolved. A diplomat observed: 'When the actual negotiations on the ATT started, it was almost from the beginning quite clear to us that because of the consensus rule, you were likely to get something, you know, the sort of *lowest common denominator* effect that consensus results in. And that in all probability the export or the international export control system created by the ATT would in all probability be less stringent or strict than our own export control system. And as it is that is exactly the way it turned out' (interview#207, 20-05-15, emphasis added by the authors). Since bargaining took place while no party had significant advantages in bargaining leverage, all actors involved were only partially successful (H6b). For example, ECOWAS failed to get the reference of the 'internal situation in the country of final destination to avoid a situation where arms transfer may aggravate existing tensions or help prolong armed conflicts' and 'consideration of the final user of the arms to prevent diversion and access of arms to non-authorized entities or groups' included into the criteria for risk assessment in the final version of Article 6.

### 6.2.9  Article 8: Import

While Article 7 specifies the responsibilities of states that are willing to export arms to another state, the exporting state needs to make a risk assessment and only if this does not turn out negative can the exporting state sell its weapons to an importing state. In this context, Article 8 defines the role of the importing state in an arms trade. Article 8§1 prescribes that the importing state needs to provide the necessary information to the exporting state so that the latter can carry out the risk assessment required by Article 7, but it must do so only upon the request of the exporter.

*Issue 1: Arms trade between states only*

The details of arms trade were of high importance to many of the regional actors and the activity level on this topic was high in the negotiations (H8). One of the main points discussed was that arms trade should take place between states, not between a state and non-state actors in a third country. In this respect, ECOWAS proposed that the transfer of arms is a 'State to State activity' and argued that the ATT should, therefore, exclude the transfer of arms to any non-state actors without the authorisation of the importing country (ECOWAS 2010). This point was hardly contested as almost all actors agreed (Bangladesh 2011a, Brazil 2010). While the final Treaty does not include a reference to non-state actors at all, the articles on export and import of arms specify that arms trade be regarded as an activity that takes place between an exporting country and an importing country.

*Issue 2: Responsibilities and rights of importing states*

On the one end of the spectrum, the African Group emphasised the rights of importing states and flagged that it should be up to the importing state to authorise transfers of conventional weapons (African Group 2010, 2011). Moreover, the African Group argued that an importing state should 'obtain its required transfers' if they comply with the parameters and criteria specified in the ATT (African Group 2012).

On the other end of the spectrum, states primarily focused on the obligations and not on the rights of importers and contended that importers should be held responsible for arms trade (e.g. Australia 2010a). The EU also put emphasis on the obligations of arms-importing states. Accordingly, state parties should be 'required to put in place adequate legislative and administrative measures that would allow them, where necessary, to monitor and control these types of transfers of arms, and to ensure compliance with relevant legally binding international obligations' (European Union 2011c). These measures should be decided at the 'national level' (European Union 2011c). In this vein, the EU favoured an ATT in which the arms importers would also be held responsible for preventing illicit arms trade once an import in their country has been finalised. In the same way, CARICOM also preferred to place obligations for the prevention of illicit arms trade on both exporters and importers (CARICOM 2011d). Similarly, a regional coalition of Latin American and Caribbean countries (Peru speaking on behalf of the Bahamas, Belize, Chile, Colombia, El Salvador, Guatemala, Jamaica, Mexico, Peru, Trinidad and Tobago, and Uruguay) voiced a common position: 'We also believe that the ATT cannot be understood as an exporters' agreement only. It must reflect an equitable balance of rights and obligations for all States

Parties. The implementation of the Treaty must address the needs of both exporters and importers' (Bahamas et al. 2013).

Yet, these normative fairness arguments were not compelling (H6c) since PIF and some states adopted a different policy frame. They were primarily concerned that the ATT would place too many responsibilities on importing states, which might not be feasible for states with limited government capacities (Brazil 2011c, Costa Rica 2011a, DPRK 2012, Indonesia 2013, Pacific Islands Forum 2012; also interview#206, 13-05-15). Acknowledging capacity differences in general, and capacity limitations of developing states in particular as a problem, some states proposed that 'an effective Arms Trade Treaty would require all States to have appropriate export and import control systems in place. In this context, promoting capacity building is a major task to be addressed' (Brazil 2012).[54] Given the hesitation among many actors to extensively engage in capacity-building via resource reallocation and redistribution of financial means via a fund within the ATT (see discussion on international assistance in this chapter), arguments lending themselves to capacity-sensitive negotiation outcomes resonated well in the ATT negotiations (H6c).

As a result, the ATT's architecture places the overwhelming responsibility for risk assessment checks on the exporting state (Article 7), while the importing state only needs to provide information relevant to risk assessment upon request of the exporting state (Article 8§1). In addition, the importing state has no strong legal obligation to set up a domestic regulatory regime to manage the arms that it imports. Article 8§2 explicates that the 'importing State Party shall take measures that will allow it to regulate, *where necessary*, imports under its jurisdiction of conventional arms covered under Article 2 §1. Such measures *may include import systems*' (United Nations General Assembly 2013a, emphasis added by the authors).

### 6.2.10  Article 9: Transit or trans-shipment

Since it regulates the trade of arms across borders, the transit and trans-shipment of arms is an important element of the ATT. According to Article 9, 'Each State Party shall take appropriate measures to regulate, where necessary and feasible, the transit or trans-shipment under its jurisdiction of conventional arms covered under Article 2§1 through its territory in accordance with relevant international law' (United Nations General Assembly 2013a).

Naturally, discussions on transit and trans-shipment of arms focused on the obligations of the state, through whose territory an arms trade between the initial exporter and the final importer passes. This issue was crucial for PIF and CARICOM, who swiftly formulated their respective regional positions and engaged in coalition-building on that basis (H6f, H8).[55] Afterwards, PIF members became active and argued that 'responsibilities must be carefully tailored so as to avoid the creation of obligations which are unduly onerous on transit and trans-shipment States – particularly Small Island Developing States – and which would, in any event, be likely to prove beyond their capacity to implement' (Pacific Islands Forum 2012). PIF and CARICOM were not the only actors pushing for a capacity-sensitive solution to responsibilities of states affected by trans-shipments. Several others also emphasised this point from the start,[56] whereas hardly any countries explicitly demanded responsibilities be put on transit states.

A notable exception represented the P5, consisting of China, France, Russian Federation, the United Kingdom and the United States. They claimed that an 'effective ATT should not hinder the legitimate arms trade or the legitimate right to self-defense under the UN Charter. It should help curb the illicit trafficking in conventional weapons that undermines peace, security and prosperity. It should create a shared responsibility in the international transfer of conventional arms between all states, be they exporters, importers, transit or trans-shipment states' (Common position of P5 2013). Yet the P5 did not win sufficient support for their position on transit and trans-shipment, not in the least since they did not invest much effort in actively negotiating with respect to this issue and did not use a broad array of negotiation strategies.

By contrast, CARICOM and especially the PIF lobbied extensively various venues by contacting third-party states to which they had ties (H6e). They also argued that capacity limitations of (developing) states needed to be taken into account as they affected the effectiveness of ATT rules and that, with respect to transit and trans-shipment, the ATT should not place unrealistic demands on affected states (interviews #211, 29-07-15, #206, 13-05-15). These arguments resonated well with other states (H6c), not in the least because many of the richer states did not approve of extensive capacity-building measures and associated retribution of resources within the ATT (see debate on international assistance in this chapter).

Thus, similar to the import issue, in the course of negotiations the actors agreed that capacity limitations of countries affected by trans-shipments might prevent them from thorough controls, and therefore opted for a rather undemanding formulation in the final ATT text (United Nations General Assembly 2013a).

### 6.2.11 Article 11: Diversion

To reach the goals of the ATT (United Nations General Assembly 2013a: Article 1), it is important to prevent diversion, defined as the process by which arms move from the legal market to the illegal market. Since diversion is an integral element of the illicit arms trade, Article 11 is solely devoted to this issue. It starts with: 'Each State Party involved in the transfer of conventional arms covered under Article 2§1 shall take measures to prevent their diversion' (Article 11§1). The measures states need to take when exporting and importing conventional arms are further specified in Article 11 §2–6.

## Issue 1: Covering 'diversion' within the ATT

Diversion was a highly salient topic for many actors, rich and poor, as it has important consequences for the effectiveness of the ATT and the ability to reach the Treaty's goals and objectives (interview#208, 20-05-15). A regional coalition of Latin American and Caribbean States[57] expressed that 'one of the primary objectives of an ATT must be preventing arms reaching the illicit market' (Argentina et al. 2010). A diplomat explained: 'Working on diversion was of the utmost importance: You could have the best systems for licensing but if at the end of the day those transfers are broken in the middle of the sea or wherever and those weapons go to end up where not intended to, then your export system doesn't work' (interview#206, 13-05-15). The United States also made this point and even regarded it as 'the second major goal' (USA 2013a).

Especially in areas in which illicit arms trade has strong negative consequences for the development and safety of the country and its population, regional group members had similar problems and thus also similar positions. CARICOM, Pacific Small Island Developing States, and the Latin American and Caribbean countries were all in favour of explicitly including the issue of diversion into the ATT text (CARICOM 2011g, Pacific Small Island Developing States 2011). Yet, only CARICOM was vocal in pushing their position. To this end CARICOM made the following factual argument: 'As a region which does not manufacture, export or re-export weapons, or import[s] them on a large scale, the diversion of weapons from legitimate to illicit purposes is a key feature of the continued proliferation of illegal arms in our societies. CARICOM Member States wish to express our full support for the inclusion of this criterion in the Chairman's working paper' (CARICOM 2011g) and explained that 'For us, the conclusion of an Arms Trade Treaty ("ATT") is a matter of priority. Our region has witnessed the deleterious effects of the illicit trade in small arms and light weapons which is due to the diversion of these weapons from the legal market to the illicit market' (CARICOM 2011f).[58] In addition to making arguments (H6c) CARICOM actively and extensively lobbied opponents, such as Russia, in order to ensure their support (H6e) (Depauw 2012): 'We were able to have bilaterals with big players like Russia, the United States . . ., China' (interview#208, 20-05-15, similar interview#206, 13-05-15).[59]

The fact that diversion became part of the ATT is due to a combination of CARICOM's persistence, the support of several states from the start and the fact that negotiators from individual countries, such as Mexico, managed to bring even initially sceptical states on board as well (interview#211, 29-07-15). Finally, 'The text was accepted by everyone. At the end of the day everybody was okay with it' (interview#206, 13-05-15). This was a substantive success for those actors who were very vocal and engaged in negotiation strategies to increase support and circumvent opposition.[60]

The EU and CSTO were also in favour of including diversion (European Union 2012b).[61] However, the EU and CSTO did not negotiate with full force (H6a). As a consequence, the incorporation of diversion into the ATT was not due to the negotiation activities of the EU or CSTO.

*Issue 2: State capacities and diversion*

Already in the first PrepCom, PIF was active with respect to countries' capacity limitations and argued that they should be addressed by the ATT in order to optimise the effectiveness of its provisions: 'The biggest problem for Island States in the Pacific is that arms proliferation is often locally sourced through illicit home production or diversion from official stocks. In this regard, a key regional priority is to improve legal and enforcement capacity for domestic weapons control' (Pacific Island Countries 2010). This point was compelling – especially to actors with similar problems – and taken up subsequently by the Pacific Small Island Developing States (PSIDS) (Pacific Small Island Developing States 2011). However, apart from Sweden and Canada (Canada 2012),[62] no other state explicitly supported the crucial role of state capacities concerning diversion. Accordingly, the issue of capacity-building in order to enable all states to set up and run effective domestic, national control systems has not been included in Article 11. Instead, it was moved into a separate article, namely Article 16 on international assistance (discussed in detail later in this chapter). Consequently, concerning the diversion Article, neither the PIF nor the PSIDS were successful.

## 6.2.12 Article 12: Record keeping

Article 12 forms part of the implementation provisions of the ATT according to which states should keep a record of their authorised arms exports, their conducted imports, as well as the transfers and trans-shipments through their territories. How exactly states keep records is up to them. The ATT only prescribes that the records should include 'the quantity, value, model/ type, authorised international transfers of conventional arms covered under

Article 2 (1), conventional arms actually transferred, details of exporting State(s), importing State(s), transit and trans-shipment State(s), and end users, as appropriate' (ATT Article 12§3) and that states need to keep them for a period of ten years (§4).

One of the first actors mentioning record keeping as an important part of the ATT implementation was the EU. Already during the first PrepCom, it stated: 'As far as the implementation and application of the Treaty is concerned, the EU believes that we should not only refer to national legislation and controls, but rather to the obligation for each State Party to establish the legal provisions and the administrative structure needed to control all transactions of conventional arms. Such a system should include an authorisation system and a record keeping mechanism for proposed transfers of conventional military equipment. The entirety of these provisions would provide for the enforcement of the Treaty at national level' (European Union 2010b, reiterated in a similar fashion on European Union 2011d). Compared to the final ATT text, the EU's suggestion was only partially incorporated. Article 12 was not formulated in a demanding manner, since it does not place any obligation upon the states to create national control systems that record the ATT-related activities of a state. This is also due to opposing proposals, such as from Brazil, which were softer in nature and less costly to all states – especially the ones with administrative and government capacity shortcomings.[63] Thus, Brazil's idea fitted better with already agreed-upon norms and rules and was therefore taken up by many others, including India,[64] Israel (which had concerns with record keeping violating confidentiality of arms trades),[65] and Zimbabwe (which regarded detailed record keeping as endangering national security),[66] and shaped the final version of Article 12.

### 6.2.13  Article 13: Reporting

Article 13 details that each state party has to deliver a report to the Secretariat stating which measures have been undertaken to implement the Treaty, within one year, as well as if the measures have changed or have been extended. These reports will be distributed to other state parties by the secretariat. Furthermore, the states are encouraged to share their experiences with other parties. Moreover, every ATT member state has to deliver annual reports on the exports or imports of conventional arms.

*Issue 1: Annual reporting requirement*

In the negotiations on the reporting requirements, there was some controversy about the extent to which states need to create reporting systems in order to comply with the ATT. On the one hand, CARICOM[67] and the African Group[68] highlighted that they are in favour of a reporting requirement in principle, but opted for a light reporting obligation rather than a comprehensive duty since the former would be less capacity-intensive than the latter. On the other hand, the EU suggested that a comprehensive reporting system be created and linked this to the objective to increase 'transparency and accountability in the international arms trade' (European Union 2011d).[69] While CARICOM and the African Group initially made functional arguments with respect to domestic bottlenecks of administrative capacities (H6c) (interview#208, 20-05-15), the EU made a functional argument with respect to the effectiveness of the ATT (H6c). A series of countries were not persuaded by either side. States such as Vietnam, Iran, the Republic of Korea (Republic of Korea 2012) or Israel objected to mandatory reporting in general on the grounds of national security[70] and stressed that the 'UNCAR – the Conventional Arms Reporting System – it's a voluntary system' (interview#210, 29-07-15). Other states emphasised that there is not necessarily a trade-off between transparent reporting and national security.[71]

Yet others, most notably South Africa and New Zealand, were responsive to the EU and preferred regular reporting, but were also sensitive to the capacity-limitation concerns: 'As far as reporting on arms transfers is concerned, the submission of such reports should be regular, but in a format that is uncomplicated and not burdensome' (South Africa 2012, similar New Zealand 2012). Next, to the EU, the PIF also supported the inclusion of a demanding reporting system (Pacific Island Countries 2010 and Pacific Islands Forum 2012), but unlike the EU, the PIF did not actively use negotiation strategies in order to seek support for its stance. Overall, the EU's point was more forceful than arguments of sceptics. Its proposal of an annual reporting requirement was also reiterated by South Africa, Guatemala, Papua New Guinea, New Zealand and Kazakhstan as well as Nepal, Namibia and Montenegro.[72] The latter three linked strong reporting to an 'adequate provision of international assistance for national capacity building for effective implementation of the Treaty' (Nepal 2012).[73]

Thus, bargaining dynamics evolved (H6b). Based on statements that point to capacity limitations, less developed states stressed that international assistance would be a welcome means to remedy capacity shortages that would prevent them from effective implementation of the ATT (interview#208, 20-05-15, also Philippines [Philippines 2012], Nepal [Nepal 2012], Namibia [Namibia 2012], Montenegro [Montenegro 2012]).

In order to accommodate these concerns whilst sticking to the EU's proposal for a demanding reporting mechanism, a package deal was proposed (interview#210, 29-07-15).[74] Thus, a strong reporting mechanism was created (in Article 13), but at the same time, the states created a new Article (16) on international assistance.[75] This compromise was acceptable to the poorer states and the final text of Article 13§3 places an obligation on all ATT member states to submit an annual report to the Secretariat in which the states list all authorised or actual exports and imports of conventional arms, and the Secretariat passes the reports on to all ATT member states.

### 6.2.14 Article 15: International cooperation

Article 15 stipulates the principles according to which states should cooperate when implementing the Treaty, such as exchanging and sharing information regarding the implementation and application of the Treaty and consulting on 'matters of mutual interest', as well as sharing 'experience and information on lessons learned in relation to any aspect of this Treaty' (ATT Article 15).

As early as the first PrepCom in 2010 the EU called for an article dedicated to international cooperation and made concrete suggestions. The EU framed the topic as being of a 'two-fold nature': cooperation among the state parties and the creation of transparency and monitoring at the international level by reports on their arms transfers. This process should be supported by an 'international structure within the UN . . . to keeps records and support the states parties in the implementation of the Treaty' (European Union 2010c). This resonated well with other actors in the ATT negotiations. For example, ECOWAS demanded that the 'ATT should provide for international cooperation, more specifically possible assistance to requesting member States by countries in position to do so but more importantly exchange of information on arms transfer' (ECOWAS 2010). Similarly, South Africa also backed the EU's proposal (interview#207, 20-05-15).

On this basis, the EU further suggested that state parties should assist each other to ensure that 'their national systems and international controls comply with the requirements of the Treaty' (European Union 2010c). More specifically, international cooperation should cover 'legislative assistance, institution-building; assistance in the development of necessary administrative measures, as well as technical assistance for the development of appropriate expertise in all national bodies involved in the transfer control system' (European Union 2010a). During the course of negotiations, there were many voices requesting the inclusion of provisions on assistance into the ATT (African Group 2010, Brazil 2010, CARICOM 2010b, East African Community 2011, ECOWAS 2010, Iran 2010, Pacific Island Countries 2010). Thus, the issue was moved into a separate Article, namely Article 16.

### 6.2.15 Article 16: International assistance

Financial and other support was frequently debated in the ATT negotiations. Article 13 on reporting and Article 15 on international cooperation were two of the instances where assistance played a role in the discussion. Hence, the topic was put into a separate article (Article 16), which describes how states may seek or offer international assistance in order to implement the ATT and comply with its monitoring and reporting requirements.

Regional actors had issues at stake in three respects. First, they were active concerning the incorporation of international assistance into the Treaty. Second, ROs participated in the discussions about the types of assistance to incorporate into the ATT. Third, some actors also pushed the topic of victim's assistance.

### *Issue 1: Incorporation of international assistance into the ATT*

ECOWAS members placed high importance on 'international assistance', formulated a regional position according to which the ATT should support states that request assistance (ECOWAS 2010) and voiced this point repeatedly during the course of negotiations. Myanmar, speaking on behalf of ASEAN, also stressed that cooperation and assistance are especially important for states that would like to implement the provisions of the Treaty, 'but lack sufficient capacity to do so' (ASEAN 2012). CARICOM members made a more specific suggestion and proposed that 'the Treaty should contain provisions on international cooperation and assistance, particularly as it relates to capacity-building and the transfer of technology to strengthen the national capacities of developing States to effectively implement the Treaty' (CARICOM 2010b). Furthermore, Australia stated on behalf of the Pacific Island Countries (a regional actor that comprises forty small countries in the Pacific), 'We recognise, too, the importance of the ATT providing for international cooperation and assistance to developing States needing help to implement their treaty obligations. We believe that States in a position to do so should strive to provide that assistance bilaterally or multilaterally to ensure that Pacific Island Countries, too, can play their part in support of an Arms Trade Treaty' (Pacific Island Countries 2010). These demands were also echoed by several individuals, mostly developing states, such as Bangladesh, the Philippines, Fiji, Nigeria, Mongolia and Saint Lucia (Bangladesh 2011b, Fiji 2011, Mongolia 2010, Nigeria 2011, Philippines 2011, Saint Lucia 2011).[76] Apart from the bargaining leading to a package deal (c.f. discussion on Article 13), these actors used a variety of negotiation strategies in order to get their point across. CARICOM made a causal argument (H6c), linking assistance to an improved implementation performance of developing states (CARICOM 2010b).[77] Other actors, notably the Pacific Island Countries, engaged in bargaining (H6b), hinting towards the inability of poor states to fully implement the ATT if they lack the capacities to do so and are not supported through capacity-building measures by more developed states (Pacific Island Countries 2010). Bangladesh used moral arguments in reminding 'donor countries of their commitments and responsibilities towards development assistance' (H6c) (Bangladesh 2011b). All of these strategies supported the finalisation of the emerging package deal.

Accordingly, richer actors also opted for including provisions on assistance into the ATT. For example, the EU regarded assistance as being of tremendous importance for the implementation of the ATT (European Union 2010b) and supported the possibility for state parties to receive help in the national implementation of the ATT (European Union 2011a).[78] In addition, several states expressed their support for developing countries. Iran, for example, deemed it appropriate to allocate one of the ATT articles to assistance to developing countries, including capacity-building, technical and financial assistance, and training (Iran 2010).

## Issue 2: Types of assistance

Besides expressing its general support for the inclusion of international cooperation in the ATT and the importance of assistance, several actors made constructive proposals on how to strengthen the position of developing states. The African Group asked for training and building of institutional and human resources in developing states (African Group 2011). CARICOM requested help in capacity building, such as in the drafting of domestic legislation for state parties that need assistance in the implementation process (CARICOM 2012c). PIF suggested the creation of an 'Implementation Support Unit' in order to work as a 'clearing house for implementation assistance, matching needs with available resources and ensuring coordination in the provision of technical assistance' (Pacific Islands Forum 2012).

Out of these three proposals, CARICOM's idea was incorporated into the final ATT, as Article 16§1 explicitly mentions 'legal or legislative assistance'. Due to the high congruity of CARICOM's proposal both with the general opinion that capacity-building is important to achieve an effective ATT, and with the general hesitation to redistribute resources between countries to this end, CARICOM achieved substantive success in making causal arguments (H6c) about how capacities would foster the effectiveness of the ATT in practice (CARICOM 2012c). This resonated well within the negotiations, especially since the states had already agreed to express their support of the principle of international cooperation and assistance in an entire Article. The two proposals by the African Group and the PIF are not as closely reflected in the final text of the ATT, as they are more demanding regarding the resource investments states would need to undertake. Thus, amongst the countries that preferred 'resource-sensitive' negotiation outcomes, such as India, South Africa, the United States and many of the EU member states, the proposals of the PIF and the African Group did not resonate as good as CARICOM's suggestion. Yet, neither point was fully disregarded. Thus §1 also refers to technical assistance and §2, while not creating an implementation support unit as proposed by PIF, lists a series of pathways through which support can be requested and provided, including 'United Nations, international, regional, subregional or national organisations, non-governmental organisations, or on a bilateral basis' (United Nations General Assembly 2013a: Article 16§2).

### *Issue 3: Victims' assistance*

Under discussion was also a paragraph dedicated to victims' assistance. The very first actor bringing up this issue was Norway: 'Norway would also like to raise the question of assistance to persons falling victims to armed violence resulting from illicit and poorly regulated arms trade. An ATT could address the rights of victims of such violence, including their rights to adequate care and rehabilitation, as well as their social and economic inclusion' (Norway 2010).

Of the regional actors, the most prominent voice with respect to the inclusion of victim's assistance was the EAC. It argued that: 'People die as a result of an arms trade poorly regulated' and that 'including this issue of assistance to the victims, we will be giving a human dimension to the future ATT' (East African Community 2011). The EAC's causal and moral arguments resonated well with a series of other states, which also started to call for victim's assistance, such as Burundi (Burundi 2011), Ghana (Ghana 2012), Malawi (Malawi 2011) and the Philippines (Philippines 2011). However, the EAC did not manage to talk developed countries into supporting its stance in the ATT negotiations (H6c). This is largely due to the very active engagement by adversaries, which also used a broad array of argumentative strategies.

Next, to Israel, Thailand and Costa Rica (Costa Rica 2011b, Israel 2011a, Thailand 2011), the EU was the most vocal opponent of the inclusion of victim's assistance in the ATT. They argued that the ATT is not the appropriate arena in which victims of armed violence and especially of violence related to the illicit trade of arms should be compensated or supported: 'An Arms Trade Treaty is not meant to be an international disarmament instrument comparable to those that ban entire categories of weapons and include provisions on victim assistance. Whilst the EU agrees that an ATT should have a positive impact in reducing human suffering and armed violence, we do not consider appropriate to envisage specific provisions on victim assistance in the articles of the Treaty. The EU is concerned by the issue of human suffering and victim assistance and remains ready to engage in consultations in more appropriate UN fora' (European Union 2011a).[79] This argumentative strategy was effective and silenced the debate in this regard (H6c). It resonated with actors who, like ECOWAS, regarded the ATT as 'a treaty to prevent . . . "human suffering" that can result from the uncontrolled circulation of arms' (interview#209, 17-07-15) and framed the issue of arms control not as an economic, but a humanitarian necessity (interview#209, 1707-15). Thus, the actors reaffirmed that the ATT's foremost purpose should be the prevention of the illicit trade of conventional weapons and the Treaty needs to achieve this aim as much as possible. Against this background, the states agreed that related, relevant topics, such as humanitarian support or victim's assistance, would better be dealt with in a separate negotiation arena and a separate treaty, as this would allow the states to concentrate on the topics most closely linked to illicit trade of conventional weapons in the ATT negotiations.[80]

### 6.2.16 Article 19: Dispute settlement

Article 19 regulates how the member states should settle potential conflicts. The dispute settlement mechanism in the ATT reflects a low level of centralisation and legalisation as it is based on mutual consent of all affected parties and rests on state–state consultations (Abbott et al. 2000). Furthermore, the access to dispute settlement is considerably limited as it is tailored to affected states only and the procedure can be started only if affected parties consent. This places states in control of dynamics and outcomes of dispute settlement, thereby limiting the effectiveness of the instrument in cases of severe conflicts.

Already in 2010, the EU argued that the ATT should include a compliance mechanism, albeit a decentralised one, in which problems are addressed by a state-based consultation mechanism: 'In the view of the EU, the monitoring, verification and compliance mechanism of the Treaty should be based on a consultation mechanism among States Party. Such a mechanism would allow comparing the actual implementation of the Treaty and interpretation of its parameters, thus leading to a progressive convergence of national practices. This mechanism would assist States Party in addressing possible concerns' (European Union 2010b).[81]

By contrast, CARICOM opted for a third-party-based dispute settlement mechanism, which would reflect a higher level of legalisation than the EU proposal: 'A dispute settlement regime for the purpose of addressing differences concerning the interpretation or application of the provisions of the Treaty would also be useful. This should also include mechanisms such as conciliation and mediation' (CARICOM 2010b). Furthermore, CARICOM argued that an independent secretariat, 'equipped with appropriate dispute resolution mechanisms', might fulfil the role of the mentioned third party (CARICOM 2011g).

However, CARICOM's arguments failed to be effective. Opposition to a centralised dispute settlement system was strong, as important P5 states 'were not interested in a treaty that set up a new international or UN organisation to enforce it' (interview#204, 16-03-15). P5 members 'were in a strong negotiation position, as pretty much every state there recognised that if the Treaty could not be supported by the United States as the world's largest arms exporter, that it would be unlikely to attract the support of Russia, China, and other major exporters' (interview#204, 16-03-15). Due to the bargaining strategies of P5 states, states and regional actors on both sides of the divide looked for compromises in order to allow an ATT to pass with all large and powerful states on board.

The resulting compromise was a partial success of the EU. Its preference for a state-based consultation procedure was reflected in Article 19§1. It was also a partial success of P5 countries since a highly legalised dispute settlement mechanism in which the dynamics and outcomes would not be controlled by the affected states was prevented. At the same time, Article 19§2 also provided the option for third-party arbitration: 'States Parties may pursue, by mutual consent, arbitration to settle any dispute between them, regarding issues concerning the interpretation or application of this Treaty'. Once it was clear that a highly legalised compliance mechanism would not find the support of ATT members, CARICOM shifted its stance and also supported the outcome. 'We opted for a third party-based [dispute settlement mechanism, insertion by the authors] and if you look at the article, you'll find that it does not exclude third party accords, but it gives the states parties themselves the opportunity to resolve disputes and to include a third party as [a] last resort. So we were happy with that compromise' (interview#213, 16-12-15).

## 6.3 CONCLUSIONS

The ATT represents an important component of the global efforts to reduce the illicit arms trade and to establish common standards for the international trade of conventional weapons. It does so by promoting accountability and transparency by state parties concerning the transfer of conventional arms. In 2006 and again in 2008, UNGA member states passed a resolution calling for an ATT and established PrepComs that met between 2010 and 2012, leading to two CoPs in 2012 and 2013. The negotiation arenas are characterised by a combination of a high number of member states and a medium level of openness for ROs, which can only obtain formal observer status. Thus, the ATT negotiations should be more conducive to RO success than the least likely negotiation environment of the IWC.

In fact, the number of ROs that actively participated in the ATT negotiations was high (eleven different ROs), and the regional actors were relatively successful overall (c.f. table 6.1). First, ROs influenced the negotiation dynamics and managed to get support for their positions from third-party actors in twenty-eight instances, and in twenty-two at least partially. Second, ROs were also substantively successful; of the fifty-four number of times that ROs tried to exert influence on the content of the ATT text, they succeeded twenty-eight times and were in fifteen instances partially successful.

Thus, regional actors played a major role in the ATT negotiations and influenced the final outcome document in numerous ways. For instance, CARICOM was one of the strongest supporters for incorporating not only small arms and light weapons but also ammunition into the ATT's scope and was – together with ECOWAS – substantively successful in achieving the inclusion of bullets and other forms of ammunition. However, not all of the regional actors' endeavours to leave regional imprints on the ATT text were successful. For instance, the EU tried to insert a 'regional organisations clause' into the ATT preamble, according to which RO would have become signatories, and thus parties, to the ATT.

Although none of the ROs had formal voting rights and although security as 'high politics' is often regarded as the prerogative of states (e.g. Waltz 1959, 1979), the ATT negotiations received the attention of numerous regional actors and were highly regionalised.

The most active and successful regional actors were the CARICOM, ECOWAS and the EU. CARICOM pushed for fifteen different text changes and succeeded in eight instances fully and in three instances partially. The EU tried to change the text twelve times, six of which were successful. ECOWAS sought to influence the text of the ATT seven times, of which four were fully and two partially successful.

CARICOM and ECOWAS not only placed enormous importance on a treaty regulating arms trade, largely because their regions are extremely affected by illicit trade of arms and light weapons, but were also highly successful in shaping the content of the ATT (in line with H8). By contrast, for ROs such as ASEAN or MERCOSUR, the arms trade topic was less salient, and these regional actors participated less actively in the ATT negotiations.

Both CARICOM and ECOWAS had high levels of internal homogeneity, respectively, and had matching positions in many instances, while considerably larger African regional actors, such as the AU or the UNAG, were often unable to speak with one voice due to differences amongst their many member states. By contrast, due to the high internal homogeneity of member state preferences, CARICOM and ECOWAS were frequently able to develop of group positions in time for the very beginning of the

**Table 6.1.   The success of ROs in the ATT negotiations**

| Issue | Active ROs | Procedural Success – Proactive | Procedural Success – Reactive | Substantive Success – Proactive | Substantive Success – Reactive |
|---|---|---|---|---|---|
| **Preamble:** RIO clause | EU | Yes | No | No | No |
| | EAC | No | No | No | No |
| **Article 1:** Inclusion of proactive objective 'to combat' illicit trade | CARICOM | | | No | |
| | PIF | No | | No | |
| | CSTO | | | Partial | |
| **Article 2:** Small arms and light weapons | ECOWAS | Yes | Yes | Yes | Yes |
| | CARICOM | Yes | Yes | Yes | Yes |
| **Article 2:** 7+1+1 formula | CARICOM | Partially | Partially | Partially | Partially |
| | ECOWAS | Partially, supported CARICOM | Partially, supported CARICOM | Partially, supported CARICOM | Partially, supported CARICOM |
| | EAC | Partially, supported CARICOM | Partially, supported CARICOM | Partially, supported CARICOM | Partially, supported CARICOM |
| **Article 2:** Re-export, technical assistance, leases, gifts and loans related to conventional weapons | EU | No | | No | |
| **Article 2:** Transit controls | CARICOM | | Yes | | Yes |
| | PIF | | Yes | | Yes |
| **Article 3:** Inclusion of ammunition under scope | CARICOM | Yes | No | No | No |
| **Article 3:** Putting ammunition into the Treaty in a separate Article | ECOWAS | Yes | | Yes | |
| | CARICOM | Yes (but second-best choice) | | Yes (but second-best choice) | |

(Continued)

**Table 6.1.    Continued**

| Issue | Active ROs | Procedural Success – Proactive | Procedural Success – Reactive | Substantive Success – Proactive | Substantive Success – Reactive |
|---|---|---|---|---|---|
| **Article 4:** Parts and components | CARICOM | Partial | No | Partial | |
| | EU | Partial | No | Partial | |
| **Article 5:** Implementation: Central or decentralised database | EU | Partial | | No | |
| | ECOWAS | Partial | | No | |
| **Article 5:** Upgrading national regulatory systems | EU | Yes | | Yes | |
| | African Group | No | | No | |
| **Article 6:** States responsible for prohibitions | African Group | Yes, but no opposition | | Yes, but no opposition | |
| | PIF | Yes, but no opposition | | Yes, but no opposition | |
| **Article 6:** Prohibition of transfers under specific violations | CARICOM | Yes | | Yes | |
| **Article 7:** Which parameters should apply to risk assessment | ECOWAS | Partial | | Partial | |
| | Arab Group | Partial | | Partial | |
| **Article 8:** Arms trade between states only | ECOWAS | Yes, no opposition | | Yes, no opposition | |
| **Article 8:** Responsibilities and rights of the importing state | African Group | Partial | | Partial | |
| | EU | No | | No | |
| | CARICOM | No | | No | |
| | PIF | | | Yes | |

| Issue | Active ROs | Procedural Success – Proactive | Procedural Success – Reactive | Substantive Success – Proactive | Substantive Success – Reactive |
|---|---|---|---|---|---|
| **Article 9:** Transit or trans-shipment: Capacity-sensitive solution for affected states | PIF | Yes | Yes | | |
| | CARICOM | Yes | | Yes | |
| **Article 11:** Inclusion of diversion in ATT | CARICOM | Yes, but little opposition | | Yes, but little opposition | |
| **Article 11:** Strengthen state capacities concerning diversion | PIF | no | | No | |
| | Pacific Small Island Developing States | no | | No | |
| **Article 12:** Record Keeping | EU | No | No | No | No |
| **Article 13:** Annual reporting | CARICOM | Partial | Partial | No | No |
| | African Group | Partial | Partial | No | No |
| | EU | Yes | Partial | Yes | Yes |
| **Article 15:** International cooperation | EU | Yes | | Yes | |
| **Article 16:** Including international assistance | ECOWAS | Yes, but limited opposition | | Yes, but limited opposition | |
| | CARICOM | Yes, but limited opposition | | Yes, but limited opposition | |
| | ASEAN | Yes, but limited opposition | | Yes, but limited opposition | |
| | Pacific Island Countries | Yes, but limited opposition | | Yes, but limited opposition | |
| | EU | Yes, but limited opposition | | Yes, but limited opposition | |

(Continued)

**Table 6.1. Continued**

| Issue | Active ROs | Procedural Success – Proactive | Procedural Success – Reactive | Substantive Success – Proactive | Substantive Success – Reactive |
|---|---|---|---|---|---|
| **Article 16:** Types of international assistance | African Group | Partially | | Partially | |
| | CARICOM | Yes | | Yes | |
| | PIF | Partially | | Partially | |
| **Article 16:** Victim's assistance | EAC | Partially | | No | |
| | EU | Yes | | Yes | |
| **Article 19:** Extent of legalisation | EU | Yes | | Yes | |
| | CARICOM | Partially | | Partial | |

negotiations. Furthermore, the internal homogeneity of CARICOM and ECOWAS increased the prospects for success of their negotiation strategies and, consequently, their ability to shape the content of the final ATT (in line with H5b).

The ATT negotiations were characterised by a high number of issues and a high level of complexity on the negotiations table. The final version of the ATT includes twenty-eight Articles. ROs pushed for one or several different changes in seventeen of these (including the preamble). Overall, ROs tried to change the ATT text in fifty-three instances and succeeded in thirty-seven of them. In general and as expected by H6a, the more active ROs are, the better their prospects to influence dynamics and outcomes of international negotiations. Yet, not all negotiation strategies used were equally effective in all cases.

The higher the saliency of the topic under negotiation (H8), the more member states are willing to negotiate for their RO and engage in burden-sharing in this respect (H5a). For instance, the member states of CARICOM negotiated on behalf of the regional actor in fifteen instances in the formal negotiation settings of the CoPs, the PrepComs as well as informal meetings. Similarly, the member states of ECOWAS spoke in seven instances on behalf of the regional group in the ATT negotiations. By contrast, the member states of the EAC or CSTO only spoke, respectively, in three instances/one instance on behalf of the regional group.

Coordination amongst group members is essential to formulate common regional positions and act on this basis. Especially when the homogeneity of member states is high with respect to the international norm on the negotiation agenda, states have not only regional positions to articulate, but also incentives to speak on behalf of the group in order to increase their lever-age in international negotiations (H5b). Moreover, internal homogeneity is an important prerequisite for RO success; argumentative strategies are not persuasive vis-à-vis third parties, when the latter notice that not even all RO members are convinced by the reasons provided. Similarly, collective bargaining and tied-hands strategies are undermined, and bargaining power declines, if the group's collective voting power is delimited. Thus, CARI-COM succeeded in eleven instances, while the much larger and more hetero-geneous African group was successful three times.[82]

Regional actors applied bargaining strategies in some instances. Since the negotiations were complex and involved many issues, cross-issue compromises were possible, such as moving ammunition or assistance into separate Articles. The creation of Article 3 on ammunition was a compromise with CARICOM and ECOWAS, who pushed for the explicit inclusion of ammunition under Article 2 (scope). Similarly, the EU pushed for a robust reporting system (Article 13), which was opposed by the PIF and other ROs. Bargaining took place, but no side was strong enough to push its preferred text without getting support from the other side. Thus, compromise dynamics emerged and the actors created Article 16 on inter-national assistance, whilst opting for relatively strong national reporting systems (Article 13), which placed capacity demands on the member states. In line with H6b, bargaining was especially conducive to success, if the RO in question had high leverage, while bargaining failed to be effective in instances in which leverage was lacking and the compromises offered could not compensate the costs (e.g. with respect to the Article on imple-mentation, the EU tried to offer ex post capacity support in exchange for supporting strong implementation measures, but failed due to the perceived high sovereignty costs).

ROs frequently applied argumentative strategies. In line with hypoth-esis 6c, regional actors were successful when using reason-based strategies, especially if they could back up their claims by good technical, scientific, political, legal or moral reasons. For instance, with respect to the Article on international assistance, CARICOM, as well as ASEAN, ensured their substantive success through causal arguments on how capacities can increase the effectiveness of the ATT. By contrast, and also in line with the argu-ing hypothesis, regional actors were not successful in using this strategy when they failed to provide well-reasoned explanations for their claims. For instance, the EU pushed for the inclusion of the 'RIO clause' into the preamble, according to which regional organisations would become signa-tory parties of the ATT. Yet, it did not provide novel information or sound scientific studies to support their point that the RIO clause would strengthen the role of ROs in external security matters.

In the ATT negotiations, the lock-in strategy by which pre-agreed language from international law is used to push a similar but somewhat different issue in another arena (H6d) was not used very often. Only CARICOM applied this strategy; it tried to link the ATT to the UN Register of Conventional Arms in respect to the ATT scope. While it failed to use the UN Register as a means to entrap the states that were against a broad ATT scope as such, CARICOM managed to use the UN Register as the argumentative baseline for the minimal definition of arms covered by the ATT with respect to implementation (Article 5) and reporting (Article 13).

The most frequently adopted strategy does not take place in the formal negotiation arenas, but in more informal settings such as coffee breaks, lunches or bilateral settings, namely the lobbying of third-party states. As expected by H6e, lobbying is capacity-intensive and very small ROs whose members have small diplomatic delegations and limited financial capacities generally use this strategy less often and are subsequently less often successful in influencing negotiation dynamics and also in pushing for specific text changes. While the EU often engaged in informal lobbying in addition to negotiation contributions in the formal settings, it was nevertheless CARICOM who used lobbying strategies the most often and the most successfully. Since CARICOM is much smaller in terms of diplomatic resources than the EU, hypothesis 6e can be qualified. The more often regional actors engage in lobbying, the greater their overall chances of influencing dynamics and outcomes of international negotiations. However, the frequency of lobbying does depend not only on the available diplomatic resources, but also on the priority of the topic at hand for the respective ROs.

Although none of the ROs is large enough to hold sufficient member states votes for passing an ATT, coalition-building happened on an ad hoc basis in very few instances in the negotiation process. For example, PIF and CARICOM formed a coalition with respect to the transit and trans-shipment of arms and succeeded against the initial opposition of the P5 with their demand that capacity limitations of developing states need to be taken into account so that the ATT should not place unrealistic demands on affected states concerning transit and trans-shipment (H6f).

In short, this chapter illustrates that activity and success of regional actors are interlinked and the extent to which international negotiation outcomes are regionalised and reflect regional positions varies as well. For regional actors to be successful in influencing dynamics and outcomes of international negotiations, it is essential that their respective member states swiftly develop national positions on the basis of which their diplomats can engage in group coordination meetings, most often taking place in the city of the IO headquarters. Regional positions can be articulated only by the members (or by RO delegates if they have speaking rights) once the regional actor manages to develop a regional position. Since RO member states can negotiate on behalf of their regional group irrespective of the formal status of the regional actor in the international negotiation arena, the formal access of ROs to IOs is not a necessary precondition for regional actorness in international negotiations. Activity is important for success, but active ROs are not automatically successful. This chapter demonstrates that regional actors influenced the ATT negotiations. The more effective RO negotiation strategies are, the more successful regional actors are in shaping international negotiation dynamics and the content of international norms. For instance, argumentative strategies are most effective if the regional actors and their member states can rely on a high level of technical, scientific and legal expertise or good, moral claims regarding the issue on the negotiation table. Similarly, lobbying strategies work best if the regional actors have sufficient resources to approach other states in various venues and through multiple channels. Moreover, the better negotiation strategies of ROs are adjusted to the opposing states and the issue under negotiation, the greater the chances of negotiation success in IOs.

*Chapter 7*

# Case Study 3: The negotiations of the Rome Declaration on Nutrition

Since 1945, the Food and Agriculture Organization (FAO) is an international organisation under the United Nations umbrella.[1] The FAO deals with the fight against poverty and food insecurity, as well as the sustainable use of natural resources. The FAO also sheds light on world's nutrition problems and seeks to remedy them. To this end, the FAO, together with the World Health Organization (WHO), organised two conferences in 1992 and 2014. At the Second International Conference on Nutrition (ICN2), which took place at the FAO headquarters in Rome and also followed the procedural rules of the FAO, the delegates discussed food, agriculture and health topics and reviewed of the progress made since the first ICN in 1992 (ICN2 Secretariat 2014, FAO/WHO 2014a).

This chapter examines the activity and success of regional actors in the ICN2 negotiations leading to the 'Rome Declaration on Nutrition' in 2014.[2] These negotiations constitute a most likely instance for RO success, as the negotiation arena is large in size (the FAO and the WHO have the same 194 member states) and regional actors have strong formal roles. In the FAO, ROs can apply for full membership or can become observers for the Conference of the Parties (CoP). The EU is the only RO with full membership rights in the FAO and in the CoPs of the ICN negotiations. In addition, regional actors have a special status in the Joint Working Groups (JWGs), in which the negotiations on the 2014 Rome Declaration started. In the JWG, regional groups are the only actors, since states cannot negotiate on their own.

## 7.1 HISTORY OF THE ROME DECLARATION ON NUTRITION

The first International Conference on Nutrition (ICN1) was held in 1992 and unanimously adopted a 'World Declaration' and a 'Plan of Action for

Nutrition' (World Declaration 1992). Both addressed the aim of reducing starvation and famine, widespread chronic hunger, undernutrition and micronutrient deficiencies (World Declaration 1992). In addition, National Plans of Action for Nutrition (NPANs) were initiated. Those plans represent priorities and strategies of member states with the aim to fight hunger and malnutrition (FAO/WHO 2013).

Following ICN1, several attempts were made to address food and nutrition security, including the World Food Summits in 1996, 2002 and 2009, which did not remedy the problems (interviews#241, 05-09-16, #243, 07-09-16).

Nutrition and food safety were high on the agendas for many Heads of States and Governments: 'People felt that there was the need for another conference, a global conference . . . to talk about the nutrition issues because it has changed so much' (interview#241, 05-09-16). In comparison to ICN1, the 'nutritional architecture changed' (interview#241, 05-09-16) and challenges, which were not present in 1992, like increasing obesity, needed to be discussed: 'It's much more complex. It's not just undernutrition and hunger; you're talking about entire food systems. . . . So that means that you're not only looking at hunger, we're looking at undernutrition, so stunting, wasting, underweight, micronutrient deficiencies involved with obesity' (interview#241, 05-09-16).

Twenty-two years after the ICN1, a second International Conference on Nutrition (ICN2) was initiated by the FAO.[3] Similar to ICN1, the FAO and the WHO cooperated again in organising and hosting ICN2. While members from FAO and WHO participated, the ICN2 was based on FAO rules (ICN2 interviews#13, 06-05-16, #231, 11-05-16).[4]

### 7.1.1 The role of regional actors in the negotiations

According to Article 2 of the FAO Constitution, regional organisations (specified as 'regional economic integration organisation') are eligible to apply for membership in the FAO, but 'must be one constituted by sovereign States, a majority of which are Member Nations of the Organisation, and to which its Member States have transferred competence over a range of matters within the purview of the Organisation, including the authority to make decisions binding on its Member States in respect of those matters' (Food and Agricultural Organization 2013: Article 2).

The European Union (EU) became a full FAO member as a 'member organisation' on 26 November 1991 (EEAS 2016). Since then the EU has the same rights as FAO member states with respect to speaking in the FAO and voting on FAO policies. So far the EU is the only regional organisation (RO) with this specific status, which is described by the EU as an 'institutional breakthrough' (EEAS 2016), as it was the first time that the EU became a

Member as such of a UN institution (Food and Agricultural Organization 2014). The status is comparable to that of a Member Nation in a UN body. The status of Membership of the European Union required changes in the Basic texts of the Organisation, which were approved by the FAO Conference of 1991 (Food and Agriculture Organization 1991).[5]

In addition, regional actors can register as observers at the FAO in order to gain access to the negotiation arenas. 'Such observer may, without vote, speak and, upon the request of the Chairperson, participate in the discussions. They may circulate to the Conference, without abridgement, the views of the organisations which they represent' (FAO General Rules 2015: 17.2). Apart from that, the FAO Director-General can grant non-observer ROs access to specific negotiation arenas so that they turn into temporary observers. In the period 2008 and 2014, between ten and sixteen ROs became active observers in the FAO, depending on which FAO committee one looks at.

The negotiations for the 2014 Rome Declaration took place under the FAO's rules of procedure. In the JWG regional groups from all across the globe were the core actors. States are obliged to work through the FAO and WHO regional groups, and cannot participate on their own in the JWG.[6]

The regional groupings in the FAO are informal groups with the purpose of discussing certain topics among each other with the aim of finding common ground, presenting a uniform position in the different governing bodies of the FAO and simplifying the negotiation processes by appointing chief negotiators. The FAO member states from seven regional groups (for details c.f. appendix table A7.1): The African regional group (AFRICA) comprises forty-nine members, the forty-eight European states meet in the European Regional Group (ERG), the Latin American and Caribbean countries, in total thirty-three states, gather in the Latin America and Caribbean group (GRULAC), the twenty-one countries of the Near East discuss their position in the Near East regional group (NEEA), the Southwest Pacific group (SWP) is composed of sixteen states of that region, and the smallest regional group is North America (NOAM), only comprising Canada and the United States (FAO 2016).

In the WHO, there are six regional groups (c.f. table A7.1): with fifty-two members, the European Region (EUR) includes the largest number of states, followed by the African Region group (AFR) with forty-six members. The Region of the Americas (AMR) includes thirty-five states (and four associated members). The twenty-seven (and one associated member) countries of the Western Pacific Region try to find a common position in the Western Pacific Region group (WPR), whereas the twenty-three countries of the Eastern Mediterranean Region meet in the Eastern Mediterranean Region group (EMR). The smallest group is the South-East Asia Region (SEAR) with eleven member states.

### 7.1.2 The negotiation arenas of the Rome Declaration on Nutrition

The Rome Declaration on Nutrition was negotiated between August and November 2014 under FAO rules of procedure (FAO/WHO 2014a). As figure 7.1 illustrates, the negotiations took place in three different settings: The JWG, the Open-Ended Working Group (OEWG) and the CoP.

The early draft was discussed in the JWG in which regional groupings had a special status. The FAO and WHO regional groups were not only observers but the core participating actors. In fact based on Article 8 of the JWG's rules of procedures, states could not voice their respective national interests in the JWG, since only regional actors had the competence to articulate positions (FAO/WHO 2014c). Each regional group selected two representatives that spoke on their behalves in the JWG (interviews#237, 12-05-16, interview#225, 06-05-16). The regional groups negotiated the first draft of the Rome Declaration on Nutrition on the basis of consensus rule, 'which is more or less the scheme followed by FAO in most of their committees' (interview#225, 06-05-16). The negotiations were difficult, and the actors 'ended up meeting like a dozen times instead of three' (interview#225, 06-05-16).[7]

Following the JWG meetings, an OEWG was established, in order to complete the negotiation on the draft outcome document. The OEWG had its own rules of procedure. It was open to all FAO and WHO members including the EU as a member organisation with full rights. In the OEWG, regional actors that had already gained observer status within UN organisations had access and also speaking rights at the OEWG (Feistritzer and Martinez 2014).[8] In addition, states could continue to act on behalf of FAO and WHO regional groupings. In the OEWG, mainly the FAO members (states and the EU) voiced positions, while other regional organisations remained silent. In addition, member states spoke on behalf of GRULAC, AFRICA, AFR, NOAM, SWP and ERG. Only FAO members (194 states and the EU) had full formal

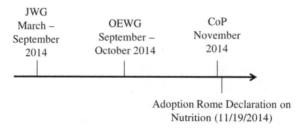

**Figure 7.1. The timeline of the negotiations of the 2014 Rome Declaration**

rights. Consensus rule applied for decisions on the outcome documents (Feistritzer and Martinez 2014). In October 2014, the OEWG finalised its draft and submitted it for the formal adoption to the Conference of the Parties of the ICN2, in which the EU was again operating as a full member.

The Conference of the Parties (CoP) took place in Rome at the FAO Headquarter from the 19th to 21st of November 2014. The general FAO rules of procedure applied, according to which 'plenary meetings of the Conference shall be open to attendance by all delegations, the representatives of participating international organisations, and such members of the staff of the Organisation as the Director-General may designate' (FAO General Rules 2015: rule 5). At the 2014 CoP, seven regional organisations – namely the African Union, Arab Maghreb Union, Eurasian Economic Community, Latin American Economic System, Nordic Council, Pacific Community and the Organisation for Economic Cooperation and Development – participated as observers. The observer may speak in negotiations upon the invitation by the Chairperson, only full members have voting rights (the member states and the EU) and decisions can be made by a simple majority.[9] While this casts a shadow of voting over the negotiations, the parties achieved consensus for the ICN1's outcome documents and wanted to pass the 2014 Rome Declaration without formally voting as well (International Institute for Sustainable Development 2014).

## 7.2 EMPIRICAL ANALYSIS: THE NEGOTIATION DYNAMICS ON THE TEXT OF THE ROME DECLARATION ON NUTRITION

How was the Rome Declaration negotiated, which regional actors were active and how did activity translate into success?

The Rome Declaration on Nutrition of 2014 is divided into three substantive parts and a declaratory one. The declaratory part includes three Articles. The first specifies the overall purpose, which is to 'address the multiple challenges of malnutrition in all its forms and identify opportunities for tackling them in the next decades' (Rome Declaration 2014, Article 1).[10] Article 2 reaffirms the aim to fight malnutrition.[11] Article 3 reaffirms 'the right of everyone to have access to safe, sufficient, and nutritious food, consistent with the right to adequate food and the fundamental right of everyone to be free from hunger' (FAO/WHO 2014b, article 3). Unlike the many of the substantive parts, the declaratory part as well as Articles 4,[12] 6,[13] 7,[14] 12,[15] and 16[16] were not contested amongst regional actors and are therefore not examined in this case study.

### 7.2.1 First part on multiple challenges of malnutrition to inclusive and sustainable development and health: Articles 4 to 12

The *first substantive part* of the 2014 Rome Declaration is titled 'Multiple challenges of malnutrition to inclusive and sustainable development and to health' and outlines the threats to nutrition (Rome Declaration 2014). These include the lack of access to food, factors aggravating poor child feeding practices, such as poor sanitation standards or polluted drinking water or food, and epidemics. Moreover, it recognises the influence of socioeconomic and environmental changes and the connection to obesity and noncommunicable diseases, the impact of climate change and conflicts over food security, the challenges of food scarcity and unbalanced distribution of goods. It identifies trade and trade policies as one of the main components of food security and nutrition. This substantive part comprises Article 4 to 12 in the final version of the Rome Declaration adopted by the CoP in 2014. Several components were contested, and major cleavages often run through developed and less developed countries as well as producers and consumers.[17]

### *Article 5*

Article 5 of the Rome Declaration stresses the variety of causes of malnutrition. It was considerably more disputed and called regional actors into action. The final version 'recognizes that the root of and factors leading to malnutrition are complex and multidimensional . . . malnutrition is often aggravated by poor infant and young child feeding and care practices, poor sanitation and hygiene, lack of access to education, quality health systems and safe drinking water, foodborne infections and parasitic infestations, ingestion of harmful levels of contaminants due to unsafe food *from production to consumption*' (Rome Declaration 2014, emphasis added by the authors).

The last part of Article 5 was added based on the negotiation efforts of the EUR group, which used argumentative negotiation strategies (H6c). From early on, the EUR[18] pointed out that one cause of malnutrition is the ingestion of unsafe food and argued that this stems from mistakes in 'production, processing and storage' (JWG August 27th 2014). Delegates from the Global South opposed the EUR's position concerning the importance of handling of food, not in the least since it entailed an element of blame-shifting, by making it clear that at least a part of the responsibility for malnutrition rests on the affected country itself. Yet, countries from the Global South, such as Sudan, regarded the lack of resources as *the* core factor for malnutrition, especially for countries in Africa (e.g. interview#242, 06-09-16). They preferred Article 5 to be linked only to the lack of access to sufficient and affordable food (interview#224, 05-05-16, also #242, 06-09-16 and interview#243, 07-09-16, also Bain 2013) and preferred language in the text that speaks of 'victims of malnutrition' in a passive manner (interview#224, 05-05-16).[19] Nevertheless, the EUR's preferred position prevailed. Its argument was linked to widely known scientific insights and could be backed up by reports on health-related implications of unsafe food and the variety of its origins and resonated well with developed countries, such as the United States, Japan and Mexico (interview#225, 06-05-16; also FAO/WHO 2014b). Regional groups, such as GRULAC, also supported the EU's text insertion.[20] A diplomat reported that what 'GRULAC supported was the recognition of why malnutrition exists and it says that it comes from different areas, it's not only poverty in like developing but also like knowledge of what to eat' (interview#226, 06-05-16).

*Article 8*

In the final version of Article 8 the members 'recognise the need to address the impacts of climate change and other environmental factors on food security and nutrition, in particular on the quantity, quality and diversity of food produced, taking appropriate action to tackle negative effects' (FAO/WHO 2014b). By contrast, the initial draft of the ICN2 Secretariat did not include a separate article on climate change, but only mentioned climate change as one of the challenges food systems face in Article 3 (Zero Draft 2014).

The North America group (NOAM) and the African group (AFRICA) proposed text changes and the EU became vocal as well. Other ROs were not active regarding climate change, as their members did not agree on common group positions[21] or regarded the issue as not being of high saliency.

AFRICA proposed the first version of Article 8,[22] thus upgrading the link between climate change and food security to an own Article that stresses that climate change affects the quantity, quality and diversity of food produced and calls for appropriate action to tackle negative effects. In contrast, NOAM did not want to upgrade the climate change topic (JWG August 27th 2014), but suggested to delete these parts (JWG August 27th 2014). Yet, they failed in this respect, which was due to limited group homogeneity (H5b). While the United States was strongly in favour of deleting this text (interview#240, 02-09-16), the Canadian interests were more moderate (Government of Canada 2017). While both countries agreed to act in concert, the other members of the ICN2 negotiation arenas understood that Canada was not strongly behind this proposal, which reduced the persuasiveness of deletion-arguments. At the same time, AFRICA was united and used argumentative as well as lock-in strategies to promote a separate climate-change Article (H6c, 6d). There had already been an FAO conference in 2008, which linked climate change to nutrition (FAO 2008).[23] References to prior agreed language in the FAO Declaration of 2008 provided a means with which AFRICA advocates of a new Article 8 were able to reduce opposition in the ICN2 negotiations (H6d). In line with the lock-in strategy, actors, such as the United States, would have risked damaging their reputation had they continued to oppose formerly agreed linkages and principles. Hence, they gave in as 'it's hard to disagree that climate change has an impact on food security' (interview#242, 06-09-16). The EU also supported the position of the African group, but did not become active in this respect, since it wanted to avoid that the ICN2 negotiations become overshadowed by UNFCCC issues and cleavages (interviews#240, 02-09-16, #220, 04-02-16).

After it had become clear that NOAM could not prevent Article 8 altogether, it tried to weaken the link between climate change and food security and wanted to see only a reference to a 'potential impact' in the text. This proposal caused resistance among other regional groupings in the JWG and members in the OEWG. Especially the EU was against the term 'potential impact' and used lobbying and argumentative strategies to bring its point across (H6c, H6e). The EU pointed out that 'the impacts of climate change are actual and not potential' and made this argument in the formal negotiation arenas as well as on the basis of (EU 2014).[24] Given that scientific evidence is available for climate change and its connection to agricultural yields, the EU's argument resonated well amongst states and other regional groups (H6c).[25] By contrast, NOAM's internal homogeneity on the climate change issue was limited, since Canada is more progressive in this respect than the United States, which hampered the group's ability to act in concert (H5b). Thus, NOAM failed to succeed with its proposal, whereas the EU prevailed.

*Article 9*

The ICN2 delegates also discussed the adverse effects of civil disturbances on food security and whether a paragraph or article should be included in the Rome Declaration to this end.

The topic first came up in the JWG, when AFRICA proposed including a paragraph into the then Article 8 (on climate change) stating that access to food is also aggravated by 'civil disturbances' (FAO/WHO 2014b). The issue was of particular importance to AFRICA, as they are one of the world's regions that suffer most severely from conflicts (interview#224, 05-05-16). Thus, due to the high issue saliency, AFRICA was very active in the negotiations on Article 9 (H8) and argued that conflict-prone regions face great difficulties in providing access to food (interview#243, 07-09-16). This factual argument was compelling as it resonated well with the prior knowledge of the Parties (H6c) and therefore not contested by in the course of negotiations. While the inclusion of a passage on conflict and its negative effects on nutrition was accepted, the initial proposed wording 'civil disturbances' caused confusion among the parties (EU 2014). The EU was against this specific wording, arguing that it politicises the Rome Declaration, and suggested that the term be replaced by 'conflict emergencies and protracted crises' (EU 2014). This suggestion resonated well with the other actors, as this wording had already been agreed upon in other UN arenas, most notably in the ICN1 negotiations (interview#239, 22-08-16). Yet, instead of re-stating the ICN1 text 1:1, the delegates agreed on re-phrasing it into 'Recognize that conflict and post conflict situations, humanitarian emergencies and protracted crises, including, inter alia, droughts, floods and desertification as well as pandemics, hinder food security and nutrition' (interview#240, 02-09-16).

*Article 10*

Article 10 deals with food systems and environmental challenges. It summarises a variety of difficulties for providing healthy food, which is, in the final version of the Rome Declaration, 'resource scarcity and environmental degradation, . . . unsustainable production and consumption patterns, food losses and waste, and unbalanced distribution' (FAO/WHO 2014b).

Since this Article was touching on a series of different topics (interview#242, 06-09-16), several regional actors suggested changes, namely the Western Pacific regional group (WPR), the European regional group (ERG), GRULAC and the EU. Mainly, two issues were under discussion: whether to opt for a quantitative or a qualitative notion of food security (and which one) and also whether to incorporate ecological sustainability as a challenge to current food systems.

The first contested element was a recurring issue in the ICN2 and depicts one of the crucial conflict lines in the negotiations: some actors define food security as the pure quantity of food inter alia calories provided by day, whereas others go beyond that and stress also the need of healthy food in order to provide the human system with adequate vitamins and minerals and therefore speak of 'nutritious' food.

The WPR's twenty-seven member states coordinated swiftly on this topic, agreeing that they wanted to see 'nutritious' in the text and made a proposal in the negotiations to this end. This proposal was supported by AFRICA. They argued that just referring to food without the emphasis on nutritious food allows 'business people to manipulate the nutrition aspect of food to make it open for people to choose whether they want to eat nutritious or non-nutritious food' (interview#224, 05-05-16). Similarly, individual states from the Global South also placed emphasis on nutritious food (e.g. Cambodia 2014, Kenya 2014, Kiribati 2014, Pakistan 2014, Zimbabwe 2014).

By contrast, the ERG opposed the quality element and opted for the quantity-based framing. Consequently, they suggested deleting 'nutritious' from the draft of the Article altogether (JWG August 27th 2014).[26] Yet, the ERG was not successful with this radical position. It neither made arguments for a quantitative definition that resonated well with third parties, nor did it have formal bargaining power, since voting did not take place in the JWG. In addition, the group homogeneity was limited, since the EU members had a more nuanced position than the ERG at large going beyond mere calorie counting (interview #238, 22-08-16).

While the EU members also belonged to the ERG, which had a formal role in the JWG, the EU had a full member status in the OEWG and the CoP and did, thus, actively promote its own position in these arenas. In addition to making formal speeches in the later stages of the ICN2 negotiations, the EU delegation and its member states engaged in burden-sharing and lobbied third-party states inside and outside the JWG (H5a, H6e). The EU supported a qualitative notion of food security but opposed wording such as 'nutritious food, healthy/unhealthy food', arguing that healthy food in abundance can be unhealthy and cause obesity (interview#235, 11-05-16). Instead, the EU promoted terms such as 'healthy diets' and 'balanced diets', as they argued that these terms relate to a wholesome approach (interview#235, 11-05-16).[27] In addition, the EU was reluctant to agree to the term "nutritious' because 'the idea of nutritious food, it's more of a North American concept that a single element of food must provide all the nutritional elements. And this of course in our point of view also opens doors for GMOs and things like that' (interview#225, 06-05-16). Yet, the EU's arguments did not resonate widely in the ICN2 arena, as WPR members and states from the Global South regarded the term 'nutritious' as a qualitative criterion as crucial.

It became evident that no side could persuade the other side from its own position based on argumentative strategies (H6c). Compromise dynamics emerged since the actors wanted to pass the Rome Declaration by acclamation rather than putting it to a formal vote. Hence, the parties finally agreed on including both type of terms, 'healthy diets' and 'nutrient rich food'. Accordingly, the final version of Article 10 starts with 'Acknowledge that current food systems are being increasingly challenged to provide adequate, safe, diversified and nutrient rich food for all that contribute to healthy diets'.

The second topic under negotiation regarding Article 10 related to environmental sustainability and resource scarcity and their roles with respect to current food production. These two environmental political aims could turn into challenges for food systems. While large-scale farming might provide large quantities of food, it could place environmental sustainability at risk and could in the long run lead to resource scarcity.

The Western Pacific regional group brought this issue to the negotiation table. They argued for a reference acknowledging that current food systems are challenged in the longer run by shortages of key resources and lack of ecological sustainability (JWG August 27th 2014). Yet, the WPR did not circulate scientific reports on linkages between both elements and did not systematically use epistemic communities in order to strengthen their argument. Instead of gaining support, they were immediately opposed by GRULAC, for which the issue saliency was very high (H8). Because of their large-scale farms, GRULAC members wanted to delete 'ecological sustainability' (JWG August 27th 2014, interview#225, 06-05-16). Thus, the debate began focusing on the question of whether to replace the term 'ecological sustainability' with the weaker and less demanding concept 'environmental degradation' as suggested by GRULAC members (interview#225, 06-05-16). Similar to WPR, GRULAC did not make causal or scientific arguments, and bargaining dynamics started (H6b). No side was de facto in a pivotal position. Although all parties preferred a consensual Rome Declaration (similar to the ICN1 outcome documents), FAO rules applied so that the Rome Declaration could have been passed by simple majority vote. Yet, no group was large enough to constitute a blocking majority in the CoP. Hence it became necessary for both sides to make compromises. WPR succeeded partially in getting 'resource scarcity' into the text, while GRULAC succeeded partially in replacing 'environmental sustainability' with 'environmental degradation' (interview#225, 06-05-16). Accordingly, the final version of Article 10 states: 'Acknowledge that current food systems are being increasingly challenged . . . due to, inter alia, constraints posed by resource scarcity and environmental degradation, as well as by unsustainable production and consumption patterns, food losses and waste, and unbalanced distribution'.

*Article 11*

A major conflict emerged on how to frame the role of trade in the Rome Declaration (Article 11). One side preferred a negative framing, regarding trade as a potential challenge for current food systems (in the JWG draft), while the other side framed it positively and emphasised that trade is a 'key element in achieving food security' (in the final Rome Declaration). The parties also disagreed whether to flag that 'trade distorting economic measures' and/or whether 'unilateral coercive economic measures' are problems to be included in the list of challenges to the food systems.

Article 11 signifies a north–south divide in the negotiations where regional actors and countries from the Global South implicitly blamed the more developed states and their respective trade systems for their protected markets.[28] The AFR, SWP, GRULAC and NEEA regarded current trade practices as a potential obstacle to food systems. In line with this negative framing, they wished to emphasise the negative effect of 'trade distorting economic measures' (JWG August 27th 2014). In addition, Bolivia and Argentina proposed

exemplifying 'distorting economic measures' by adding 'subsidies for agricultural products' (Bolivia) and 'protectionism' (Argentina) and therewith
emphasised the existing conflict line even more (OEWG September 24th
2014). Cuba, Iran, Bolivia and Venezuela pushed statements that 'the use of
unilateral coercive economic measures adversely affects economies and the
development efforts of developing economies and have a generally negative
impact on international economic cooperation and on the worldwide effort
to move towards an open and non-discriminatory trading system' and called
for 'international cooperation and solidarity' (OEWG September 24th 2014).
The FAO European Regional group (ERG), the WHO European Region
(EUR), the North America regional group (NOAM) and also the EU – all
regions with highly protected agricultural markets – were fiercely against the
mentioning of any trade-distorting economic measures into the text of the
Rome Declaration. The negotiations on the trade article were highly disputed,
and both sides initially showed 'little flexibility' and insisted on their respective positions (EU Delegation Geneva 2014, also interview#225, 06-05-16).
This changed when the EU took the argumentative lead and stressed that the
term 'trade-distorting support' is used in the WTO arena and contested there
(interviews#229, 10-05-16, #239, 22-08-16).[29] The EU made the point that
non-agreed language should not be transferred from one arena into the other
(interview#235, 11-05-16), as this would pre-empt constructive negotiation
dynamics in the ICN2,[30] in the formal negotiation arenas as well as on the
basis of bilateral lobbying. The EU additionally argued that the facts behind
the AFR, SWP, GRULAC and NEEA's proposal are uncertain as there is no
hard evidence that trade practices do indeed challenge food systems (H6c)
(interview#235, 11-05-16). The argument resonated well and the text of the
draft Rome Declaration was changed accordingly since the initial proposal of
AFR, SWP, GRULAC and NEEA was deleted.

In addition to pushing for the inclusion of 'trade distorting economic
measures' GRULAC and AFR also proposed stressing the negative effects
of trade for food systems by mentioning 'unilateral coercive economic measures' (JWG August 27th 2014). WPR wanted to delete this insertion (JWG
August 27th 2014), but did not use bargaining or argumentative strategies to
this end. The EU, however, used arguing and lobbying strategies and pointed
out that the UN resolution on unilateral economic measures and coercion was
not passed by consensus in the UNGA, as the United States and EU members
abstained (interview#235, 11-05-16). Again they emphasised the point that
the ICN2 parties should not transfer non-consensual language from another
arena into the Rome Declaration on Nutrition. This EU intervention resonated
well in the discussions, and the proposed language from GRULAC and AFR
was dropped in the final text of the Declaration (interview#235, 11-05-16).

Along with these two achievements, the EU accomplished a major nego-tiation success in changing the whole framing of the trade Article 11. In the initial drafts and the draft of the JWG, trade was framed negatively as a challenge to food systems, yet, in the draft of the OEWG and the final text of the Rome Declaration, trade was framed in a positive manner. Article 11 stated that 'trade is a key element in achieving food security and nutrition' (OEWG September 24th 2014, Rome Declaration 2014). In order to re-frame the trade issue, the EU resorted to a lock-in strategy (H6d). The EU, with the support of NOAM, emphasised that there is already agreed-upon language on trade and food security, which does not even originate in a different IO, but is part of the outcome document of the World Food Summit of 1996, the 'Rome Declaration on World Food Security' (ICN2 interview#16, 10-05-16, interview#235, 11-05-16). This Rome Declaration on World Food Security' states: 'Trade is a key element in achieving food security. We agree to pursue food trade and overall trade policies that will encourage our producers and consumers to utilise available resources in an economically sound and sus-tainable manner' (World Food Summit 1996).[31] As a consequence, members from AFR, SWP, GRULAC and NEEA could not disregard the positive con-notation of trade and food security that had previously been accepted by all ICN2 member states. Opposing their former agreement would have resulted in loss of reputation, which these actors wanted to avoid. As a result, the EU, with the support of the North America group, succeeded in changing the essence of Article 11 (Rome Declaration 2014).

### 7.2.2 The second part on a common vision for global action to end all forms of malnutrition: Articles 13 and 14

In the second substantive part of the Declaration (Article 13 and 14), the ICN2 members reaffirm their 'common vision for global action to end all forms of malnutrition' (Rome Declaration 2014), on the basis of which policy implications and activities are outlined in part three of the Declaration (Rome Declaration 2014, Articles 15–17).

*Article 13*

Article 13 covers a broad range of topics related to malnutrition, which has implications for how to combat it effectively (e.g. concerning target groups, areas and levels). It was contested in several parts. Several ROs became active in the negotiations and proposed text changes.

The first instance in which a regional actor had substantive, rather than merely rhetorical, issues[32] at stake and acted accordingly was the issue of 'food as a means of political or economic pressure'. GRULAC proposed putting this phrase into Article 13 of the Rome Declaration (interview#235, 11-05-16) and succeeded in doing so even against the opposition of the United States and the EU (JWG August 27th 2014, OEWG September 24th 2014 and Rome Declaration 2014). The issue 'was contested quite a lot. But then they [GRULAC, insertion by the authors] were very strong on this one' (interview#240, 02-09-16).

The issue saliency was high for GRULAC who even regarded this element as a 'red line' (interview#225, 06-05-16), and was effective in their bargaining threat (H6b) (interview#225, 06-05-16). Although the United States demanded the deletion of the phrase 'food as a means of political or economic pressure' initially (OEWG September 24th 2014), they did not risk a voted agreement in the end. The EU was slower in responding to GRU-LAC's bargaining move. Yet, the EU stopped opposing the phrase 'food as a means of political or economic pressure' once GRULAC was supported by Egypt. They used lock-in strategies (H6d), pointing out that the 1992 World Declaration on Food Security already included similar consensual language. Paragraph 15 of the 1992 Declaration explicitly states that 'in the context of international humanitarian law that food must not be used as a tool for political pressure. Food aid must not be denied because of political affiliation, geographic location, gender, age, ethnic, tribal or religious identity' (OEWG September 24th 2014). Had the EU members continued to reject the phrase 'food as a means of political or economic pressure' in the 2014 Declaration, they would have risked to lose international credibility and reputation. Thus, the EU ended up in agreeing to GRULAC's insertion.

Both African groups – the AFR and AFRICA – proposed that the phrase 'right to development' should be incorporated into the text of Article 13. Yet, its group coherency was not too strong on this issue (H5b), as some members became active on their own. Most notably, Zambia proposed 'adding the phrase "in the context of nutrition" instead' (interview#235, 11-05-16). Consequently, the African groups did not succeed in obtaining this text change, especially since many actors, amongst them the EU, argued that a 'right to development' is not relevant in the context of the Rome Declaration, which seeks to identify and fight challenges of malnutrition. Thus, 'The right to development . . . was removed' from Article 13 and 'only the non-discriminatory treatment and in terms of access of food' remained in Articles 14 and 15, respectively (both quotes interview#242, 06-09-16).

A third issue focused on the special role of women. ASIA[33] and GRU-LAC proposed mentioning in the Declaration that nutrition policies 'should consider and address special care for women' (JWG August 27th 2014, also ICN2 interview#26, 05-09-16). This proposal was included in the final text version of Article 13, although it did not meet opposition in the negotiations.

Instead, many states and also some of the other regional actors[34] were favourable to the ASIA–GRULAC suggestion.

## Article 14

Article 14 is a collection of several topics related to food and nutrition which the Head of States and Governments 'recognize' (JWG August 27th 2014). For instance, according to Article 14a, international cooperation should be in line with national policies in order to be effective.

Proclaiming a 'right to food' has been a long-standing position of AFR and AFRICA members,[35] and became a major issue in Article 14b, because of its potential normative and re-distributional implications. NOAM wanted to delete the 'right to food' as such (JWG August 27th 2014). However, its group coherency was limited, since it was the United States who had a rigid policy concerning the 'right to food', namely objecting to it,[36] which was not in line with Canada's more open position (e.g. interviews#225, 06-05-16, #228, 09-05-16). Thus, the North American group was not successful in achieving an omission of this right in the Declaration (H5b). The United States soon started to negotiate on its own in this respect, which showcased the limited coherency of the North American group. The United States engaged in bargaining and highlighted that it would not agree to this formulation. Yet, since it did not issue a threat of no-vote, which would have put the consensual passing of the Declaration at risk, its bargaining stance was not particularly strong (H6b). Instead of threatening to block the Declaration altogether, the United States made it clear that it would issue a reservation in order to flag that it differs from the other ICN2 members with respect to the right to food.[37] Yet, the United States was not the only actor opposing the African groups' endeavour to insert a right to food into the document. Initially, in the JWG negotiations, the ERG also asked for the right to food to be deleted.

Yet, AFR and AFRICA could entrap the critics in the ERG by highlighting that it is already pre-agreed language (H6d). Most notably, Article 11 of the International Covenant on Economic, Social and Cultural Rights explicates a right to food. Since many of the ERG members have ratified this Treaty, they would have faced reputational losses, had they insisted on opposing the African groups' push for the inclusion of a 'right to food' into the Rome Declaration.[38] In the wake of this argument, both sides agreed on a middle ground: While the final version of the Rome Declaration included the 'right to food' it did so by stating a 'right to *adequate* food', which was slightly less demanding (Rome Declaration 2014, emphasis by the authors).

Another point of discussion was the inclusion of a reference to 'culturally acceptable' food systems, which was pushed by countries with Muslim majorities, especially Iran and Sudan (interviews#240, 02-09-16, #242, 06-09-16).[39]

They argued that 'food should be adequate not only from the nutrition point of view but also from the cultural' points of view (interview#242, 06-09-16), but did not provide normative or factual reasons to support their stance. Accordingly, the argument didn't resonate well with opponents (H6c). The ERG rejected the notion of 'culturally acceptable' food, as it was afraid that this could affect trade to those countries, for example in the form of trade restrictions (interview#224, 05-05-16). However, the internal homogeneity in the ERG was not very high. Russia strongly opposed any reference to 'culturally acceptable' food as they objected to 'giving a lot of concessions to some local minorities', while most other ERG members did not have a similarly strong stance on the issue (interview#225, 06-05-16). For instance, the EU wanted to keep 'culturally acceptable' in the text (interview#235, 11-05-16). Showcasing this internal disagreement, it does not come as a surprise that the ERG was not successful (H5b). Although NOAM was firmly against any reference to culture, it did not resort to bargaining threats in order to bring their point across (interview#242, 06-09-16). Instead, argumentative dynamics unfolded and focused on whether 'culturally acceptable food systems' can be misused in order to distort free trade.[40] In the course of this debate, a new and softer formulation evolved. Thus, the final version of the Declaration speaks of food which 'conforms with the beliefs, culture, traditions, dietary habits and preferences of individuals' and therefore picks up the proposal of countries such as Iran and Sudan, which gained support from Tanzania, Italy, the Netherlands, Finland and also the EU (Finland 2014, Netherlands 2014, Organization 2014, Tanzania 2014, interview#236, 11-05-16).

An additional contested issue related to how to define the groups affected by malnutrition, more specifically whether the term 'nutritionally vulnerable groups' should be used and whether the affected groups should be listed explicitly (JWG August 27th 2014, OEWG September 24th 2014, interview#235, 11-05-16). AFR proposed the following wording: 'Refugees, displaced persons, war-affected populations, indigenous populations, people under foreign occupation and migrants are among the most nutritionally vulnerable groups and should be supported adequately' (JWG August 27th 2014, similar interview#235, 11-05-16). In this list of groups, the term 'people under foreign occupation' was most disputed, because it referred to the Israel–Palestine conflict, taking sides with the Palestinians[41] (interview#240, 02-09-16, ICN2 interview#11, 05-05-16, interviews#234, 11-05-16, #229, 10-05-16).

By contrast, 'The U.S. and EU wanted to keep the reference general' (interview#235, 11-05-16). The United States preferred not listing vulnerable groups at all and initially managed to get the support of Canada, so that it could try to leverage up through the North American group (JWG August 27th 2014). However, the group coherency of the NOAM group was – again – rather limited. This became evident, as Canada suggested its own additional groups that should be listed in the Declaration as 'nutritionally vulnerably', namely 'people living under governments that include designated terror organisations and under governments that use civilian infrastructure for terrorist-related activities' (OEWG September 24th 2014). Accordingly, the North American group's initial attempt to avoid a list of nutritionally vulnerable groups failed (H5b). Due to the limited importance put on this issue, the EU did not negotiate with full force and did not make arguments or bargaining threats in the formal negotiation arenas or through informal lobbying in an effort to avoid cataloguing groups vulnerable to malnutrition altogether (H6a).[42]

In the end, AFR was successful to a considerable extent. It argued that some groups are nutritionally more exposed than others and therefore need suitable support (interview#233, 11-05-16). In general, this argument resonated well with the other regional groups. Consequently, the African group's initial list of vulnerable groups was mostly adopted (Rome Declaration 2014).

Yet, the EU took a stronger stance on the issue of including 'people under foreign occupation' into the Declaration and negotiated more actively in this respect. The EU cautioned that an issue linkage to the Israel–Palestine conflict would complicate the ICN2 negotiations unnecessarily. It argued that 'one should also not overdo it [making such references] . . . as we need a balanced treatment' (interview#229, 10-05-16). Thus, the EU called for moderation in this respect, but was not very effective in doing so.[43]

With respect to the most controversial issue, namely whether to include people living under occupation in the list of the vulnerable groups, a stalemate between the United States and the African group materialised. While the United States objected to 'occupation', the African group was unwilling to delete this term. Based on Canada's initial proposal to include people affected by terror into the list of nutrition vulnerable groups (OEWG September 24th 2014), an unusual compromise finally emerged. As a diplomat recalls, 'I think that the eventual agreement was to include anything. Because either, you put everything or you remove everything . . . and the end result was: "Ok, let's put everything", which eventually doesn't make a lot of sense out of this paragraph but this is the compromise, and it's put in a lot of completely different things in the same place' (interview#242, 06-09-16).[44] Thus, while the United States finally accepted the term 'occupation' in the list of vulnerable groups (referring implicitly to Israel), the compromise was that people suffering from terrorism (referring implicitly to Palestine) were listed as well (United Nations General Assembly 2013a).

AFR and GRULAC wanted to emphasise the strong position of 'small holders and family farmers' in fighting malnutrition and promoted special programmes in order to strengthen their position (JWG August 27th 2014).

Especially in Africa and Latin/South America, smallholding and family farms are widespread. Therefore, the regions wanted to see a reference included. In contrast, ERG, EUR, ASIA and NOAM wished to maintain the original text, with no special attention given to smallholding and family farming, largely due to the fear that any claims for financial aid could subsequently arise through this paragraph. However, the EU whose members are in the ERG and the EUR is internally divided on this issue, as some of its member states have small family farms, while others have larger farms (Fouilleux 2010, Patterson 1997).[45] A similar observation is in order with respect to ASIA members (Cornia 1985, Fan and Chan-Kang 2005). Accordingly, the ERG, the EUR and ASIA were not very active in the negotiations in this respect and did not use a broad array of strategies in order to oppose the AFR and GRULAC proposal. That left NOAM facing GRULAC and AFR, which both combined much more votes than the two of NOAM, which only consists of the United States and Canada. Thus, the latter was not in any way in a stronger bargaining position than the former, especially since all actors were interested in passing the ICN2 Declaration similar to the ICN1 Declaration, namely by acclamation instead of formal voting. Hence, the AFR and GRU-LAC prevailed, and the final text reads: 'Family farmers and small holders, notably women farmers, play an important role in reducing malnutrition and should be supported by integrated and multisectoral public policies, as appropriate, that raise their productive capacity and incomes and strengthen their resilience' (Article 14f).

A further issue under discussion amongst regional groups was the EXPO article (Article 14p), which promoted the world exhibition in Milan, Italy, in 2015 (Rome Declaration 2014). Entitled 'Feeding the Planet, Energy for Life', the world fair was linked to the ICN2 topic. EXPO was perceived as a chance to promote the ICN2 outcomes, to 'raise public awareness' and 'to foster the international debate' (Rome Declaration 2014). This paragraph was pushed by Italy, as the host of the 2015 EXPO (interviews#225, 06-05-16, #232, 11-05-16, #240, 02-09-16).[46] GRULAC, AMR and WPR were against its inclusion into the Rome Declaration (JWG August 27th 2014). They made the argument that the Declaration should not advertise to a specific single event taking place only some months after the ICN2 conference in only one of the member states (interviews#233, 11-05-16, #242, 06-09-16), but should be of universal character (interview#238, 22-08-16). At first, this argument resonated well, and countries such as Switzerland and Venezuela agreed that this reference should be deleted from the Declaration text (interview#240, 02-09-16). Despite these criticisms, GRULAC, AMR and WPR did not succeed. Instead, Italy prevailed, and the EXPO reference was maintained (interviews#225, 06-05-16, #240, 02-09-16). Due to spontaneous lobbying of

Italy in the negotiation arena (H6e) 'people felt that it was sort of courtesy to Italy hosting the FAO and ICN2' (interview#242, 06-09-16).

### 7.2.3 The third part on commitment to action: Articles 15 to 17

*The last part of the Declaration* covers the self-commitment to the action of the ICN2 Parties and specifics how they seek to 'eradicate hunger and prevent all forms of malnutrition' (Rome Declaration 2014). This part is comprised of Articles 15 to 17.

*Article 15*

Article 15 starts with the commitment to 'eradicate hunger and prevent all forms of malnutrition' followed by a commitment to 'increase investments for effective interventions and actions to improve people's diets and nutrition, including in emergency situations' which were not controversial between regional actors in the JWG and the OEWG (JWG August 27th 2014, OEWG September 24th 2014, Rome Declaration 2014).

Regional actors came into play with respect to Article 15f, which focused on intergovernmental cooperation to improve nutrition. It explicates a commitment to 'strengthen and facilitate contributions and action by all stakeholders to improve nutrition and promote collaboration within and across countries, including North–South cooperation, as well as South-South and triangular cooperation' (Rome Declaration 2014). Initially, GRULAC proposed adding 'on the basis of solidarity at national, regional, international and global levels' (JWG August 27th 2014). Yet, the group did not provide novel moral, normative or other arguments, why solidarity should be explicitly incorporated into Article 15. Also, not in the least since the issue was not highly salient (H8), GRULAC did not engage in lobbying or bargaining strategies in order to promote the insertion.

The GRULAC proposal of including solidarity into Article 15f was met with opposition from EUR and NOAM which all wanted it to be deleted. EUR and NOAM were concerned that the term 'solidarity' would open doors for redistributive claims and argued for its removal in order to avoid an unnecessary politicisation of the Declaration. The Africa and Asia groups were also not enthusiastic about inserting national and regional solidarity. They argued that the solidarity references are redundant, since the paragraph already flags the importance of North–South cooperation, South–South and triangular cooperation (OEWG September 24th 2014, Rome Declaration 2014).

Given that these four groups represent an overwhelming majority of the ICN2 members (128 out of the 194 member states), whilst GRULAC only embodies thirty-three countries, the bargaining leverage of the former was considerably higher. Although the bargaining leverage was not used as a negotiation asset as such, their stance against the insertion prevailed, and the GRULAC proposal was deleted (OEWG September 24th 2014).

## Article 17

Article 17, the last article of the Declaration, calls on the UNGA to 'to endorse the Rome Declaration on Nutrition, as well as the Framework for Action which provides a set of voluntary policy options and strategies for use by governments, as appropriate, and to consider declaring a Decade of Action on Nutrition from 2016 to 2025 within existing structures and available resources'.

The Decade on Nutrition was proposed by GRULAC and supported by AFRICA (interviews#226, 06-05-16, #224, 05-05-16, ICN2 interview#15, 09-05-16), while the EU, supported by ERG and NOAM, opposed it and called for its deletion (JWG August 27th 2014). GRULAC pushed the Decade on Nutrition, as it would serve 'as a strong sign of commitment towards action in nutrition' (interview#235, 11-05-16). In contrast, the EU did not back the idea of a Decade of Action on Nutrition.

GRULAC argued that a decade of action on nutrition would be beneficial for the effectiveness of the ICN2 outcomes and as it would push the 'agencies based in Rome to work around this at least for ten years' (interview#226, 06-05-16).[47] This resonated well with the African regional group, which added that 'it was important to put at least a title of ten years to concentrate our efforts, so that after ten years at least you have to evaluate what you have achieved and what you haven't' (interview#224, 05-05-16). In contrast, the EU argued against such an inclusion because of the 'ambiguity surrounding the content added value and cost of such an initiative' (interview#235, 11-05-16).[48] While ERG and NOAM sided with the EU, they did not become active themselves on this issue. Thus, after the exchange of the pro- and contras, an argumentative deadlock manifested itself, and no side could persuade the other from the rightfulness of its reasons (H6c).

Accordingly, the actors started to engage in bargaining (H6b). GRULAC used bargaining strategies and 'pushed very hard' indicating its red lines (interview#236, 11-05-16). The EU also engaged in bargaining but did not indicate that they would not support the entire Rome Declaration if the decade issue was maintained (interview#236, 11-05-16). Although the issue was 'not a red line' (interview#236, 11-05-16), the EU flagged that it had serious problems with the notion of having a 'decade on nutrition'. Therefore, and because of the support from the ERC and NOAM, in the course of the final negotiations both sides reached a compromise, which was tilted only slightly towards GRULAC's position.

Accordingly, the final Declaration asks for a Decade of Action on Nutrition. Yet, it does so with two qualifications. First, instead of saying that the Rome Declaration is 'recommending' a Decade of Action on Nutrition, the text is now softened and asks the UNGA to 'consider declaring a Decade of Action on Nutrition'.[49] Second, the Decade of Action on Nutrition should be limited to take place 'within existing structures and available resources' (Rome Declaration 2014) and therefore without any additional financial resources or institutional set-up such as a secretariat (interview#242, 06-09-16).[50]

## 7.3 CONCLUSIONS

The case study on the negotiation of the Rome Declaration exemplifies a most likely case for regional actor success. This is due to the combination of the access and formal role of regional actors (H7a) as well as the size of the negotiation arena (H7b), both of which are conducive to regional actor success. The negotiation arena was larger than in the SAWS case since the negotiations on the 2014 Rome Declaration included 194 member states (which are in the FAO and the WHO) and the EU. In addition, the negotiations were more open to regional actors than the IWC and the ATT. Since the negotiations took place at the FAO headquarters and based on FAO rules, the EU was a full member, and between ten and sixteen other ROs were granted full or temporary observer status varying from committee to committee. In addition, regional actors were institutionally built into the ICN2 negotiations in another manner, since the first negotiation arena, the JWG, was an exclusive forum for regional actors. In the JWG, states could not negotiate by themselves and were not able to voice national positions. Instead, the JWG negotiations were exclusively conducted by a total of thirteen regional groups.[51] States could only voice national positions in the subsequent OEWG and the CoP, as could the EU as the only regional actor with full member status in the FAO.

In line with hypotheses 7a and 7b, regional actors played a prominent role in the ICN2 negotiations and left imprints on twenty different aspects of the Rome Declaration on Nutrition of 2014. Regional actors succeeded in changing the text of the document in twenty-two instances fully in line with their respective regional group positions and partially in line with their regional position in ten instances (c.f. table 7.1). For instance, the African groups managed to insert the 'right to food' into the Rome Declaration and also succeeded in explicitly listing nutritionally vulnerable groups. GRULAC successfully pushed for the recognition that 'food should not be used as an instrument for political or economic pressure'. The EU changed the spin of the trade-related article from a negative into a positive framing so that the

2014 outcome document now emphasises the positive role of trade for food security.

While IO openness and IO size are important, the possibility of majority decisions was not (H7c). Formally, the FAO rules of procedures would have allowed passing the Rome Declaration by majority voting. Hypotheses 7c would have expected that this rule increased the prospects of larger regional actors to be successful due to the number of votes they carry. On this basis, EUR with its fifty-two members should have been most successful AFRICA with forty-eight and ERG with forty-eight member states. Yet, the two European regional groups were considerably less successful in the ICN2 negotiations (EUR three instances, ERG one instance), than the much smaller EU (eight instances). AFR succeeded four times and AFRICA six times. Also, NOAM was relatively successful (four substantive text changes), although it has only two member states. Thus, hypothesis 7c needs to be rejected.

In general, the negotiations revealed that activity is a crucial stepping stone for regional actor success (H6a). The most active regional actors were the EU (concerning twelve issues), NOAM (in ten instances), followed by GRU-LAC (nine instances), AFR and AFRICA (seven issues each). By contrast, the Western Pacific regional group (four issues) and the Asian group (three issues) were less active, preceded only by the Near East Regional Group and the Southwest Pacific group (one issue each). In absolute terms, the most successful regional actors influencing the final content of the Declaration were the EU and the AFRICA group (with eight and five text changes, respectively) followed by AFR, GRULAC and NOAM (four substantive text changes each). The Western Pacific regional and the Asian groups were less active overall and, as expected, also less successful, influencing the Rome Declaration in only three and two instances, respectively.

The case study also illustrated that varying success of regional actors is also linked to issue saliency. Working through regional groups is time- and resource-intensive. Hence, regional actors develop positions and invest diplomatic capacities in pushing them in the international negotiations especially when the issue on the IO negotiation table is of high importance to them (H8). Consequently, the African groups were very engaged in the ICN2 negotiations, whenever food security was linked to developmental issues and vulnerable groups. Likewise, the EU and NOAM became particularly involved when issues touched trade aspects.

Apart from successfully altering negotiation outcomes, regional actors also succeeded in changing negotiation dynamics in thirty-one instances, thus influencing third-party actors to support their regional positions. Yet, not all negotiation strategies were equally prominent and equally effective. In the negotiations of the Rome Declaration of 2014, the most used strategies were arguing and lock-in, while informal lobbying and coalition-building were not prominent at all.

**Table 7.1. The success of ROs in the negotiations on the Rome Declaration on Nutrition**

| Issue | Active ROs | Procedural Success – Proactive | Procedural Success – Reactive | Substantive Success – Proactive | Substantive Success – Reactive |
|---|---|---|---|---|---|
| **Article 5:** Causes for malnutrition | EUR | Yes | | Yes | |
| **Article 8:** Climate change: own article | AFRICA | Yes | | Yes | |
| | NOAM | | No | | No |
| **Article 8:** Climate change: insertion of 'potential impact' | NOAM | No | | No | |
| | EU | | Yes | | Yes |
| **Article 9:** Civil disturbances | AFRICA | Yes | | Partially | |
| | EU | | Yes | | Partially |
| **Article 10:** Quantitative or a qualitative definition of food security | WPR | Partially | | Partially | |
| | AFRICA | Partially | | Partially | |
| | ERG | | No | | No |
| | EU | | Partially | Partially | |
| **Article 10:** Ecological sustainability and resource scarcity as challenges to current food systems | WPR | Yes | | Partially | |
| | GRULAC | | Yes | | Partially |
| **Article 11:** Trade as obstacle to food systems | AFR | No | | No | |
| | SWP | No | | No | |
| | GRULAC | No | | No | |
| | NEEA | No | | No | |
| | EU | | Yes | | Yes |
| | ERG | | Not active | | Yes |
| | EUR | | Not active | | Yes |
| | NOAM | | Not active | | Yes |
| **Article 11:** Inclusion of 'unilateral coercive economic measures' | GRULAC | No | | No | |
| | AFR | No | | No | |
| | EU | | Yes | | Yes |
| | WPR | | Not active | | Yes |
| **Article 11:** Positive framing: trade as key element in achieving food security | EU | Yes | | Yes | |

(Continued)

**Table 7.1. Continued**

| Issue | Active ROs | Procedural Success – Proactive | Procedural Success – Reactive | Substantive Success – Proactive | Substantive Success – Reactive |
|---|---|---|---|---|---|
| **Article 13:** 'Food as a means of political or economic pressure' | GRULAC | Yes | | Yes | |
| | EU | | Not active | | No |
| **Article 13:** 'Right to development' | AFRICA | Yes | | No | |
| | AFR | Yes | | No | |
| | EU | | Yes | | Yes |
| **Article 13:** Inclusion of 'special care for women' | GRULAC | Yes | | Yes, but no opposition | |
| | ASIA | Yes | | Yes, but no opposition | |
| **Article 14:** Inclusion of 'right to food' | AFR | Yes | | Yes | |
| | AFRICA | Yes | | Yes | |
| | NOAM | | No | | No |
| | ERG | | No | | No |
| **Article 14:** Notion of 'culturally acceptable' | ERG | | No | | No |
| | NOAM | | partially | | partially |
| **Article 14:** Listing nutritionally vulnerable groups | AFR | Yes | | Yes | |
| | NOAM | | No | | No |
| | EU | | No | | No |
| **Article 14:** Inclusion of the term 'occupation' | AFR | Yes | | Yes | |
| | EU | | No | | No |
| | NOAM | | No | | No |
| **Article 14:** Emphasise position of 'small holders and family farmers' | AFR | Yes | | Yes | |
| | GRULAC | Yes | | Yes | |
| | ERG | | Not active | | No |
| | EUR | | Not active | | No |
| | EU | | Not active | | No |
| | ASIA | | Not active | | No |
| | NOAM | | No | | |
| **Article 14:** Against inclusion of EXPO reference | GRULAC | | No | | No |
| | WPR | | No | | No |
| | AMR | | No | | No |
| **Article 15:** Inclusion of 'on the basis of solidarity at national, regional, international and global levels' | GRULAC | Yes | | No | |
| | EUR | | Yes | | Yes |
| | NOAM | | Yes | | Yes |
| | AFRICA | | Yes | | Yes |
| | ASIA | | Yes | | Yes |

| Issue | Active ROs | Procedural Success – Proactive | Procedural Success – Reactive | Substantive Success – Proactive | Substantive Success – Reactive |
|---|---|---|---|---|---|
| **Article 17:** 'Decade of Action' | GRULAC | Yes | | Partially successful | |
| | EU | | Yes | | Partially successful |
| | AFRICA | Limited activity | | Partially successful | |
| | NOAM | | Limited activity | | Partially successful |

Bargaining strategies, by which regional actors use their collective leverage in order to issue threats (e.g. with no votes) and seek concessions from others, were not used extensively in the ICN2 negotiations. Bargaining is effective only if the respective actor also possesses leverage, for instance in being pivotal for the passing of the negotiation outcome. Since the FAO rules of procedure were used for the ICN2 negotiations, the parties could have passed the Rome Declaration by majority voting. Accordingly, no regional group was large enough to block the Rome Declaration. In line with the bargaining hypothesis (H6b), the lack of formal pivotal positions in the ICN2 negotiations rendered the usage of bargaining strategies less effective, so it was rarely used by regional actors.

Compared to bargaining, arguing strategies were much more prominent in the 2014 negotiations of the Rome Declaration. All regional actors used arguments in order to persuade third-party actors to support them at different points in the ICN2 negotiations. Yet, not all of them linked their positions to factual, scientific or normative reasons. This, and the varying extent to which the provided reasons resonated with the other actors, impacted the effectiveness of the argumentative strategy (H6c).

Especially the cases of NOMA and ERC illustrate that group homogeneity (H5b) is important for the prospects of a group's negotiation strategies to be successful. Whenever it is obvious that group members are not fully on one page, the effectiveness of their argumentative or bargaining efforts in the international negotiation arena is hampered.

ICN1 and its outcome documents covered in parts similar topics as were on the ICN2 negotiation table. Thus, regional actors frequently adopted lock-in strategies and were frequently successful on this basis in pushing specific text elements or preventing changes (H6d). Thereby they used textual elements from the previous outcome document to silence opponents of specific elements with respect to the Rome Declaration on Nutrition of 2014.

While lock-in strategies were used more often in the FAO than in the IWC and the ATT negotiation arenas, lobbying and systematic coalition-building were strikingly less often applied. In fact, there is not much evidence on informal lobbying, by which groups reached out to third parties during workshops, dinners at the FAO and in Rome, or at the various capitals of non-group members in order to promote a regional position. This is in line with the expectation that informal lobbying requires capacities of regional groups to be conducted on a sufficiently large scale to be effective in talking a sufficient number of other actors into supporting the regional position (H6e). FAO and the WHO regional groups have no supporting capacities on their own, such as secretariats, administrators and policy experts, which could have orchestrated and supported informal lobbying. The EU, in contrast, has a comprehensive administrative and policy apparatus in Brussels which can aid the negotiations in Rome and thereby also support informal lobbying. Thus, the observation that the EU used lobbying more than the other regional actors is in line with the theoretical expectation.

Fitting to the observation of the lack of informal lobbying is another phenomenon. Compared to the ATT and the IWC case studies, it is apparent that there was hardly any systematic burden-sharing amongst member states of regional actors in the FAO case (H5a). This is most likely due to the specific institutional set-up of the ICN2 negotiation arenas. Especially at the early stage of the negotiations on the Rome Declaration, FAO and WHO regional groups had prominent formal roles and the states had to work through them in the JWG. Yet, FAO and WHO regional groups are not as highly institutionalised as regional organisations, such as the EU, in which a similar set of actors cooperate over a long period of time. Thus, the member states of the EU had advantages over members of the WHO and FAO regional groups in this respect.

Similar to lobbying, systematic coalition-building did also not take place in the ICN2 negotiations. While especially in the JWG regional groups sometimes happened to be on the same side, thus forming ad hoc coalitions, there is no indication that the groups reached out to one another prior to the negotiations in order to act in concert in the international negotiation arena from the start. This is in line with the coalition-building hypothesis (H6f), which expects that such a strategy requires additional regional actor capacities in order to develop the strategy and carry it out. While FAO and WHO regional groups have no capacities on their own to become active in this respect, the EU has capacities, but operated in the JWG within the EUR and ERG regional groups so that it could not reach out to other regional actors on its own. In the OEWG and the CoP, in contrast, FAO and WHO regional groups had no formal status, so they were not 'natural allies' that the EU could have approached to form coalitions.

# Conclusions

This book started from the observation that international cooperation has proliferated after WWII, leading to an ever-increasing number of international and regional organisations. This development has created a situation in which states are not only members in multiple IOs and ROs, but in which the policy themes covered by ROs and IOs increasingly overlap. Thus, this book examined the regionalisation of today's international negotiations. It examines how active regional actors participate in international negotiations and explains why some ROs are more vocal than others. It also studies how ROs can be successful in IOs and shape international negotiation outcomes. This chapter summarises the answers to these questions, and the key findings of the book. It also provides an outlook of how ROs could make their voices better heard in international negotiations, and ends with outlining avenues for future research.

Studying the activity as well as the success of regional actors in international negotiations is important and timely, since we currently witness an era of regionalisation. Not only has the number of regional organisations increased from two in 1945 to more than seventy in 2015 (Panke and Stapel under review), states also cooperate in various regional groups, such as the UN groups or the regional groups in the FAO. Although many of these ROs have no official standing in IOs and most have no formal speaking rights on their own, let alone formal votes, states can and do voice regional positions in international negotiations. On average, almost 12 per cent of the speech acts made in international negotiations in IOs are regional in character. This changes not only the dynamics of international negotiations, which are no longer exclusive state–state exchanges of national interests, but also the policy outcomes of IO negotiations if ROs manage to leave regional imprints on international norms and rules. In short, global governance today has an inherently regional component, in which ROs turn into actors in IOs as the former arena of state–state interactions. This has the potential to render international negotiations more effective since the number of positions at the negotiation table is reduced when a few regional, rather than many, national positions are expressed. Moreover, the regionalisation of international negotiations also has the potential to increase the legitimacy of global governance, since ROs give voices to states which might be too poor or too small to participate in international negotiations on their own actively.[1]

In short, this book illustrates that the activity and success of ROs in international relations are linked. Without actively voicing regional positions, ROs cannot influence negotiation outcomes. Yet, to become active, ROs need capacities for the construction of regional positions concerning the issues on the IO negotiation agenda, and their members need to be motivated to act on the basis of developed regional positions subsequently in the international negotiations. RO activity has greater chances to translate into RO success in IOs, when the latter grant ROs formal status and are large. In addition, ROs increase their prospects for negotiation success when the RO members act in concert, are motivated to invest their negotiation resources for the RO and collectively use negotiation strategies for which they possess the required capacities (e.g. veto power or other leverage for bargaining, expertise for arguing). Figure C.1 summarises the major findings with respect to activity

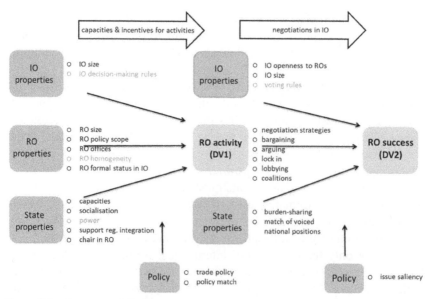

**Figure C.1.   Summary of findings**

and success of ROs in IO negotiations. This illustrates not only that variables driving RO activity and RO success are located at the state, the regional, the international as well as the policy levels of EMLG systems, but also that most hypotheses are empirically supported (in dark black colour), while only a few need to be rejected (in light grey colour).

## C.1 MAJOR FINDINGS

Two research questions formed the core of this book. Are some ROs more active than others, and, if so, why? Can ROs exert influence over international norms although they are not usually full members of IOs, and, if so, under what conditions are regional actors successful?

In order to answer these questions, chapters 2–7 looked at the active participation and the effective participation of ROs in IOs. Thus, the book combines comprehensive quantitative analysis with in-depth comparative case studies. This combination allows detecting and examining broader patterns of RO activity as well as zooming into the nexus between active and effective participation and study how and under what conditions ROs are most successful in shaping international norms and rules.

### C.1.1 The active participation of ROs in IOs

Concerning the *activity of ROs* in international negotiations, a series of interesting empirical patterns emerge (c.f. chapter 3). First, although almost 12 per cent of all speeches made in the 512 international negotiations under scrutiny are regional in character, not all states are equally inclined to act on behalf of their ROs in IOs. Second, not all ROs are equally vocal in IOs. Third, some IOs attract greater shares of regional positions than others. Fourth, not all policy issues are regionalised to the same extent. As table C.1 illustrates, this variation can be accounted for by the EMLG approach put forward in chapter 2, which in essence captures how state-, regional- and international-level factors, as well as policy variables, shape the propensity to which ROs develop regional positions that their members subsequently voice in IO negotiations, if they have incentives and capacities to do so.

Not all states are equally vocal for their ROs in international negotiations. In absolute terms, Denmark, South Africa, Sweden, followed by Benin voiced regional positions the most often with 175, 129, 118 and 103 instances, respectively. In contrast, countries such as Macedonia, Romania, Bolivia, Guinea and Gambia did not get active on behalf of an RO at all. The variation of states to negotiate in the name of ROs in international negotiations can be accounted for by the EMLG state-level hypotheses (c.f. figure C.1,

**Table C.1. Overview of findings for RO activity (DV1)**

| Level | Hypothesis | IV | Expected Effect on DV | Findings Focused Level Analysis | Findings Comprehensive Multilevel Analysis | Comments |
|---|---|---|---|---|---|---|
| Member state | H1a | Administrative capacities | Positive | √ | √ | |
| | H1b | Democratic socialisation | Positive | √ (in tendency) | √ | |
| | H1c | Power | Negative | – | – | No linear IV DV relationship |
| | H1d | Support regional integration | Positive | √ | √ | |
| RO | H2a | RO size | Positive | √ (in tendency) | – | Comprehensive multilevel finding statistical artefact due to burden-sharing between RO member states |
| | H2b | RO policy scope | Positive | √ (in tendency) | √ | |
| | H2c | RO offices at IO | Positive | √ | √ | |
| IO | H3a | IO size | Positive | √ | – | Comprehensive multilevel finding statistical artefact due to burden-sharing between RO member states |
| | H3b | IO decision making per majority vote | Positive | – | – | |
| Policy properties | H4 | Trade policies | Positive | √ | n.a. | |
| Cross-level effects | Hca | RO member homogeneity | Positive | n.a. | – | |
| | Hcb | RO chair | Positive | n.a. | √ | |
| | Hcc | RO–IO policy match | Positive | n.a. | √ | |
| | Hcd | RO formal status in IO | Positive | n.a. | √ | |
| | Hce | RO resource allocation regarding IO | Positive | n.a. | √ | |

table C.1). The more administrative capacities countries have (H1a), and the more strongly their diplomats are democratically socialised (H1b), the easier the construction of common regional positions become, that these states can subsequently articulate in IO negotiations. Incentives matter as well for the motivation of states to voice a formulated regional position. Most notably, the stronger the states support regional integration, the more likely they are to act on behalf of an RO (H1d). Power is also a motivator for states, but the linear relationship as expected by the hypothesis 1c does not hold empirically. While the most powerful states, such as the United States and China, can act unilaterally and do not need the RO in order to leverage up in international negotiations, the least powerful states (e.g. Tuvalu, Burundi, or the Central African Republic) do not vocalise regional positions the most often, because they simply lack the capacities necessary to actively participate in many international negotiations at all.

On the regional level, the European Union, followed by the UN African Group and the UN GRULAC are most prevalent in the negotiations (absolute number of speeches made for and by these regional actors are 1,052, 655 and 207, respectively), while others such as the East African Community, the Organisation for American States or the European Free Trade Association only spoke up once. RO-level properties impact the likelihood that positions of particular ROs are articulated in international negotiations. In general, the size of ROs (H2a), the scope of policy competencies of ROs (H2b), and the number of RO offices at IO headquarters (H2c) tend to increase the probability for regional activity (c.f. table C.1). Thus, well-equipped ROs with broad policy scopes and many member states, such as the EU, are more active in international negotiations than ROs with few or no offices in New York and the other IO headquarters, with a more limited scope of competencies as well as fewer member states, such as the Shanghai Cooperation Organisation or the European Free Trade Association.

The examination of the international level revealed that not all IOs attract regional actor activity to an equal extent. In some IOs, multilateral negotiations are more strongly regionalised than in others. For instance, the ILO, the UNCTAD or the WHO features more than twice the share of regional positions that are voiced in the IWC, the IOM or UNESCO. The larger IOs are, the more strongly they attract regional positions (H3a). At the same time, the formal decision-making rules do not have a systematic impact on regional actor activity, and the expectation that ROs are more active in majority-vote IOs (H3b) is not the case (c.f. table C.1). When IOs grant formal status as observers or members to ROs, this increases the incentives of their members to become active on behalf of the RO and, thus, contributes to the regionalisation of the negotiations in the respective IO (Hcd).

Policy themes also impact the propensity of regional actor activity. When trade issues are on the negotiation agenda of an IO, the vocality of ROs increases (H4). Likewise, the greater the match between the policy competencies of an RO and the policy issues at stake in IO negotiations, the more active the respective RO becomes in these negotiations (Hcc).

These findings of the focused level analysis also hold, when all level variables are incorporated in a comprehensive, multilevel model (c.f. table C.1). In addition to testing the effect of the individual-level variables on the likelihood that states voice specific RO positions in specific negotiations while controlling for state, RO, IO and policy effects, the comprehensive analysis also examines cross-cutting effects. This takes the nested character of state, regional and international levels into consideration. Most importantly this reveals that states are more likely to speak on behalf of a specific RO in international negotiations when they chair the RO at the time being (Hcb). Thus, Denmark, Hungary and France often expressed EU positions during the time in which they served as Presidency of the EU, and Brazil was very active on behalf of MERCOSUR, whilst chairing this RO. Also, the stronger the competencies of an RO overlap with the policy issues under negotiation in an IO, the easier the development of regional positions for these negotiations becomes and the more likely it is that the positions of the former are articulated in the latter (Hcc). The formal status that IOs grant ROs also matters (Hcd). The prospect that positions of a particular RO are voiced in international negotiations increases, when RO members are committed to acting on behalf of the RO, which is the case when the RO has invested resources in getting the latter accredited as observers or member in an IO. Moreover, whenever an RO has invested coordination resources into preparing for negotiations in a specific IO, its activity increases in this IO (Hce). However, the homogeneity amongst RO member states does not impact the likelihood that states voice positions of the respective RO more often, although Hca would have expected such an effect.

### C.1.2 The successful participation of ROs in IOs

Chapters 5–7 show that activity is an essential prerequisite for negotiation *success of ROs* in IOs, but not sufficient in itself. Not every instance in which a regional actor actively participates in international negotiations translates into a successful change of negotiation dynamics (e.g. talking third-party states into supporting a specific position) and outcomes (e.g. influencing the text of international rules and norms). Moreover, not all ROs are equally successful, and RO success varies within and across international negotiations. This variation can also be captured by the EMLG approach put forward in chapter 2 since factors conducive to RO success are located on the state, the regional as well as the international level. Three case studies on negotiations of the SAWS, the ATT and the 2014 Rome Declaration taking place in the IWC, the ATT regime, the FAO negotiation arenas, respectively, reveal that ROs can play an important role In the international level, especially under certain scope conditions.

Concerning state-level properties, the case studies showed that furthering regional interests, burden-sharing amongst RO member states, by which they coordinate themselves and divide the negotiation activities for their RO amongst them, is not a common practice in international negotiations. It is also highly conducive to being successful in influencing negotiation dynamics and outcomes in line with regional preferences (H5a). This is especially the case when negotiations are complex and cover a vast array of Articles and when the members of a specific RO have individually too few capacities to do the leg work of negotiating on behalf of an RO in the informal (e.g. coffee breaks, workshops) and formal negotiation arenas alone. Another insight of the case studies is that in line with hypothesis 5b, showcasing internal disagreement of RO members in the IO counteracts the RO's collective efforts to influence negotiation dynamics and outcomes. While national positions of RO member states are usually far from being in natural alignment with one another, it is quite rare that after group coordination meetings have developed a regional position an individual member state voices dissent or even contrary national positions in IO negotiations.

Being active is a necessary condition for success in negotiations. Accordingly, the case studies illustrated that the ROs that are more vocal tend to be more successful to alter dynamics and outcomes of negotiations that the ones that take a backseat (H6a). The case studies also revealed that not each activity is equally effective in all situations. Bargaining strategies allow ROs to make use of their collective leverage. Yet, bargaining is effective only when ROs have bargaining power in a specific negotiation setting, such as possessing enough votes to turn a positive into a negative vote (H6b). However, without being in a pivotal position, bargaining remains an ineffective strategy and is, therefore, less frequently used than arguing strategies. Unlike bargaining, argumentative strategies are not based on threats and promises, but on persuasion by the better argument (H6c). This works well if the RO that uses arguments can recur to unchallenged expertise. However, whenever two or more policy frames clash, the effectiveness of argumentative strategies have their limits. Especially in argumentative or bargaining stalemates, lock-in strategies are promising pathways for influence in international negotiations. Lock-in strategies link a contested issue under negotiation to pre-agreed language from other international norms, rules and treaties and threaten thus the opponents with losses of reputation, should they oppose formerly agreed norms, rules or treaties (H6d). Thus, through lock-in strategies, RO members can exert influence over negotiation dynamics in breaking stalemates and thereby also influence negotiation outcomes, as, for instance, the FAO case illustrated. Apart from these negotiation strategies, all of which are prominent in the official negotiation settings (Conferences of the Parties, preparatory committees or official working groups), ROs can also recur to lobbying in informal settings. This includes approaching third-party states informally during coffee breaks, lunches, receptions or workshops at the IO headquarter or even the ministries or embassies of third parties in different countries in order to talk them into supporting a specific regional position. Thus, lobbying is highly capacity-intensive (e.g. diplomatic manpower) and is the more effective, the better the RO is equipped in this respect (H6e). Finally, especially in international negotiations in which an RO is not in a pivotal position, reaching out to other collective actors to construct coalitions could be a promising strategy (H6f), which is, however, not very prominent amongst ROs in practice. When coalition-building between ROs happens, it usually takes places on ad hoc basis, as the ATT case study illustrates. The FAO case further illustrates that regional actors with hardly any own capacities are not using this strategy at all.

In sum, the case studies revealed that there is not the one superior strategy for ROs that is always effective. Rather, the scope conditions for the effectiveness of negotiation strategies vary from strategy to strategy and are often also contingent upon contextual variables, such as the distribution of votes and positions in an international negotiation or the number of policy frames used by third-party actors. Thus, the case studies revealed that ROs are most successful if they consecutively adopt a mix of different negotiation strategies during an international negotiation rather than just sticking with one.

Shifting to the IO level, which IOs are most conducive to RO success? In general, the EMLG approach expects high levels of regionalisation of international negotiations taking place in IOs, the more ROs possess important formal competencies in IOs decision-making processes (H7a), the larger IOs are (H7b), and if decisions are taken by vote in an IO (H7c) (c.f. chapter 2).

Regarding openness to ROs, the FAO ranges before the ATT and the IWC negotiation arenas. In the FAO, regional organisations can not only become observers to the Conference of the Parties, but also full members. Moreover, the FAO is very open to regional actors, as the first working group that prepared the draft Rome Declaration had exclusive regional group memberships. While the EU is the only full member RO in the FAO, several ROs have registered as observers and have thus also formal access to negotiations. Compared with this, the ATT negotiation arena is formally less open to regional actors. The latter cannot obtain full membership right, but can – and in many instances do – become observers. Also, in the ATT negotiation regime, there are no working groups or committees in which regional actors are the prime actors. Compared to the ATT negotiation arena, the IWC is the least open to ROs. Only one regional actor, namely the European Union, has observer status (in the negotiation in 2011, 2012 and 2014). Thus, hypothesis 7a expects that the IWC is the institutional negotiation arena in which RO success should be the weakest, preceded by the ATT and the FAO. As expected by H7a, ROs were least successful in the IWC. Only the BAG and the EU did seek to exert influence. The BAG drafted the SAWS proposal. It managed to strengthen it, whilst fighting off weakening text changes. However, the SAWS proposal was not passed. In the ATT, ROs were very active regarding many of the articles under negotiation and succeeded in leaving their imprints on the final outcome document in several respects. Comparing the FAO and the ATT cases, it becomes evident that which regional actors are involved in the negotiations is influenced by the IO institutional design. In the 2014 Rome Declaration case, FAO and WHO regional groups were the exclusive actors in one negotiation arena, the JWG. Accordingly, they played an important role and the most active ROs were also often successful. In line with H7a, the EU, which had an even stronger formal role due to its full membership status, was even more successful than the institutional regional groups. While ROs with formal status were very active and also highly successful, other ROs did not actively participate in the negotiations on the 2014 Rome Declaration. In contrast, in the ATT case, the institutional design does not privilege certain ROs over others, which leads to a higher diversity of active ROs, but also a somewhat lower prospect for average RO success.

Comparing the size of the three negotiation arenas, the order is the following. The FAO has 194 member states, closely followed by the ATT with 193 and the IWC with 88 members in the period of examination. Thus, based on hypothesis 7b, we would expect that the IWC is considerably less conducive to RO success, than the ATT and the FAO. The reason behind this expectation is that the FAO and the ATT are large IOs, in which negotiations would be lengthy and inefficient if each member state would take the floor individually. This provides a window of opportunity for ROs to become active and in turn also successful. When states – instead of voicing their own individual position – negotiate either through ROs or when RO delegates negotiate directly in international negotiations, the negotiations become more efficient. This effect is considerably less strong in the IWC, which has less than half the member states of the ATT and the FAO. Hence, the empirical findings of the three case studies support hypothesis 7b. Compared to the IWC, ROs were considerably more successful in influencing dynamics and outcomes of international negotiations in the ATT and the FAO.

Finally, when it comes to IO decision-making rules, the three negotiation arenas differ as well. In the IWC, a qualified majority would have been required to adopt the SAWS. In the ATT arena, the Treaty needed to be passed by consensus (while it could be adopted by majority vote in the UNGA). Finally, although the FAO's rules of procedure would also have allowed majority voting, the Rome Declaration on Nutrition of 2014 was passed per acclamation. Hypothesis 7c expects that if decisions are taken by vote in an IO, ROs should be more successful the more member states they have. By contrast, in consensus IOs, all actors have equal weight, and each IO member state can veto a decision, which reduces the prospects of regional actors to be successful based on the fact that they bundle votes. Thus, looking at the formal procedural rules of the respective international negotiation arenas, the IWC and the FAO should have been most conducive to RO success, while the ATT negotiation arena is less favourable. The empirical findings from the case studies do not support this expectation on the aggregate level, since regional actors were least successful in the IWC and most successful in the FAO. When zooming into the one IO in which voting took place, the IWC, large ROs should be have more successful than smaller ROs. However, this is not the case, since the BAG is smaller but scored more procedural successes in the SAWS negotiations than the larger EU. Thus, H7c needs to be rejected.

Taken together, in line with H7a and 7b of the EMLG approach the IWC negotiation dynamics and outcomes are the least regionalised, while ROs are considerable more successful in FAO negotiations, closely followed by the ATT negotiations. By contrast, the formal decision-making mode in an IO has no bearings on the regionalisation of international negotiation outcomes.

Finally, policy properties are also of importance for the prospects of ROs to exert influence in international negotiations. The higher the saliency of an issue on the international negotiation table for a specific RO, the more motivated its members are to invest their time and resources in negotiation on behalf of the RO (H8). Thus, under conditions of high issue salience, it is more often the case that RO members use burden-sharing to multiply the usage of formal negotiation strategies as well as informal lobbying efforts and approach as many third-party states as possible to further their regional position. For instance, the IWC case study illustrated how an actor attributing high saliency (BAG) negotiates with full, while an actor with more capacities but lower saliency concerning whaling issues (EU) was less active and thus less successful than the BAG.

## C.2  ROs IN IOs: HOW TO IMPROVE ACTIVE AND SUCCESSFUL PARTICIPATION

The quantitative analysis and the qualitative case studies (chapters 3–7) have not only demonstrated that international negotiations are regionalised to a

**Table C.2. Overview of findings for RO success (DV2)**

| Level | Hypothesis | IV | Expected Effect on DV | Case Study 1 IWC | Case Study 2 ATT | Case Study 3 FAO | Comments |
|---|---|---|---|---|---|---|---|
| Member state | H5a | Burden-sharing | Positive | ✓ | ✓ | ✓ | Especially important if negotiations are complex or if RO members have little capacities |
| | H5b | Heterogeneity of national positions | Negative | ✓ | ✓ | ✓ | Showcasing internal RO disagreement is rare |
| RO | H6a | RO activity | Positive | ✓ | ✓ | ✓ | Important prerequisite for success, but not sufficient |
| | H6b | Bargaining | Positive | ✓ | ✓ | ✓ | |
| | H6c | Arguing | Positive | ✓ | ✓ | ✓ | Effectiveness reduced when two policy frames compete |
| | H6d | Lock-in | Positive | ✓ | ✓ | ✓ | Not used in IWC, rarely used in ATT, but important in FAO |
| | H6e | Lobbying | Positive | ✓ | ✓ | ✓ | Especially important if negotiations are complex and lengthy and require a lot of negotiation capacities |
| | H6f | Coalitions | Positive | ✓ | ✓ | n.a. | Rarely used |
| IO | H7a | Openness to ROs | Positive | ✓ | ✓ | ✓ | |
| | H7b | IO size | Positive | ✓ | ✓ | ✓ | |
| | H7c | IO voting | Positive | – | – | – | |
| Policy properties | H8 | Issue salience | Positive | ✓ | ✓ | ✓ | |

significant extent today. They also revealed that the regionalisation of negotiation dynamics and outcomes is not driven by all regional actors to an equal
extent. Instead, the EU and CARICOM are not only considerably more active
than CIS or the SAARC, but also more successful in influencing the content
of international norms and rules.

The primary reasons behind variation in the propensity of regional positions in international negotiations relate to the ability of states and ROs to
construct regional positions and their incentives to voice them, respectively,
as well as the opportunity structures to do so, provided by IOs themselves.

To become active on behalf of an RO in an IO, states need to know what
the regional position is in the first place. Thus, the process by which states
develop regional positions in RO coordination meetings is important. In
general, states are more likely to voice regional positions when they have
administrative capacities to participate in regional group coordination meetings and are oriented towards accepting compromises when formulating a
regional position. Regional positions can furthermore be developed more
easily, when regional organisation cover the same policy issues that are on the
IO negotiation table and past regional policies serve as vocal points. Also, the
more coordination capacities a regional actor has invested for negotiations in
specific IOs, the better regional positions can be developed and subsequently
articulated.

States are especially motivated to voice regional positions when they support regional integration, chair the RO in question and are invested into getting the RO accredited as observer or member in an IO. The most powerful
states have very limited incentives to voice regional positions, as they are
not in need of leveraging up through groups in international negotiations and
can afford to act on their own. While the least powerful states have strong
incentives to voice regional positions in order to leverage up in international
negotiations, they are not often active on behalf of an RO as they lack the
capacities to actively participate in all IOs they have joined.

Finally, opportunity structures also play a role for regional actor activity in
international negotiations. In larger IOs aggregating national statements into
group statements improves the speed and effectiveness of the international
negotiation dynamics. Thus, larger IOs attract more regional positions than
smaller IOs.

In general, ROs have the greatest prospects for successfully furthering their
regional positions in international negotiations, when the group homogeneity
is high so that member states do not showcase RO internal heterogeneity, and
when the ROs are very active in international negotiations and apply a broad
variety of different strategies vis-à-vis third-party states. Thus, similar to RO
activity (DV1) variation in RO success (DV2) is related to capacities, incentives and opportunity structures as well.

Capacities matter for the number of times ROs can get active, the number of negotiation formal strategies they can employ during an international negotiation and the extent of informal lobbying. As the ATT and the FAO cases illustrated; international negotiations are oftentimes complex and cover a series of different issues across a large number of articles and paragraphs. Thus, a single state acting on behalf of an RO would soon reach its capacity limits and would need to pick and choose which issues to follow and which ones to drop. In this context, burden-sharing amongst RO members helps to overcome capacity shortages, as ROs divide the negotiation tasks amongst some of their members rather than relying on a single delegation.

Incentives are also important since RO members need to be willing to invest their own time and resources to promote the regional position in the IO. The case studies illustrated that this motivation is particularly high when the issue at the IO negotiation table has a high level of saliency for the RO. Another incentive of RO members to invest their own resources for the RO lies in a contextual factor, the size of IOs. The larger IOs are, the slower and the less effective international negotiations are, should each IO member state voice its own position during a tour de table. Thus, especially in larger IOs, RO members should be motivated to work through regional groups.

Finally, opportunity structures in the form of the openness of IOs for ROs also impact the prospects of RO success as well. The more ROs have formal access to negotiations, speaking rights or even formal votes, the more opportunity RO delegates have to become active themselves, rather than only relying on their member states to promote the regional position.

These findings allow for an *outlook* of how regional actors could make their voices better heard in international negotiations, since being vocal is an important prerequisite for the ability of regional actors to influence negotiation dynamics and outcomes in line with their regional preferences. The first set of recommendations focuses on the ability of ROs to become vocal in the first place, either through their member states or RO institutional actors (e.g. the RO delegation, secretariat or executive actor). The second set of recommendations zooms into the nexus between negotiation activities and negotiation resources on the one hand, and the chances of regional actors to leave regional imprints on dynamics and outcomes of international negotiations.

Without the existence of regional positions concerning the issues on IO negotiation agendas, states or regional actor delegate cannot get active on behalf of the RO. Thus, to maximise the prospects for shaping international negotiations, regional actors need to first to support the ability and incentives of its members to act in concert and develop and voice regional positions in IOs.

There are no immediate remedies, but in the mediate and longer term, ROs can improve the prerequisites of turning into actors in IOs. In the mediate term, regional actors could boost the effective and swift construction of regional positions by setting up offices at IO headquarters to provide administrative support and possibly also policy expertise to the member states, and help setting up and conducting regional group coordination meetings. The resource allocation of ROs to aid their members when they are trying to organise collective action can be adjusted in the mediate term. This would increase the RO's prospects to ultimately be successful in multilateral negotiations within IOs. Changing the formal status of ROs in IOs, increasing RO's policy scope internally and optimising RO enlargement processes are long-term strategies to the same end.

In the longer term, enlargement criteria are important, since larger ROs tend to be more active in general and since member state properties influence the prospects of developing regional positions. When states with high levels of administrative capacities and support regional integration strongly join an RO, they are able to actively participate in RO coordination meetings and international negotiations. When they are also highly democratic they are used to making compromises, which increases the chance that states can agree on a common regional position, and are subsequently motivated to act on behalf of the RO in IOs. Compared to that, ROs, which enlarged by accepting new member states with limited administrative capacities, limited willingness to compromise and limited incentives to voice regional positions, have fewer chances that the positions of the regional actors are voiced. Moreover, when new member states are very powerful, they have limited incentives to leverage up through regional groups, while very weak states have incentives to operate through groups, but often lack the capacities to do so. Thus, the ideal new RO member state would be of medium power. The second type of long-time reform could also impact the prospects of regional actors to become vocal on the international level. The larger the RO's scope of policy competencies, the more vocal points are available for the development of regional positions, and the greater the chances that the regional positions are articulated in IO negotiations. Hence, when ROs broaden their policy mandates through treaty changes or amendments, it has the potential to benefit the regional actor in the longer run in international negotiations. Last but not least, accrediting the RO as an observer or even full member increases the commitment of its members to act coherently in the respective IO. Thus, when ROs invest resources and political clout to improve their official standing in IOs, their prospects for having their voices articulated in the respective international negotiations increases as well. Yet, not all IOs are equally open to regional actors. As a consequence, this strategy to maximise RO activity and ultimately RO influence in IOs is contingent upon the opportunity structures provided by the different institutional contexts.

The discussion of RO success determinants has revealed that ROs are more successful the more capacities they possess collectively and use based on burden-sharing for a broad variety of different formal and informal negotiation strategies. Hence, in the short and mediate term, ROs without burden-sharing practices could set up an informal process for dividing the international negotiation work and placing it on more than one shoulder. In the longer term, ROs can use enlargement processes to attract capacity-wise well-equipped new member states that could subsequently support the RO in IO contexts on the basis of burden-sharing. Moreover, another long-term approach to improve the prospects for RO success would be to get the RO accredited, ideally as a full member or, as the second-best option, as an observer. The other contextual factors conducive for RO success, IO size and issue saliency, cannot be manipulated by an immediate- or long-term RO improvement approach as they are outside of its control.

In sum, while there are plenty of toeholds for ROs to improve their performance concerning active participation in IOs, the number of issues they can address to optimise their prospects for the success of negotiations as such is more limited. But, since RO activity is an important prerequisite for RO success, regional actors wishing to maximise their abilities to leave regional imprints on international norms can always work on improving their prospects for activity, though improving their ability to develop regional positions and act on that basis in a coherent manner.

## C.3 OUTLOOK: AVENUES FOR FUTURE RESEARCH

Based on the insights of this book, there are basically three promising avenues for future research, including a longitudinal approach to study the regionalisation of international negotiations, a comparative regionalism agenda for the comparative analysis of ROs as external actors all over the globe, as well as a research agenda that puts the complexity of international and regional regimes at centre stage.

The first avenue for research is most closely related to the theme of this book. This book provides a snapshot as it studies a five-year time frame. This offers novel and valuable insights into the current state of regionalisation of negotiations within IO arenas and its underlying causes. Yet, it does not enquire whether regionalisation is an increasing trend over time and, if so, how the temporal patterns look like and can be accounted for. Thus, a longitudinal analysis of the regionalisation of international negotiations would be a fruitful endeavour to uncover long-term trends and complement the study of this book.

The second avenue for future research is studying ROs as external actors in a broad, comparative perspective. The increase in the number of regional organisations and the broadening of their policy scopes and memberships in the post-WWII and again in the post–Cold War era have contributed to a changing role of ROs, since they have increasingly turned into external actors themselves. This includes not only the participation in international negotiations within IOs, but also RO's foreign policy towards neighbouring states or the near abroad (Freyburg et al. 2009, Kelley 2006, Knodt and Princen 2003, Lavenex 2008, Lavenex and Schimmelfennig 2011, Wetzel et al. 2015) and the ROs' promotion and diffusion of norms and rules into other regions (Börzel and Risse 2012b, a, Grabbe 2001, Jetschke and Lenz 2013, Jetschke and Murray 2012). These examples indicate that the field of comparative regionalism and its interplay with the field of international relations provides a rich research field, which, however, currently is still suffering from an EU bias. The EU bias manifests itself as most studies examine how the EU acts towards third-party states or other ROs, while the other more than seventy regional organisations of today are considerably less often studied as external actors in their own right. Consequently, a fertile future strand of research could study ROs as external actors in a comparative manner. In addition, there are no comparative longitudinal studies of ROs as external actors as of yet. We know very little of how RO capacities and capabilities for external action as well as the ROs' external activities have changed over time and across the globe. Do we see a trend towards a world of regions and a region-alisation of international affairs in general?

Finally, with the increase in the number of international as well as regional organisations came about an increasing complexity of governance beyond the nation-state. Today, IOs overlap with respect to both member states and policy competencies. The combination of membership and policy overlap provides opportunity structures for actors who can engage in forum-shopping and arena selection as the emerging literature on regime complexity has pointed out (Alter and Meunier 2009, Betts 2013, Crump and Zartman 2003, Drezner 2009, Hafner-Burton 2009, Morin and Orsini 2013, Oberthür and Stokke 2011). Concerning ROs in IOs, overlapping membership and policy mandates are rarely under scrutiny (for an exception c.f. Panke et al. 2017). Similarly, overlapping regionalism and, more specifically, its patterns, causes and consequences for effective and legitimate governance of both ROs and their member states have not yet received much scholarly attention. This is despite the timeliness of the phenomenon and the importance of its potential consequences (for an exception c.f. Panke and Stapel 2016).

Today regional actors from all over the globe form an integral part of the global governance architecture. Thus, a broadening of the comparative regionalism research agenda seems to be a worthwhile endeavour.

# Notes

## Chapter 2

1. Benz 2000, Christiansen 1997, Enderlein et al. 2010, Falkner 1999, Grande 2000, Jachtenfuchs 2001, Kohler-Koch and Eising 1999, Levi-Faur 2012, March and Olsen 1994, Marks 1993, 1997, Marks and Hooghe 2001, Marks et al. 1996, Neyer 2003, Scharpf 1997b, 2000, Schuppert 2005, von Krause 2008.

2. Others have used the term before (e.g. Falkner 2002, Frennhoff Larsen 2007, Patterson 1997), but not to capture how and under which conditions ROs can turn into active and potentially also into influential actors in IOs.

3. For instance, UNGA, UNCTAD, UNFCCC, UNESCO, HRC, ECOSOC, UNEP, UNHCR, ILO, WHO, WIPO, IAEA.

4. For instance, WTO, IBRD/IMF, IOM.

5. There is dissent in the literature on the status of this variable, as some regard member state position homogeneity as necessary, but not sufficient, while others tend to regard it as sufficient condition (c.f. Macaj and Nicolaïdis 2014, Smith 2013b).

6. Typically, lower-level actors such as US state or German Länder representatives negotiate and pass common policies on higher levels such as on the federal level or the Bundesebene either among themselves, like in the US Senate or the German Bundesrat, or with higher-level actors such as the Senate with the House of Representatives or the Bundesrat with the Bundestag. Accordingly, actors in multilevel systems face a joint decision trap due to the high number of veto points (Benz 1985, 1999, Elazar 1994, Kincaid 1990, König and Bräuninger 1997, Michelmann and Soldatos 1990, Scharpf 1988, Smiley and Watts 1985, Tsebelis 2002, Tsebelis and Garrett 1997, Wälti 1996, Watts 1999, Wheare 1963, Whitaker 1983).

7. In the EU, as in other regional supranational organisations, governance takes place on the member state and the regional levels, which are institutionally interlinked concerning agenda setting, decision making and the implementation and enforcement of common norms (Benz 2003, 2004 Benz et al. 1992, Christiansen 1997, Conzelmann 1998, Falkner 1999, Grande 2000, Hooghe and Marks 2001, Koslowski 2001,

Marks and Hooghe 2001, McKay 2002, Neyer 2003, Scharpf 1997b, 1999, Schmidt 1999).

8. To this end, it draws on approaches of RO decision making and liberal theory. The former emphasises the role of institutional structures and intergovernmental practices for the development of RO policies (e.g. Eising and Kohler-Koch 1999, Enderlein et al. 2010, Jachtenfuchs and Kohler-Koch 1996, Kohler-Koch and Eising 1999, Marks and Hooghe 2001). Liberal approaches flag that national positions are not just out there but need to be constructed domestically in the first place to allow for subsequent active participation in negotiations (e.g. Evans et al. 1993, Putnam 1988). While current research applies these insights to state involvement in IO or in RO negotiations, this book also applies them to RO involvement in IOs.

9. Two reasons stick out. First, state coordination in ROs reduces the number of positions at the IO negotiation table, especially in IOs with broad membership, and speeds up and simplifies the negotiations, which is essential for the chances of producing international norms (e.g. interview#159, 15-03-12). Second, most IOs are based on the principle of sovereign equality, which is expressed in one-state, one-vote decision making. In such contexts, states might increase their bargaining leverage and their chances of influencing international norms considerably if they express the position of an RO rather than an individual state interest (e.g. interview#39, 07-03-11).

10. While the three-level game metaphor has been used by others before (Collinson 1999, Falkner 2002, Paarlberg 1997, Patterson 1997), they do not apply the analytical framework to the role of ROs in IO negotiations. Two-level game theory focuses on the interplay between the domestic and the international levels. Prior to international negotiations, states must develop their preferences in the domestic realm. In this context, states with a high number of veto points (e.g. coalition governments, bicameralism, federalism) can be empowered vis-à-vis other states. By using a 'tied-hands' strategy, negotiators can point to their narrow win-sets and argue that their ability to make concessions is constrained by the presence and interests of domestic veto players who would not accept particular solutions, thereby asking other states with fewer or less strong veto players for concessions (Lehman and McCoy 1992, Mo 1995, Putnam 1988). At the same time, international negotiations empower governments vis-à-vis domestic actors (e.g. veto players) and allow them to de facto broaden their win-set (cutting slack strategy). International negotiations often take place behind closed doors, so that parliaments or line ministries have limited information about the negotiation dynamics. If the government wishes to pursue a position or support a negotiation outcome that differs from the position preferred by domestic actors, they can do so and defend the outcome as the best possible achievement.

11. For example Benz 1998, Reissert 1976, Scharpf 1988, Scharpf et al. 1976, Zintl 1992.

12. For example Delreux 2009a, 2013, Groenleer and Schaik 2007, Kaunert 2010, Kissack 2010, Monar 2004, Oberthür 1999, Panke 2014b, Peterson and Smith 2003, Söderbaum and Van Langenhove 2005, Wunderlich 2012, Zwartjes et al. 2012, Xiarchogiannopoulou and Tsarouhas 2014

13. Moreover, this also applies to studies on states in international negotiations. They often focus on the success or lack of success of states or alliances (Bailer 2004,

Keohane and Nye 1989, Powell 1999, Selck and Kaeding 2004), but hardly on the varying extent to which different actors actively participate in negotiations and voice their positions (for an exception see Panke 2011b, 2012b, 2013c).

14. It does not, however, eradicate the problem of subjective perceptions. Even in surveys, answer categories, such as very often, often, regularly, hardly, not at all, and continuous answer options, such activity of voicing a position in % with daily = 100% and never = 0% are subject to interpretation of the survey respondent and can vary between individuals.

15. While triangulation is not possible systematically, the intersubjective quality of survey data can be checked by complementing a survey with a range of semi-structured interviews whereby diplomats are asked to assess the activity/performance of other actors.

16. Similarly, within the ILO the EU performs better in negotiations on items in the technical domain, than on political issues (Kissack 2011).

17. While activity is essential for success, it is not sufficient (Panke 2013c). For example, an actor can actively voice his or her own positions and use a broad array of bargaining strategies in order to shape the final policy outcome, but if the actor lacks bargaining leverage it is unlikely that the strategy will be effective and the actor is most likely not influential.

## Chapter 3

1. Moreover, this also applies to studies on states in international negotiations. They often focus on influence or success of states or alliances (Bailer 2004, Keohane and Nye 1989, Powell 1999, Selck and Kaeding 2004), but hardly on the varying extent to which different actors actively participate in negotiation and voice their positions (for an exception see Panke 2011b, 2012b, 2013c).

2. Examples include the Organization of the Petroleum Exporting Countries, the International Union for the Conservation of Nature or International Telecommunications Satellite Organization.

3. Due to the unavailability of reliable and comparative data access for all selected IOs, we did not map negotiation activities of ROs in informal settings (e.g. coffee breaks or lunches) or in preparatory committees without or with only limited member state access (e.g. the Joint Working Group [JWG] of the FAO and WHO, c.f. chapter 7).

4. The discrepancy between observations and statements is due to the fact that actors can speak up more than once during a negotiation.

5. Regional organisations are responsible directly or indirectly for 1,378, or 6.76 per cent, of the recorded activity, while regional groups account for 1,063 regional positions voiced (5.18 per cent).

6. When statements by RO delegates themselves are omitted, this results in a total number of 2.097 positions voiced by states on behalf of their RO. For example, the EU's Commission and, since May 2011, the EU delegation can make statements directly for the EU in the UNGA, in which the EU has observer status and an enhanced observer status since May 2011. While the enhanced observer status of

the EU is a special case, most regional actors do speak up for themselves. Further examples for vocal ROs are the AU and the LAS, both speaking up exclusively for themselves through delegates in the sampled negotiations.

7. Compared to the case study on the Rome Declaration on Nutrition (c.f. chapter 7), in which regional actors were very active, the FAO's percentage of 3.66 in table 3.5 seems to be very low. However, while the case study also captures negotiations in informal settings (workshops, receptions, etc.) and in preparatory committees to which not all or no member states have access (the JWG), the mapping in chapter 3 only captures formal negotiations in the main legislative arenas (e.g. CoPs, member state committees). Thus, the mapping and the quantitative analysis of RO negotiation activity (chapter 4) is conservative and captures only the tip of an iceberg.

8. The twelve categories are agriculture, development, education, environment, finance/economy, health, human rights, internal issues, security, social affairs, technology and trade.

9. The factor analysis shows that internal issues are, similar to security, rarely discussed isolated, but mostly part of discussions on other policy fields. C.f. Annex table A3.2.

## Chapter 4

1. Developing a regional position in group coordination meetings in a manner that brings all member states on board is essential for RO activity in international negotiations. A diplomat explained: 'We are in GRULAC, that's Latin America and the Caribbean, we're a very active participant in that group and usually the way we work here is that we reach consensus within the group, and we go with the GRU-LAC position to the plenary. If there is no consensus, every country will just ask for the floor and give its position on the matter. But generally we reach consensus' (interview#215, 03-02-16). Another diplomat reported: 'there is no secretariat of the group that develops a statement and then speaks. If the group wants to speak and have meaning, not a single word will be spoken unless everyone in the group has endorsed it. So, for example, we have important meetings coming up and the chair's responsibility, and this changes every year, is that he would present a draft and circulate it to the group and wait for comment. After the comments come, he revises it accordingly, then passes it back as a final version. Once it is endorsed by each and all members, then the group will deliver a statement on behalf of the group' (interview#69, 22-03-11).

2. For example: 'There're others where they may really not have a position because the bureaucracy is such that it's one of those issues where they never really had to concern themselves about. . . . I think an organised government, and organised bureaucracy does lead to a more organised mission putting our more consistent positions' (interview#7, 22-10-10).

3. Such states are not always participating in group coordination meetings: 'Of course it takes a lot of time, but at the same time, we attach great importance to the EU as an organisation, so we have to be there, that is a political decision by our ambassador or by our Ministry of Foreign Affairs, that we have to be present at all EU

coordination meetings. It is also because if there is a split, for one reason or another, we need to communicate that back to the capital. But smaller countries like Luxembourg, Cyprus, they are definitely not there all the time. I can only imagine that they experience those time constraints even more with our limits of resources, because they simply do not have the time to follow everything. Some of the Missions are only four or five people; it is impossible for them to be at six committees in parallel that coordinate pretty much all the time. They try to be there only when there are only big decisions to be made within the EU, and as soon as that decision has been made, they stop following it, because their interest is taken care of by the presidency' (interview#5, 05-05-10). Concerning states with ineffective government apparatuses, a diplomat reported: 'They don't know what their position is, so they don't participate, it happens a lot' (interview#7, 22-10-10). Another interviewee stated, 'You could say . . . political, administrative capacity determine the absent rates, I would definitely agree with that, and maybe even say that that is the most determining factor when it comes to being present at GA meetings' (interview#5, 05-10-10). Also, 'You have the big countries who really have great capacity and that, of course, is a determining factor when it comes to absent rates' (interview#5, 05-10-10). Similarly, 'Intuitively, I'm guessing that quite a few of the absentees are people who don't have somebody to attend those negotiations. And if they do then they're not at the negotiations. So they're not in a position to write instructions, for their capitals to be fair to them are at a disadvantage. And maybe they don't even want to tell their capital because then it'll just highlight the fact that they haven't been reporting on them previously. So yes, I think that it does come down to that. There's a lack of resources on the New York end, and that kind of has a chances are if they're poorly resourced in New York, then they're often poorly resourced in the capital. It's a kind of vicious cycle of under-resourceness' (interview#10, 15-11-10). 'Obviously, if the government is ineffective, they're really not going to care about some little resolution that in the UN and taking a position on it, quite frankly' (interview#7, 22-10-10). 'If a country is not getting any direction from home, people don't want to take a chance on voting and irritate somebody at home' (interview#18, 26-11-10). 'If you don't have an instruction and you're not sure how to vote, you can also decide not to be there, because you didn't have the instruction from back home, because lack of preparedness you didn't have the right instruction, or if it came, it came too late. And that has to do with capacity because people with more capacity will certainly give instructions on all issues, on time, so that you're able to do the full thing' (interview#11, 16-11-10).

4. A diplomat from a democratic country explained: 'There are times there are certain positions that are taken on board in regard to the larger group position that wouldn't necessarily be your own national position but for the sake of consensus we all agree to keep a particular reference keep a particular paragraph in a statement or in a resolution of whatever we are discussing' (interview#44, 08-03-11). Similarly, a colleague from another democratic country explained: 'One of the weaknesses of the regional group is that normally it's the weakest link that determines the position of the group, sometimes. And that has been used sometimes as an argument by saying that it forces other group members because of group loyalty to go along with that position' (interview#120, 29-09-11).

5. For example: 'Not all states have the same interests and have the same capacities and resources to follow and be active in the very long deliberations. . . . I think that small states have only a few notes of vital national interest, and probably a few others that are probably related to more or less our neighbourhood and what impacts it directly. And so, it is only natural that they focus on only a few notes of their foreign policy priorities' (interview#14, 24-11-10).

6. A diplomat reported: 'One voice in regional group has impact more than one country speaking alone. From what I have seen here, one country is not going to affect an issue. This still depends on what country. If you are big, powerful, and you speak with your voice, it still makes difference. Others don't. For a small country . . . speaking as one voice with the group makes more influence than alone' (interview#68, 18-03-11) and 'If you do have a group position, it is always more influential than an individual country. That might be different with the big players, the French or the British. They are a big country with lots of influence. Smaller countries like ours don't have that influence' (interview#66, 16-03-11). Other diplomats from small states also reported that 'regional groups give you more weight in negotiations' (interview #111, 25-07-11), that regional groups 'help us to make the world hear our voice' (#161, 16-03-12) or that 'the biggest advantage for us . . . is you have an amplifier of your voice' (interview #106, 19-07-11). Another diplomat stated: 'We have found that speaking as CARICOM it makes us stronger, it gives us a stronger voice and people and sit up and listen because it is 14 as opposed to 1. I think that type of coordination helps, it also helps the smaller countries within the regional group because like myself, a lot of people are carrying more than one committee. So there may be clashes of meetings so you aren't able to participate as well as you would like in one meeting but because again there is a CARICOM statement your voice is not lost. Even if you can't deliver your own national statement you are able to make inputs into a regional statement' (interview#44, 08-03-11). Another diplomat stated: 'The small countries benefit tremendously because they immediately magnify their interest from one of a small state to one of a large group' (interview#135, 30-11-11).

7. For example: 'I am quite thankful that I am not a member of the EU, and having to take my instructions from capital, go into a consultation with my colleagues, come up with a common position there, which then gets negotiated in the room with other delegations. That adds a layer which I cannot imagine' (interview#3, 08-09-10). Another diplomat stated: 'The active countries benefit because they really project their policy priorities, but also the small countries benefit tremendously because they immediately magnify their interest from one of a small state to one of a large group' (interview#135, 30-11-11).

8. For example: 'Most of the countries joining a regional group are interested in the region' (interview#68, 18-03-11).

9. Similarly, another interviewee said: 'There will be issues on which they cannot reach a common position and then they all go in their national capacities. So, solidarity is a bit stronger within the EU than for instance in the African group – it really depends on the issue, but I have perhaps more often seen an African group not voting as a block as I do see the EU, but I suppose the EU has much more coordination mechanisms amongst itself' (interview#3, 08-09-10). Also, 'Well what we will have

is an African Group position. We would have determined who is the spokesman for Africa and that person . . . would then be told this is the point of view of the African Group and then we have one spokesperson for that rather than that being all the 54 states saying the same thing we would say this is the African Group position' (interview#154, 26-01-12). Another interviewee explained: 'GRULAC doesn't always have . . . you know we are not a group that coordinates to have a unified position all the time. We coordinate only on some positions, for example the right of a child . . . that is always an issue that we have a unified position. And on an ad-hoc basis, we have a unified position around some of the issues. But you can see if you follow the discussions, GRULAC not always has a unified position' (interview#113, 29-07-11). A diplomat explained with respect to CARICOM that 'typically on those agenda items where we have had common positions, the focal point or the chair of the caucus will deliver statements' (interview#49, 09-03-11).

10. For example, an interviewee reported: 'We are asking Member States of the European Union to burden share for the EU a specific resolution. So instead of EU delegation to represent, for example, the European Union in a specific negotiation we ask a Member State to do it on behalf of the European Union. And this is a system which is working quite well. It is the role of the EU delegation to identify which Member State would be the most suitable to negotiate on behalf of the European Union for a specific resolution, and if this Member State is agreeable, so this role is given to him, and this is helping us tremendously because obviously, we cannot be in different rooms at the same time' (interview#157, 02-03-12). Another diplomat added, 'We're able to speak on behalf of the CARICOM states and I can give you examples of others, but, yes on occasions, the focal point is empowered to speak on behalf of CARICOM member states' (interview#49, 09-03-11). 'Normally I do one or two burden sharing myself, this year I did on migration, last year I did on the drugs. So that takes, of course, your own resources of course because you have to be you speak on behalf of 27 so you have to be the one to tell the others what is going on' (interview#35, 07-03-11).

11. In line with this, a diplomat explained: 'I think it's important if it is a large number of countries, if we have a large number of countries in our group' (interview#171, 25-07-14). Yet, while larger groups have more members and can be more active, they also have greater difficulties adjusting their group positions during ongoing negotiations as 'it is more difficult for the larger group to show flexibility' (interview#27, 06-12-10).

12. A diplomat reported that the EU, as an active RO on the international level, has a broad array of policy competencies, while ROs such as the PIF are narrower in scope and are more selective regarding the topics on which they voice a regional position: 'They are looked to for more input for more contribution on sustainable development issues and those kinds of things. They do carry some weight in terms of particular areas and what is being discussed' (interview#61, 11-03-11, similarly interviews#77, 28-03-11 and #106, 19-07-11). A CARICOM member explained: 'Because the shared history of the region, shared experiences, and comparable in some instances, some levels of development you share a lot of common positions and so there is a lot of cooperation between states' (interview #162, 16-03-12) and another

diplomat stated, regarding Latin American ROs, 'I think that the biggest advantage is that we are a group with shared common values, I would say, with no big cultural differences and adhere pretty much to the same set of principles of external policy that have shaped our history, or recent history because we have been . . . we have a lot of common history' (interview#118, 23-09-11). In this regard, a member of the African Union stressed 'We share very similar heritage, culture, etc' (interview#161, 16-03-12).

13. Another example would be the African Union in the negotiations on the Rome Declaration (c.f. chapter 7). In this respect a diplomat stated: 'If you have to make any reference to the African Union, it has to be a member state, making reference to the African Union as a regional grouping. And that was done, yes it was done. For example, the issues, the African Union policy or maybe food security and nutrition. I say this, so everyone could add this, it's an object, that is the African Union as the regional organisation has already a policy which is very clear on the issues of nutrition. But by itself, it can't say, because it's not an accredited' (interview#224, 05-05-16).

14. An interviewee explained, 'It doesn't bring good psychological effect, when you hear 70 times the same argument . . . it's a question of efficiency' (interview #78, 28-03-11). Similarly, another diplomat reported: 'So, you have NAM or African States or Arab League States or whatever format. But it's a much more effective way of doing business and to be frank also for the sake of the negotiation itself it's important, because if you have 5 or 7 actors, then you can have some voice outside the choir, but not to the extent that, you know, you don't want to try to compose 193 positions, it's fairly impossible, almost impossible. So, I would say that yes, the regional approach, the EU approach is the only effective way we can deal with the current state of international affairs' (interview#203, 27-02-15).

15. A diplomat reported: 'If you want your position to be heard in multi-lateral fora, then it is always better to associate yourself with a big group' (interview #115, 09-08-11) and a colleague from another country stressed 'One voice in regional group has impact more than one country speaking alone. From what I have seen here, one country is not going to affect an issue . . . speaking as one voice with the group makes more influence than alone' (interview#68, 18-03-11).

16. For instance, a diplomat stated, 'Consensus is good so that you don't have to vote on certain issues' (interview#154, 26-01-12). With respect to the UNGA another interviewee reported, 'The budgetary negotiations always concluded by consensus, and it would be absolutely unacceptable if this tradition was to be broken' (interview#155, 15-02-12) and a colleague from another state explained: 'No, not that often because it is also a very high political cost for a delegation to break the consensus on a resolution, and whenever a resolution is adopted by consensus traditionally you will see that everyone will make the utmost to retain that consensus because no one wants to bear the burden of saying "I was the one that called for a vote"' (interview#151, 08-12-11).

17. A diplomat stated: 'Well the process, it begins in Brussels with meetings of the so called, the working group on the human rights issues so I would say that the general objective aims and in general the main principle of our positions are already

prepared well before the beginning of the third committee in the GA. Then it's up to the experts here in New York through the EU coordination to elaborate further about the details of the strategic decisions taken in Brussels, and of course the other contribution we give from New York is that we are always updated on the developments ongoing and the positions which are put forward by other regional groups or specific delegations. Let's say that the strategic priorities are set in Brussels and then the content and the elaboration I would say, of the strategic lines are defined here in New York through the coordination' (interview#92, 01-04-11). The same diplomat continued after being asked whether the positions of the EU can be developed more quickly if there was a common position in Brussels on a similar theme with: 'Of course, if there is a common position in Brussels, these speed up enormously the process. The problem sometimes is there are no common positions on specific subjects and in that case we have a lengthy and not easy coordination meeting. I would say on human rights, the occasions on which we see difficulty, the positions are divided are rare' (interview#92, 01-04-11).

18. For example: 'ASEAN . . . is evolving from an economic grouping to a political one. . . . But then, in other multi-lateral issues like broad issues of disarmament, nuclear weapons, chemical weapons, biological weapons . . . well we have the non-aligned movement' (interview #115, 09-08-11).

19. Information on model fit and the results of the outlier analysis is given in the annex (A4.2 and A4.3 respectively).

20. An interviewee explained: 'We had done a lot of sort of burden sharing, so one didn't have to cover all of the field, but we had divided various agenda items so that one of us would be responsible for certain issues and then look after that particular agenda item and dossier throughout the General Assembly' (interview#104, 14-07-11). Similarly, 'The EU delegation would not be able to cover all the items or the questions, therefore we have this burden sharing exercise or burden sharing practice whereas the people from member states can also join, you know the EU delegation in negotiating different resolutions, but obviously the burden sharer from a member state has to rely on the mandate given by the 27 as well. So there is no difference in this regard between an EU delegation negotiator or a burden sharer from a member state, it's all in the, I would say the only difference is the origin that the person comes from a member state and you know we are from the EU delegation but the mandate, the objective, the tactics are exactly the same, identical' (interview#155, 15-02-12). Also, 'How is lobbying made? We ask our PR to send letters to specific countries we divide this with burden sharing, between ourselves this is the first way. There are phone calls, we may also organise meetings with representatives from the country concerned but let's say representative with the civil society concerned with ambassadors or specific missions to work on advocacy' (interview#39, 07-03-11). Another diplomat reported that burden-sharing also takes place along the lines of priorities: 'We are a peace keeper country, so we will be following peace keeping related meetings but then there will be a whole other range of things, that are priorities of other countries so we let those countries shepherd the processes or be active in those processes. So I think there is at the end of the day there is a division of labour' (interview#150, 15-03-12).

21. For example, a diplomat reported: 'We also have a system of burden sharers because again no matter how many members we have here we cannot do it all, so on certain issues sometimes some member states that have a very keen interest in the subject may offer to assist. So that's also a very helpful system which also allows member states who feel that they have an ownership in the process and sometimes apart from the system of burden sharers you may have ad hoc cases where member states can be useful' (interview#156 21-02-12). Similarly, a European diplomat explained: 'We are asking Member States of the European Union to burden share for the EU a specific resolution. So instead of EU delegation to represent, for example, the European Union in a specific negotiation we ask a Member State to do it on behalf of the European Union. And this is a system which is working quite well. It is the role of the EU delegation to identify which Member State would be the most suitable to negotiate on behalf of the European Union for a specific resolution, and if this Member State is agreeable so this role is given to him and this is helping us tremendously because obviously we cannot be in different rooms at the same time' (interview#157, 02-03-12, similar interview#155, 15-02-12).

22. For instance, several member states of the African Union reported that they are not very active individually in international negotiations (e.g. interviews#2, 03-06-10, #6, 21-10-10, #11, 16-11-10, #119, 23-09-11, #154, 26-01-12).

23. A diplomat reported that homogeneity in a group makes it easier to turn into a collective actor 'because the shared history of the region, shared experiences, and comparable in some instances, some levels of development you share a lot of common positions and so there is a lot of cooperation between states' (interview#162, 16-03-12). By contrast, low homogeneity renders collective action more difficult: 'CELAC is a very new institution. It's still trying to find its way, time to build within the diversity we have in Latin America, it's time to build a political consensus. Because of the diversity, we have different political, economic roots, we cannot always reach consensus' (interview#214, 03-02-16).

24. Another member of the generally homogenous EU explained that 'there are issues on which we are doomed to be split' (interview#158, 06-03-12).

25. For example, a diplomat explained: 'If they try to get more approvals for one specific resolution normally they try to do this in a coordinated matter so the chair is given a mandate by the group to approach that and that country' (interview#43, 08-03-11).

26. For example: 'I think a strong chair is very important, in the EU we're mostly singing off the same hymn sheet on a lot of issues so it's maybe not as difficult than other regional groupings, you come together on one cause but you have varying national positions on other issues. I don't think it's easy to coordinate all 27 members of the EU but if you take a strong approach as I have witnessed it makes it a lot easier and the results are going to be better' (interview#107, 20-07-11). Another diplomat reported with respect to GRULAC: 'There is a lot of influence. Definitely. On how the chair presents the issues, how he manages the meetings, how strong he is in steering the group towards a unified position, definitely, yah. I mean the group needs to trust the chair and to . . . he needs to be transparent and at the same time strong, otherwise it just becomes very disunited' (interview#113,

29-07-11). And with respect to the Latin American group in the UN, an interviewee noted: 'The personality of the chair, the knowledge of the chair of the issues which are being discussed, the importance of the country which is chairing the group. All those aspects do have influence. I mean, of course, the general logic is that all the countries belonging to a certain group do accept and support the management of the chair. But, of course if the chairman is a very, is someone who is very knowledge-able . . . has a good knowledge of the issue and he's directly involved in the issue as such, then there a number of factors that influence the importance of the chair of the group. In general, as I said, there is an agreement to respect and to follow and to support whoever is chairing the various groups' (interview#114, 04-08-11). Another interviewee explained: 'And the chair really is important, because the chair has to provide the guidance and the leadership and, if necessary, try and reach compromise on issues where there are differences within the group. So, it's a dif-ficult task, and it's very important. If you have a chair who doesn't seem to exercise much leadership or interest, then what happens is sometimes, you know, well, there would be less coherence in the group . . . each country would start voicing out its own view, and it may be hard to reach a common group position' (interview#120, 29-09-11).

27. An interviewee reported that before the start of international negotiations, 'We'll sit down as a group and look at the key range of issues and decide who's interested in what and who will take leadership on certain things. Quite often the chair himself of the Forum speaks on behalf of the countries' (interview#25, 03-12-10). A colleague from a different RO explained: 'If you have a strong chair there's going to be more activity' (interview#107, 20-07-11). Another diplomat reported: 'You have to leave the speaking role to chair of the group and . . . professionally the most rewarding and interesting 6 months I had was during our EU presidency, you're speaking on behalf of your group, you're leading, advising, basically nothing goes on unless you're involved more or less' (interview#105, 19-07-11).

28. Another diplomat explained that for the EU it additionally makes a difference whether the policy field is an exclusive or a shared EU competence, as the demand for coordination is higher in the second: 'The ATT, there was a mix of competence: You have the trade elements which were obviously EU competence, but you also had a full range of conflict prevention aspects to it, of humanitarian aspects, of, you know, the very notion of setting up a new international regime. So it had a whole range of complexities to it, that meant it had to be a genuine effort of coordination between the Brussels institutions and the member states, because both competences were live. And that very much, I think, changes the way the EU acts and can act. To give you a bit of a flavour of what that might look like practically, obviously there is the EU common position on the trade in arms, I cannot remember its name, but it was originally a code of conduct that then was upgraded. . . . So there was already a pretty clear view of how the EU approaches these sorts of issues. So that was, sort of, our starting point' (interview#197, 23–02–15). A CARICOM member also explained that RO policy competencies for the issues at stake in international negotiations are important in enabling the RO to become vocal. The diplomat stated, 'When we coordinate to have a common foreign policy, the revised Treaty . . . establishing the

Caribbean single market and economy . . . provides some measure of coordination in foreign policy, not totally, we haven't reached the level of the European Union on the Lisbon Treaty, but there's a measure of coordination of foreign policy, I think one of the shining examples, of the most brilliant examples of that coordinated foreign policy was the ATT' (interview#208, 20-05-15).

29. For instance, the EU tried to become a full member of the UNGA and obtained an enhanced observer status after lengthy and contested negotiations: 'When we had, we just to have this rotating presidency, it was the member states carrying the flag of the EU, so it was no problem, now with the new system in Brussels and the Lisbon treaty, we're saying, it would be normal and logical that the EU delegation takes the floor but in order to do that we have to change rules of the GA and we have to improve the status of the EU as an observer, a resolution was presented last September, and it was defeated and blocked by a no action motion. It is a challenge for the EU because for the moment it's Hungary who is reading the EU statement and if it doesn't change it's going to be Poland in the next semester' (interview#53, 10-03-11).

30. For example: 'Definitely the EU is always active in the negotiations' (interview#48, 09-03-11) and 'the EU is very active' (interview#36, 07-03-11) or 'the EU had a strong position, very active, coordinated and professional but they're EU' (interview#20, 29-11-10).

31. Often RO delegates with observer status are silent and rely on the member states to articulate the group positions: 'We really do practice our title which is observer, we don't participate in the negotiations, we're more a coordinating body but we are present for negotiations to you know, be able to assist our group if there needs to be a position' (interview#130, 29-11-11).

32. Accordingly, a diplomat reported: 'If you're a member of a regional group . . . with, you know, ideally a seat, whereby you can, you know, even an observer seat, it certainly helps' (interview#212, 28-10-15).

33. For example, an interviewee reported: 'We had coordination meetings probably at least twice a week and we attended each one of these. And I would say that there were even times that we met every day. That is, I would say, a disadvantage of belonging to a regional group, because you spend too much time . . . and I think this is something you would hear over and over – we spend too much time on our internal coordination and too little time to actually advance our position within the UN' (interview#110, 21-07-11). Another diplomat explained 'you have your CARICOM meetings you have your group meetings you have your issues to attend to, even the coordination itself sometimes puts you in a bit of a bind and as I said you can't be everywhere at once so sometimes you have to depend on faith that the statement will be when your Capital sees it won't be something that they won't go it's time for you to come home. So it's, even the coordination as good as it is sometimes it places you in a bit of bind when you resource strapped. It's better I guess to have a voice in a large group than not at all' (interview#44, 08-03-11). Similarly, a European diplomat explained: 'Well the EU coordination meetings cannot be read independent from what happens in the negotiations because we negotiate at the beginning of the process and many times during the process. You don't have just one co-ordination meeting at the beginning, and once the EU delegation receives the mandates they can go down

the road up to the end of the negotiations with that mandate. Most of the times they have to come back to the EU coordination group to report on developments around the negotiating table and ask for an adjusted mandate in light of those developments. That's a work in progress. It starts with an initial coordination meeting in order to define an initial common position which translates to a mandate for the EU negotiation team but then the team needs to come back most of the time, it's rare they can go till the end of the process with just the initial mandate, they come back to the group, report on developments and check on what is the updated common position and what is the updated mandate for the rest of the negotiations' (interview#29, 10-12-10).

34. For example, 'The EU delegation is rather active in the EU coordination as such' (interview#36, 07-03-11) and 'I mean if you have a proactive EU delegation that puts a lot of things on the table in New York' (interview#158, 06-03-12): Another interviewee stated 'One problem that we have and hopefully after the Lisbon Treaty, the European External Action Service, now the role that the EU delegations play around the world will help mitigate is we continue to spend too much time in introspection if I may say, meaning we spend too much time agreeing on a common position rather than actively lobbying for that position' (interview#156, 21-02-12). The same interviewee continued, 'We have received the reinforcements [more staff, insertion by the authors] now and so I think we are relatively well-staffed to be able to fulfil our function'.

## Chapter 5

1. According to the proponents of the proposal, this is important as around 80 per cent of the world's whales go to the South Atlantic each summer to feed.

2. For an overview of the supporters and proponents of the SAWS proposal, c.f. figure 5.1.

3. As of January 2015 the member states of the IWC are: Antigua and Barbuda, Argentina, Australia, Austria, Belgium, Belize, Benin, Brazil, Bulgaria, Cambodia, Cameroon, Chile, People's Republic of China, Colombia, Republic of the Congo, Costa Rica, Côte d'Ivoire, Republic of Croatia, Cyprus, Czech Republic, Denmark, Dominica, Dominican Republic, Ecuador, Eritrea, Estonia, Finland, France, Gabon, Gambia, Germany, Republic of Ghana, Grenada, Guatemala, Guinea-Bissau, Republic of Guinea, Hungary, Iceland, India, Ireland, Israel, Italy, Japan, Kenya, Kiribati, Republic of Korea, Laos, Lithuania, Luxembourg, Mali, Republic of the Marshall Islands, Mauritania, Mexico, Monaco, Mongolia, Morocco, Nauru, Netherlands, New Zealand, Nicaragua, Norway, Oman, Republic of Palau, Panama, Peru, Poland, Portugal, Romania, Russian Federation, San Marino, Saint Kitts and Nevis, Saint Lucia, Saint Vincent and The Grenadines, Senegal, Slovak Republic, Slovenia, Solomon Islands, South Africa, Spain, Suriname, Sweden, Switzerland, Tanzania, Togo, Tuvalu, United Kingdom, Uruguay and the United States (International Whaling Commission 2015b).

4. When it comes to the admission of new members, the Convention sets no limitations: 'Any Government which has not signed this Convention may adhere thereto after it enters into force by a notification in writing to the Government of the United States of America' (International Whaling Commission 1946: Article X.2).

5. "Contracting Government" means any Government which has deposited an instrument of ratification or has given notice of adherence to this Convention' (Contracting Governments to the International Convention for the Regulation of Whaling 1946: Art. 2§4).

6. EU member states which are not part of the IWC are Greece (left the IWC in 2013), Latvia and Malta.

7. The IWC has a full-time Secretariat with headquarters located in the City of Cambridge, United Kingdom. In 2012 the Commission changed the rules of procedure regarding the frequency of the Commission Meeting to a biennial cycle. Besides that, the Scientific Committee shall meet annually. Other committees and sub-committees shall meet biennially, prior to the meeting of the Commission (IWC 2012: 1).

8. Article 3(a) describes, 'Where a vote is taken on any matter before the Commission, a simple majority of those casting an affirmative or negative vote shall be decisive, except that a three-fourths majority of those casting an affirmative or negative vote shall be required for action in pursuance of Article V of the Convention' (IWC 2012:4).

9. A member state can lodge an objection to a new regulation and then this regulation is not binding for the country concerned.

10. Of these, the United Nations Convention on the Law of the Sea (UNCLOS) is the most universal, with 165 signatory states. It gives only vague general guidelines regarding the conservation of marine mammals and encourages coastal states and international organisations to implement stricter regulations, all the while emphasising the sovereign right of these states to exploit the marine resources of their own maritime territories (Art. 56, 61, 65). The article does not specifically acknowledge the IWC's authority in this matter leaving IWC members with the possibility of searching for other, more favourable, institutions to legitimise their activities (Forkan unknown).

11. Examples are the 1972 United Nations Conference on the Human Environment where a proposal was adopted which recommends a ten-year moratorium.

12. For a comprehensive definition of a sanctuary see, for instance, Hoyt 2005 and Stoett 1997.

13. It states, 'The Commission may amend from time to time the provisions of the Schedule by adopting regulations with respect to the conservation and utilisation of whale resources, fixing: . . . open and closed waters, including the designation of Sanctuary areas' (Contracting Governments to the International Convention for the Regulation of Whaling 1946: Article 2).

14. The first sanctuary, which was in force from 1948 to 1955, encompassed the Southern Ocean south of 40°S between 70°W and 160°W (Argentina, Brazil, South Africa, Uruguay 2014).

15. States coastal to the proposed sanctuary are IWC members Argentina, Brazil, Congo, Equatorial Guinea, Gabon, South Africa and Uruguay, and non-members Angola, Democratic Republic of Congo, Namibia and Sao Tome and Principe.

16. The SAWS proposal divides the marine population into different categories, such as 'populations which are depleted but known to be recovering' or 'populations whose current trends and size are unknown' (Argentina, Brazil, South Africa, Uruguay 2014).

17. Map of IWC Sanctuaries: The Indian Ocean Sanctuary, the Southern Ocean Sanctuary and the proposed South Atlantic Whaling Sanctuary (SAWS). Source: Zacharias et al. 2006 (edited by the authors).

18. For example: interviews #170, 22-07-14, #173, 18-08-14, #184, 17-09-14, #193, 19-09-14.

19. Already present as observers at that founding meeting were Colombia, Ecuador and Uruguay (which later joined the BAG).

20. Already in 2005 Argentina hosted a meeting for Latin American States to discuss whale conservation (Bailey 2012). In 2008 the following countries signed a Declaration as BAG: Argentina, Brazil, Chile, Costa Rica, Ecuador, Nicaragua, Panama, Peru and Uruguay in which the states supported the moratorium, whale sanctuaries as well as the non-lethal use of whales (Buenos Aires Group 2008).

21. In Brazil commercial whaling has been legally forbidden since 1987 (Muello 2002).

22. Compilation on the basis of IWC Annual/Chair Reports: International Whaling Commission 2002, 2003, 2004, 2005, 2006, 2007, 2008, 2009, 2010, 2011a, 2012a, 2013, Compton-Antoine 2014.

23. A diplomat explained that 'the first draft of the SAWS proposal was made by Brazil and then was sent to scientist of the co-sponsoring countries in order to revise the text and add comments' (interview#189, 18-09-14).

24. The 'Future of the IWC' process was an attempt at a consensus decision package (including, inter alia, the SAWS proposal) that was intended to secure the functional efficiency of a deeply divided and seemingly irreconcilable organisation. While being negotiated for nearly three years (from IWC 59 in 2007 to IWC 62 in 2010), no consensus was found and no decision adopted (International Whaling Commission 2014a).

25. At the IWC meetings 61 and 62 (in 2009 and 2010 respectively) the proposed SAWS Schedule amendment was neither discussed nor put to a vote, although it was included in these meetings' Agendas. The proposal's sponsors chose not to bring the matter up so as not to compromise the efforts undertaken to defuse the tensions between the pro-whaling and anti-whaling factions in the 'Future of the IWC' process (Hogarth 2009, Liverpool 2010).

26. Several states bordering the South Atlantic have already established strict conservation rules for cetaceans in their jurisdictional waters: Brazil, Argentina and Uruguay prohibited whaling activities. Also, South Africa introduced strict conservation rules and Gabon committed to do so as well (Governments of Argentina 2014).

27. 'When you negotiate something, whatever it is, you really need to get groups together and get things done' (interview#193, 19-09-14).

28. An interviewee stated, 'In Buenos Aires Group we coordinate our positions in every issue' (interview#189, 18-09-14).

29. For example: 'Uruguay has its own waters named as sanctuary protected areas, Argentina did the same, Brazil did the same, but all these countries, they're using the whale in a very nonlethal method as there are very big developments with the tourist

sector and so that makes it very important for us to get the sanctuary, because we want to ensure that the whales are not touched there' (interview#178, 16-09-14).

30. Thus, the BAG supported the insertion of this part into the 2012 text of the SAWS norm: 'With the exception of Brazil, this provision does not apply to waters under the national jurisdiction of coastal states within the area described above, unless those States notify the Secretariat to the contrary and this information is transmitted to the Contracting Governments' (see table 5.2).

31. For example, a small BAG member state noted that it has strong incentives for burden-sharing 'because we are too small in the world' (interview#178, 16-09-14), while working with regional coalitions increases the bargaining power (H6b) (see also interview#185, 17-09-14). In contrast, a representative of a small EU state explained that before the internal EU coordination and the rule to speak with one voice, 'We felt more important', as they directly engage with other states instead of negotiating via the EU Presidency (interview#175, 01-09-14).

32. The BAG was furthermore criticised by some opposing states as well as NGOs for distributing factual and scientific information either with delay or insufficiently (interview#175, 01-09-14).

33. The EU coordinated as frequently as two to three times a day (interviews #188, 18-09-14, #175, 01-09-14). This is because 'if you want to operate as one and be more powerful by operating as a block, then the downside of that is that you have to spend time talking and trying to come to a common position' (interview#188, 18-09-14). In the EU Council the Working Party on International Environmental Issues (WPIEI) is the place where national experts from the EU member states meet in preparation of the IWC meetings and discuss their position and statements (interview#175, 01-09-2014).

34. At the start of EU coordination, the Presidency of the Council seeks to explore the positions of the various member states and, on this basis, proposed compromises in an impartial manner: 'As a presidency you have to be as much as possible neutral' (interview#193, 19-09-14). Only if the member states are not voicing specific problems or making specific suggestions does the Council Presidency base its draft common position on its own national position (interview#193, 19-09-14).

35. An EU diplomat explained that 'it allows us to have a frank airing of views, to understand other countries' positions, without having to have those discussions or arguments in public' (interview#188, 18-09-14).

36. For example, in its 2011 opening statement Denmark stressed that whales are a renewable resource and part of the culture of whale hunting nations: 'Within the Kingdom of Denmark whaling is confined to the waters of the Faroe Islands and Greenland in the North Atlantic, where marine mammals have long been – and continue to be – valuable renewable resources and an important part of the cultures and needs of the Faroe Islands and Greenland' (Denmark 2011b).

37. The only country which was initially not in line with the other EU member states when it comes to whaling was Denmark, as it also represents Greenland, where whale hunting is common. This was described as a recurrent point of discussion among the EU member states by a EU diplomat (interview#175, 01-09-14) and already apparent in the EU's opening statement to the IWC 2011 meeting

which stated: 'At this meeting, Poland, currently holding the Presidency of the Council of the European Union, will be speaking on behalf of the European Union and its Member States. In this context, we note that Greenland and the Faeroe Islands are Danish Overseas Territories but not European Union Territories. Should divergences arise between the interests of the European Union and those of the afore-mentioned territories, Denmark may need to intervene on their behalf to pursue the latter's interests' (Poland on behalf of the European Union 2011). In fact, while the BAG was homogenous already in earlier years, the EU's internal homogeneity has been limited previously as well: 'Nakamae said the success or failure of the initiative depends on the cooperation of the EU and the Buenos Aires group. He added the Buenos Aires group will be easier to manage because of its clear goal (a whale sanctuary in the South Atlantic). However, he sees some dissent within the EU based on individual countries' reaction during the vote at the Santiago IWC meeting on Greenland's proposal to take humpback whales' (Embassy Tokio 2008).

38. A diplomat of an EU member state explained: 'I started contacting the relevant countries outside the EU beforehand, maybe discussing over the telephone' (interview#193, 19-09-14). Lobbying third parties also continues during IWC negotiations, taking place also in 'coffee breaks, . . . lunches, dinners' and the diplomat continued to mention, 'That's why we never stop working actually, . . . talking to someone and even if it's a friendly talking' (interview#193, 19-09-14).

39. For example: 'We had a discussion we wanted to have with the BAG, for example, we may nominate one or two or ask one or two member states or individuals to actually go and make contact with certain individuals of a group we know in there and start to try that discussion. And then at the later stages, it may become a bit more formally, and you would arrange a so called working groups in order to discuss. Most of it is really done is done bilaterally, informally' (interview#188, 18-09-14, similar interview#175, 01-09-14).

40. The United Kingdom made a supplementary technical point, stating 'that sanctuaries were a key element in the conservation of whales as they protect feeding and breeding grounds and it hoped the IWC would attach a high priority to creating this Sanctuary and to respecting existing ones' (International Whaling Commission 2012a: 9.2.2). 'On occasion, you may agree with the presidency, or you feel as a member state that you can come in and supplement beyond of what they said. And that's allowed, there's no hard and far set of rules of when you can and can't. It's just: You have to judge the situation. But of course, if the presidency came in and said something and then UK came in and said exactly the same or something different that would not be cooperating and therefore there would normally be a discussion behind closed doors about what we should or shouldn't have done. So it's about presenting a united single front. You can get away with a certain amount of interventions. You'll see that most of the UK's interventions have been on technical points or we've had the courtesy of discussing with the presidency that we would like to help and intervene and we have agreed that we will do that. Some of that is in order that we can show to civil society that we are not dissipating' (interview#188, 18-09-14). In general, the United Kingdom can be

described as one of the most vocal member states of the EU in the IWC, both when it comes to the internal coordination meetings and to statements in the IWC arena: 'The UK is usually the most vocal on the conservation agenda' (interview#174, 29-08-14).

41. Few states claimed that a statement made by an EU member other than the one holding the EU Presidency allows the calling of attention to a specific factor and supports the arguments made by the latter (interviews #175, 01-09-2014, #193, 18-09-14, #181, 11-12-14). However, whenever the content of the speeches made, and arguments presented, deviated and did not fit together, the negotiation contributions showcase EU internal dissent and do not add to a greater negotiation effectiveness of the regional group as a whole.

42. More precisely, the EU is aware of its ability to almost block any proposals in the IWC: 'As a block, have more of a say in what happens. The EU as given the number of countries – twenty-five that we have here – can operate almost as a blocking minority' (interview#188, 18-09-14), or stressed even stronger by another EU member state delegate: 'Sometimes the whole issue depends on whether the EU is supporting or opposing' (interview#174, 29-08-14). This potential blocking power of the EU is not perceived as positive by all EU member states. One interviewee explained that 'the power EU is having is sometimes not very helpful in the process . . . in IWC things are getting more . . . black and white' (interview#174, 29-08-14).

43. 'We provided comments within the scientific committee and our views on it [SAWS proposal, insertion by the author]' (interview#188, 18-09-14). Asked for the basis of being influential a diplomat responded: 'It's expertise and reputation build up over a long time. Because expertise changes over time' (interview#188, 18-09-14).

44. Yet, the EU invested time and negotiation resources to overcome difficulties and to, in the end, cooperate with the BAG. 'We discuss very much and very often with Mexico and with Argentina – two key players and quite influential in the BAG. And we have regular discussions with . . . this meeting we had a number of bilaterals with the mobile phone just in order to explain what our position was and where we felt the EU was going without jeopardising the EU's position. And in turn, understanding where they were in order to make us more powerful, more effective when we reach the meeting itself' (interview#188, 18-09-14).

45. A member of the EU stated: 'When you get to go with other blocks then you got quite the powerful abilities and can drive decisions in the way you want them to be driven' (interview#188, 18-09-14).

46. These were Costa Rica, Colombia, the United States, Australia, Poland, Mexico, Ecuador, UK, Hungary, Chile, India, Panama, Uruguay, Germany, New Zealand, Denmark, Israel, Monaco, Switzerland, Portugal and Spain. By contrast Japan, Cambodia, Cameroon, Côte d'Ivoire, the Gambia, Iceland, Norway, Nauru, Mongolia, Mauritania, Guinea-Bissau, Grenada, Kiribati, Morocco, Republic of Korea, Ghana, Palau, Togo, the Russian Federation, Tuvalu, Saint Kitts and Nevis, and Saint. Lucia were against the 2011 proposal (International Whaling Commission 2012a: 9.2.2).

47. Japan participates with a very large and growing delegation in the IWC. In 2011, twenty-six people were part of the official delegation; in 2012 the Japanese delegation already included thirty-four persons, and in 2014 forty-one persons supported

the Japanese Commissioner Joji Morishita (International Whaling Commission 2011b, 2012b, 2014b).

48. The opponents of the SAWS proposal also argued that the proposal was biased by the Latin American states on the Atlantic coast, while the East African countries are not actively involved as not all of them are IWC members (interview#175, 01-09-14). In fact, some even argued that the African states bordering the Atlantic would need to join the IWC prior to passing the SAWS (interview#175, 01-09-14). An EU member state representative explained that 'you need the support of the territory you try to protect' and thereby favours the inclusion of African States ranging the planned SAWS (interview#174, 29-08-14).

49. The Brazilian Commissioner Marcus Henrique Paranagua explained, 'We didn't come here to win the sanctuary on the vote, but we wanted to put it to a vote, we believe our conservation agenda cannot be put forward, be stressed, be highlighted, be defended in some issues without a vote'. Japan, on the contrary, stated that 'this was not a hostile move to the Latin American countries' (Black 2011).

50. Furthermore, 'The question was . . . when do you decide on a quorum? Is it in the morning, or is it at the beginning of a meeting, or is it the beginning of a vote, so there's a lot of legal questions been ask, so it became very legal' (interview#170, 22-07-14).

51. For example, the BAG presented their coordinated position in other arenas as well, such as a meeting of pro-conservationist countries in order to maximise support for the 2012 SAWS norm: 'We always try to have a common position on several issues. So that is the way that we move here, and in other meetings, for example, in the like-minded meeting we have a common position' (interview#189, 18-09-14).

52. Only Denmark spoke after the vote in order to explain its position (International Whaling Commission 2013: 4.1.2), and to point out the position of Greenland, which has historically been given an Aboriginal Subsistence Whaling quota by the IWC (International Whaling Commission 2015a, McGwin 2013).

53. Similarly, an interviewee reported that 'the EU is an important player . . . it can lead and does often lead the way . . . yet it is considered quite an important decision maker in these situations' (interview#188, 18-09-14).

54. In line with this, a diplomat explained that the EU is 'a very large player just on that front and so working with them as a regional block, if you will, is important not just for the South Atlantic Whale Sanctuary but for any country who wants to get something passed' (interview#168, 10-07-14).

55. While the EU engaged in collective bargaining, individual states, such as Monaco, had limited bargaining power. Due to the distribution of votes, no individual state was in a pivotal position. Therefore, 'smaller countries . . . will look towards . . . this bigger groups', such as the 'the Sustainable-Use-Group . . . the EU-group and then the Buenos-Aires-Group, which is basically the three groups formed in the IWC context' (interview#170, 22-07-14).

56. Furthermore, Japan argues that its work in the Southern Ocean is not meant to supply commercial markets with whale meat, but to conduct scientific research. Their stated aim is actually the preservation of whale populations – they argue that by following the 1986 moratorium on commercial whaling, they were compelled to

collect data that would help them learn more about whale populations. Japan claims that they would use this data to pursue whaling in a more sustainable fashion (Fortin 2012). Also, 'Japan and Antigua and Barbuda noted there was no support from the Scientific Committee for the proposal, and as such was contrary to the intention of Article 5§2(b) of the ICRW 1946 which required amendments to the Schedule to be based on scientific findings' (International Whaling Commission 2013).

57. Brazil argued, 'That the primary intention in creating the Sanctuary was to support the biodiversity, conservation and non-lethal use of whale resources in the South Atlantic Ocean. The Sanctuary was intended to maximise the rate of recovery of whale populations and to promote the long term conservation of whales with particular emphasis on breeding and calving areas and migratory pathways. The Sanctuary would also: (1) stimulate co-ordinated research programmes between developing countries and the IWC; (2) develop the sustainable and non-lethal utilisation of whales through ecotourism and whale watching; (3) provide a framework for the development of measures at an ocean-basin level; and (4) integrate national and regional conservation and management strategies while taking into account the rights and responsibilities of coastal states' (International Whaling Commission 2013).

58. Diplomats support the proposal as they regard it as an 'incredibly positive and successful tool for marine conservation management and stewardship' (interview#168, 10-07-14).

59. The Australian delegate stated that the 'Prime Minister had recently reaffirmed the importance of area-based conservation measures at the United Nations Conference on Sustainable Development' and continued 'that no commercial whaling or special permit whaling should be allowed in this proposed new Sanctuary or any other IWC Sanctuary' (International Whaling Commission 2013: 4.1.2). Furthermore, Australia 'believed the Commission should adopt an integrated approach to conservation with the moratorium being complementary to, rather than an alternative to whale sanctuaries' (International Whaling Commission 2013: 4.1.2).

60. However, Article 10.2 of the ICRW states that 'any Government which has not signed this Convention may adhere thereto after it enters into force by a notification in writing to the Government of the United States of America' (1946).

61. Brazil insisted on a vote in order to document the voting behaviour of the IWC member states (interview#175, 01-09-14).

62. Thirty-eight votes in support, twenty-one votes against and two abstentions.

63. Japan has frequently been accused of exchanging official development aid for support in IWC voting. For example, an article in *The Guardian* stated: 'Hopes of creating two whale sanctuaries in the south Atlantic and the south Pacific were dashed last week at the International Whaling Commission (IWC) annual meeting in London amid new claims that Japan has been buying votes from Caribbean nations' (Bowcott 2001). Similarly, a diplomatic cable indicated that Japan might use ODA to obtain voting support and ensure that Japan can engage in whaling in the future as well: 'The Japanese are actively lobbying him to change Nicaragua's position. Nicaragua is the recipient of Japanese assistance, and this was the reason Fagoth gave why Nicaragua will listen to Japan's proposals and might shift its position more favourably toward their perspective' (Embassy Managua 2008).

64. Since Denmark also represents Greenland (which has an Aboriginal Subsistence Whaling quota) (International Whaling Commission 2015a), there are regularly intense discussions in the EU coordination meetings between Denmark and the other EU member states, in order to bring Denmark more closely in line with the general conservationist position of the EU.

65. Gabon was not named as a co-sponsor on the proposal distributed by the IWC in June 2014, but was named as a co-sponsor in the introduction of the proposal on the first day of the IWC65 meeting. This suggests that Gabon shifted into strongly supporting the 2014 SAWS proposal between June and September 2014.

66. Moreover, the IWC is not the only forum where negotiations on the topic happened; members of the BAG, for example, used the forum of the South Atlantic Zone of Peace and Cooperation (ZPCAS) in order to convince African countries of the proposal: 'Uruguay had the presidency of the . . . ZPCAS and they circulated notes remembering that . . . African countries committed to support the SAWS. Uruguay circulated notes to foreign embassies of members of ZPCAS in Uruguay recalling that commitment' (interview#196, 22-12-14).

67. The workshop had the aim to 'present the benefits of the proposal and ask about their opinions, what are their concerns about their proposal in order to improve it, because this was one of the things they highlighted, that the proposal should take in consideration their concerns' (interview#189, 18-09-14). During the workshop, the BAG's lobbying was effective as it was able to talk Gabon into support (H6f). However, although Gabon agreed to become a co-sponsor in response to Brazil's lobbying, Gabon's position shift happened too late for the formal submission of the 2014 SAWS proposal to the IWC (interview#196, 22-12-14). Thus, in the document from 5 June 2014 Gabon is not listed as a co-sponsor (Government of Argentina 2014).

68. Brazil stated, 'That the primary goal of the Sanctuary was to promote biodiversity, conservation and the non-lethal use of whale resources in the South Atlantic Ocean. It would also maximise the rate of recovery of whale populations within ecologically meaningful boundaries; promote long-term conservation of whales throughout their life cycle and their habitats, with special emphasis on breeding, calving and feeding areas and migratory paths. In addition, it would: stimulate coordinated research; develop the sustainable and non-lethal utilisation of whales for the benefit of coastal communities in the region; provide an overall framework for the development of measures at an ocean basin level; and integrate national research, conservation and management efforts and strategies in a cooperative framework, taking into account the rights and responsibilities of coastal States under the United Nations Convention on the Law of the Sea (UNCLOS). Brazil considered that, as whales are highly migratory animals, a concerted multilateral effort is required to guarantee their conservation and the recovery of their populations. The Sanctuary would result in the creation of an important preserved area in the Southern Hemisphere with three contiguous whale sanctuaries (South Atlantic – Indian Ocean – Antarctica)' (Compton-Antoine 2014: 10).

69. The interviewee expects incomes of around US$16 million from whale-watching-activities for his country (interview#189, 18-09-14).

70. In line with a EU member (interview#195, 22-12-14), a diplomat from a BAG state explained, 'During the long history all the countries that are proposing the creation

of the sanctuary participated in the seminars or via email. That was how the proposal was finally made' (interview#196, 22-12-14).

71. The strong role of the EU Commission in the EU coordination meetings was not welcomed by all members equally: some representatives would have liked to raise their voice more often in order to underline a specific point or put more weight on a statement of a third party (interview#193, 19-09-14).

72. A diplomat explained that the EU has to 'be very careful, you don't cut across what others are doing, obviously the proponents, if they are negotiating with others, you don't want to intervene and cut across that, you have to care for balance, really' (interview#195, 22-12-14).

73. A BAG member stressed that 'the process was that Brazil has the leadership on this, so they sent the first draft to other scientists, that first write all information on that and then, of course, we need to discuss internally among governments on that. So in this proposal, if I could say, the body of the proposal is the same. We are doing updates, and we are incorporating what other countries request or these kind of things' (interview#189, 18-09-14). This was corroborated by an EU member, who explained that the process of modifying the text of the proposal is a 'collaborative approach, so something would be circulated, and yeah, experts and others will make suggestions and comments and then the authors will take these comments on board' (interview#195, 22-12-14).

74. Argentina, Australia, Chile, Colombia, Dominican Republic, Ecuador, Gabon, Germany, Italy on behalf of the EU, Mexico, Monaco, New Zealand, Panama, Peru, South Africa, Uruguay and the United States.

75. Antigua and Barbuda, Côte d'Ivoire, Grenada, the Republic of Guinea, Iceland, Japan, Norway, the Russian Federation and Saint Lucia.

76. The following countries referred to the SAWS proposal in their opening statements and indicated their support for its establishment: the Members of the Buenos Aires Group, Italy on behalf of the European Union, New Zealand, the United States, as well as two NGOs (WWF and Animal Welfare Institute).

77. An NGO representative described that some of the African States present at the IWC65 meeting could not remember that their state officials signed this declaration (interview#177, 16-09-14).

78. In 2012 twenty-one countries opposed the proposal, while in 2014 eighteen countries did not support it. The number of countries abstaining remained the same, with two countries abstaining in each case. As the numbers suggest, the perceived win in supporters by members of the BAG and the rise in percentage on the supporting side can be explained by the countries present/not present and their voting behaviour. Nothing actually changed the balance of power between the two camps: in 2012 four potentially supporting countries did not attend the proposal, namely Croatia, Hungary, Oman and Slovakia, whereas in 2014 India and Cyprus were not present; therefore, two potential yes votes were missing. In 2012 three countries potentially opposing the proposal did not attend the meeting: Côte d'Ivoire, Guinea and Vietnam. In 2014 several countries voting against the proposal over the past several years were not present, namely Benin, China, Nauru, Palau, Togo. In total, this leads to forty-two countries in the IWC supporting the proposal and twenty-four opposing it, had all IWC member states been present and eligible to vote.

# Chapter 6

1. The UN Register of Conventional Arms of 1991 defines seven categories of weapon systems, namely battle tanks, armoured combat vehicles, large-calibre artillery systems, combat aircraft, attack helicopters, warships, missiles and missiles launchers. All UN member states are asked to report on export and import of these arms. Additionally, countries can report on small armed and light weapons (also referred to as the '7+1+1' formula) (United Nations Office for Disarmament Affairs 2013). Unlike trade in chemical, biological and nuclear weapons, trade in conventional weapons is not regulated by a comprehensive treaty at the international level (CARICOM 2010b).

2. There have been several attempts in various international fora to agree on common standards for the trade in arms throughout the twentieth century, for example the Conventions of the Second Hague Conference of 1907, the League of Nations 'Convention for the Control of the Trade in Arms and Ammunition' of 1919, the 'Arms Traffic Convention' of 1925, the NGO-led 'Campaign Against Arms Trade' of 1974, 'UN Resolution 43/75: General and Complete Disarmament' of 1988, the 'UN Register of Conventional Arms (UNROCA)' established by 'UN Resolution 4/361: Transparency in Armaments' 1991 or the 'Wassenaar Arrangement on Export Controls for Conventional Arms and Dual-Use Goods and Technologies' of 1995. However, none of these attempts has seen universal ratification, and hence their regulatory effect has remained marginal (Prakash 2013).

3. The UNGA meets throughout the year, but the main sessions of the assembly are held at the headquarters in New York from early September to mid-December, starting with a two-week general debate attended by the Heads of States and/or ministers. More than 150 agenda items are discussed, either in the plenary session of the UNGA or in one of the six committees (Panke 2013b).

4. Non-binding recommendations bearing in mind the views and recommendations expressed in the replies of Member States (see A/62/278 [Parts I and II] and Add. 1–4) and those contained in the report of the Group of Governmental Experts and the report of the Open-ended Working Group, and to present a report containing those elements to the Assembly at its sixty-sixth session (United Nations General Assembly 2009).

It was decided to transform the remaining sessions of the Open-Ended Working Group in 2010 and 2011 as a preparatory committee for the conference (United Nations General Assembly 2009).

Section 7 of the UNGA resolution 64/48 determines the purpose of the PrepComs by requesting that the committee should 'make recommendations to the United Nations Conference on the Arms Trade Treaty on the elements that would be needed to attain an effective and balanced legally binding instrument on the highest possible common international standards for the transfer of conventional arms' (United Nations General Assembly 2009: §7).

5. The following countries abstained: Bahrain, Belarus, Bolivia, China, Cuba, Egypt, India, Iran, Kuwait, Libya, Nicaragua, Pakistan, Qatar, Russia, Saudi Arabia, Sudan, Syria, United Arab Emirates, Venezuela and Yemen. In total 151 countries

voted 'YES', 1 country 'No', 20 countries abstained and 20 countries did not vote. The total voting membership was 192 member states.

6. Resolution 67/234 that included the adoption of the Arms Trade Treaty was introduced to the General Assembly by the representative of Costa Rica on 1st April on behalf of the following states: Albania, Antigua and Barbuda, Argentina, Australia, Austria, the Bahamas, Belgium, Bulgaria, Chile, Colombia, Costa Rica, Cote d'Ivoire, Croatia, Cyprus, Czech Republic, Denmark, Dominican Republic, Estonia, Finland, France, Germany, Ghana, Greece, Grenada, Guatemala, Guyana, Haiti, Hungary, Iceland, Italy, Jamaica, Japan, Kenya, Latvia, Liberia, Liechtenstein, Lithuania, Luxembourg, Mali, Mexico, Montenegro, Morocco, Namibia, the Netherlands, New Zealand, Nigeria, Norway, Peru, Poland, Portugal, Republic of Korea, Romania, Rwanda, Saint Lucia, Saint Vincent and the Grenadines, Slovakia, Slovenia, Spain, Sweden, Switzerland, Trinidad and Tobago, Turkey, United Kingdom of Great Britain and Northern Ireland and the United States of America (Agence France Presse 2014).

7. As of 28 April 2015, sixty-six states have ratified the Treaty, and a further sixty-four states have signed but not ratified it.

8. Some states were in favour of a strong and comprehensive treaty, which means the inclusion of human rights obligation or references to humanitarian law. Other delegations interpreted the treaty as 'solely a trade treaty and sought to limit its scope' (Control Arms 2013).

9. The resolution passed by a vote of 133 in favour to none against, with 17 abstentions. The following countries abstained: Bahrain, Belarus, Bolivia, Cuba, Egypt, Iran, Kuwait, Myanmar, Nicaragua, Oman, Qatar, Saudi Arabia, Sudan, Syria, United Arab Emirates, Venezuela, and Yemen. In total 133 countries votes 'YES', 17 countries abstained, and 43 countries did not vote. The total voting membership was 193 member states.

10. Abstaining were the following countries: Angola, Bahrain, Belarus, Bolivia, China, Cuba, Ecuador, Egypt, Fiji, Haiti, India, Indonesia, Kuwait, Lao PDR, Myanmar, Nicaragua, Oman, Qatar, Russia, Saudi Arabia, Sri Lanka, Sudan, Swaziland, Yemen. In total 154 countries voted 'YES', three countries with 'No' and 23 countries abstained. The total voting membership was 193 member states.

11. Amendments to the Treaty may be proposed six years after entry into force of the Treaty, and will be adopted by a three-quarters majority if efforts to achieve consensus have failed.

12. Article 17: Conference of States Parties; Article 18: Secretariat.

13. The Articles are: Article 20: Amendments; Article 21: Signature, Ratification, Acceptance, Approval or Accession; Article 22: Entry into Force; Article 23: Provisional Application; Article 24: Duration and Withdrawal; Article 25: Reservations; Article 26: Relationship with other International Agreements; Article 27: Depositary and Article 28: Authentic Texts (United Nations General Assembly 2013a).

14. For example, all states and ROs that took the floor with respect to brokering expressed that this issue should be included in the ATT (Africa 2012, Canada 2011, CARICOM 2011d, Germany 2012, Japan 2012, Rwanda 2013, Switzerland 2012), but apart from Russia (Russian Federation 2010c) and Egypt (Egypt 2011b), hardly anyone made specific proposals that were more demanding than noting that the issue

needs to be included in the ATT and that states shall make regulations for brokerage taking place in their respective jurisdiction.

15. Article 14 is very concise and does not reflect a high level of legalisation (Abbott et al. 2000). Thus, international courts play no role, and there is no ATT dispute settlement mechanism in case a state suspects another one of violating the ATT. Article 14 states: 'Each State Party shall take appropriate measures to enforce national laws and regulations that implement the provisions of this Treaty' (United Nations General Assembly 2013a, Article 14). While several ROs articulated positions regarding enforcement (Arab Group 2011b, CARICOM 2011f, 2012a), they were all in tune with the general positions of the other states.

16. Thomas Mayr-Harting stated during CoP2 that 'we should also take into account the specific responsibilities that some regional organisations have acquired or could acquire in regulating arms transfers in several regions of the world. Consequently, we consider that the future Treaty should also be open for signature to relevant regional and international organisations, in accordance with [the] practice followed for similar international instruments, such as the UN Firearms Protocol' (European Union 2012a).

17. The EU failed to persuade other regional actors. For example, the Pacific Islands Forum (PIF) did not react to the EU's proposal and continued to emphasise that the ATT relates to state parties (Pacific Islands Forum 2012).

18. 'In Brazil's view, this instrument shall also provide the international community with efficient tools to prevent, combat and eradicate the illicit trade in conventional weapons and small arms and light weapons and their ammunition' (Brazil 2010) and also 'On Section III (Goals and Objectives), it must be underlined that one purpose of an ATT would be that of promoting cooperation and assistance among States Parties to prevent, combat and eradicate the illicit trade in conventional weapons. The reference to international cooperation and assistance here is of great relevance' (Brazil 2011b).

19. For example: 'The Russian Federation believes that it is a rather important task to settle the problems related to the uncontrolled proliferation of arms, especially in such a way as not to undermine the legitimate trade' (Russian Federation 2013).

20. The EU was also rather cautious with regard to the depth of the ATT as such. For example, an EU representative emphasised the right of states to self-defence and stressed that an ATT should not hinder states from buying weapons or to 'produce, manufacture, import, export weapons' as long as states comply with international law, including human rights and humanitarian law.

21. CARICOM member states gathered in three 'Preparatory Regional Workshops' in 2010, 2011 and 2012 with the aim to 'develop common negotiation positions', a 'negotiation strategy', as well as to 'provide delegates with the necessary background information' before the PrepCom meetings and the Negotiation Conferences (Callixtus 2013).

22. CARICOM made twelve formal statements over the course of negotiations in the PrepComs and the CoPs (CARICOM 2010 b, d, e, 2011 b, d, e, f, g, 2012 a, b, c, 2013).

23. '1. To prevent and combat the excessive and destabilising accumulation of small arms and light weapons within ECOWAS; 2. To continue the efforts for the

control of small arms and light weapons within ECOWAS; 3. To consolidate the gains of the Declaration of the Moratorium on the importation, exportation and manufacture of small arms and its Code of Conduct; 4. To promote trust between the Member States through concerted and transparent action on the control of small arms and light weapons within ECOWAS; 5. To build institutional and operational capacities of the ECOWAS Executive Secretariat and the Member States in the efforts to curb the proliferation of small arms and light weapons, their ammunitions and other related materials; 6. To promote the exchange of information and cooperation among the Member States' (Article 2; ECOWAS 2006).

24. 'ECOWAS is very committed to not go to a treaty without small arms and light weapons; we cannot do it alone. We are only 15 member states. So we started building an alliance at the continental level. ECOWAS pushed seriously to have, even if it was not strong, at least a partnership agreement at the regional level which includes small arms and light weapons at the continental level. We also discussed with groupings like the EU, like Latin American states, knowing clearly that they too want to see small arms into the Treaty. . . . And I think that it succeeded because EU was not against the inclusion of small arms into the Treaty and we, by bringing this number from the PrepCom and insisting that small arms and light weapons including ammunitions should be part of the Treaty, I think we succeeded' (interview#209, 17-07-15).

25. In line with this, Kenya which is not a member of ECOWAS, also explained: 'In our part of the world the impact of illicit weapons transfers on peace and development, is very evident by the thousands of innocent lives lost and others maimed but also the broader impact on society cannot go unmentioned, including the undermining of economies, over burdening of healthcare systems, displacement of entire communities and disruption of education for millions of children' (Kenya 2010). Thus, many African states were very empathetic to the argument made by ECOWAS in favour of including SALWS into the ATT.

26. CARICOM systematically maximised the expertise in order to boost their argumentative negotiation strategy. For instance, the RO worked closely together with civil society representatives and benefited from their expertise as they represented an 'invaluable source of research, support and public diplomacy', especially as many CARICOM member states had to deal with limited human and financial resources (Callixtus 2013). The CARICOM delegation included two Civil Society representatives (Callixtus 2013). In total twenty-seven diplomats of CARICOM Member States participated (or partly participated) in the UN ATT Conferences in 2012; partly diplomats from the UN mission in New York (fourteen diplomats) and thirteen from the capitals (Callixtus 2013).

27. ECOWAS was also among the supporters of the inclusion of SALWS and ammunition in the ATT (ECOWAS 2010). This is largely due to the fact that ECOWAS had a regional treaty passed in 2006 titled 'ECOWAS Convention on Small Arms and Light Weapons' (ECOWAS 2006).

28. 'They were certainly vocal and instrumental in the group of countries to push their ideas. . . . It has to have SALW in it. They had a lot of support from the Africans, ECOWAS' (interview#15, 29-07-15).

29. 'China had already had to back down on not having . . . on accepting small arms and light weapons. Originally they didn't want to, and it was the Africans and the

African Union that said: Hey, hang on, this is a real problem for us, we need SALW in there and guess what, we're doing a lot of trade on this. So the Africans were a very powerful group, when they put their mind to it' (interview#15, 29-07-2015).

30. For example: 'There was, however, disagreement between EU member states with regard to sports and hunting weapons. Italy would have liked to see these explicitly excluded from the ATT, while other member states did not' (Depauw 2012)

31. 'As for its scope, the ATT should cover the seven categories of the UN Conventional Arms Register, Small Arms and Light Weapons (SALW) and Ammunition' (ECOWAS 2010).

32. 'On the issue of scope, CARICOM has always advocated the 7 + 1 + 1 formula, *i.e.* the seven categories of the conventional arms register, small arms and light weapons and ammunition. From CARICOM's perspective, this is the only way to meet the goal of achieving a comprehensive and effective ATT' (CARICOM 2011e).

33. 'The rationale for the necessity of the inclusion of SALW and ammunition into a future ATT is overwhelming. In countries with high incidents of armed violence, resulting from the proliferation of gangs and the prevalence of transnational organised crime, the overwhelming majority of deaths result from the use of small arms. The latest figures from the Geneva Declaration posit that over 490,000 innocent civilians lose their lives each year, the vast majority by small arms, in countries that are not in a situation of armed conflict. This figure far exceeds the number of soldiers and other combatants that are killed fighting wars. In countries impacted by high levels of gun crime the economic cost of the treatment of gunshot wounds, the monies expended on national security measures have a long term negative impact on a country's long-term development prospects. Without bullets, small arms are virtually rendered useless as instruments of death. Small arms and light weapons and ammunition, as well as their parts and components, must, therefore, be considered in tandem and both must be included in a future ATT. For far too long, ammunition has been relegated to the periphery of international discussions concerning the arms trade. Because of their single-use quality, ammunition is produced in large quantities. Like small arms and light weapons, ammunition is at risk [of] diversion to the illicit market. The continued flow of ammunitions through the illicit market into the hands of criminals, and non-state armed groups, fuels fighting and poses enormous risk to civilian populations. By including ammunition within [the] scope of the future ATT, we will close this existing hole' (CARICOM 2011e).

34. CARICOM had adopted 'a CARICOM Declaration on Small Arms and Light Weapons by the CARICOM Heads of Government which in part seeks to harmonise the regions- efforts towards combating the illicit trade in these weapons as well as their ammunition' (CARICOM 2011a, 2012c). This declaration is a 'significant expression of commitment from CARICOM States to eradicate the illicit trade in SALW in the region while supporting the Region's push for a legally binding ATT covering SALW' (Callixtus 2013).

35. For example, 'CARICOM cannot contemplate an ATT that excludes small arms and light weapons and ammunition. These are the weapons of mass destruction in our region and the trade in them must be regulated' (CARICOM 2012c).

36. 'We continue to witness high levels of gun violence and other crimes, such as the illicit trade in narcotics which are linked to the illegal trade in small arms

and light weapons and their ammunition. Our economies are hampered by exogenic shocks. Nevertheless, we have had to divert scarce resources from programs aimed at improving the quality of life of our people, especially in terms of poverty reduction and improvement of health care and education systems, in order to tackle the effects of the illegal trade in these weapons' (CARICOM 2012c).

37. In 2012, PIF also supported 'the conclusion of an ATT which is broad in scope, and capable of comprehensively covering the full range of conventional weapons which are traded on the international market, including small arms and light weapons and ammunition' (Pacific Island Forum 2012).

38. 'It was clear from the big, from the powerful countries that ammunition will not be in the Treaty. But the Treaty was to be adopted by consensus. I remember a region coming to us saying that, no, we should give up on the ammunition issue' (interview#209, 17-07-15, similar Russian Federation 2010b).

39. The EU was also sceptical whether ammunition should be treated as part of the ATT's scope. Out of a total of eight statements made during the first PrepCom by the EU, Belgium, speaking on behalf of the regional group, only once demanded that ammunition should be covered by an ATT (European Union 2010d), whilst all other EU statements suggested dealing with the issue of ammunition in ways other than integrating it into ATT (e.g. European Union 2010a, b, c, e, h). In addition, some states claimed that ammunition should not be part of the ATT scope, because, unlike arms trade, ammunition trade is harder to control on the ground, and states with limited capacities would therefore not be able to implement demanding standards (Geneva Academy 2013, interview#199, 24-02-15).

40. Although Article 3 exclusively covers ammunition, it flags that 'each State Party shall establish and maintain a national control system to regulate the export of ammunition/munitions fired, launched or delivered by the conventional arms covered under Article 2 (1), and shall apply the provisions of Article 6 and Article 7 prior to authorizing the export of such ammunition/munitions' (Article 3 ATT; United Nations General Assembly 2013a). Thus, Article 3 in the ATT as passed in 2013 is less demanding than including ammunition under Article 2 (scope) would have been. It now requires that states regulate the trade of ammunition on their own, rather than explicitly regulating it in the same manner as the items explicitly placed under the ATT's scope.

41. And welcomed by other ROs as well. For instance, the EAC supported the compromise, although moving ammunition into a separate article and placing the regulation of trade with ammunition into the responsibility of the ATT member states leads to a less-demanding ATT (East African Community 2012).

42. Thus, CARICOM delegates stressed that they support 'the conclusion of a legally binding, robust, effective and nondiscriminatory Treaty that will set the highest possible international standards governing the transfer of conventional weapons, including small arms and light weapons, and the ammunition for these weapons' (CARICOM 2012a).

43. States which supported CARICOM were, for example, Switzerland, Canada, Lesotho, Costa Rica or the UK (Canada 2011, Costa Rica 2013, Lesotho 2012, Switzerland 2011, UK 2013).

44. A diplomat explained, 'Obviously, ammunitions and parts and components [were] always gonna be difficult to discuss, but I think we . . . there was a lot of things in the language that still [was] fixe[d] that we found through the course of the final conference' (interview ATT #14, 29-07-15, insertions by the authors).

45. Thus, the ROs had partial success. An interviewee reported that 'the EU, was just making sure that if it [the elements of the ATT relating to parts and components, insertion by the authors] couldn't be at least better, that it at least matches what their needs are and that makes sense' (interview ATT #14, 29-07-15).

46. The same diplomat continued: 'It was: It might sound daunting now, but we'll help you with the implementation. The EU has buckets of money; everybody knows the EU has buckets of money and they throw it at lots of things. And the EU were already doing, previously to all this; they were doing these outreach seminars, the regional seminars. So they were already out in the regions saying: "This is what we want from the ATT. It's like the Code of conduct, but it's not really. We wanna help you. And this is the reasons why we want it" (interview#211, 29-07-15). Similarly, in a speech, Germany elaborated, 'We stand ready to assist countries in setting up or improving their respective control systems. Once we have been successful here in New York experts from future States Parties will need to cooperate with each other to implement an ATT at national level in the best and most appropriate way. Germany has already made available funds for these purposes, for example for two seminars in Windhoek and Abuja as well as in Addis Ababa, and will continue to do so' (Germany 2013).

47. There were only a few exceptions. For example, Papua New Guinea, speaking for Pacific Small Island Developing States, welcomed assistance regarding ATT implementation: 'We recognise the importance of the ATT providing for international cooperation and assistance to developing States needing help to implement their treaty Obligations' (Pacific Small Island Developing States 2011).

48. Since each UN member state is already required to respect a Security Council embargo, this provision reiterates an existing obligation (Geneva Academy 2013).

49. Venezuela explained that 'we must remember that, despite the existence of an arms embargo by the Security Council, imperial powers supplied heavy weapons to rebel groups in Libya. The consequences are obvious: the illegal transfer of weapons has endangered the entire region' (Venezuela 2012).

50. For example, Indonesia stated that 'the language in old Article 3§1 (prohibited transfers) with regard to the Security Council measures should be crafted carefully so that the ATT will not create new interpretations or additional obligations beyond Article 25 of the UN Charter'(Indonesia 2013).

51. Regarding the *second cleavage*, Belize, whilst generally supporting the notion of state risk assessment or arms export, emphasised that 'the parameters reflected in the ATT should be carefully crafted so as to achieve the balance between the sovereign rights of States to trade in arms and the collective interests of the international community to combat the destructive impact of the illicit trade in arms. To achieve this fine balance the criteria incorporated in the ATT, to guide the decisions of States on whether to authorise a transfer of arms, must have practical applicability, must be specific and unambiguous so as not to lend itself to widely and wildly differing

interpretations and outcomes, and the criteria must result in fairly predictable outcomes. Only parameters which are objective, nondiscriminatory, transparent and non-political will ensure that the balance is permanently maintained' (Belize 2011). Cuba argued for a low level of ambiguity: 'Any Criterion or Parameter for the arms transfer included in the Treaty should be precise, objective, transparent, predictable and applicable in a consistent manner. Cuba will not support any Criterion that can be discriminatorily and selectively applied or easily manipulated by some to establish conditionality and exert pressure' (Cuba 2012). Italy also argued that 'parameters are essential for the effectiveness of an ATT. We need clear, strong and comprehensive criteria against which to assess exports' (Italy 2012).

*Third*, the debate focused on who would be responsible for the risk assessment, but dissent was very limited in this regard. The United States used this opportunity to emphasise once more that they would not accept an ATT which would interfere with their domestic arms trade. The United States diplomat explained: 'We must acknowledge and respect that this negotiation is not an attempt to intrude, either in principle or process, into states' internal activities, laws, or practices concerning the domestic possession, use, or movement of arms. Rather, this treaty will regulate only the international trade in arms. Any attempt to include provisions in the Treaty that would interfere with each state's sovereign control over the domestic possession, use, or movement of arms is clearly outside the scope of our mandate' (USA 2012). Yet, in this instance, it was not necessary to refer to tied hands in order to obtain concessions as there was already a large majority of states in favour of handling the responsibility for risk assessment to the arms exporting states.

52. For example, Italy argued, 'Should a transfer be in violation of international obligations, such as embargoes decided upon by the UN Security Council, then the ATT should contain a provision on its automatic ban. Similarly, in cases where a risk of serious violations of international human rights law or international humanitarian law may emerge from a possible transfer of arms, then such transfer must be prohibited' (Italy 2012). Also, 'The United States supports establishing additional criteria that each government must consider carefully before authorising the export of conventional arms, to ensure that international transfers even to legitimate end users are not made capriciously, without deliberation, or contrary to longstanding international principles' (USA 2012).

53. For example, Iran claimed that it would not be adequate to apply the same criteria for authorising arms exports to all states and all regions. 'In regard to the principles and criteria for conventional arms transfer, we believe that the ATT process shall not be abused to forcibly globalise the narrow national agendas or regional doctrines. Quite the contrary, ATT process shall take into account different national and regional realities and needs and the current security asymmetries in the world' (Iran 2010).

54. The diplomat continued: 'Brazil believes that, whenever requested, States shall have the opportunity of benefiting from international assistance in building operational and administrative capacities, including the development of appropriate legislation and regulations. As such, an ATT should require the identification of national bodies or points of contact to act as liaison among State Parties. Modalities of

technical assistance, including the exchange of experience and training among competent officials, including customs, police, intelligence and arms control officials, at the national, regional and global levels, would enhance the adequate implementation of an ATT. This technical assistance could also include the exchange of equipment, and of scientific and technological information' (Brazil 2012).

55. A diplomat reported that, regarding trans-shipment, PIF 'would then join forces with CARICOM and you'd find some of the Pacific's speaking up and saying "This is a big issue for us as well!" ' (interview#211, 29-07-15).

56. For example, India stated, 'With regard to transit, we have to be mindful of the potential burden on transit states from record keeping, etc. and consider how exporting countries can share that burden and reduce the chances of illicit transfers by measures such as marking and record keeping that they could take' (India 2011a). Similarly, a Swedish diplomat expressed that 'there should be an obligation to have the necessary legislation and administrative capacity in place to prevent the diversion or arms to the illegal market or the shipment of such arms' (Sweden 2012, similar DPRK 2012). Also, a diplomat from a big country pointed out that trans-shipment countries often 'don't have the capacity to check every single container' (interview#206, 13-05-15).

57. This coalition consisted of Argentina, Chile, Colombia, Guatemala, Jamaica, Mexico, Peru, Trinidad and Tobago and Uruguay (Argentina et al. 2010).

58. Similarly, CARICOM sought to 'indeed eventually eliminate the diversion of these weapons that cause tremendous suffering to populations worldwide, on a daily basis, including within our own region' (CARICOM 2012a). 'CARICOM supports the goals and objectives of the ATT outlined in your text of July 2011 and remains convinced that one of the key aims of the ATT should be the prevention of the diversion of these weapons to the illicit market, through the establishment of adequate controls' (CARICOM 2012a). A CARICOM member state representative also explained that CARICOM members 'are small importers, but we are disproportionately affected by the illegal trade, the diversion of arms and ammunition, coming from the north and the south, mixing together with illegal drug trade and other trans boundary crimes' (interview#208, 20-05-15).

59. Another diplomat reported that 'CARICOM, I mean they were all very active as well in advocating the need for the Treaty, you know, in representing the states affected most by the illicit trade and diversion of arms . . . coalition-building does help, highlights on issues. It's not always necessarily a regional construction either, often it is. So like the issues of diversion, you know, kind of stand out to me as being a real Latin-American issue, I mean as well as Africa, but like that kind of global south, sort of region saying the issue of diversion is what we're trying to tackle here' (interview#210, 29-07-15).

60. A CARICOM member reported: 'We were able to get a separate provision on diversion in the Treaty. That was a big victory fought together with like-minded states like Mexico, New Zealand and so on and so forth and some of the Latin American countries' (interview#208, 20-05-15).

61. A representative of the CSTO elaborated: 'The main purpose of this mechanism, in our view, is to prevent the diversion of arms from legal trade to illicit traffic by strengthening or establishing, where not in place, national systems of

governmental controls over arms transfers' (Collective Security Treaty Organization 2012) and 'We are interested in adopting at the outcome of the Conference a strong and effective, but also concise, clear and implementable document based on highest possible standards for the transfer of conventional arms. This implies specific practical measures that could contribute to their integrity to strengthening governmental controls over all types of activities related to transfers of conventional arms, primarily in the areas of higher risks of diversion of arms into the illicit traffic. The document should establish general rules and principles with the modalities of their implementation to be determined by the Governments themselves based on the specific character of their national legislation and existing practice' (Collective Security Treaty Organization 2012).

62. Sweden demanded 'that there should be an obligation to have the necessary legislation and administrative capacity in place to prevent the diversion or arms to the illegal market or the shipment of such arms' (Sweden 2012).

63. This was important as especially poorer states repeatedly stressed the financial burden that the ATT would place upon them and requested support to be able to fully comply with the ATT. For example, Tanzania stated, 'In order to ensure the implementation of the Treaty universally, we cannot avoid using financial resources to undertake some activities including training or provision of equipment for record keeping and conducting patrols to facilitate sporting or arresting of violators. A small Fund and a limited group of staff may be availed to assist member states in implementation' (Tanzania 2013).

64. The Indian delegation was much less modest: 'While transparency is a laudable goal and regular national reports of value in assessing compliance by all states parties, we do not believe that detailed and burdensome reporting and record keeping obligations serve our collective interest. There are obvious national security, foreign policy and commercial sensitivities involved' (India 2011b).

65. The Israeli delegation explained, 'With regard to the issue of transparency and related issues – record keeping, reporting and notifications – We believe that these require careful consideration. While well balanced mechanisms in this regard could serve to promote effective implementation and application by states of their obligations, special care should be taken so as not to create a mechanism which will be' (Israel 2011c).

66. 'This provision is intrusive and has a potential to compromise national security of importing States particularly the landlocked ones. It may be used to monitor other States' rearmament and self-defense programs. As it is we do not find this provision acceptable for the above mentioned reasons' (Zimbabwe 2011).

67. CARICOM was generally in favour of the creation of a reporting system; however, it also stressed that the workload attached to it is a 'burdensome nature of such reporting requirements on developing States' (CARICOM 2010b).

68. The African Group emphasised that in the interest of transparency, reporting may be seen as an essential ingredient of an ATT, but favoured a reporting template that should be 'simple and simplified' in order to 'lessen the burden on States and to ensure timely compliance' (African Group 2012).

69. Regarding reporting, the EU made very concrete suggestions: 'Concerning the implementation of the Treaty, States Parties should be required to report on

measures undertaken to control arms transfers according to the relevant provisions of the Treaty. After the first submission of the implementation report, for instance within 180 days following the ratification of the Treaty, States Parties should submit further report updates as appropriate and in advance of Review Conferences. Reports on implementation could contain, inter alia, information on relevant administrative, enforcement, and legal measures, national provisions on [the] criminalization of unauthorised transfers, and other elements of national arms transfer control systems. Reports on implementation of the Treaty should provide an overview of how each State Party controls transfers of arms in accordance with the Treaty's requirements' (European Union 2011d).

70. 'ATT should not establish procedures for the submission of information that endanger the national security of States. At the same time, any possible reporting or exchange of information shall be on voluntary basis' (Iran 2010) and 'Well-balanced mechanisms could enable states to effectively implement their obligations, under a future ATT. We must take special care not to create a mechanism that will impede states' national security interests. In this regard, on the issue of reporting, Israel considers the UN Register of Conventional Arms as an important confidence building measure among states, particularly in our region' (Israel 2013).

A Vietnamese diplomat demanded that 'there should be a balance between the need for transparency and legitimate security needs of states in its provisions on transparency mechanism, including regulations on reporting responsibility of states, which are established in accordance with the primary objective of ATT, namely to prevent illicit transfer of conventional arms. Overlapping and complicated reporting mechanism would create unnecessary burden for States Parties, especially developing ones. It is our view that to ensure the universality of the Treaty; the reporting mechanism should be based on a voluntary basis' (Vietnam 2013).

71. For example, Lesotho: 'Needless to mention that inherent in the ATT should be the aim to promote transparency without compromising the legitimate security interests of States. National reporting and structured meetings of State Parties are, therefore, key to achieving our objective for an ATT. There is no doubt that a well-managed and regulated international trade in conventional weapons will go a long way in promoting peace, freedom, observance of human rights and prosperity' (Lesotho 2012).

72. For example, Guatemala 2012, Kazakhstan 2013, Montenegro 2012, Namibia 2012, Nepal 2012, New Zealand 2012, Papua New Guinea 2012, South Africa 2012.

73. Similar: 'We foresee a Treaty that is transparent, and this can only be verified by clearly defined reporting mechanisms. Reporting under the ATT should be simple, to encourage States to report on their obligations. In this regard, we wish to emphasise the importance of international cooperation and assistance, to help developing countries in their reporting obligations under the envisaged Treaty. This can go a long way in ensuring that the Treaty achieves its major objective of greater transparency in international arms transfers' (Namibia 2012).

74. A diplomat characterised the negotiations concerning the reporting dispute in the following manner: 'I think it was more just maintaining the momentum on that and making sure that that doesn't slip away for some, you know, as a compromise for something else' (interview#210, 29-07-15).

75. Article 16 ' International Assistance' states:

> 1 In implementing this Treaty, each State Party may seek assistance including legal or legislative assistance, institutional capacity-building, and technical, material or financial assistance. Such assistance may include stockpile management, disarmament, demobilisation and reintegration programmes, model legislation, and effective practices for implementation. Each State Party in a position to do so shall provide such assistance, upon request.

> 2 Each State Party may request, offer or receive assistance through, inter alia, the United Nations, international, regional, subregional or national organisations, non-governmental organisations, or on a bilateral basis.

> 3 A voluntary trust fund shall be established by States Parties to assist requesting States Parties requiring international assistance to implement this Treaty. Each State Party is encouraged to contribute resources to the fund. (United Nations General Assembly 2013a, Article 16)

76. A diplomat of the Philippines suggested that 'specific mention be made on assistance to developing and less developed countries that do not possess the capacity and expertise or even resources to effectively implement a future ATT' (Philippines 2011).

77. 'The Treaty should contain provisions on international cooperation and assistance, particularly as it relates to capacity- building and the transfer of technology to strengthen the national capacities of developing States to effectively implement the Treaty' (CARICOM 2010b).

78. The EU repeatedly offered to support other states in their implementation of the Treaty (European Union 2011e). Moreover, the EU described itself as extremely active regarding international cooperation (and also assistance) by its involvement in several projects, such as the regional outreaching seminars (European Union 2011a).

79. An EU representative elaborated: 'Let me also seize this opportunity to recall our position on victim assistance. In the view of the EU, an Arms Trade Treaty is not meant to be an international disarmament instrument comparable to those that ban entire categories of weapons and include provisions on victim assistance. Whilst the EU agrees that an ATT should have a positive impact in reducing human suffering and armed violence, we do not consider appropriate to envisage specific provisions on victim assistance in the articles of the Treaty' (European Union 2011e).

80. For example, Malaysia stated, 'An ATT should not makes references to issues dealt with by separate legal regimes and laws or other international mechanisms, for example such as corruption, money-laundering, or mutual legal assistance. We must not tack on auxiliary issues covered elsewhere, and must continue to view the ATT through a trade and security perspective only. Additionally, "Victim Assistance" is a matter that would require much further deliberations' (Malaysia 2012).

81. Some EU member states were explicitly opposing a more legalised dispute settlement mechanism in the ATT. Sweden stated: 'We would have no problem with a dispute settlement mechanism relating to the implementation of Treaty obligations, but would oppose the idea of a dispute settlement mechanism for the transfer control decisions taken by sovereign nations. That would introduce a supranational element into this Treaty that so far has not been entertained by anyone' (Sweden 2011).

82. An example for internal group heterogeneity inhibiting an RO to be successful provides the EU with respect to the discussions on ATT scope.

## Chapter 7

1. The Food and Agricultural Organization (FAO), founded in 1945, has its Head-quarters in Rome/Italy. The agency is directed by the Conference of Member Nations, which meets every two years to review the work carried out by the organisation and to approve a Programme of Work and Budget for the next two-year period. Besides nego-tiating agreements and debate on specific topics, the FAO also serves as a source of knowledge to improve agriculture, forestry and fisheries practices as well as ensuring good nutrition and food security for all. As of October 2017, the FAO has 194 member states, along with the European Union (a 'member organisation' with full speaking and voting rights), and the Faroe Islands and Tokelau, which are associate members.

2. The Rome Declaration on Nutrition consists of seventeen Articles and has three major parts, namely multiple challenges of malnutrition to inclusive and sustain-able development and health, a common mission for global action to end all forms of malnutrition and a commitment to action (Rome Declaration 2014).

3. In June 2013 the 38th FAO Conference decided to hold a Preparatory Techni-cal Meeting to establish the ICN2 (International Institute for Sustainable Develop-ment 2014).

4. An FAO official explained, 'If you're negotiating with WHO and you say, let's set up ad-hoc rules, we would've spent more time talking about the process that on the document. So it just seemed easier to adopt one set of rules which were the rules of this house' (interview#231, 11-05-16). Another argument for the decision of the FAO rules was that 'the conference itself took place at FAO. So when you do it at FAO the FAO rules apply' (interview#229, 10-05-16).

5. The EU membership introduced the concept of the 'alternative exercise of Membership rights' between the EU and its member states, which applies not only to voting rights but also to speaking rights. This means that whenever the EU exercises its right to vote, its member states shall not exercise theirs, and conversely. On this specific point, the FAO constitution required the submission of a general statement specifying the matters in which competence has been transferred to the EU by its Member States. Before the opening of a session of the Council, the EU has to indicate whether the organisation or its Members have competencies with respect to items on the Provisional Agenda. Such a declaration of competence is issued as an information document (Food and Agriculture Organization 2013: rule XLII.2). One of the reasons why the EU initially pursued full membership in the FAO is its common policy in the area of agriculture and fisheries (interview#234, 11-05-16).

6. In the subsequent Open-Ended Working Group (OEWG), FAO and WHO regional groups have no formal speaking or voting rights. In this arena, only the 194 member states of the FAO and the WHO and the EU, which is a full member of the FAO, have access, speaking and voting rights. The same rules apply to CoP, in which the outcome document was formally adopted. It was held at the FAO Headquarters in Rome, Italy from the 19th to the 21st of November 2014 under the motto 'Better Nutrition, Better Lives' (International Institute for Sustainable Development 2014).

7. This process was described by many actors involved as difficult, especially in the beginning (interviews#231, 11-05-16, #232, 11-05-16, #238, 22-08-16): A member of the FAO secretariat said that 'in terms of communications sometimes it was a bit challenging . . . because the body language etc. may be much more telling than just the video conferences. It was also not easy to have quieter private consultations. It's a bit limited, but that was the agreement, also because of financial reasons, it would have costed much, much more [to bring the FAO and WHO representatives together in one city for the negotiations – addition by the authors]' (interview#242, 06-09-16).

8. The OEWG 'was opened for all member states to contribute. It was not limited now to the spokesperson from the regions to speak. So, everyone now could bring the issues on the table' (interview#224, 05-05-16).

9. 'The required majority for any decision or for any election shall be more than one half of the votes cast' (Rule XII Quorum and Voting Arrangements at Meetings of Conference and Council, 3a).

10. It states, 'We, Ministers and Representatives of the Members of the Food and Agriculture Organisation of the United Nations (FAO) and the World Health Organisation (WHO), assembled at the Second International Conference on Nutrition in Rome from 19 to 21 November 2014, jointly organised by FAO and WHO, to address the multiple challenges of malnutrition in all its forms and identify opportunities for tackling them in the next decades' (Rome Declaration 2014).

11. 'Reaffirming the commitments made at the first International Conference on Nutrition in 1992, and the World Food Summits in 1996 and 2002 and the World Summit on Food Security in 2009, as well as in relevant international targets and action plans, including the WHO 2025 Global Nutrition Targets and the WHO Global Action Plan for the Prevention and Control of Noncommunicable Diseases 2013–2020' (Rome Declaration 2014).

12. Article 4 lists different forms of malnutrition, such as undernutrition, but also obesity, and its negative effects to health and wellbeing. It also mentions negative 'social and economic consequences' of malnutrition.

13. Article 6 identifies different forms of malnutrition within countries and stresses that large inequalities exist in the nutritional status between countries.

14. Article 7 describes the link of 'socioeconomic and environmental changes' which influence life habits, for example the ingestion of food which is rich in fat, and might lead to obesity and/or noncommunicable diseases (Rome Declaration 2014).

15. Article 12 summarises numerous figures, which illustrate that the fight against hunger and malnutrition is one of the most prevailing issues of our time. Due to its balanced and factual nature, Article 12 was hardly contested in the ICN2 negotiations.

16. Article 16 refers to the assistance of international organisations, especially the UN agencies, the FAO and the WHO, to assist states with the implementation of specific programs and policies upon request (Rome Declaration 2014). Apart from minor rhetorical questions ('to develop, strengthen, and implement their national policies' instead of 'developing, strengthening and implementing their policies' brought to the table by ERG, EUR; NOAM, WPR and ASIA), the debate on this Article was not controversial amongst regional actors.

17. A diplomat explained that 'in these negotiations, the main issues were between G77 and non-G77. . . . You can agree on some policy message, but of course, the main issue is: How are we going to implement these policies. And it's a question of the resources. And that's where the big differences are' (interview#227, 09-05-16).

18. The EUR group was a regional group that regularly met in the WHO context and therefore had formal access to the ICN2 JWG. The European group has fifty-two member states from Europe (broadly defined), amongst them Kirgizstan, Russia, Turkey, Azerbaijan, the Ukraine and Armenia, as well as the EU members. Thus, group coordination was challenging in general due to the large number of partially heterogeneous states. However, concerning the topic of who carries blame for mal- and undernutrition in the Global South, the positions of the EUR group members were not far apart in agreeing that malnutrition is caused not only by a lack of access to food but also by problems and insufficiencies in the food production and consumption chain (e.g. hygiene, cooling) (interview#239, 22-08-16). Thus, group coordination was effective and allowed the EUR group to act in concert in the JWG in this respect.

19. This is also reflected in the societal discussions on the topic (e.g. Fickling 2005, Perry 2008).

20. The GRULAC member states managed to coordinate a common position, even though it evoked 'very hard discussions' (interview#228, 09-05-16). A diplomat from a GRULAC member explained: 'Inside GRULAC exists an informal mechanism to coordinate. There exists a plenary, maybe, that includes all permanent representatives of GRULAC that are based in Rome. And then in the plenary, we discuss about topics, for example, we revise the document and give input based on our national positions in order to reach a consensus around a regional position. When I took the floor in the negotiations . . . I spoke on behalf of GRULAC' (interview#228, 09-05-16). Another diplomat from a GRULAC country explained that 'the way we work here (at the FAO Headquarter, added by the authors) is that we reach consensus within the group and we go with the GRULAC position to the plenary. If there is no consensus, every country will just ask for the floor and give its position on the matter. But generally, we reach consensus. If we have very different opinions we take one or two positions or, like I said before, each country would give its own position and try to find other countries that will be like-minded or we simply would not deal with the issue' (interview#214, 03-02-16).

21. For instance, in GRULAC especially big countries with huge agriculture industries were not interested in a strong climate change reference as 'agricultural practices also accelerate climate change' and therefore 'They don't want to talk about that . . . and don´t want to alter some practice' (interview#226, 06-05-16).

22. The African Group was very interested in the adoption of the Declaration as 'malnutrition is prevailing . . . in most of the countries in Sub-Saharan Africa' (interview#224, 05-05-16). Thus, its member states met frequently to find common positions, which was difficult for many topics (interviews#224, 06-05-16, #225, 06-05-16), but not the climate change one. A diplomat explained that 'for the ICN2, we were forced to be very organised' (interview#224, 06-05-16), especially since the African group was the only option for some of the poorer countries to have a voice in Rome at all. The poorer members grapple with 'limited human resource, they don't

have people to stick to that subject, follow up' (interview#224, 05-05-16, also #226, 06-05-16).

23. The 'High-Level Conference on World Food Security: The Challenges of Climate Change and Bioenergy' took place at the FAO Headquarters in Rome in June 2008.

24. The EU was perceived as being one of the most active regional actors in the ICN2 negotiations with a 'prominent and constant presence' (interview#238, 22-08-16) and described as a 'specific animal' due to its status as a member organisation in FAO (interview#239, 22-08-16). Its member states coordinated its common position very extensively, which was 'on several topic[s] . . . difficult' (interview#237, 12-05-16, also #229, 10-05-16). The EU was part of the ERG in Rome and the EUR in Geneva, and it appointed key delegates for the negotiations, namely the Italian representative Luca Fratini, who was, together with his Russian colleague, Ivan Konstantinopolskiy, appointed as the two negotiators for the ERG. In the WHO, the EUR was represented by Finland and Switzerland, in order to 'take on board the positions of the EU and non-EU-member states' (interview#239, 22-08-16). EU Members felt that, as the EU combines twenty-eight voices, 'the impact of any European Union position is very strong' and that the EU was 'driving the exercise' (interview#225, 06-05-16), also because other regions such as 'many Africans or even Latin Americans and sometimes Asians will refer to the EU positions' (interview#225, 06-05-16). Besides coordinating a common position amongst the EU member states in Rome, the EU and some member state representatives were in close contact with the EU member states in Geneva 'in order to forward the same line' (interview#230, 10-05-16), doing so by holding 'phone talks or phone conferences' (interview#239, 22-08-16).

25. A diplomat explained that NOAM 'saw that six other regional groups were definitely in favour [of deleting the term "potential", insertion by the authors] and then they had to accept it' (interview#240, 02-09-16). Similarly, in later stages of the negotiations, the EU's preferred position was reiterated by many non-EU member states which for instance emphasised the importance of the connection between climate change and food security (Kiribati 2014, Philippines 2014, Seychelles 2014), for instance in framing the former as threat to the latter (Vietnam 2014).

26. The ERG members frequently meet in Rome to coordinate a common position and succeed in doing so for the topic at hand (interviews#225, 06-05-16, #233, 11-05-16, #216, 03-02-16, #225, 06-05-16, #227, 09-05-16, #232, 11-05-16).

27. A diplomat explained, 'So one piece of food can be healthy or unhealthy depending on how much you eat of it. So the most important is the balance of the diet' (interview#225, 06-05-16). Another EU diplomat explained that 'there is nothing like healthy nutrition, it's a healthier lifestyle or there's a healthy diet' (interview#229, 10-05-16).

28. A diplomat explained that for some countries, for example in Central America or Africa, 'trade is everything, they grow the products but it doesn't get to the market, and they are colonised by huge multinationals' (interview#225, 06-05-16).

29. A diplomat was stressing that the ICN2 'was on nutrition, not a forum for discussing our trade' (interview#230, 10-05-16) and therefore 'no language that would compromise any of the discussions that were ongoing in the frame of the Doha' should be used and that the EU member states 'did not want was any text that could

be used through the back door in the Geneva setting' (interview#229, 10-05-16). Another diplomat reported, 'On trade related issues there were always some sensitivity and so it's like, the world summit should not substitute the WTO' (interview#217, 03-02-16).

30. This also carried an implicit bargaining threat, as it implied that a prevailing negative trade framing could prevent progress in furthering a new international agreement on nutrition (H6b). The EU was not in pivotal position, and its threat did not work out.

31. A diplomat explained that the paragraph 'was taken from the previous compromise' (interview#230, 10-05-16) and another one that this part represents a 'reconfirmation of an existing text' (interview#229, 10-05-16).

32. For example, the WPR substituted the term 'nutrition policies should target' with 'nutrition policies should encourage', and the EU proposed 'stages of life' instead of 'all age groups' (JWG August 27th 2014).

33. The Asia Group was rather silent in the negotiations (interview#234, 11-05-16). In the OEWG it became clear that finding common ground in the regional group was difficult (interview#226, 06-05-16), as the member states became very vocal in expressing their diverse country positions, as 'this was the first opportunity he [a diplomat from a Asia group member state, added by the authors] had to say things' (interview#225, 06-05-16).

34. For instance, a diplomat reported 'the gender aspect was very strong for the EU' (interview#225, 06-05-16).

35. The 'right to food' is, for example, included in the Constitutions of South Africa (Chapter 2/Section 27), Uganda (Objective 14), Nigeria (Article 16), Malawi (Article 13) or the Congo (Article 47) (South Africa 1996, Uganda 1995, Nigeria 1999; Malawi 1994, Congo 2005). See also the 'Voluntary Guidelines to Support the Progressive Realisation of the Right to Adequate Food in the Context of National Food Security' (FAO 2005).

36. For example, a diplomat reported, 'The reaffirmation of the right to food. You may know, I mean this is not controversial, the vast majority of countries would not object to this. But the policy of the US is not to recognise formally the right to food' (interview#242, 06-09-16).

37. A diplomat reported, 'There was a reservation by the US which I think referred to the right to food, but they stated in the beginning that they would put the reservation, but they would not object to the consensus. So, the declaration went' (interview#225, 06-05-16).

38. This does not apply to the United States 'because they aren't part of the covenant . . ., the covenant on social, economic and cultural rights, which proclaims the right to food, adequate level of eating, right to food etc. So not being part of that, they think: Ok, we have our own legislation, we are not bound by this covenant and therefore we cannot agree on a declaration which states formally the right to food. I think it's critical position and they don't want to change it' (interview#242, 06-09-16).

39. However, no direct reference was made to halal or kosher food (interview#240, 02-09-16).

40. For example, 'Because it came to the light that some of the cultures doesn't allow some food that has been treated in a certain way. So it was easier to express it

that maybe you make it available in a nutritious way which is culturally acceptable. Then it brought a lot of problems phrasing culturally acceptable because the others are open and say: 'No, no if you say culturally acceptable, it will attract some sentiment of the trade barriers' (interview#224, 05-05-16).

41. A diplomat explained that 'it has always been a reference to Palestine although there are more situations of occupation in the world' (interview#229, 10-05-16).

42. A diplomat from an EU member state explained that 'in this case, there was no strong EU positioning here' (interview#229, 10-05-16).

43. The Middle East group hardly voiced a common position, as the member states have diverging positions on various issues and therefore it was 'very difficult for them . . . to speak with one voice' (interview#232, 11-05-16). Moreover, some member states of this group also belong to the African Group, and therefore had the possibility to be active in this regional grouping. If expressing a position at all, it related to salient issues (interview#239, 22-08-16). Yet with respect to the inclusion of the term 'occupation' in the Rome Declaration, the Middle East group's position was very moderate in nature and, thus, 'in contradiction to what other regions expected' (interview#239, 22-08-16). The Middle East group – similar to the ICN2 secretariat and the EU – wanted to prevent politicising the Rome Declaration (interview#234, 11-05-06).

44. Similarly, 'Those who don't like this occupation would at least accept to have it if you have terrorism, so it was a compromise . . . it was a trade-off' (interview#234, 11-05-16).

45. C.f. Eurostat 2007.

46. An EU member state described the Expo as an 'ideal platform to disseminate whatever messages came from ICN2 (interview#225, 06-05-16).

47. A diplomat explained that the issue was important for the African regional group and that 'it was important to put at least a title of ten years to concentrate our efforts, so that after ten years at least you have to evaluate what you have achieved and what you haven't' (interview#224, 05-05-16).

48. Moreover, another diplomat stated that for the EU the 'added value and cost of such an initiative' was not clear to many actors (ICN2 interview#30, 11-05-16). Another colleague explained that 'you have to make sure you'll find the resources necessary to implement the decade' (interview#242, 06-09-16). Another diplomat from an EU country asked, 'Who's going to pay for that, what are the benefits'? and explained that 'there was no plan, there was nothing on the table, so we were very reluctant to support it' (interview#229, 10-05-16). A representative of an EU country explained that many EU countries were reluctant on that issue as it was the 'G77 who wanted more funds to be brought in, because of course, the funds come from us' (interview#225, 06-05-16).

49. The wording was *"consider declaring"* although *"we recommend to the UN"* is standard language because we cannot instruct the General Assembly what to do. But this says: *Consider declaring* because of the language that we would have preferred is "We recommend the regional Assembly to declare". And this is the trick: To consider declaring. And that was the compromise because the Europeans didn't want it. . . . Because generally what you say when you have full agreement, and you

send something to other bodies we recommend to declare' (interview#226, 06-05-16; emphasis added by the authors).

50. A diplomat from an EU member explained that this addition 'is an EU phrase that came in because of us and we wanted it' (interview#229, 10-05-16).

51. These are the African Regional Group (AFRICA), the European Regional Group (ERG), the Latin America and Caribbean Group (GRULAC), the Near East Regional Group (NEEA), the Southwest Pacific group (SWP) and North America (NOAM) of the FAO, as well as the six regional groups of the WHO, namely the European Region (EUR), the African Region group (AFR), the Region of the Americas (AMR), the Western Pacific Region group (WPR), the Easter Mediterranean Region group (EMR) and the South-East Asia Region (SEAR).

## Conclusions

1. For instance, a diplomat reported, 'Most of the countries have got representation here. I know for Africa only, maybe one tenth of countries are not represented in Rome, so are unable to attend the day-to-day-meetings. So it was decided that because the, to make the process efficient, some. . . . The region, the regional groups, proposed the representatives of the countries to represent their regions in the negotiation' (interview#224, 05-05-16).

# Literature

Abbott, K. W., Keohane, R. O., Moravcsik, A., Slaughter, A. M., and Snidal, D. (2000) The Concept of Legalization. *International Organization* 54(3): 401–19.

Acharya, A. (2007) The Emerging Regional Architecture of World Politics. *World Politics* 59(4): 629–52.

African Group (2010) Statement delivered by Lawrence Olufemi Obisakin, First Session of the ATT Preparatory Committee, New York, July 12, 2010.

———— (2011) Statement delivered by Abiodun Richards Adejola, Minister, Permanent Mission of Nigeria to the United Nations, Third Session of the ATT Preparatory Committee, New York, July 11, 2011.

———— (2012) Statement delivered by Abiodun Richards Adejola, Minister, Permanent Mission of Nigeria to the United Nations, Fourth Session of the ATT Preparatory Committee, New York, February 13, 2012.

Agence France Presse (2014) Japan's Antarctic Whaling Bid Faces IWC Scrutiny after Scientific Challenge. *Japan Times*, 17 September 2010.

Aggestam, L. (2011) *European Foreign Policy and the Quest for a Global Role. Britain, France and Germany*, London: Routledge.

Albin, C., and Druckman, D. (2014) Procedures Matter: Justice and Effectiveness in International Trade Negotiations. *European Journal of International Relations* 20(4): 1014–42.

Alderson, K. (2001) Making Sense of State Socialization. *Review of International Studies* 27(3): 415–33.

Alecu de Flers, N. (2011) *EU Foreign Policy and the Europeanization of Neutral States. Comparing Irish and Austrian Foreign Policy*, London: Routledge.

Almasi, A., Eshraghian, M. R., Moghimbeigi, A., Rahimi, A., Mohammad, K., and Fallahigilan, S. (2016) Multilevel Zero-Inflated Generalized Poisson Regression Modeling for Dispersed Correlated Count Data. *Statistical Methodology* 30: 1–14.

Alter, K. J., and Meunier, S. (2009) The Politics of International Regime Complexity. *Perspectives on Politics* 7(1): 13–24.

Alvarez, J. E. (2005) *International Organizations as Law-makers*. Oxford: Oxford University Press Oxford.

Amin, A., and Thrift, N. (1994) *Globalization, Institutions, and Regional Development in Europe*. Oxford: Oxford University Press.

Arab Group (2011a) Statement of the Arab Group, delivered by Mr. Mesaid Alkulaib, First Secretary Permanent Mission of the State of Kuwait to the United Nations. Third Session of the ATT Preparatory Committee, New York, July 11, 2011.

——— (2011b) Statement on behalf of the Arab Group, delivered by Jamal Fares Alrowaiei, Permanent Mission of the Kingdom of Bahrain to the United Nations, Second Session of the ATT Preparatory Committee, New York, February 28, 2011.

Argentina, Chile, Colombia, Guatemala, Jamaica, Mexico, Peru, Trinidad and Tobago, and Uruguay (2010) Joint Statement on Elements for a Treaty. First Session of the ATT Preparatory Committee, New York, July 21, 2010.

Argentina, Brazil, South Africa, Uruguay (2014) The South Atlantic: A Sanctuary for Whales, Portoroz, Slovenia.

ASEAN (2012) Statement by Ambassador Han Thu, Deputy Permanent Representative, on Behalf of the ASEAN Member States, Fourth Session of the ATT Preparatory Committee, New York, July 3, 2012.

ATT Legal Bloggers. 'Beyond the Shadow of a Doubt? Thoughts on the first PrepCom for an Arms Trade Treaty'. http://armstradetreaty.blogspot.de/2010_07_01_archive.html

———. 'Third PrepCom'. Geneva Academy of International Humanitarian Law and Human Rights, http://armstradetreaty.blogspot.de/search?updated-min=2011-01-01T00:00:00-05:00&updated-max=2012-01-01T00:00:00-05:00&max-results=15

Australia (2010a) Statement by H. E. Gary Quinlan Ambassador and Permanent Representative of Australia to the United Nations, First Session of the ATT Preparatory Committee, New York, July 12, 2010.

——— (2010b) Statement by Mr. John Tilemann, International Security Division, Department of Foreign Affairs and Trade, First Session of the ATT Preparatory Committee, New York, July 13, 2010.

——— (2011a) Statement by Mr. James Potter, Office of International Law, Attorney-General's Department, Second Session of the ATT Preparatory Committee, New York, March 1, 2011.

——— (2011b) Statement by Mr. John Tilemann, International Security Division, Department of Foreign Affairs and Trade, Third Session of the ATT Preparatory Committee, New York, July 12, 2011.

Axelrod, R. A. (1984) *The Evolution of Cooperation*, New York: Basic Books.

Axelrod, R. A., and Keohane, R. O. (1986) Achieving Cooperation under Anarchy: Strategies and Institutions. *World Politics* 38(1): 226–54.

Baccini, L., and Dür, A. (2011) The New Regionalism and Policy Interdependence. *British Journal of Political Science* 42(1): 57–79.

Bahamas, Belize, Chile, Colombia, El Salvador, Guatemala, Jamaica, Mexico, Peru, Trinidad and Tobago, Uruguay (2013) Joint Statement. Delivered by Ambassador Enrique Roman-Morey Permanent Representative of Peru to the United Nations. New York, March 18, 2013.

Bailer, S. (2004) Bargaining Success in the European Union. *European Union Politics* 5(1): 99–123.

Bailey, J. (2012) Whale Watching, the Buenos Aires Group and the Politics of the IWC. *Marine Policy* (36): 489–94.

Bain, L. E. (2013) Malnutrition in Sub-Saharan Africa: Burden, Causes and Prospects. *The Pan African Medical Journal* 15: 120.

Bangladesh (2010) Statement by Dr. A. K. Abdul Momen, Permanent Representative of Bangladesh to the United Nations, First Session of the ATT Preparatory Committee, New York, July 13, 2010.

————— (2011a) Statement by Mr. Mohammad Sarwar Mahmood, Permanent Mission of Bangladesh to the United Nations, Second Session of the ATT Preparatory Committee, New York, March 1, 2011.

————— (2011b) Statement by Mr. Mohammad Sarwar Mahmood, Permanent Mission of Bangladesh to the United Nations, Third Session of the ATT Preparatory Committee, New York, July 11, 2011.

Baroncelli, E. (2011) The EU at the World Bank: Institutional and Policy Performance. *Journal of European Integration* 33(6): 637–50.

Basu, S. (2012) 'The European Union in the Human Rights Council', in J. Wouters, Bruynickx, H., Basu, S. and Schunz, S. (eds) *The European Union and Multilateral Governance. Assessing EU Participation in the United Nations Human Rights and Environmental Fora.* Basingstoke: Palgrave, 86–102.

Bauer, S., Beijer, P., and Bromley, M. (2014) The Arms Trade Treaty: Challenges for the First Conference of States Parties, *SIPRI Insights on Peace and Security.* http://books.sipri.org/files/insight/SIPRIInsight1402.pdf

Baylis, J., Smith, S., and Owens, P., eds. (2011) *The Globalization of World Politics.* Oxford: Oxford University Press.

Beeson, M. (2005a) Rethinking Regionalism: Europe and East Asia in Comparative Historical Perspective. *Journal of European Public Policy* 12(6): 969–85.

————— (2005b) Rethinking Regionalism: Europe and East Asia in Comparative Historical Perspective. *Journal of European Public Policy* 12(6): 969–85.

Belize (2011) Statement on Parameters/Criteria, Second Session of the ATT Preparatory Committee, New York, March 1, 2011.

Bellestri, T. E. (2011) 'International Whaling Commission (IWC)', in P. Robbins (ed) *Green Issues and Debates: An A-to-Z-Guide.* London: SAGE, 314–18.

Benz, A. (1985) *Föderalismus als dynamisches System, Zentralisierung und Dezentralisierung im föderativen Staat.* Opladen: Westdeutscher Verlag.

————— (1998) Politikverflechtung ohne Politikverflechtungsfalle – Koordination und Strukturdynamik im euroäischen Mehrebenensystem. *Politische Vierteljahresschrift* 39(3): 558–89.

————— (1999) 'Der deutsche Föderalismus', in T. Ellwein and Holtmann, E. (eds) *50 Jahre Bundesrepublik Deutschland. Rahmenbedingungen – Entwicklungen – Perspektiven.* Opladen: Westdeutscher Verlag, 135–53.

————— (2000) Two Types of Multi-Level Governance: Intergovernmental Relations in German and EU Regional Policy. *Regional and Federal Studies* 10(3): 21–44.

————— (2003) 'Mehrebenenverflechtung in der Europäischen Union', in M. Jachtenfuchs and Kohler-Koch, B. (eds) *Europäische Integration.* Opladen: Leske+Budrich, 317–52.

————— (2004) *Governance – Regieren in komplexen Regelsystemen*, Opladen: Leske + Budrich.

————— (2007) Accountable Multilevel Governance by the Open Method of Coordination? *European Law Journal* 13(4): 505–22.

Benz, A., Scharpf, F. W., and Zintl, R., eds. (1992) *Horizontale Politikverflechtung. Zur Theorie von Verhandlungssystemen.* Frankfurt a/M; New York: Campus.

Beretvas, S. N. (2011) Cross-Classified and Multiple-Membership Models, in Hox, J. J., Roberts, J. K. (eds) *Handbook for advanced multilevel analysis.* New York: Routledge, 313–334.

Berton, P., Kimura, H., and Zartman, W., eds. (1999) *International Negotiation: Actors, Structure/Process, Values.* New York: St. Martin's Press.

Betts, A. (2013) Regime Complexity and International Organizations: UNHCR as a Challenged Institution. *Global Governance: A Review of Multilateralism and International Organizations* 19(1): 69–81.

Bhagwati, J. (1994) Free Trade: Old and New Challenges. *The Economic Journal* 104(3): 231–46.

Binmore, K., and Samuelson, L. (2006) The Evolution of Focal Points. *Games and Economic Behavior* 55(1): 21–42.

Binmore, K., Swierzbinski, J., Hsu, S., and Proulx, C. (1993) Focal Points and Bargaining. *International Journal of Game Theory* 22(4): 381–409.

Black, R. (2011) Whaling Meeting 'Ignores Needs of Whales'. BBC News, Jersey, July 14, 2011. http://www.bbc.com/news/science-environment-14153779

Blavoukos, S., and Bourantonis, D. (2010) *The EU Presence in International Organizations.* London: Routledge.

————— (2011a) The EU's Performance in the United Nations Security Council. *Journal of European Integration* 33(6): 731–42.

————— (2011d) The EU's Performance in the United Nations Security Council. *Journal of European Integration* 33(6): 731–42.

————— (2014) Do Sanctions Strengthen the International Presence of the EU? *European Foreign Affairs Review* 19(3): 393–410.

Blavoukos, S., Bourantonis, D., and Tsakonas, P. (2006) Parameters of the Chairmanship's Effectiveness: The Case of the UN Security Council. *The Hague Journal of Diplomacy* 1(2): 143–70.

Böhmelt, T., and Freyburg, T. (2013) The Temporal Dimension of the Credibility of EU Conditionality and Candidate States' Compliance with the Acquis Communautaire, 1998–2009. *European Union Politics* 14(2): 250–72.

Börzel, T. A. (2006) 'Mind The Gap! European Integration between Level and Scope', in T. A. Börzel (ed) *The Disparity of European Integration. Revisiting Neofunctionalism in Honour of Ernst B. Haas.* New York: Routledge, 1–20.

————— (2010) European Governance: Negotiation and Competition in the Shadow of Hierarchy. *Journal of Common Market Studies* 48(2): 191–219.

————— (2012) 'Comparative Regionalism: European Integration and Beyond', in W. Carlsnaes, Risse, T. and Simmons, B. (eds) *Handbook of International Relations.* London: SAGE.

Börzel, T. A., and Hackenesch, C. (2013) Small Carrots, Few Sticks: EU Good Governance Promotion in Sub-Saharan Africa. *Cambridge Review of International Affairs* 26(3): 536–55.

Börzel, T. A., and Risse, T. (2012a) From Europeanisation to Diffusion: Introduction. *West European Politics* 35(1): 1–19.

———— (2012b) When Europeanisation Meets Diffusion: Exploring New Territory. *West European Politics* 35(1): 192–207.

————, eds. (2016) *The Oxford Handbook of Comparative Regionalism*. Oxford: Oxford University Press.

Bosse, G., and Korosteleva-Polglase, E. (2009) Changing Belarus? The Limits of EU Governance in Eastern Europe and the Promise of Partnership. *Cooperation and Conflict* 44(2): 143–65.

Blavoukos, S. and Bourantonis, D. (2015) Issue Salience and Controversy: Any Effect on Chair's Autonomy in Multilateral Negotiations? *International Negotiation*, 20, 199-217.

Bowcott, O. (2001) Plans for Two New Whale Sanctuaries Voted Down. The Guardian Weekly, 08.08.2001.

Bowles, P. (1997) ASEAN, AFTA and the 'New Regionalism'. *Pacific Affairs* 70(2): 219–33.

Brazil (2010) Brazil: Statement on an Arms Trade Treaty, First Session of the ATT Preparatory Committee, New York, July 12, 2010.

———— (2011a) ATT – Draft Paper on Implementation, Third Session of the ATT Preparatory Committee, New York, July 11, 2011.

———— (2011b) Chair's New Draft Paper. Third Session of the ATT Preparatory Committee, New York, July 14, 2011.

———— (2011c) Statement by the Delegation of Brazil on 'Consideration of International Cooperation and Assistance in the Context of the ATT', Second Session of the ATT Preparatory Committee, New York, March 1, 2011.

———— (2012) Statement by H. E. Ambassador Antonio Guerreiro, Permanent Representative of Brazil to the Conference on Disarmament, at the High Level Segment of the United Nations Conference on the Arms Trade Treaty. New York, July 2, 2012.

Breslin, S., and Higgott, R. (2003) New Regionalism (s) in the Global Political Economy. Conceptual Understanding in Historical Perspective. *Asia Europe Journal* 1(2): 167–82.

Breslin, S., Hughes, C. W., Phillips, N., and Rosamond, B., eds. (2013) *New Regionalism in the Global Political Economy: Theories and Cases*. London: Routledge.

Browne, W. J. (1998) Applying MCMC methods to multi-level models. Dissertation. University of Bath, Bath.

Browne, W. J., Goldstein, H., and Rasbash, J. (2001) Multiple Membership Multiple Classification (MMMC) Models. *Statistical Modelling* 1(2): 103–24.

Browne, W. J., Subramanian, S. V., Jones, K., and Goldstein, H. (2005) Variance Partitioning in Multilevel Logistic Models That Exhibit Overdispersion. *Journal of the Royal Statistical Society: Series A (Statistics in Society)* 168(3): 599–613.

Buenos Aires Group (2008) Declaration of the Buenos Aires Group: The Conservation of Cetaceans in the 21st Century and the International Whaling Commission. Ilha do Papagaio, Brazil, 24–26 April, 2008.

———— (2011) Opening Statement of the Members of the Buenos Aires Group, International Whaling Commission 63 Annual Meeting, St. Helier, Jersey, United Kingdom, 11–14 July 2011.

―――― (2012) Opening Statement of the Members of the Buenos Aires Group (GBA), International Whaling Commission 64th Annual Meeting, City of Panama, Panama, 2–6 July 2012.

―――― (2014a) Opening Statement of the Members of the Grupo Buenos Aires (GBA) Attending the 65th IWC Meeting.

―――― (2014b) Opening Statement of the Members of the Grupo Buenos Aires (GBA), 65th Annual Meeting International Whaling Commission, Portoroz, Slovenia, 15–18 September 2014.

Bull, H. (1982) Civilian Power Europe: A Contradiction in Terms? *Journal of Common Market Studies* 21(2): 149–70.

Burmester, N., and Jankowski, M. (2014) Reassessing the European Union in the United Nations General Assembly. *Journal of European Public Policy* 21(10): 1491–508.

Burundi (2011) Déclaration de la Délégation de la Republique du Burundi lors de la Troisième Conférence Préparatoire – PrepCom – des Nations Unies relative aux Négociations sur le Traité sur le Commerce des Armes (ATT).

Burundi on Behalf of the East African Community (2011). Scope, International Cooperation and Assistance, Second Session of the ATT Preparatory Committee, New York, March 2, 2011.

Busby, L., and Holt, S. (2012) South Atlantic Whale Sanctuary. Securing a Future for Whales through Cooperation, Research and Non-Consumptive Use. International Fund for Animal Welfare, London.

Busch, M. L. (2007) Overlapping Institutions, Forum Shopping, and Dispute Settlement in International Trade. *International Organization* 61(4): 735–61.

Busch, M. L. and Reinhardt, E. (2000) Bargaining in the Shadow of the Law: Early Settlement in GATT/WTO Disputes. Fordham International Law Journal 24 (1): 158–172.

Callixtus, J. (2013) Reflections from the Arms Trade Treaty Negotiations: CARICOM Punching and Succeeding above Its Weight. *Caribbean Journal of International Relations & Diplomacy* 1(1): 93–109.

Cambodia (2014) Statement by Sok Silo, Rome. Food and Agriculture Organization, Rome.

Canada (2011) Statement by the Delegation of Canada. Third Session of the ATT Preparatory Committee, New York, July 14, 2011.

―――― (2012) Statement by the Delegation of Canada at the Opening of the Arms Trade Treaty Diplomatic Conference, New York, July 5, 2012.

CARICOM (2010a) Statement of Antigua and Barbuda on behalf of CARICOM Member States, First Session of the ATT Preparatory Committee, New York, July 13, 2010.

―――― (2010b) Statement on behalf of CARICOM Member States, First Session of the ATT Preparatory Committee, New York, July 13, 2010.

―――― (2010c) Statement on behalf of CARICOM Member States by H. E. Henry Mac Donald, Permanent Representative of Suriname to the United Nations, irst Session of the ATT Preparatory Committee, New York, July 13, 2010.

―――― (2010d) Statement on behalf of CARICOM Member States by H. E. Henry Mac Donald, Permanent Representative of Suriname to the United Nations, First Session of the ATT Preparatory Committee, New York, July 14, 2010.

———— (2010e) Statement on behalf of CARICOM Member States by H. E. Henry Mac Donald, Permanent Representative of Suriname to the United Nations, on the Issue of Principles for Inclusion in the Arms Trade, First Session of the ATT Preparatory Committee, New York, July 14, 2010.

———— (2011a) CARICOM Declaration on Small Arms and Light Weapons, Issued by the Thirty-Second Meeting of the Conference of Heads of Government of the Caribbean Community, 30 June–4 July 2011, Basseterre, St. Kits and Nevis, Basseterre.

———— (2011b) Draft CARICOM Statement. International Cooperation and Assistance in the Context of the ATT, Second Session of the ATT Preparatory Committee, New York, March 2, 2011.

———— (2011c) Draft CARICOM Statement to the 2nd Meeting of the Preparatory Committee for the United Nations Conference on an Arms Trade Treaty. 28 February–3 March 2011. International Cooperation and Assistance in the Context of the ATT (3rd CARICOM Statement), New York.

———— (2011d) Intervention by H. E. Mr. Joseph Goddard. Permanent Representative of Barbados to the United Nations on behalf of The Caribbean Community (CARICOM), Third Session of the ATT Preparatory Committee, New York, July 11, 2011.

———— (2011e) Second Meeting of the ATT Preparatory Committee. 28 February–4 March. Talking Points on Scope, New York.

———— (2011f) Statement by H. E. Mr. Joseph Goddard, Permanent Representative of Barbados to the United Nations on Behalf of the Caribbean Community (CARICOM) at the Third Session of the Preparatory Committee for the United Nations Conference on the Arms Trade Treaty, New York.

———— (2011g) Statement Delivered on Behalf of CARICOM during the Second Preparatory Committee, New York, Second Session of the ATT Preparatory Committee, New York, March 1, 2011.

———— (2011h) Talking Points on Scope, Second Session of the ATT Preparatory Committee, New York, February 2, 2011.

———— (2012a) Statement by Mr. Eden Charles, Counsellor, Permanent Mission of the Republic of Trinidad and Tobago, to the United Nations on behalf of CARICOM, on Substantive Elements of the future ATT, Fourth Session of the ATT Preparatory Committee, New York, February 13, 2012.

———— (2012b) Statement by Mr. Eden Charles. Counsellor, Permanent Mission of Trinidad and Tobago on behalf of CARICOM on Draft Rules of Procedure, Fourth Session of the ATT Preparatory Committee, New York, February 15, 2012.

———— (2012c) Statement by the Honourable Winston Dookeran, Minister of Foreign Affairs of the Republic of Trinidad and Tobago, First UN Conference on the Arms Trade Treaty, New York, July 5, 2012.

———— (2013) Statement by H. E. Eden Charles, Ambassador Extraordinary and Plenipotentiary, Deputy Permanent Representative of the Republic of Trinidad and Tobago to the United Nations, 'General Exchange of Views', Second UN Conference on the Arms Trade Treaty, New York, March 18, 2013.

Carlsnaes, W., and Smith, S., eds. (1994) *European Foreign Policy. The EC and Changing Perspective in Europe*. London: SAGE.

Cass, L. (2005) Norm Entrapment and Preference Change: The Evolution of the European Union Position on International Emissions Trading. *Global Environmental Politics* 5(2): 36–60.

Chandra, A. C. (2004) Indonesia's Non-State Actors in ASEAN: A New Regionalism Agenda for Southeast Asia? *Contemporary Southeast Asia* 26(1): 155–74.

Chayes, A., and Handler-Chayes, A. (1995) *The New Sovereignty. Compliance and International Regulatory Agreements.* Cambridge; London: Harvard University Press.

China (2012) Statement by the Chinese Delegation at the General Debate of United Nations Conference on the Arms Trade Treaty. First UN Conference on the Arms Trade Treaty, New York, July 9, 2012.

Christiansen, T. (1997) 'Reconstructing European Space: From Territorial Politics to Multi-Level Governance', in K. E. Jorgensen (ed) *Reflective Approaches to European Governance.* London: Macmillan, 51–68.

Christiansen, T., and Tonra, B., eds. (2004) *Rethinking EU Foreign Policy.* Manchester: Manchester University Press.

Chung, H., and Beretvas, S. N. (2012) The Impact of Ignoring Multiple Membership Data Structures in Multilevel Models. *The British Journal of Mathematical and Statistical Psychology* 65(2): 185–200.

Coleman, J. S. (1970) The Benefits of Coalition. *Public Choice* 8(1): 45–61.

Collective Security Treaty Organization (2012) Statement by the Delegation of the Collective Security Treaty Organization (CSTO) Member States at the 2012 United Nations Conference on the Arms Trade Treaty, First UN Conference on the Arms Trade Treaty, New York, July 6, 2012.

Collinson, S. (1999) Issue-Systems, Multi-Level Games, and the Analysis of the EU's External Commercial and Associated Policies: A Research Agenda. *Journal of European Public Policy* 6(2): 206–24.

Colombia (2012) Statement by H. E. Miguel Camilo Ruiz, First UN Conference on the Arms Trade Treaty, New York, July 3, 2012.

Common Position of P5 (2013) Declaration by H. E. Jean-Hugues Simon-Michel. Ambassador, Permanent Representative of France to the Conference of Disarmament, on Behalf of the People's Republic of China, the Russian Federation, the United Kingdom, the United States of America and France March 18, 2013, New York.

Compton-Antoine, J. (2014) International Whaling Commission. Chair's Report of the 65th Meeting. Portoroz, Slovenia.

Congo (2005) The Constitution of the Democratic Republic of the Congo.

Control Arms. 'The Story So Far'. http://controlarms.org/en/about-controlarms/

Conzelmann, T. (1998) 'Europeanisation' of Regional Development Policies? Linking the Multi-Level Governance Approach with Theories of Policy Learning and Policy Change. *European Integration Online Papers* 2(4), http://eiop.or.at/eiop/texte/1998-004a.htm

Cornia, G. A. (1985) Farm Size, Land Yields and the Agricultural Production Function: An Analysis for Fifteen Developing Countries. *World Development* 13(4): 513–34.

Costa Rica (2011a) Statement of Costa Rica. Third Session of the ATT Preparatory Committee, New York, July 11, 2011.

——— (2011b) Statement of Costa Rica at the Third Session of the ATT Preparatory Committee, New York, March 2, 2011.

———— (2013) Statement at the Opening of the Second United Nations Conference on the Arms Trade Treaty, New York, March 18, 2013.

Cowles, M. G., Caporaso, J. A., and Risse, T., eds. (2001) *Transforming Europe. Europeanization and Domestic Change*. Ithaca, NY: Cornell University Press.

Crump, L., and Zartman, I. W., eds. (2003) *International Multilateral Negotiation: Approaches to the Management of Complexity*. Vol. 8, 1, International Negotiation – Special Issue.

Cuba (2012) Statement by Ambassador Rodolfo Benitez Verson, Representative of Cuba to the United Nations Conference on the Arms Trade Treaty. First UN Conference on the Arms Trade Treaty, New York, July 5, 2012.

Cyprus on Behalf of the European Union (2012) 64th Annual Meeting of the International Whaling Commission. Opening Statement by Cyprus on Behalf of the EU and Its Member States, https://archive.iwc.int/pages/view.php?ref=3311&search=! collection82&order_by=relevance&sort=DESC&offset=0&archive=0&k=&cur pos=19

da Conceição-Heldt, E. (2014) When Speaking with a Single Voice Isn't Enough: Bargaining Power (A)symmetry and EU External Effectiveness in Global Trade Governance. *Journal of European Public Policy* 21(7): 980–95.

da Conceição-Heldt, E., and Meunier, S. (2014) Speaking with a Single Voice: Internal Cohesiveness and External Effectiveness of the EU in Global Governance. *Journal of European Public Policy* 21(7): 961–79.

Damro, C. (2012) Market Power Europe. *Journal of European Public Policy* 19(5): 682–99.

Dashwood, A., and Maresceau, M. (2011) *Law and Practice of EU External Relations. Salient Features of a Changing Landscape*, Cambridge: Cambridge University Press.

Debaere, P., De Ville, F., Orbie, J., Saenen, B., and Verschaeve, J. (2014) 'Membership. The Evolution of the EU Membership in Major International Organizations', in A. Orsini (ed) *The European Union with(in) International Organisations. Commitments, Consistency and Effects across Time*. Farnham/Burlington: Ashgate, 34–53.

Dee, M. (2012) Standing Together or Doing the Splits? Evaluating European Union Performance in the Nuclear Non-Proliferation Treaty Review Negotiations. *European Foreign Affairs Review* 17(2): 189–212.

———— (2015) 'The European Union and Its Performance in the NPT Negotiations: Consistency, Change and Challenges', in D.e. Bourantos, Blavoukos, S.e. and Portela, C.e. (eds) *The EU and the Non-Proliferation of Nuclear Weapons: Strategies, Policies, Actions*, Basingstoke/New York: Palgrave Macmillan, 77–94.

Deitelhoff, N., and Müller, H. (2005) Theoretical Paradise – Empirically Lost? Arguing with Habermas. *Review of International Studies* 31: 167–79.

Delreux, T. (2008) The EU as a Negotiator in Multilateral Chemicals Negotiations: Multiple Principals, Different Agents. *Journal of European Public Policy* 15(7): 1069–86.

———— (2009a) Cooperation and Control in the European Union The Case of the European Union as International Environmental Negotiator. *Cooperation and Conflict* 44(2): 189–208.

———— (2009b) The European Union in International Environmental Negotiations: An Analysis of the Stockholm Convention Negotiations. *Environmental Policy and Governance* 19(1): 21–31.

———— (2011) *The EU as International Environmental Negotiator*, Farnham/Burlington: Ashgate.

———— (2012) 'The EU in Negotiations on the Cartagena Protocol on Biosafety', in J. Wouters, Bruyninckx, H., Basu, S. and Schiunz, S. (eds) *The European Union and Multilateral Governance. Assessing EU Participation in United Nations Human Rights and Environmental Fora*. Houndmills: Palgrave, 214–31.

———— (2013) *The EU as International Environmental Negotiator*, London: Ashgate Publishing, Ltd.

Delreux, T., Drieskens, E., Kerremans, B., and Damro, C. (2012) 'The External Institutional Context Matters: The EU in International Negotiations', in O. Costa and Jörgensen, K. E. (eds) *The Influence of International Institutions on the EU. When Multilateralism Hits Brussels*. Basingstoke: Palgrave Macmillan, 58–75.

Denmark (2011a) Danish statement on the scope of the ATT, Second Session of the ATT Preparatory Commiittee, New York, February 28, 2011.

———— (2011b) Denmark. Opening Statement, Third Session of the ATT Preparatory Commiittee, New York, July 15, 2011.

Depauw, S. (2012) The European Union's Involvement in Negotiating an Arms Trade Treaty. Non-Proliferation Papers No.23, EU Non-Proliferation Consortium, December 2012. https://www.sipri.org/sites/default/files/EUNPC_no-23.pdf

Dosch, J., and Wagner, C. (1999) *ASEAN und SAAR. Entwicklungen und Perspektiven regionaler Zusammenarbeit in Asien*. Hamburg: Abera.

DPRK (2012) Statement by H. E. Mr. Sin Son Ho, Ambassador and Permanent Representative of the Democratic People's Republic of Korea to the United Nations.

Drahos, P. (2003) When the Weak Bargain with the Strong: Negotiations in the World Trade Organization. *International Negotiation* 879–109.

Draper, D. (2008) 'Bayesian Multilevel Analysis and MCMC', in J. D. Leeuw and Meijer, E. (eds) *Handbook of Multilevel Analysis*. New York: Springer, 77–140.

Drezner, D. W. (2009) The Power and Peril of International Regime Complexity. *Perspectives on Politics* 7(1): 65–70.

Drieskens, E. (2010) Beyond Chapter VIII: Limits and Opportunities for Regional Representation at the UN Security Council. *International Organizations Law Review* 7(1): 149–69.

Drieskens, E., and van Schaik, L. G., eds. (2014) *The EU and Effective Multilateralism. Internal and External Reform Practices*. Abingdon/New York: Routledge.

Druckman, D. (1997) Dimensions of International Negotiations: Structures, Processes, and Outcomes. *Group Decision and Negotiation* 6(5): 395–420.

Dür, A. (2007) EU Trade Policy as Protection for Exporters: The Agreements with Mexico and Chile. *Journal of Common Market Studies* 45(4): 833–55.

———— (2008) Measuring Interest Group Influence in the EU: A Note on Methodology. *European Union Politics* 9(4): 585–602.

Dür, A., and Mateo, G. (2010) Choosing a Bargaining Strategy in EU Negotiations. Power, Preferences and Culture. *Journal of European Public Policy* 17(5): 680–93.

Dür, A., and Zimmerman, H. (2007) Introduction: The EU in International Trade Negotiations. *Journal of Common Market Studies* 45(4): 771–87.

East African Community (2011) Second Session of the Arms Trade Treaty Preparatory Committee. Statement Made by Burundi on Behalf of the East African Community. Scope, International Cooperation and Assistance, Second Session of the ATT Preparatory Committee, New York, March 2, 2011.

———— (2012) Statement by Dr. Julius T. Rotich, Deputy Secretary General, First UN Conference on the Arms Trade Treaty, New York, July 12, 2012.

ECOWAS (2006) ECOWAS Convention on Small Arms and Light Weapons, Their Ammunition and Other Related Materials, Abuja, Nigeria, adopted on June 14th, 2006.

———— (2010), Statement by Economic Community of West Africa States (ECOWAS), First Session of the ATT Preparatory Committee, New York, July 14, 2010.

———— (2012) Décleration de S.E.M. Kadré Désiré Ouedraogo, Président de la Commission de la Communauté Economique des Etats de l' Afrique de l'Ouest (CEDEAO), First UN Conference on the Arms Trade Treaty, New York, July 9, 2012.

EEAS (2016) The UN in Rome and the EU: EU Status in FAO. May 12, 2016. https://eeas.europa.eu/delegations/un-rome_en/1704/The%20UN%20in%20Rome%20and%20the%20EU.

Egypt (2011a) Egypt – Chair's Non-Paper on Criteria/Parameters, Second Session of the ATT Preparatory Committee, New York, February 1, 2011.

———— (2011b) Egypt – Chair's Non-Paper on Scope, Second Session of the ATT Preparatory Committee, New York, February 28, 2011.

———— (2012) Statement by H. E. Ambassador Mootaz Ahmadein Khalil, Permanent Representative of Egypt to the United Nations in New York, First UN Conference on the Arms Trade Treaty, New York, July 5, 2012.

Eising, R., and Kohler-Koch, B. (1999) 'Governance in the European Union. A Comparative Assessment', in B. Kohler-Koch and Eising, R. (eds) *The Transformation of Governance in the European Union*. London: Routledge, 267–85.

Elazar, D., ed. (1994) *Federal Systems of the World: A Handbook of Federal, Confederal and Autonomy Arrangements*. Second Edition, New York: Grove's Dictionaries.

Elgström, O. (2000) Norm Negotiations. The Construction of New Norms Regarding Gender and Development in EU Foreign Aid Policy. *Journal of European Public Policy* 7(3): 457–76.

Elster, J. (1992) 'Arguing and Bargaining in the Federal Convention and the Assemblée Constituante', in R. Malnes and Underdal, A. (eds) *Rationality and Institutions. Essays in Honour of Knut Midgaard*. Oslo: Univeritetsforlaget, 13–50.

Embassy Managua (2008) Nicaragua: International Whaling Commission (IWC) Demarche, Managua.

Embassy Tokyo (2008) Whaling Commission Chair Discusses Upcoming IWC Working Group with Japan.

Enderlein, H., Wälti, S., and Zürn, M., eds. (2010) *Handbook on Multilevel Governance*. Cheltenham: Edward Elgar.

EU (2014) EU Lines to Take. ICN2 OEWG (Geneva, 22–23 September 2014), Rome.

EU Commission (2007) Proposal for a Council Decision Establishing the Position to Be Adopted on Behalf of the European Community with Regard to Proposals for

Amendments to the Schedule of the International Convention on the Regulation of Whaling, COM(2007) 821 final, Brussels, December 19, 2007.

EU Delegation Geneva (2014) Subject: Second International Conference on Nutrition – Preparatory Working Group Concludes without Finalizing Outcome Document, Geneva.

European Union (2010a) EU Statement on International Cooperation and Assistance, First Session of the ATT Preparatory Committee, New York, July 14, 2010.

——— (2010b) EU Statement on the Chair's Draft Elements of an Arms Trade Treaty, First Session of the ATT Preparatory Committee, New York, July 15, 2010.

——— (2010c) EU Statement on the Elements of the Arms Trade Treaty, New York.

——— (2010d) EU Statement on the elements of the Arms Trade Treaty. Statement by H. E. Mr. Werner Bauwens, Special Envoy for Disarmament and Non-Proliferation, First Session of the ATT Preparatory Committee, New York, July 14, 2010.

——— (2010e) EU Statement on the Implementation and Application of the Arms Trade Treaty, First Session of the ATT Preparatory Committee, New York, July 19, 2010.

——— (2010h) EU Statement on the Scope of an ATT, First Session of the ATT Preparatory Committee, New York, July 15, 2010.

——— (2011a) Statement on behalf of the European Union by Mr. Attila Zimonyi, Deputy Permanent Representative of the Republic of Hungary to the United Nations, International Cooperation and Assistance, Second Session of the ATT Preparatory Committee, New York, March 2, 2011.

——— (2011b) Statement on Behalf of the European Union by Mr. Attila Zimonyi, Deputy Permanent Representative of the Republic of Hungary, to the United Nations, Parameters of an Arms Trade Treaty, Second Session of the ATT Preparatory Committee, New York, March 1, 2011.

——— (2011c) Statement on Behalf of the European Union by Ms. Annalisa Gianella, Director for Non-Proliferation and Disarmament on Specific Aspects of the Implementation Mechanism of the Arms Trade Treaty, Third Session of the ATT Preparatory Committee, New York, July 11, 2011.

——— (2011d) Statement on Behalf of the European Union by Ms. Annalisa Gianella, Director for Non-Proliferation and Disarmament on Provisions and Implementation Support Unit of the Arms Trade Treaty, Third Session of the ATT Preparatory Committee, New York, July 12, 2011.

——— (2011e) Statement on behalf of the European Union by Ms. Eszter Sándorfi, Director General, Department for Security Policy and Non Proliferation, Ministry of Foreign Affairs of the Republic of Hungary, Comments on the Revised Chair's Draft Paper, Second Session of the ATT Preparatory Committee, New York, March 3, 2011.

——— (2011f) Statement on behalf of the European Union by H. E. Mr. Csaba Körösi, Permanent Representative of the Republic of Hungary to the United Nations, Scope of an Arms Trade Treaty, Second Session of the ATT Preparatory Committee, New York, February 28, 2011.

——— (2012a) EU Opening Statement by Mr. Thomas Mayr-Harting, Head of Delegation of the European Union to the United Nations, First UN Conference on the Arms Trade Treaty, New York, July 5, 2012.

———— (2012b) Opening Statement on Behalf of the European Union and Its Member States by Ms. Mara Marinaki, Managing Director, Global and Multilateral Issues, European External Action Service, First UN Conference on the Arms Trade Treaty, New York, July 5, 2012.

Eurostat. 'Farm Structure Survey'. http://ec.europa.eu/eurostat/statistics-explained/index.php/Archive:Farm_structure_survey_2007

Evans, P. B., Jacobson, H. K., and Putnam, R.D., eds. (1993) *Double-Edged Diplomacy: International Bargaining and Domestic Politics*. Berkeley: University of California Press.

Epstein, L., and Segal, J. A. (2000) Measuring Issue Salience. *American Journal of Political Science* 44(1): 66–83.

Executive Office of the Secretary-General, P.a.L.S. (2010) *United Nations Blue Book – Permanent Missions to the UN*. New York: United Nations.

Falk, R. (2003) 'Regionalism and World Order: The Changing Global Setting', in F. Söderbaum and Shaw, T. (eds) *Theories of New Regionalism*. Houndmills: Palgrave, 63–80.

Falkner, G. (1999) 'European Social Policy: Towards Multi-Level and Multi-Actor Governance', in B. Kohler-Koch and Eising, R. (eds) *The Transformation of Governance in the European Union*. London: Routledge, 83–97.

———— (2002) Introduction: EU Treaty Reform as a Three-Level Process. *Journal of European Public Policy* 9(1): 1–11.

Fan, S., and Chan-Kang, C. (2005) Is Small Beautiful? Farm Size, Productivity, and Poverty in Asian Agriculture. *Agricultural Economics* 32(1): 135–46.

FAO (2005) Voluntary Guidelines to Support the Progressive Realization of the Right to Adequate Food in the Context of National Food Security. Food and Agriculture Organization of the United Nations, Rome. http://www.fao.org/3/a-y7937e.pdf

———— (2008) Declaration of the High-Level Conference on World Food Security: The Challenges of Climate Change and Bioenergy, 2008. Report of the Conference. Food and Agriculture Organization of the United Nations, Rome.

———— (2013) Preparations for the Second International Conference on Nutrition (ICN2), Rome.

———— (2014) Priorities for FAO Activities in the African Region, Tunis, Tunisia.

———— (2016) FAO Member Nations by region for Council Election, Rome.

FAO General Rules (2015) Basic Texts of the Food and Agriculture Organization of the United Nations. Volume I and II. 2015 Edition, Rome.

FAO/WHO (2013) Second International Conference on Nutrition (ICN2) Concept Note, 1 March 2013.

FAO/WHO (2014a) Arrangements for the Second International Conference on Nutrition.

———— (2014b) Conference Outcome Document of the Second International Conference on Nutrition: Rome Declaration on Nutrition, Rome.

———— (2014c) Mandate and Arrangements for the ICN2 Joint Working Group (JWG): Food and Agriculture Organization of the United Nations and World Health Organization.

Farrell, M. (2009) EU Policy towards Other Regions: Policy Learning in the External Promotion of Regional Integration. *Journal of European Public Policy* 16(8): 1165–84.

Fawcett, L. (2004) Exploring Regional Domains: A Comparative History of Regionalism. *International Affairs* 80(3): 429–46.

Fawcett, L., and Hurrell, A., eds. (1995) *Regionalism in World Politics. Regional Organization and International Order*. Oxford: Oxford University Press.

Fearon, J. D. (1998) Bargaining, Enforcement and International Cooperation. *International Organization* 52(2): 269–305.

Featherstone, K., and Radaelli, C., eds. (2003) *The Politics of Europeanisation*. Oxford: Oxford University Press.

Feistritzer, N., and Martinez, M. (2014) Co-Chairs' Summary: Resumed Meeting of the Open-Ended Working Group (OWEG) on the Second International Conference on Nutrition (ICN2).

Fickling, D. (2005) Sub-Saharan Malnutrition Worse than 10 Years Ago. *The Guardian*, November 22, 2005. https://www.theguardian.com/world/2005/nov/22/hearafrica05.development

Fiji (2011) Statement by Mr. Sainivalati Navoti, Head of Fiji Delegation, Third Session of the ATT Preparatory Committee, New York, July 15, 2011.

——— (2013) Intervention Statement by Mr. Joji Dumukoro, Second United Nations Conference on the Arms Trade Treaty, New York, March 18, 2013.

Finland (2014) Statement by Jaana Husu-Kallio, ICN2 Conference, Rome, November 19, 2014.

Food and Agricultural Organization (2013) General Rules of the Organization, Rome.

——— (2014) FAO and EU: Unlocking Rural Potential, Rome.

Food and Agriculture Organization (1991) Report of the Conference of FAO: Twenty-Sixth Session, Rome, 9–27 November 1991, Rome.

——— (2013) Basic Texts of the Food and Agriculture Organization of the United Nations, Rome.

Forkan, P. (unknown) The Legislative History and Interpretation of Article 65 of the Law of the Sea Convention.

Fortin, J. (2012) Whale Sanctuary In South Atlantic Shot Down: Why Japan Still Hunts, *International Business Times*. http://www.ibtimes.com/whale-sanctuary-south-atlantic-shot-down-why-japan-still-hunts-722520.

Fouilleux, E. (2010) 'The Common Agricultural Policy', in M. Cini and Borragàn, P.-S. (eds) *European Union Politics*. Oxford: Oxford University Press, 340–56.

Frennhoff Larsen, M. (2007) Trade Negotiations between the EU and South Africa: A Three-Level Game. *Journal of Common Market Studies* 45(4): 857–81.

Freyburg, T., Lavenex, S., Schimmelfennig, F., Skripka, T., and Wetzel, A. (2009) EU Promotion of Democratic Governance in the Neighbourhood. *Journal of European Public Policy* 16(6): 916–34.

Gamble, A., and Payne, A. (1996) *Regionalism and World Order*, London: Macmillan.

Gehring, T., Oberthür, S., and Mühleck, M. (2013) European Union Actorness in International Institutions: Why the EU Is Recognized as an Actor in Some International Institutions, but Not in Others. *Journal of Common Market Studies* 51(5): 849–65.

Gehring, T. O., Sebastian; Mühleck, Marc (2013) European Union Actorness in International Institutions: Why the EU Is Recognized as an Actor in Some International Institutions, but Not in Others. *Journal of Common Market Studies* 51(5): 849–65.

Gelman, A., Carlin, J.B., Stern, H. S., Dunson, D. B., Vehtari, A., and Rubin, D. B. (2013) *Bayesian Data Analysis, Third Edition*, Hoboken: CRC Press.

Geneva Academy (2012) The Draft Arms Trade Treaty, Academy Briefing No. 2, October 2012, Geneva.

——— (2013) The Arms Trade Treaty, Academy Briefing No. 3, June 2013, Geneva.

George, A. L., and Bennett, A. (2005) *Case Studies and Theory Development in the Social Sciences*. Cambridge: MIT Press.

Germany (2012) Statement by H. E. Ambassador Dr. Peter Wittig, Permanent Representative of Germany to the United Nations, First UN Conference on the Arms Trade Treaty, New York, July 9, 2012.

——— (2013) Statement by H. E. Ambassador Jörg Ranau, Head of the German Delegation to the UN Conference on the Arms Trade Treaty, Second UN Conference on the Arms Trade Treaty, New York, March 18, 2013.

Ghana (2012) Statement by Ambassador Chris Kpodo, Deputy Minister for Foreign Affairs and Regional Integration of Ghana, First UN Conference on the Arms Trade Treaty, New York, July 10, 2012.

Ginsberg, R. H. (1999) Conceptualizing the European Union as an International Actor: Narrowing the Theoretical Capability-Expectations Gap. *Journal of Common Market Studies* 37(3): 429–54.

Goetz, K. H., and Hix, S., eds. (2000) *Europeanised Politics? European Integration and National Political Systems*. London: Frank Cass.

Goldstein, H. (1995) *Multilevel Statistical Models*, London: Wiley.

Goldstein, H., Browne, W. J. (2014) Multilevel Models, in Balakrishnan, N., Colton, T., Everitt, B., Piegorsch, W., Ruggeri, F., Teugels, J. F. (eds) Wiley StatsRef. Statistics Reference Online. Chichester, UK: John Wiley & Sons, Ltd, 1–8.

Goldstein, H., Rasbash, Jon (1996) Improved Approximations for Multilevel with Binary Responses. *Journal of the Royal Statistical Society: Series A (Statistics in Society)* 159(3): 505–13.

Gómez-Mera, L. (2008) How 'New' is the 'New Regionalism' in the Americas? The Case of Mercosur. *Journal of International Relations and Development* 11(3): 279–308.

Goodin, R. E., ed. (1995) *The Theory of Institutional Design*. Cambridge: Cambridge University Press.

Götz, N., and Haggrén, H., eds. (2008) *Regional Cooperation and International Organizations. The Nordic Model in Transnational Alignment*. London: Routledge.

Government of Canada (2017) Canada's Action on Climate Change. http://www.climatechange.gc.ca/default.asp?lang=En

Governments of Argentina, South Africa and Uruguay (2014) The South Atlantic: A Sanctuary for Whales. Portorož, Slovenia.

Governments of Argentina, Brazil and South Africa (2005) The South Atlantic: A Sanctuary For Whales. Ulsan, Republic of Korea.

Grabbe, H. (2001) How Does Europeanization Affect CEE Governance? Conditionality, Diffusion and Diversity. *Journal of European Public Policy* 8(6): 1013–31.

——— (2006) *The EU's Transformative Power : Europeanization through Conditionality in Central and Eastern Europe*, New York: Palgrave Macmillan.

Græger, N., and Gaugevik, K. M. (2011) The EU's Performance with and within the NATO: Assessing Objectives, Outcomes and Organisational Practices. *Journal of European Integration* 33(6): 743–57.

Grande, E. (2000) 'Multi-Level-Governance: Institutionelle Besonderheiten und Funktionsbedingungen des europäischen Mehrebenensystems', in E. Grande and Jachtenfuchs, M. (eds) *Wie problemlösungsfähig ist die EU*. Baden-Baden: Nomos, 1–16.

Greenpeace Essen (2011) 63. Jahrestagung der Internationalen Walfangkommission (IWC) in St. Helier (Kanalinsel Jersey), 11–14 July 2011, Überblick und Ergebnisse.

Grenada (2012) Statement by Mr. Marlon Glean, Crown Counsel, Ministry of Legal Affairs on Substantive Elements of the future ATT. Fourth Session of the ATT Preparatory Committee, New York, February 16, 2012.

Groenleer, M. L. P., and Schaik, L.v. (2007) United We Stand? The European Union's International Actorness in the Cases of the International Criminal Court and the Kyoto Protocol. *Journal of Common Market Studies* 45(5): 969–98.

Guatemala (2012) Statement by Ambassador Gert Rosenthal, Permanent Representative of Guatemala to the United Nations High-Level Segment of the United Nations Conference on the Arms Trade Treaty. First UN Conference on the Arms Trade Treaty, New York, July 6, 2012.

Guyana (2012) Statement by Ambassador George Talbot, Permanent Representative, Republic of Guyana, First UN Conference on the Arms Trade Treaty, New York, July 5, 2012.

Haas, E. B. (1970) The Study of Regional Integration: Reflections on the Joy and Anguish of Pretheorizing. *International Organization* 24(4): 607–46.

Habeeb, W. M. (1988) *Power and Tactics in International Negotiation: How Weak Nations Bargain with Strong Nations*, Baltimore: John Hopkins University Press.

Hafner-Burton, E. M. (2009) The Power Politics of Regime Complexity: Human Rights Trade Conditionality in Europe. *Perspectives on Politics* 7(01): 33–37.

Hampton, M., and Christensen, J. (2014) 'Looking for Plan B: What Next for Island Hosts for Offshore Finance?', in A. Narlikar (ed) *Small States in Multilateral Economic Negotiations*. London: Routledge, 35–48.

Hanson, B. T. (1998) What Happened to Fortress Europe? External Trade Policy Liberalization in the European Union. *International Organization* 52(1), 55–79.

Hayes, A. F., and Krippendorff, K. (2007) Answering the Call for a Standard Reliability Measure for Coding Data. *Communication Methods and Measures* 1(1): 77–89.

Hettne, B., and Söderbaum, F. (1998) The New Regionalism Approach. *Politeia* 17(3): 6–21.

——— (2000) Theorising the Rise of Regionness. *New Political Economy* 5(3): 457–72.

——— (2005) Civilian Power or Soft Imperialism? The EU as a Global Actor and the Role of Interregionalism. *European Foreign Affairs Review* 10(4): 535.

Hivonnet, J. (2012) 'The European Union in the 2009 Durban Review Conference', in J. Wouters, Bruyninckx, H., Basu, S. and Schiunz, S. (eds) *The European Union and Multilateral Governance. Assessing EU Participation in United Nations Human Rights and Environmental Fora*. Houndmills: Palgrave, 122–42.

Hoef, J., and Boveng, P. (2007) Quasi-Poisson vs Negative Binomial Regression: How Should We Model Overdispersed Count Data? *Ecology* 88(11): 2766–72.

Hogarth, B. (2008a) International Whaling Commission, Capitol Hill Hearing Testimony. Washington D.C.

――――― (2008b) IWC 60 Chair Report 2008, Santiago, Chile.

――――― (2009) IWC 61 Chair Report 2009, Madeira, Portugal.

Hojnacki, M., and Kimball, D.C. (1999) The Who and How of Organizations' Lobbying Strategies in Committee. *The Journal of Politics* 61(4): 999–1024.

Holzinger, K. (2004) Bargaining through Arguing: An Empirical Analysis Based on Speech Act Theory. *Political Communication* 21(1): 195–222.

Hooghe, L., and Marks, G. (2001) *Multi-Level Governance and European Integration*. Lanham, MD: Rowman & Littlefield Publishers.

Hooghe, L., and Marks, G. (2014) Delegation and Pooling in International Organizations. *Review of International Organizations* 10(3): 305–328.

Hox, J. J., and Roberts, J. K., eds. (2011) *Handbook for Advanced Multilevel Analysis*. New York: Routledge.

Hoyt, E. (2005) *Marine Protected Areas for Whales, Dolphins and Porpoises*. London: Earthscan.

Huber, J. D., and McCarty, N. (2004) Bureaucratic Capacity, Delegation, and Political Reform. *American Political Science Review* 98(3): 481–94.

Hurd, I. (2011) *International Organizations. Politics, Law, Practice*. Cambridge: Cambridge University Press.

――――― (2012) Almost Saving Whales: The Ambiguity of Success at the International Whaling Commission. *Ethics & International Affairs* 26(1): 1–10.

ICN2 Secretariat (2014) Report of the Joint FAO/WHO Secretariat on the Conference, Rome.

India (2011a) Intervention by Amandeep Singh Gill of India. Third UN Conference on the Arms Trade Treaty, New York, July 12, 2011.

――――― (2011b) Intervention by Amandeep Singh Gill of India. Third UN Conference on the Arms Trade Treaty, New York, July 14, 2011.

Indonesia (2013) Statement by Member of the Parliament of the Republic of Indonesia Hon. Mr. Muhammad Najib, Delegate of Indonesia, Second UN Conference on the Arms Trade Treaty, New York, March 18, 2013.

International Institute for Sustainable Development (2014) Summary of the International Conference on Nutrition (ICN2). *International Conference on Nutrition Bulletin* 226(1).

International Whaling Commission (1946) The International Convention for the Regulation of Whaling. Founding Document. Washington D.C.

International Whaling Commission (2005) Annual Report of the International Whaling Commission 2004. Cambridge, 2005.

――――― (2002) Annual Report of the International Whaling Commission 2001, Cambridge.

――――― (2003) Annual Report of the International Whaling Commission 2002, Cambridge.

――――― (2004) Annual Report of the International Whaling Commission 2003, Cambridge.

――――― (2005) Annual Report of the International Whaling Commission 2004, Cambridge.

—— (2006) Annual Report of the International Whaling Commission 2005, Cambridge.

—— (2007) Annual Report of the International Whaling Commission 2006, Cambridge.

—— (2008) Annual Report of the International Whaling Commission 2007, Cambridge.

—— (2009) Annual Report of the International Whaling Commission 2008, Cambridge.

—— (2010) Annual Report of the International Whaling Commission 2009, Cambridge.

——. (2011) Participation List of the 63rd Annual Meeting, St Helier/ Jersey, 2014.

—— (2011a) Annual Report of the International Whaling Commission 2010, Cambridge.

—— (2012a) Annual Report of the International Whaling Commission 2011, Cambridge.

——. (2012) Participation List of the 64th Annual Meeting, Panama City/ Panama, 2012.

—— (2012c) Rules of Procedure and Financial Regulations, as Amended by the Commission at the 64th Annual Meeting, July 2012.

—— (2012d) Schedule to the 1946 International Convention for the Regulation of Whaling, 64th IWC Annual Meeting, Panama City, Panama.

—— (2013) Annual Report of the International Whaling Commission 2012, Cambridge.

—— 'Future of the IWC'. https://iwc.int/future

—— (2014) Participation List of the 65th Annual Meeting, Portoroz/ Slovenia, 2014.

—— (2014c) Rules of Procedure and Financial Regulations as Amended by the Commission at the 65th Meeting, September 2014.

—— (2015a) Aboriginal Subsistence Whaling, Cambridge. https://iwc.int/aboriginal.

—— (2015b) Membership and Contracting Governments, Cambridge. https://iwc.int/members

—— (2014) Scientific Permit Whaling, Cambridge. http://iwc.int/permits.

Iran (2010) Statement of H. E. Ambassador Eshagh Al Habib, Deputy Permanent Representative of the Islamic Republic of Iran to the UN, First Session of the ATT Preparatory Committee, New York, July 12, 2010.

—— (2012) Statement by H. E. Ambassador Mohammad Khazaee. First UN Conference on the Arms Trade Treaty, New York, July 10, 2012.

Israel (2011a) Israel's Statement. Second Session of the ATT Preparatory Commiittee, New York, March 3, 2011.

—— (2011b) Israeli Statement (28 February 2011). Second Session of the ATT Preparatory Commiittee, New York, February 28, 2011.

—— (2011c) The State of Israel. Opening Statement. Third Session of the ATT Preparatory Commiittee, New York, July 11, 2011.

—— (2013) Opening Statement by Mr. Eran Yuvan, Deputy Director, Arms Control Policy Department, Ministry of Foreign Affairs, Israel. Second United Nations Conference on the Arms Trade Treaty, New York, March 18, 2013.

Italy (2012) Statement by H. E. Ambassador Cesare Maria Ragaglini, Permanent Representative of Italy to the United Nations. First United Nations Conference on the Arms Trade Treaty, New York, July 9, 2012.

IWC (2012) Rules of Procedure and Financial Regulations, as Amended by the Commission at the 64th Annual Meeting, July 2012, as amended by the Commission at the 64th Annual Meeting, Panama City/ Panama, July 2012.

———— (2014) Rules of Procedure and Financial Regulations, as amended by the Commission at the 65thMeeting, Portoroz/ Slovenia, September 2014.

Jachtenfuchs, M. (2001) The Governance Approach to European Integration. *Journal of Common Market Studies* 39(2).

Jachtenfuchs, M., and Kohler-Koch, B. (1996) 'Einleitung: Regieren im dynamischen Mehrebenensystem', in M. Jachtenfuchs and Kohler-Koch, B. (eds.) *Europäische Integration*. Opladen: Leske und Budrich, 15–44.

Jackman, S. (2000) Estimation and Inference via Bayesian Simulation: An Introduction to Markov Chain Monte Carlo. *American Journal of Political Science* 44(2): 375–404.

———— (2004) Bayesian Analysis for Political Research. *Annual Review of Political Science* 7(1): 483–505.

Jacoby, W. (2004) *The Enlargement of the European Union and NATO: Ordering from the Menu in Central Europe*. Cambridge; New York: Cambridge University Press.

Japan (2012) Statement by H. E. Mr. Joe Nakano, Parliamentary Vice-Minister for Foreign Affairs of Japan, First UN Conference on the Arms Trade Treaty, New York, July 9, 2012.

Jetschke, A., and Lenz, T. (2011) Vergleichende Regionalismusforschung und Diffusion: Eine neue Forschungsagenda. *Politische Vierteljahresschrift* 52(3): 448–74.

———— (2013) Does Regionalism Diffuse? A New Research Agenda for the Study of Regional Organizations. *Journal of European Public Policy* 20(4): 626–37.

Jetschke, A., and Murray, P. (2012) Diffusing Regional Integration: The EU and Southeast Asia. *West European Politics* 35(1): 174–91.

Jin, X., and Hosli, M. O. (2013) Pre- and Post-Lisbon: European Union Voting in the United Nations General Assembly. *West European Politics* 36(6): 1274–91.

Joergensen, K. E., Oberthür, S., and Shahin, J. (2011) Introduction: Assessing the EU's Performance in International Institutions – Conceptual Framework and Core Findings. *Journal of European Integration* 33(6): 599–620.

Johnstone, I. (2003) Security Council Deliberations: The Power of the Better Argument. *European Journal of International Law* 14(3): 437–80.

Jönsson, C., and Tallberg, J. (1998) Compliance and Post-Agreement Bargaining. *European Journal of International Relations* 4(4): 371–408.

Jung, M. (2010) *Stimmenkauf in Internationalen Organisationen*. Basel: Helbing Lichtenhahn Verlag.

JWG August 27th (2014) Proposed Draft Declaration, Second International Conference on Nutrition, 27 August 2014, Rome.

Katzenstein, P. (1996) Regionalism in Comparative Perspective. *Cooperation and Conflict* 31(2): 123–59.

Kaunert, C. (2010) Europol and EU Counterterrorism: International Security Actorness in the External Dimension. *Studies in Conflict & Terrorism* 33(7): 652–71.

Kazakhstan (2013) Statement by H. E. Ambassador Byrganym Aitimova, Permanent Representative of the Republic of Kazakhstan to the United Nations, Second UN Conference on the Arms Trade Treaty, New York, March 18, 2013.

Keating, M. (1998) *The New Regionalism in Western Europe. Territorial Restructuring and Political Change*. Cheltenham: Edward Elgar.

Keating, M., and Loughlin, J., eds. (1997) *The Political Economy of Regionalism.* London: Frank Cass.

Kelemen, R. D. (2001) The Limits of Judicial Power. Trade-Environment Disputes in the GATT/WTO and the EU. *Comparative Political Studies* 34(6): 622–50.

Kelley, J. (2006) New Wine in Old Wineskins: Promoting Political Reforms through the New European Neighbourhood Policy. *Journal of Common Market Studies* 44(1): 29–55.

Kellow, A. (2012) Multi-Level and Multi-Arena Governance: The Limits of Integration and the Possibilities of Forum Shopping. *International Environmental Agreements: Politics, Law and Economics* 12(4): 327–42.

Kenya (2010) Statement by Mr. Salim M. Salium, Second Counselor, First Session of the ATT Preparatory Committee, New York, July 13, 2010.

———— (2014) Statement by Fred H. Segor, ICN2 Conference, November 19, 2014.

Keohane, R. O. (1967) The Study of Political Influence in the General Assembly. *International Organisations* 21(2): 221–37.

———— (1984) *After Hegemony. Cooperation and Discord in the World Political Economy*, Princeton, NJ: Princeton University Press.

———— (1989) *International Institutions and State Power*. Boulder, CO: Westview.

———— (2001) Governance in a Partially Globalized World. *American Political Science Review* 95(1): 1–13.

Keohane, R. O., and Nye, J. S. (1989) *Power and Interdependence*. Glenview: Scott, Foresman and Company.

Kincaid, J. (1990) 'Constituent Diplomacy in Federal Polities and the Nation-State: Conflict and Cooperation', in H. J. Michelmann and Soldatos, P. (eds.) *Federalism and International Relations*. Oxford: Clarendon Press, 54–75.

Kiribati (2014) Statement by Kautu Tenaua, ICN2 Conference, Rome, November 20, 2014.

Kissack, R. (2010) *Pursuing Effective Multilateralism. The European Union, International Organisations and the Politics of Decision Making*, Houndmills: Palgrave.

———— (2011) The Performance of the European Union in the International Labour Organization. *Journal of European Integration* 33(6): 651–65.

———— (2012) 'The EU in the Negotiations of a UN General Assembly Resolution on a Moratorium on the Use of the Death Penalty', in J. Wouters, Bruynickx, H., Basu, S. and Schunz, S. (eds) *The European Union and Multilateral Governance. Assessing EU Participation in the United Nations Human Rights and Environmental Fora*. Basingstoke: Palgrave, 103–21.

———— (2014) 'Labour Standards. An Historical Account of the EU Involvement with(in) the ILO', in A. Orsini (ed) *The European Union with(in) International Organisations. Commitment, Consistency and Effects across Time*. Burlington: Ashgate, 75–93.

Kleine, M., and Risse, T. (2005) Arguing and Persuasion in the European Convention, unpublished manuscript Berlin.

Knelangen, W. (2013) *Die Europäische Union als internationaler Akteur*. Wiesbaden: VS Verlag für Sozialwissenschaften.

Knodt, M. (2000) 'Europäisierung à la Sinatra: Deutsche Länder im europäischen Mehrebenensystem', in M. Knodt and Kohler-Koch, B. (eds) *Deutschland zwischen Europäisierung und Selbstbehauptung*. Frankfurt a/M; New York: Campus, 237–64.

Knodt, M. (2005) *Regieren im erweiterten europäischen Mehrebenensystem. Internationale Einbettung der EU in die WTO*. Baden-Baden: Nomos.

Knodt, M., and Princen, S. (2003) *Understanding the European Union's External Relations*. London: Routledge.

Kohler-Koch, B., and Eising, R., eds. (1999) *The Transformation of Governance in Europe*. London: Routledge.

König, T., and Bräuninger, T. (1997) Wie wichtig sind die Länder für die Politik der Bundesregierung bei Einspruchs- und Zustimmungsgesetzen? *Zeitschrift für Parlamentsfragen* 1997(4): 605–28.

König, T., Dannwolf, T., and Luetgert, B. (2012) 'EU Legislative Activities and Domestic Politics', in S. Brouard, Costa, O. and König, T. (eds) *The Europeanization of Domestic Legislatures: The Empirical Implications of the Delors' Myth in Nine Countries*. New York: Springer, 21–37.

König, T., Tsebelis, G., and Debus, M., eds. (2010) *Reform Processes and Policy Change: Veto Players and Decision-Making in Modern Democracies*. New York: Springer.

Koremons, B., Lipson, C., and Snidal, D. (2001) The Rational Design of International Institutions. *International Organization* 55(4): 761–99.

Koschut, S. (2014) Regional Order and Peaceful Change: Security Communities as a Via Media in International Relations Theory. *Cooperation and Conflict* 49(4): 519–35.

Koslowski, R. (2001) 'Understanding the European Union as a Federal Policy', in T. Christiansen, Jörgensen, K. and Wiener, A. (eds) *The Social Construction of Europe*. London: SAGE, 32–49.

Krasner, S.D. (1991) Global Communications and National Power: Life on the Pareto Frontier. *World Politics* 43(3): 336–66.

Kremenyuk, V., ed. (1991) *International Negotiation: Analysis, Approaches, Issues*. San Francisco, CA: Jossey-Bass.

Krippendorff, K. (2011a) Agreement and Information in the Reliability of Coding. *Communication Methods and Measures* 5(2): 93–112.

——— (2011b) 'Computing Krippendorff's Alpha-Reliability'. http://repository.upenn.edu/asc_papers/43

Kydd, A. (2001) Trust Building, Trust Breaking: The Dilemma of NATO Enlargement. *International Organization* 55(4): 801–28.

Langan, M., and Scott, J. (2014) The Aid for Trade Charade. *Cooperation and Conflict* 49(2): 143–61.

Lavenex, S. (2008) A Governance Perspective on the European Neighbourhood Policy: Integration Beyond Conditionality? *Journal of European Public Policy* 15(6): 938–55.

Lavenex, S., and Schimmelfennig, F. (2007) EU Rules Beyond EU Borders: Theorizing External Governance in European Politics. *Journal of European Public Policy* 16(6): 791–812.

———— (2011) EU Democracy Promotion in the Neighbourhood: From Leverage to Governance? *Democratization* 18(4): 885–909.

Leckie, G. (2013a) Cross-Classified Multilevel Models, 1–60 (https://www.cmm.bris.ac.uk/lemma/pluginfile.php/14922/mod_resource/content/1/C12%20Cross-Classified%20Multilevel%20Models.pdf).

———— (2013b) Multiple Membership Multilevel Models, 1–61 (https://www.cmm.bris.ac.uk/lemma/pluginfile.php/14925/mod_resource/content/1/C13%20Multiple%20Membership%20Multilevel%20Models.pdf).

Lehman, H. P., and McCoy, J. L. (1992) The Dynamics of the Two-Level Bargaining Game. The 1988 Brazilian Debt Negotiations. *World Politics* 44(4): 600–44.

Lenz, T. (2012) Spurred Emulation: The EU and Regional Integration in Mercosur and SADC. *West European Politics* 35(1): 155–73.

Lesotho (2012) Statement by Mr. Mafiroane Motanyane, Chargé d'Affaires of the Permanent Mission of the Kingdom of Lesotho to the United Nations, First UN Conference on the Arms Trade Treaty, New York, July 10, 2012.

Levi-Faur, D., ed. (2012) *The Oxford Handbook of Governance*. Oxford: Oxford University Press.

Lewis, J. (2005) The Janus Face of Brussels: Socialization and Everyday Decision Making in the European Union. *International Organization* 59(4): 937–71.

Lewis, P. (2001) 'The Enlargement of the European Union', in S. Bromley (eds.) *Governing the European Union*. London: SAGE, 221–54.

Leyland, A. H., and Goldstein, H., eds. (2001) *Multilevel Modelling of Health Statistics*, Wiley series in Probability and Statistics. Chichester: Wiley.

Lightfoot, S. (2012) 'The European Union in the World Summit on Sustainable Development', in J. Wouters, Bruynickx, H., Basu, S. and Schunz, S. (eds) *The European Union and Multilateral Governance. Assessing EU Participation in the United Nations Human Rights and Environmental Fora*. Basingstoke: Palgrave, 232–51.

Liverpool, A. (2010) IWC 62 Chair Report 2010. Agadir, Marocco.

Macaj, G., and Nicolaïdis, K. (2014) Beyond 'One Voice'? Global Europe's Engagement with its Own Diversity. *Journal of European Public Policy* 21(7): 1067–83.

MacLeod, G. (2001) New Regionalism Reconsidered: Globalization and the Remaking of Political Economic Space. *International Journal of Urban and Regional Research* 25(4): 804–29.

Move this entry before the reference: Jönsson, C., and Tallberg, J. (1998) Juli 2012. Vollmer, Patrick M., "Debate 15th May: Development of the International Arms. Trade Treaty," *House of Lords* - Library Note, LLN 2008/013, 2008.

Malawi (1994) Constitution of the Republic of Malawi.

———— (2011) Statement by Malawi, Delivered by Lt Col (Dr.) Dan Kuwali. Second Session of the ATT Preparatory Committee, New York, March 3, 2011.

Malaysia (2012) Statement by Malaysia on Substantive Matters Relevant to a potential Arms Trade Treaty, Fourth Session of the ATT Preparatory Committee, New York, February 14, 2012.

Manners, I. (2006) Normative Power Europe Reconsidered: Beyond the Crossroads. *Journal of European Public Policy* 13(2): 182–99.

Mansfield, E., and Milner, H. (1999) The New Wave of Regionalism. *International Organization* 53(3): 589–627.

March, J. G., and Olsen, J. P. (1984) The New Institutionalism: Organizational Factors in Political Life. *American Political Science Review* (78): 734–49.

———— (1994) 'Institutional Perspectives on Governance', in H.-U. Derlien, Gerhardt, U. and Scharpf, F. W. (eds) *Systemrationalität und Partialinteresse*. Baden-Baden: Nomos, 249–69.

Marks, G. (1993) 'Structural Policy and Multilevel Governance in the European Community', in A. Cafruny and Rosenthal, G. (eds) *The State of the European Community II: Maastricht Debates and Beyond*. Boulder, CO: Lynne Rienner, 391–410.

———— (1997) 'An Actor-Centred Approach to Multi-Level Governance', in C. Jeffery (ed) *The Regional Dimension of the European Union. Towards a Third Level in Europe?*, London: Frank Cass, 20–40.

Marks, G., and Hooghe, L. (2001) *Multi-Level Governance and European Integration*. Lanham, MD: Rowman & Littlefield.

Marks, G., Scharpf, F. W., Schmitter, P. C., and Streeck, W., eds. (1996) *Governance in the European Union*. London; Thousand Oaks; New Delhi: SAGE.

Martens, K. (2007) 'NGOs and the United Nations System: Evaluating Theoretical Approaches', in P. Opoku-Mensah, Lewis, D. and Tvedt, T. (eds) *Reconceptualising NGOs and Their Roles in Development – NGOs, Civil Society and the International Aid System*. Aalborg: Aalborg University Press, 55–84.

Martin, L. L., and Simmons, B. A., eds. (2001) *International Institutions. An International Organization Reader*. Cambridge: MIT Press.

Martin, R., and Sunley, P. (2006) Path Dependence and Regional Economic Evolution. *Journal of Economic Geography* 6(4): 395–437.

Mattli, W. (1999) *The Logic of Regional Integration*, Cambridge: Cambridge University Press.

Mayring, P. (2007). Qualitative Inhaltsanalyse. Grundladen und Techniken. Weinheim: Beltz Verlag.

McGwin, K. (2013) Denmark to Remain in IWC, *The Arctic Journal*. https://www.arcticnow.com/arctic-journal/

McKay, D. (2002) *Federalism and European Union*. Oxford: Oxford University Press.

Meerts, P. W. (2005) 'Entrapment in International Negotiations', in I. W. Zartman and Faure, G. O. (eds) *Escalation and Negotiation in International Conflicts*. Cambridge: Cambridge University Press, 111–40.

Mehta, J., Starmer, C., and Sugden, R. (1994) Focal Points in Pure Coordination Games: An Experimental Investigation. *Theory and Decision* 36(2): 163–85.

Meunier, S. (2000) What Single Voice? European Institutions and EU-U.S. Trade Negotiations. *International Organization* 54(1): 103–35.

Mexico (2010) Intervention of the Mexican Delegation Regarding the Basic Elements That Should Be Included in the ATT. First Session of the ATT Preparatory Committee, New York, July 13, 2010.

———— (2011) Intervention on Scope of an Arms Trade Treaty. Second Session of the ATT Preparatory Committee, New York, February 28, 2011.

Michelmann, H. J., and Soldatos, P., eds. (1990) *Federalism and International Relations. The Role of Subnational Units.* Oxford: Clarendon Press.

Miller, A. R., and Dolšak, N. (2007) Issue Linkages in International Environmental Policy: The International Whaling Commission and Japanese Development Aid. *Global Environmental Politics* 7(1): 69–96.

Mo, J. (1995) Domestic Institutions and International Bargaining: The Role of Agent Veto in Two-Level Games. *American Political Science Review* 86(4): 914–24.

Monar, J. (2004) The EU as an International Actor in the Domain of Justice and Home Affairs. *European Foreign Affairs Review* 3/2004, 395–415.

Mongolia (2010) Statement by Mongolia. First Session of the ATT Preparatory Committee, New York, July 13, 2010.

Montenegro (2012) Statement by H. E. Mr. Milorad Scepanovic, Permanent Representative of Montenegro to the United Nations, First UN Conference on the Arms Trade Treaty, New York, July 10, 2012.

Moravcsik, A. (1991) Negotiating the Single European Act: National Interests and Conventional Statecraft in the European Community. *International Organization* 45(1): 19–56.

––––––– (1993) Preferences and Power in the European Community: A Liberal Inter-Governmental Approach. *Journal of Common Market Studies* 31(4): 473–524.

––––––– (1998) *The Choice for Europe. Social Purpose & State Power from Messina to Maastricht.* Ithaca, NY: Cornell University Press.

Morgenthau, H. J. (1948) *Politics among Nations.* New York: McGraw Hill.

Morgera, E. (2004) Whale Sanctuaries: An Evolving Concept within the International Whaling Commission. *Ocean Development & International Law* 35(4): 319–38.

Morin, J.-F., and Gold, E. R. (2010) Consensus-Seeking, Distrust and Rhetorical Entrapment: The WTO Decision on Access to Medicines. *European Journal of International Relations* 16(4): 563–87.

Morin, J.-F., and Orsini, A. (2013) Regime Complexity and Policy Coherency: Introducing a Co-Adjustments Model. *Global Governance: A Review of Multilateralism and International Organizations* 19(1): 41–51.

Moritán, R. G. (2011) Chairman's Draft Paper, Third Session of the ATT Preparatory Committee, New York, July 14, 2011.

Muello, P. (2002) Brazil Tracks Humpbacks with Eye to Future Whale Sanctuary. The Associated Press, November 28, 2002.

Müller, H. (2004) Arguing, Bargaining and All That. Reflections on the Relationship of Communicative Action and Rationalist Theory in Analysing International Negotiations. *European Journal of International Relations* 10(3): 395–435.

Murithi, T. (2005) *The African Union: Pan-Africanism, Peacebuilding and Development.* Farnham: Ashgate.

Namibia (2012) Statement by H. E. Mr. Wilfried I. Emvula, Ambassador & Permanent Representative at the United Nations Diplomatic Conference on Arms Trade Treaty. First UN Conference on the Arms Trade Treaty, New York, July 5, 2012.

Nepal (2012) Statement by H. E. Gyan Chandra Acharya, Ambassador/PR of Nepal to the United Nations, First UN Conference on the Arms Trade Treaty, New York, July 6, 2012.

———— (2012) Statement made by Ambassador Paul van den IJssel, HoD of the Netherlands, Fourth Session of the ATT Preparatory Committee, New York, February 14, 2012.

Netherlands (2014) Statement by Sharon Dijksma, Rome.

New Zealand (2010) Statement by Ambassador Dell Higgie, Permanent Representative to the United Nations in Geneva.

———— (2012) Opening Statement. First United Nations Conference on the Arms Trade Treaty, New York, July 3, 2012.

Neyer, J. (2003) Discourse and Order in the EU. A Deliberative Approach to Multi-Level Governance. *Journal of Common Market Studies* 41(4): 687–706.

Nicaragua (2012) Statement delivered by Nicaragua. First UN Conference on the Arms Trade Treaty, New York, July 5, 2012.

Nicolaidis, K., and Meunier, S. (1999) Who Speaks for Europe? The Delegation of Trade Authority in the EU. *Journal of Common Market Studies* 37(3): 477–501.

Nigeria (1999) Constitution of the Federal Republic of Nigeria.

———— (2011) Nigerian Intervention on Implementation and Final Provisions during the 3rd PrepCom. Third Session of the ATT Preparatory Committee, New York, July 13, 2011.

Norway (2010) Statement by Ms. Annette Abelsen, Head of Delegation. First Session of the ATT Preparatory Committee, New York, July 12, 2010.

Nuttall, S. (2000) *European Foreign Policy*. Oxford: Oxford University Press.

Nye, J. S. (1965) Comparative Regional Integration. *International Organization* 22(4): 855–80.

———— (1968) Patterns and Catalysts in Regional Integration. *International Organization* 19(4): 870–84.

Oberthür, S. (1999) The EU as an International Actor: The Protection of the Ozone Layer. *Journal of Common Market Studies* 37(4): 641–59.

———— (2011) The European Union's Performance in the International Climate Change Regime. *Journal of European Integration* 33(6): 667–82.

Oberthür, S., and Stokke, O. S. (2011) *Managing Institutional Complexity: Regime Interplay and Global Environmental Change*. Boston, MA: MIT Press.

OEWG September 24th (2014) Proposed Draft Declaration, Rome.

Orsini, A. (2014) 'Membership. The Evolution of EU Membership in Major International Organisations', in A. Orsini (ed) *The European Union with(in) International Organisations: Commitment, Consistency and Effects across Time*. Farnham; Burlington: Ashgate, 35–53.

Oye, K., ed. (1986) *Cooperation under Anarchy*. Princeton, NJ: Princeton University Press.

Paarlberg, R. (1997) Agricultural Policy Reform and the Uruguay Round: Synergistic Linkage in a Two-level Game? *International Organization* 51(2): 413–44.

Pacific Island Countries (2010) Statement on Behalf of Pacific Island Countries. Statement by Mr. Philip Kimpton, First Secretary, Australian Permanent Mission to the United Nations, First Session of the ATT Preparatory Committee, New York, July 13, 2010.

Pacific Island Forum (2012) New Zealand Permanent Mission to the United Nations,Common Principles on the Key Elements of the Arms Trade Treaty, First UN Conference on the Arms Trade Treaty, New York, July 3, 2012.

Pacific Small Island Developing States (2011) Statement by H. E. Mr. Robert
    G. Aisi, Ambassador and Permanent Representative of Papua New Guinea on
    behalf of Pacific Small Island Developing States, Second Session of the ATT Pre-
    paratory Committee, New York, March 2, 2011.

Pakistan (2014) Statement by Rizwan Bashir Khan, ICN2 Conference, Rome,
    November 19, 2014.

Panke, D. (2009) Why Discourse Matters Only Sometimes. Effective Arguing beyond
    the Nation-State. *Review of International Studies* 35(1): 145–68.

———— (2010) *Small States in the European Union: Coping with Structural Disad-
    vantages*. Farnham: Ashgate.

———— (2011a) Microstates in Negotiations beyond the Nation-State: Malta, Cyprus
    and Luxembourg as Active and Successful Policy Shapers? *International Negotia-
    tion* 16(2): 297–317.

———— (2011b) Small States in EU Negotiations. Political Dwarfs or Power-Brokers?
    *Cooperation and Conflict* 40(3): 123–43.

———— (2012a) Dwarfs in International Negotiations: How Small States Make Their
    Voices Heard. *Cambridge Review of International Affairs* 25(3): 313–28.

———— (2012b) Explaining Differences in the Shaping Effectiveness. Why Some
    States Are More Effective in Making Their Voices Heard in International Negotia-
    tions. *Comparative European Politics* 10(1): 111–32.

———— (2012c) Lobbying Institutional Key Players. How States Seek to Influence
    the European Commission, the Council Presidency, and the European Parliament.
    *Journal of Common Market Studies* 50(1): 129–50.

———— (2012d) Negotiation Effectiveness. Why Some States Are More Effective in
    Making Their Voices Heard in International Negotiations. *Comparative European
    Politics* 10(1): 111–32.

———— (2012e) Small States in Multilateral Negotiations. What Have We Learned?
    *Cambridge Review of International Affairs* 25(3): 387–98.

———— (2013a) Getting Ready to Negotiate in International Organizations? On the
    Importance of the Domestic Construction of National Positions. *Journal of Inter-
    national Organizations Studies* 4(2): 25–38.

———— (2013b) Regional Power Revisited. How to Explain Differences in Coherency
    and Success of Regional Organisations in the United Nations General Assembly.
    *International Negotiation* 18(2): 265–91.

———— (2013c) *Unequal Actors in Equalising Institutions. Negotiations in the United
    Nations General Assembly*. Houndmills: Palgrave.

———— (2014a) Communicative Power Europe? How the EU Copes with Opposition
    in International Negotiations. *European Foreign Affairs Review* 19(3): 357–72.

———— (2014b) The European Union in the United Nations. An Effective External
    Actor? *Journal of European Public Policy* 21(7): 1050–66.

———— (2014c) Is Bigger Better? Activity and Success in Negotiations in the United
    Nations General Assembly. *Negotiation Journal* 30(4): 367–92.

———— (2015) Lock-in Strategies in International Negotiations. The Deconstruction
    of Bargaining Power. *Millennium* 43(2): 375–91.

———— (2016) Living in an Imperfect World? Incomplete Contracting & the Ratio-
    nal Design of International Organizations. *Journal of International Organizations
    Studies* 7(1): 25–38.

Panke, D., Lang, S., and Wiedemann, A. (2015) Regional Actors in the United Nations. Exploring the Regionalization of International Negotiations. *Global Affairs* 1(4–5): 431–40.

———— (2017) State & Regional Actors in Complex Governance Systems. Exploring Dynamics of International Negotiations. *British Journal of Politics and International Relations* 19(1): 91–112.

Panke, D., and Haubrich Seco, M. (2016) 'EU and supranational governance', in J. Torfing and Ansell, C. (eds) Handbook on Theories of Governance Cheltenham: Edward Elgar, 499–513.

Panke, D., and Stapel, S. (2016) Exploring Overlapping Regionalism. *Journal of International Relations & Development*. DOI: 10.1057/s41268-016-0081-x.

Papua New Guinea (2012) Statement by H. E. Mr. Robert G. Aisi, Ambassador and Permanent Representative of Papua New Guinea to the United Nations. First UN Conference on the Arms Trade Treaty, New York, July 5, 2012.

Patterson, L.A. (1997) Agricultural Policy Reform in the European Community: A Three-Level Game Analysis. *International Organization* 51(1): 135–65.

Pentland, C. (1975) The Regionalization of World Politics: Concepts and Evidence. *International Journal* 30(4): 599–630.

Perry, A. (2008) Why Africa Is Still Starving. Time Magazine, August 18, 2008. http://content.time.com/time/magazine/article/0,9171,1830392,00.html?iid=sr-link2

Peters, B. G. (1999) *Institutional Theory in Political Science. The 'New Institutionalism'*. London: Printer.

Peterson, J. (2012) 'The EU as a Security Actor', in E. Bomberg, Peterson, J. and Corbett, R. (eds) *The European Union. How Does It Work?* Oxford: Oxford University Press, 185–202.

Peterson, J., and Smith, M.E. (2003) 'The EU as a Global Actor', in E. Bomberg and Stubb, A. (eds) *The European Union: How Does It Work?* Oxford: Oxford University Press, 195–215.

Peterson, M. J. (1992) Transnational Activity, International Society, and World Politics. *Millennium* 21(3).

Petitjean Roget, B. (2002) Socio-Economic and Political Aspects of the Aid Provided by Japan to the Fishing Industry in the Small Independent Islands in the East Caribbean. Swiss Coalition for the Protection of Whales.

Philippines (2014) Statement by Maria-Bernardita T. Flores, Rome.

Philippines (2010) Statement by His Excellency Libran N. Cabactulan, Philippine Permanent Representative to the United Nations, ICN2 Conference, Rome, November 20, 2014.

Philippines (2010) Statement by His Excellency Libran N. Cabactulan, Philippine Permanent Representative to the United Nations, First Session of the ATT Preparatory Committee, New York, July 13, 2010.

———— (2011) Intervention for Debate on International Cooperation and Assistance and Criteria and Parameters. Second Session of the ATT Preparatory Committee, New York, March 2, 2011.

———— (2012) Philippine Statement. First UN Conference on the Arms Trade Treaty, New York, July 10, 2012.

Pierson, P. (2000) The Limits of Design: Explaining Institutional Origins and Change. *Governance. An International Journal of Policy and Administration* 13(4): 475–799.

Plantey, A. (2007) *International Negotiation in the Twenty-First Century*. New York: Routledge.

Poland on Behalf of the European Union (2011) 63rd Annual Meeting of the International Whaling Commission. Opening Statement by Poland on Behalf of the EU and Its Member States. St Helier, Jersey.

Powell, R. (1999) *In the Shadow of Power: States and Strategies in International Politics*. Princeton, NJ: Princeton University Press.

Prakash, R. (2013) India's Security Interests and the Arms Trade Treaty, *ORF Occasional Papers*. http://www.orfonline.org/research/indias-security-interests-and-the-arms-trade-treaty/ (11 January 2016).

Pruitt, D. G. (1991) 'Strategy in Negotiation', in V. Kremenyuk (ed) *International Negotiation: Analysis, Approaches, Issues*. San Francisco, CA: Jossey-Bass, 78–89.

Putnam, R. (1988) Diplomacy and Domestic Politics. The Logic of Two-Level Games. *International Organization* 42(2): 427–60.

Quaglia, L., and Moxon-Browne, E. (2006) What Makes a Good EU Presidency? Italy and Ireland Compared. *Journal of Common Market Studies* 44(2): 349–68.

Rabe-Hesketh, S. and Skrondal, A. (2012) *Multilevel and Longitudinal Modelling Using Stata – 2: Categorical Responses, Counts and Survival*. College Station: Stata Press.

Rasbash, J., and Browne, W. J. (2008) 'Non-Hierarchical Multilevel Models', in J. d. Leeuw and Meijer, E. (eds) *Handbook of Multilevel Analysis*. New York: Springer Science+Business Media LLC, 301–34.

Rasbash, J., and Goldstein, H. (1994) Efficient Analysis of Mixed Hierarchical and Cross-Classified Random Structures Using a Multilevel Model. *Journal of Educational and Behavioral Statistics* 19(4): 337–50.

Raudenbush, S. W., and Bryk, A. S. (2010) *Hierarchical Linear Models: Applications and Data Analysis Methods*. Thousand Oaks: SAGE.

Regelsberger, E., ed. (1997) *Foreign Policy of the European Union. From EPC to CFSP and Beyond*. London: Lynne Rienner.

Reissert, B. (1976) Politikverflechtung als Hindernis staatlicher Aufgabenerfüllung. *Wirtschaftsdienst* VIII413–17.

Republic of Korea (2012) Statement on Arms Trade Treaty, Fourth Session of the ATT Preparatory Committee, New York, February 14, 2012.

Ringquist, E. J., Worsham, J., and Eisner, M. A. (2003) Salience, Complexity, and the Legislative Direction of Regulatory Bureaucracies. *Journal of Public Administration and Research Theory* 13(2): 141–64.

Risse, T. (2000) 'Let's Argue!': Communicative Action in World Politics. *International Organization* 54(1): 1–39.

――― (2001) 'Transnational Actors, Networks, and Global Governance', in W. Carlsnaes, Risse, T. and Simmons, B. (eds.) *Handbook of International Relations*. London: SAGE, pp. 426–52

Rodríguez, G. 'Models for Count Data with Overdispersion'. http://data.princeton.edu/wws509/notes/c4a.pdf

Romanyshyn, I. (2013) The European Union and the Arms Trade Treaty: An Analysis of the EU's Effectiveness in Multilateral Security Governance. Bruges Regional Integration & Global Governance Papers, 3/2013.

Rome Declaration (2014) ICN2 Conference Outcome Document: Rome Declaration on Nutrition, Rome.

Rosenau, J. N., and Czempiel, E.-O., eds. (1992) *Governance without Government: Order and Change in World Politics*. Cambridge: Cambridge University Press.

Rothwell, D. R. (2010) Australia v. Japan: JARPA II Whaling Case before the International Court of Justice. The Hague Justice Portal, http://www.haguejusticeportal. net/Docs/Commentaries%20PDF/Portal%20HJJ_Rothwell_Aust_Japan_EN.pdf.

Russian Federation (2010a) Elements to Be Discussed in the Context of a Potential. ATT. Introductory Remarks by the Delegation of the Russian Federation. First Session of the ATT Preparatory Committee, New York, July 12, 2010.

——— (2010b) A Potential Arms Trade Treaty – Scope and Parameters (Non-Paper). First Session of the ATT Preparatory Committee, New York, July 15, 2010.

——— (2010c) Towards an Arms Trade Treaty – Brokering (Food-for-Thought Paper). First Session of the ATT Preparatory Committee, New York, July 19, 2010.

——— (2013) Statement by the Head of Delegation of the Russian Federation. Second UN Conference on the Arms Trade Treaty, New York, March 18, 2013.

Rwanda (2013) Arms Trade Treaty Final Conference, Rwanda Statement. Second UN Conference on the Arms Trade Treaty, New York, March 19, 2013.

Saint Lucia (2011) Speech delivered during the Third Session of the ATT Preparatory Committee, New York, July 12, 2011.

Sanchez Bajo, C. (1999) The European Union and Mercosur: A Case of Interregionalism. *Third World Quarterly* 20(5): 927–41.

Scanzoni, J., and Godwin, D. D. (1990) Negotiation Effectiveness and Acceptable Outcomes. *Social Psychology Quarterly* 53(3): 239–51.

Schalk, J., Torenvlied, R., Weesie, J., and Strokman, F. (2007) The Power of the Presidency in EU Council Decision-Making. *European Union Politics* 8(2): 229–50.

Scharpf, F. W. (1988) The Joint-Decision Trap: Lessons from German Federalism and European Integration. *Public Administration Review* 66: 239–78.

——— (1997a) *Games Real Actors Play. Actor-Centered Institutionalism in Policy Research*. Boulder, CO: Westview Press.

——— (1997b) Introduction: The Problem-Solving Capacity of Multi-Level Governance. *Journal of European Public Policy* 4(4): 520–38.

——— (1999) *Regieren in Europa. Effektiv und demokratisch?* Frankfurt a/M: Campus Verlag.

——— (2000) *Interaktionsformen: Akteurzentrierter Institutionalismus in der Politikforschung*. Opladen: Leske + Budrich.

Scharpf, F.W., Reissert, B., and Schnabel, F. (1976) *Politikverflechtung. Theorie und Empirie des kooperativen Föderalismus in der Bundesrepublik*. Kronberg/Ts.

Schimmelfennig, F., Engert, S., and Knobel, H. (2003) Costs, Commitment and Compliance. The Impact of EU Democratic Conditionality on Latvia, Slovakia and Turkey. *Journal of Common Market Studies* 41(3): 495–518.

Schmidt, V. A. (1999) 'European Federalism' and Its Encroachments on National Institutions. *Publius* 29(1): 19–44.

Schmitter, P. C. (1970) A Revised Theory of Regional Integration. *International Organization* 24(4): 836–68.

Schröder, U. (2011) *The Organization of European Security Governance – Internal and External Security in Transition*, London: Routledge.

Schunz, S. (2012) 'The European Union in the United Nations Climate Change Regime', in J. Wouters, Bruynickx, H., Basu, S. and Schunz, S. (eds) *The European Union and Multilateral Governance. Assessing EU Participation in the United Nations Human Rights and Environmental Fora*. Basingstoke: Palgrave, 191–213.

Schunz, S., Basu, S., Bruynickx, H., Keukeleire, S., and Wouters, J. (2012) 'Analysing the Position of the European Union in the United Nations System: Analytical Framework', in J. Wouters, Bruynickx, H., Basu, S. and Schunz, S. (eds) *The European Union and Multilateral Governance. Assessing EU Participation in the United Nations Human Rights and Environmental Fora*. Basingstoke: Palgrave, 25–47.

Schuppert, G. F. (2005) *Governance Forschung – Vergewisserung über Stand und Entwicklungslinien*. Baden-Baden: Nomos.

Sedelmeier, U. (2012) Is Europeanisation through Conditionality Sustainable? Lockin of Institutional Change after EU Accession. *West European Politics* 35(1): 20–38.

Selck, T. J., and Kaeding, M. (2004) Divergent Interests and Different Success Rates: France, Germany, Italy, and the United Kingdom in EU Legislative Negotiations. *French Politics* 4(2): 81–95.

Seventh Ministerial Meeting of the Zone of Peace and Cooperation of the South Atlantic (2013) Montevideo Declaration, Montevideo.

Seychelles (2014) Statement by Mitcy Larue, ICN2 Conference, Rome, November 19, 2014.

Shahin, J. (2011) The European Union's Performance in the International Telecommunication Union. *Journal of European Integration* 33(6): 683–98.

Simmons, B., and DiSilvestro, A. (2014) 'Human Trafficking. The European Union Commitment to Fight Human Trafficking', in A. Orsini (ed) *The European Union with(in) International Organisations. Commitment, Consistency and Effects across Time*. Farnham; Burlington: Ashgate, 137–55.

Sjursen, H. (2006) The EU as a 'Normative' Power: How Can This Be? *Journal of European Public Policy* 13(2): 235–51.

Smiley, D. V., and Watts, R. L. (1985) *Intrastate Federalism in Canada*, Toronto: McGraw-Hill Ryerson.

Smith, K. E. (2005) The Outsiders: The European Neighbourhood Policy. *International Affairs* 81(4): 757–73.

Smith, K. E. (2006) Speaking with One Voice? European Union Co-Ordination on Human Rights Issues at the United Nations. *Journal of Common Market Studies* 44(1): 113–37.

——— (2010) The European Union at the Human Rights Council: Speaking with One Voice But Having Little Influence. *Journal of European Public Policy* 17(2): 224–41.

Smith, K. E. (2013a) The European Union and the Politics of Legitimization at the United Nations. *European Foreign Affairs Review* 18(1): 63–80.

——— (2013b) *European Union Foreign Policy in a Changing World*. New York: John Wiley & Sons.

Smith, M. E. (2008) *Europe's Foreign and Security Policy: The Institutionalisation of Cooperation*. Cambridge: Cambridge University Press.

Snijders, T. A. B., and Bosker, R. J. (2012) *Multilevel Analysis: An Introduction to Basic and Advanced Multilevel Modeling*. Los Angeles, CA: SAGE.

Söderbaum, F., and Sbragia, A. (2010) EU Studies and the 'New Regionalism': What Can Be Gained from Dialogue? *European Integration* 32(6): 563–82.

Söderbaum, F., and Shaw, T. M., eds. (2003) *Theories of New Regionalism*. Basingstoke: Palgrave Macmillan.

Söderbaum, F., and Van Langenhove, L. (2005) Introduction: The EU as a Global Actor and the Role of Interregionalism. *European Integration* 27(3): 249–62.

South Africa (1996) The Constitution of the Republic of South Africa.

———— (2012) Statement by Mr. Johann Kellerman, Director: Disarmament and Non-Proliferation Department of International Relations and Cooperation, First UN Conference on the Arms Trade Treaty, New York, July 5, 2012.

Stein, J. G., ed. (1989) *Getting to the Table. The Processes of International Prenegotiations*. Baltimore, MD: Johns Hopkins University Press.

Stoett, P. J. (1997) *The International Politics of Whaling*. Vancouver: UBC Press.

Strand, J. R. T., John P. (2012) Foreign Aid and Voting Behavior in an International Organization: The Case of Japan and the International Whaling Commission. *Foreign Policy Analysis* 8(4): 409–30.

Sweden (2011) Statement on Implementation by the Head of the Delegation of Sweden Ambassador Paul Beijer. Third Session of the ATT Preparatory Committee, New York, July 12, 2011.

———— (2012) Statement by Ambassador Paul Beijer Ministry for Foreign Affairs of Sweden, Fourth Session of the ATT Preparatory Committee, New York, February 16, 2012.

Switzerland (2011) Statement by Mr. Simon Plüss, Head of the Swiss Delegation, Second Session of the ATT Preparatory Committee, New York, February 28, 2011.

———— (2012) Statement by the Delegation of Switzerland delivered by Mr. Erwin Bollinger, Ambassador, Head of Delegation. First UN Conference on the Arms Trade Treaty, New York, July 9, 2012.

Tallberg, J. (2000) The Anatomy of Autonomy: An Institutional Account of Variation in Supranational Influence. *Journal of Common Market Studies* 38(5): 843–64.

———— (2003) The Agenda-Shaping Powers of the EU Council Presidency. *Journal of European Public Policy* 10(1): 1–19.

Tallberg, J., Sommerer, T., Squatrito, T., and Jönsson, C. (2013) *The Opening Up of International Organizations: Transnational Access in Global Governance*. Cambridge: Cambridge University Press.

Tanner, M. A. (1996) *Tools for Statistical Inference: Methods for the Exploration of Posterior Distributions and Likelihood Functions*. New York: Springer.

Tanzania (2010) Statement by Mr. Justin N. Seruhere, Minister Plenipotentiary at the Permanent Mission of the United Republic of Tanzania, First Session of the ATT Preparatory Committee, New York, July 12, 2010.

———— (2013) Statement by H. E. Ambassador Ramadhani M. Mwinyi, Deputy Permanent Representative of the United Republic of Tanzania, Second UN Conference on the Arms Trade Treaty, New York, March 18, 2013.

———— (2014) Statement by Mohammed Gharib Bilal, ICN2 Conference, Rome, November 19, 2014.

Telò, M., ed. (2001) *European Union and New Regionalism : Regional Actors and Global Governance in a Post-Hegemonic Era*. Aldershot: Ashgate.

Thailand (2011) Consideration of International Cooperation and Assistance in the Context of the ATT. Second Session of the ATT Preparatory Committee, New York, March 2, 2011.

Themnér, L., and Wallensteen, P. (2013) Armed Conflicts, 1946–2012. *Journal of Peace Research* 50(4):509–21.

Thomas, D. C. (2011) Still Punching Below Its Weight? Coherence and Effectiveness in EU Foreign Policy. *Journal of Common Market Studies* 50(3): 457–74.

Thomson, R. (2011) *Resolving Controversy in the European Union. Legislative Decision-Making before and after Enlargement*. Cambridge: Cambridge University Press.

Thomson, R., and Stokman, F. (2006) 'Research Design: Measuring Actor's Positions, Saliencies and Capabilities', in R. Thomson, Stokman, F. N., Achen, C. H. and Koenig, T. (eds) *The European Union Decides*. Cambridge: Cambridge University Press, 24–53.

Thomson, R., Stokman, F., and Torenvlied, R. (2003) Models of Collective Decision-Making. *Rationality and Society* 15(1): 5–14.

Thomson, R., Stokman, F. N., Achen, C. H., and Koenig, T., eds. (2006) *The European Union Decides*. Cambridge: Cambridge University Press.

Tsebelis, G. (1990) *Nested Games: Rational Choice in Comparative Politics*. Berkeley: University of California Press.

——— (2002) *Veto Players: How Political Institutions Work*. Princeton, NJ: Princeton University Press.

Tsebelis, G., and Garrett, G. (1997) Agenda Setting, Vetoes and the European Union's Co-Decision Procedure. *The Journal of Legislative Studies* 3(3):74–92.

Tsoukalis, L. (2011) 'Managing Interdependence. The EU in the World Economy', in C. Hill and Smith, M. (eds) *International Relations and the European Union*. Oxford: Oxford University Press, 225–46.

Tunaru, R. (2002) Hierarchical Bayesian Models for Multiple Count Data. *Austrian Journal of Statistics* 31(2&3): 221–29.

Uganda (1995) The Constitution of the Republic of Uganda.

UK (2011) Statement by Ambassador John Duncan, UK Intervention on Scope of an ATT, Second Session of the ATT Preparatory Committee, New York, February 28, 2011.

——— (2013) Opening Statement by Ambassador Joanne Adamson, Head of Delegation, Second UN Conference on the Arms Trade Treaty, New York, March 18, 2013.

Ukraine (2013) Statement by the Delegation of Ukraine, Second UN Conference on the Arms Trade Treaty, New York, March 18, 2013.

UNIDO (2014) Second International Conference on Nutrition, Rome.

Union of International Associations, ed. (2005/2006) *Yearbook of International Organizations*, http://www.brill.nl/publications/yearbook-international-organizations

United Nations. 'Permanent Observers – Intergovernmental Organizations'. http://www.un.org/en/members/intergovorg.shtml

United Nations Coverage and Press Releases. 'Overwhelming Majority of States in General Assembly Say "Yes" to Arms Trade Treaty to Stave off Irresponsible

Transfers that Perpetuate Conflict, Human Suffering', http://www.un.org/press/en/2013/ga11354.doc.htm

United Nations General Assembly (2009) Resolution Adopted by the General Assembly on 2 December 2009: 64/48. The Arms Trade Treaty, New York.

———— (2010) Preparatory Committee for the United Nations Conference on the Arms Trade Treaty. First Session: List of Participants, New York.

———— (2011a) Preparatory Committee for the United Nations Conference on the Arms Trade Treaty. Second Session: List of Participants, New York.

———— (2011b) Preparatory Committee for the United Nations Conference on the Arms Trade Treaty. Third Session: List of Participants, New York.

———— (2012a) First UN Conference on the Arms Trade Treaty. List of Participants, New York.

———— (2012b) Preparatory Committee for the United Nations Conference on the Arms Trade Treaty. Fourth Session: List of Participants, New York.

———— (2012c) Provisional Rules of Procedure of the Conference. New York.

———— (2012d) United Nations Conference on the Arms Trade Treaty: Provisional Rules of Procedure of the Conference, New York.

———— (2013a) The Arms Trade Treaty, New York.

———— (2013b) The Arms Trade Treaty (draft version).

———— (2013c) List of Participants. Second UN Conference on the Arms Trade Treaty, New York.

———— (2013d) Resolution adopted by the General Assembly 67/234. The Arms Trade Treaty, New York, 4 January 2013.

United Nations General Assembly, n.p.M. (2012e) General Assembly Sixty-Seventh Session. Official Records, New York.

United Nations Office for Disarmament Affairs. 'The Global Reported Arms Trade. The UN Register of Conventional Arms', http://www.un-register.org/Background/Index.aspx

Uruguay (2010) Presentation of the Uruguay Delegation, First Session of the ATT Preparatory Committee, New York, July 14, 2010.

USA (2012) United States of America Statement by the Honorable Thomas M. Countryman. First UN Conference on the Arms Trade Treaty, New York, July 6, 2012.

———— (2013a) Statement of Assistant Secretary of State Thomas Countryman. Second UN Conference on the Arms Trade Treaty, New York, March 25, 2013.

———— (2013b) The United States Supports the Arms Trade Treaty. Press Statement, John Kerry, Secretary of State, March 15, 2013, Washington D.C.

van Schaik, L. (2011) The EU's Performance in the World Health Organization: Internal Cramps after the 'Lisbon Cure'. *Journal of European Integration* 33(6): 699–713.

———— (2013) *EU Effectiveness and Unity in Multilateral Negotiations. More than the Sum of Its Parts?* Basingstoke; New York: Palgrave Macmillan.

van Schaik, L., and Schunz, S. (2012) Explaining EU Activism and Impact in Global Climate Politics: Is the Union a Norm- or Interest-Driven Actor? *Journal of Common Market Studies* 50(1): 169–86.

Venezuela (2012) Statement Delivered by Ambassador Jorge Valero. First United Nations Conference on the Arms Trade Treaty, New York, July 5, 2012.

Verdier, D., and Breen, R. (2001) Europeanization and Globalization. Politics against Markets in the European Union. *Comparative Political Studies* 34(1): 227–62.

Vietnam (2011) Statement by Mr. Hoang Chi Trung, Director General, Department of International Organisations, Ministry of Foreign Affairs of Viet Nam, Second Session of the ATT Preparatory Committee, New York, February 28, 2011.

——— (2012) Statement by H. E. Ambassador Le Hoai Trung, Permanent Representative of the Socialist Republic of Viet Nam to the United Nations, First UN Conference on the Arms Trade Treaty, New York, July 9, 2012.

——— (2013) Statement by H. E. Ambassador Le Hoai Trung, Permanent Representative of the Socialist Republic of Viet Nam to the United Nations, Second UN Conference on the Arms Trade Treaty, New York, March 18, 2013.

——— (2014) Statement by H. E. Nguyen Hoang Long, Rome. ICN2 Conference, Rome, November 21, 2014.

von Krause, U. (2008) *Mehrebenengovernance in der EU*. Wiesbaden: VS Verlag für Sozialwissenschaften.

Wälti, S. (1996) Institutional Reform of Federalism: Changing the Players Rather Than the Rules of the Game. *Swiss Political Science Review* 2(2): 113–41.

Waltz, K. (1959) *Man, the State, and War*. New York: Columbia University Press.

——— (1979) *Theory of International Politics*. New York: McGraw-Hill Publishing Company.

Warleigh, A., and Rosamond, B. (2010) Across the EU-Studies-New Regionalism Frontier: Invitation to Dialogue. *Journal of Common Market Studies* 48(4): 993–1013.

Warntjen, A. (2008) The Council Presidency: Power Broker or Burden? An Empirical Analysis. *European Union Politics*, 9(3): 316–38.

Watts, R. L. (1999) *Comparing Federal Systems*. Kingston: Queen's University, Institute of Intergovernmental Relations.

Weiffen, B., Wehner, L., and Nolte, D. (2013) Overlapping Regional Security Institutions in South America: The Case of OAS and UNASUR. *International Area Studies Review* 16(4): 370–89.

Weiss, T. G., and Gordenker, L., eds. (1996) *NGOs, the UN and Global Governance*. Boulder, CO: Lynne Rienner.

Wenzelburger, G., Jäckle, S., and König, P. (2014) *Weiterführende statistische Methoden für Politikwissenschaftler: Eine anwendungsbezogene Einführung mit Stata*. München: De Gruyter Oldenbourg.

Wessel, R. (2011) The Legal Framework for the Participation of the European Union in International Institutions. *Journal of European Integration* 33(6): 621–35.

Western, B., and Jackman, S. (1994) Bayesian Inference for Comparative Research. *The American Political Science Review* 88(2): 412–23.

Wetzel, A. 2011. 'Enter the EU – or Not? The EU's Participation in International Organisations'. Paper Presented at the Workshop 'Regional Organizations as Global Players: Active = Influential?', KFG 'The Transformative Power of Europe', Berlin, 28–29 October 2011.

Wetzel, A., Freyburg, T., Lavenex, S., Schimmelfennig, F., and Skripka, T. (2015) *Democracy Promotion by Functional Cooperation. The European Union and Its Neighbourhood*. London: Palgrave.

Wheare, K. C. (1963) *Federal Government*. London; New York: Oxford University Press.

Whitaker, R. (1983) *Federalism and Democratic Theory*. Kingston, ON: Institute for Intergovernmental Relations, Queens University.

Williams, I. 'The Arms Trade Treaty at a Glance'. Arms Control Association, http://www.armscontrol.org/factsheets/arms_trade_treaty

Woolcott, P. (2012) Draft of the Arms Trade Treaty Submitted by the President of the Conference, New York.

———— (2013) Report to the General Assembly of the President of the Final United Nations Conference on the Arms Trade Treaty Ambassador Peter Woolcott of Australia, New York.

World Declaration (1992) International Conference on Nutrition: World Declaration and Plan of Action for Nutrition, Rome.

World Food Summit (1996) Rome Declaration on World Food Security, Rome.

Wouters, J., Bruynickx, H., Basu, S., and Schunz, S., eds. (2012a) *The European Union and Multilateral Governance. Assessing EU Participation in the United Nations Human Rights and Environmental Fora*. Basingstoke: Palgrave.

Wouters, J., Bruyninckx, H., Basu, S., and Schunz, S., eds. (2012b) *The European Union and Multilateral Governance*. Basingstoke; New York: Palgrave Macmillan.

Wunderlich, J.-U. (2012) The EU an Actor Sui Generis? A Comparison of EU and ASEAN Actorness. *Journal of Common Market Studies* 50(4): 653–69.

Xiarchogiannopoulou, E., and Tsarouhas, D. (2014) 'Flexicurity. The EU Actorness at the ILO on Flexicurity', in A. Orsini (eds.) *The European Union with(in) International Organisations. Commitment, Consistency and Effects across Time*. Farnham; Burlington: Ashgate, 115–35.

Xinhua General News Service (2008) International Whaling Commission Runs into Stalemate over New Proposals.

Young, A. R. (2011) The Rise (and Fall?) if the EU's Performance in the Multilateral Trading System. *Journal of European Integration* 33(6): 715–29.

Young, O. R. (1999) *Governance in World Affairs*. Ithaca, NY: Cornell University Press.

Zacharias, A., Gerber, L. R., and Hyrenbach, K. D. (2006) Review of the Southern Ocean Sanctuary: Marine Protected Areas in the Context of the International Whaling Commission Sanctuary Programme. *Journal of Cetacean Research and Management* 8(1): 1–12.

Zartman, I. W., and Rubin, J. Z., eds. (2009) *Power and Negotiation*. Ann Arbor: University of Michigan Press.

Zero Draft (2014) Zero Draft of the Framework for Action: Second International Conference on Nutrition (ICN2), Rome.

Zimbabwe (2011) Statement by Group Captain A. V. Murove to the 3rd Preparatory Committee Meeting for the Arms Trade Treaty, New York.

———— (2014) Statement by David Parirenyatwa, Rome. ICN2 Conference, Rome, November 19, 2014.

Zimmermann, H. (2007) Realist Power Europe? The EU in the Negotiations about China's and Russia's WTO Accession. *Journal of Common Market Studies* 45(4): 813–32.

Zintl, R. (1992) 'Kooperation und Aufteilung des Kooperationsgewinns bei horizon-taler Politikverflechtung', in A. Benz, Scharpf, F. W., and Zintl, R. (eds) *Horizontale Politikverflechtung. Zur Theorie von Verhandlungssystemen*. Frankfurt a/M: Campus Verlag, 97–146.

Zürn, M. (2012) 'Global Governance as Multi-Level Governance', in D. Levi-Faur (ed) *Oxford Hand-Book of Global Governance*. Oxford: Oxford University Press, 70–744.

Zwartjes, M., Van Langenhove, L., Kingah, S., and Maes, L. (2012) Determinants of Regional Leadership: Is the European Union a Leading Regional Actor in Peace and Security? *Southeast European and Black Sea Studies* 12(3): 393–405.

# Annex (Chapter 3)

**Table A3.1.** List of mapped negotiations

| IO | Year | Neg. | Start Date | End Date | Topic |
|---|---|---|---|---|---|
| ATT | 2010 | 1 | 12.07.2010 | 21.07.2010 | Scope; Universality |
| ATT | 2011 | 1 | 28.02.2011 | 04.03.2011 | Scope; Criteria and Parameters; International Cooperation and Assistance |
| ATT | 2011 | 2 | 11.06.2011 | 15.06.2011 | Implementation |
| ATT | 2012 | 1 | 13.02.2012 | 16.02.2012 | Discussion of Importance of Civil Society and NGOs |
| ATT | 2012 | 2 | 03.07.2012 | 27.07.2012 | Implementation and Scope of ATT |
| CD | 2008 | 1 | 23.01.2008 | 27.03.2008 | Fissile Material Cut-Off Prevention of Arms Race in Outer Space, Strategic Arms Reduction |
| CD | 2008 | 2 | 15.05.2008 | 25.06.2008 | Deadlock of CD |
| CD | 2008 | 3 | 29.07.2008 | 09.09.2008 | Fissile Material Cut-Off Treaty |
| CD | 2009 | 1 | 20.01.2009 | 26.03.2009 | Deadlock of CD |
| CD | 2009 | 2 | 09.05.2009 | 02.07.2009 | Fissile Material Cut-Off Treaty |
| CD | 2009 | 3 | 04.08.2009 | 17.09.2009 | Fissile Material Cut-Off Treaty |
| CD | 2010 | 1 | 18.01.2009 | 26.03.2010 | Non-Proliferation Treaty and Fissile Material Cut-Off Treaty |
| CD | 2010 | 2 | 31.05.2010 | 16.07.2010 | Prevention for an Arms Race in Outer Space |
| CD | 2010 | 3 | 09.08.2010 | 24.09.2010 | Strategic Arms Reduction Treaty, Fissile Material Cut-Off Treaty, Non-Proliferation Treaty |
| CD | 2010 | 4 | 24.09.2010 | 24.09.2010 | Issues Related to Fissile Material Cut-Off Treaty and Non-Proliferation Treaty |
| CD | 2011 | 1 | 27.07.2011 | 29.07.2011 | Fissile Material Cut-Off Treaty |

*(Continued)*

**Table A3.1.  Continued**

| IO | Year | Neg. | Start Date | End Date | Topic |
|---|---|---|---|---|---|
| CD | 2011 | 2 | 04.08.2011 | 15.09.2011 | Developments in the CD and Fissile Material Cut-Off Treaty |
| CD | 2011 | 3 | 17.02.2011 | 30.03.2011 | Non-Proliferation Treaty |
| CD | 2011 | 4 | 17.05.2011 | 28.06.2011 | Fissile Material Cut-Off Treaty |
| CD | 2012 | 1 | 31.07.2012 | 13.09.2012 | Revitalization of the CD |
| CD | 2012 | 2 | 21.08.2012 | 28.08.2012 | Revitalization of the CD |
| CD | 2012 | 3 | 24.01.2012 | 27.03.2012 | Fissile Material Cut-Off Treaty |
| CD | 2012 | 4 | 15.05.2012 | 26.06.2012 | Fissile Material Cut-Off Treaty |
| ECOSOC | 2008 | 1 | 25.07.2008 | 25.07.2008 | Emergency Assistance, Least Developed Countries, Human Trafficking |
| ECOSOC | 2008 | 2 | 24.07.2008 | 24.07.2008 | Strengthening Humanitarian Assistance, Support for Non Self-Governing Territories |
| ECOSOC | 2008 | 3 | 23.07.2008 | 23.07.2008 | Mandate of Ad-Hoc Advisory Group on Haiti |
| ECOSOC | 2008 | 4 | 22.07.2008 | 22.07.2008 | Enhance Interaction with Post-Conflict Countries |
| ECOSOC | 2009 | 1 | 27.04.2009 | 27.04.2009 | Reforming World Economic System |
| ECOSOC | 2009 | 2 | 12.02.2009 | 12.02.2009 | Potential of Traditional Medicine |
| ECOSOC | 2009 | 3 | 28.01.2009 | 28.01.2009 | Suspension of NGOs |
| ECOSOC | 2009 | 4 | 27.01.2009 | 27.01.2009 | Discussion on NGOs |
| ECOSOC | 2010 | 1 | 22.07.2010 | 22.07.2010 | Social Issues and Human Rights |
| ECOSOC | 2010 | 2 | 23.07.2010 | 23.07.2010 | Global Jobs Pact, Haiti |
| ECOSOC | 2010 | 3 | 20.07.2010 | 20.07.2010 | Palestinian Women |
| ECOSOC | 2010 | 4 | 16.07.2010 | 16.07.2010 | Cybersecurity |
| ECOSOC | 2011 | 1 | 10.03.2011 | 10.03.2011 | International Development Architecture |
| ECOSOC | 2011 | 2 | 04.11.2011 | 04.11.2011 | Right to Development |
| ECOSOC | 2011 | 3 | 28.04.2011 | 28.04.2011 | Education Priorities from Access to Quality |
| ECOSOC | 2011 | 4 | 11.03.2011 | 11.03.2011 | Partnership for Development |
| ECOSOC | 2012 | 1 | 25.07.2012 | 25.07.2012 | Decolonization, Regional Cooperation, Environment |
| ECOSOC | 2012 | 2 | 11.07.2012 | 11.07.2012 | Youth Employment |
| ECOSOC | 2012 | 3 | 20.07.2012 | 20.07.2012 | Strengthening Humanitarian Assistance |
| ECOSOC | 2012 | 4 | 27.07.2012 | 27.07.2012 | Least-Developed Countries |
| FAO | 2008 | 1 | 20.08.2008 | 21.08.2008 | FAO Reform, Global Food Security |
| FAO | 2008 | 2 | 20.08.2008 | 21.08.2008 | Food Price, Global Food Security |
| FAO | 2009 | 1 | 19.11.2009 | 20.11.2009 | Global Food Security, Climate Change, FAO Reform |
| FAO | 2009 | 2 | 19.11.2009 | 20.11.2009 | Global Strategy for Agricultural and Rural Statistics |
| FAO | 2009 | 3 | 19.11.2009 | 20.11.2009 | Status of the Global Plan of Action for Animal Genetic Resources for Food and Agriculture |

| IO | Year | Neg. | Start Date | End Date | Topic |
|---|---|---|---|---|---|
| FAO | 2009 | 4 | 30.09.2009 | 30.09.2009 | International Investment |
| FAO | 2010 | 1 | 17.05.2010 | 17.05.2010 | FAO Reform |
| FAO | 2010 | 2 | 29.11.2010 | 03.12.2010 | Livestock |
| FAO | 2010 | 3 | 29.11.2010 | 03.12.2010 | Forestry |
| FAO | 2010 | 4 | 29.11.2010 | 03.12.2010 | Food Security |
| FAO | 2011 | 1 | 27.06.2011 | 29.06.2011 | Women's Role in Agriculture, Rural Development |
| FAO | 2011 | 2 | 27.06.2011 | 27.06.2011 | The State of Land and Water |
| FAO | 2011 | 3 | 28.06.2011 | 28.06.2011 | Declaration on Rinderpest Eradication |
| FAO | 2011 | 4 | 04.07.2011 | 04.07.2011 | Developments in Fora of Importance for the Mandate of FAO |
| FAO | 2012 | 1 | 03.12.2012 | 03.12.2012 | Debate on Recommendations of the 39th Session of the World Food Security Committee |
| FAO | 2012 | 2 | 03.12.2012 | 03.12.2012 | International Code of Conduct on the Distribution and Use of Pesticides |
| FAO | 2012 | 3 | 03.12.2012 | 03.12.2012 | Debate on Conclusions and Recommendations of the 30th Session of the Committee on Fisheries |
| FAO | 2012 | 4 | 03.12.2012 | 03.12.2012 | Debate on Conclusions and Recommendations of the 21st Session of the Committee on Forestry |
| HRC | 2008 | 1 | 22.05.2008 | 22.05.2008 | Special Session on World Food Crisis |
| HRC | 2008 | 2 | 01.12.2008 | 01.12.2008 | Immediate End to All Human Rights Violations in the DRC |
| HRC | 2008 | 3 | 12.08.2008 | 12.08.2008 | Reviews Mandate on Toxic Waste |
| HRC | 2008 | 4 | 18.09.2008 | 18.09.2008 | Human Rights Situation in Palestine |
| HRC | 2009 | 1 | 09.01.2009 | 09.01.2009 | Crisis Situation in Gaza |
| HRC | 2009 | 2 | 20.02.2009 | 20.02.2009 | Special Session on the Impact of the Global Crisis on Human Rights |
| HRC | 2009 | 3 | 27.05.2009 | 27.05.2009 | Resolution on Assistance to Sri Lanka in the Promotion and Protection of Human Rights |
| HRC | 2009 | 4 | 15.10.2009 | 15.10.2009 | Situation in the Occupied Palestinian Territory and East Jerusalem |
| HRC | 2010 | 1 | 01.10.2010 | 01.10.2010 | Establishes Working Group on Discrimination against Women in Law and Practice |
| HRC | 2010 | 2 | 27.09.2010 | 27.09.2010 | Human Rights Situation in Palestine and Other Occupied Arab Territories |

(Continued)

| IO | Year | Neg. | Start Date | End Date | Topic |
|---|---|---|---|---|---|
| HRC | 2010 | 3 | 27.01.2010 | 28.01.2010 | Recovery Process in Haiti |
| HRC | 2010 | 4 | 23.12.2010 | 23.12.2010 | Human Rights in Côte d'Ivoire |
| HRC | 2011 | 1 | 25.02.2011 | 25.02.2011 | Human Rights Council Debates Situation of Human Rights in Libya |
| HRC | 2011 | 2 | 15.06.2011 | 15.06.2011 | Best Practices in the Fight Against Racism |
| HRC | 2011 | 3 | 15.06.2011 | 15.06.2011 | Debate on Racism, Racial Discrimination, Xenophobia and Related Forms of Intolerance |
| HRC | 2011 | 4 | 22.08.2011 | 22.08.2011 | Human Rights in Syrian Arab Republic |
| HRC | 2012 | 1 | 01.06.2012 | 01.06.2012 | Deteriorating Situation of Human Rights in the Syrian Arab Republic |
| HRC | 2012 | 2 | 01.06.2012 | 01.06.2012 | Deteriorating Situation of Human Rights in the Syrian Arab Republic |
| HRC | 2012 | 3 | 25.09.2012 | 25.09.2012 | General Debate on Racism, Racial Discrimination, Xenophobia and Related Forms of Intolerance |
| HRC | 2012 | 4 | 24.09.2012 | 24.09.2012 | Discussion on the Human Rights Situation in Palestine and Other Occupied Arab Territories |
| IAEA | 2008 | 1 | 30.09.2008 | 30.09.2008 | Strengthening the Agency's Activities Related to Nuclear Science, Technology and Applications |
| IAEA | 2008 | 2 | 30.09.2008 | 30.09.2008 | International Cooperation in Nuclear Radiation, Transport Safety and Waste Management |
| IAEA | 2008 | 3 | 29.09.2008 | 29.09.2008 | General Debate and Annual Report for 2007 |
| IAEA | 2008 | 4 | 03.10.2008 | 03.10.2008 | Implementation of the NPT Safeguards Agreement |
| IAEA | 2009 | 1 | 14.09.2009 | 14.09.2009 | Non-Proliferation |
| IAEA | 2009 | 2 | 18.09.2009 | 18.09.2009 | Nuclear Security |
| IAEA | 2009 | 3 | 17.09.2009 | 17.09.2009 | Strengthening the Agency's Activities Related to Nuclear Science, Technology and Applications |
| IAEA | 2009 | 4 | 18.09.2009 | 18.09.2009 | Implementation of the NPT Safeguards Agreement |
| IAEA | 2010 | 1 | 21.09.2010 | 21.09.2010 | Strengthening the Agency's Activities Related to Nuclear Science, Technology and Applications |
| IAEA | 2010 | 2 | 22.09.2010 | 22.09.2010 | Nuclear Security |
| IAEA | 2010 | 3 | 21.09.2010 | 21.09.2010 | Strengthening the Effectiveness and Improving the Efficiency of the Safeguards Systems |

| IO | Year | Neg. | Start Date | End Date | Topic |
|---|---|---|---|---|---|
| IAEA | 2010 | 4 | 22.09.2010 | 22.09.2010 | Strengthening of the Agency's Technical Cooperation Activities |
| IAEA | 2011 | 1 | 23.09.2011 | 23.09.2011 | Application of IAEA Safeguards in the Middle East |
| IAEA | 2011 | 2 | 23.09.2011 | 23.09.2011 | Israeli Nuclear Capabilities |
| IAEA | 2011 | 3 | 20.09.2011 | 20.09.2011 | Strengthening the Agency's Activities Related to Nuclear Science, Technology and Applications |
| IAEA | 2011 | 4 | 20.09.2011 | 20.09.2011 | International Cooperation in Nuclear Radiation, Transport Safety and Waste Management |
| IAEA | 2012 | 1 | 19.09.2012 | 19.09.2012 | Nuclear Security |
| IAEA | 2012 | 2 | 18.09.2012 | 18.09.2012 | Strengthening the Effectiveness and Improving the Efficiency of the Safeguards Systems |
| IAEA | 2012 | 3 | 17.09.2012 | 17.09.2012 | International Cooperation in Nuclear Radiation, Transport Safety and Waste Management |
| IAEA | 2012 | 4 | 21.09.2012 | 21.09.2012 | Promotion of Efficiency and Effectiveness of the IAEA Decision-Making Process |
| IBRD IMF | 2008 | 1 | 13.10.2008 | 13.10.2008 | General Statements: Financial Crisis |
| IBRD IMF | 2008 | 2 | 11.10.2008 | 11.10.2008 | The Global Economy and Financial Markets – Outlook, Risks, and Policy Responses |
| IBRD IMF | 2008 | 3 | 30.09.2008 | 30.09.2008 | World Bank Group Voice Reform |
| IBRD IMF | 2008 | 4 | 27.03.2008 | 27.03.2008 | Overcoming Poverty in the Poorest Countries |
| IBRD IMF | 2009 | 1 | 06.10.2009 | 06.10.2009 | General Statements: Financial Crisis, Economic Turnaround |
| IBRD IMF | 2009 | 2 | 04.10.2009 | 04.10.2009 | The Global Economy and Financial Markets – Outlook, Risks, and Policy Responses |
| IBRD IMF | 2009 | 3 | 05.10.2009 | 05.10.2009 | World Bank Group Voice Reform |
| IBRD IMF | 2009 | 4 | 13.04.2009 | 13.04.2009 | Implications of the Global Economic Crisis for Developing Countries |
| IBRD IMF | 2010 | 1 | 08.10.2010 | 10.10.2010 | General Statements: Jobless Recovery, Financial Sector |
| IBRD IMF | 2010 | 2 | 24.02.2010 | 24.02.2010 | Financial, Infrastructure Reforms |
| IBRD IMF | 2010 | 3 | 06.04.2010 | 06.04.2010 | Safety Nets Work: During Crisis and Prosperity |
| IBRD IMF | 2010 | 4 | 13.04.2010 | 13.04.2010 | World Bank Group Voice Reform |
| IBRD IMF | 2011 | 1 | 23.09.2011 | 23.09.2011 | General Statements: Role of the IMF, Financial Crisis |
| IBRD IMF | 2011 | 2 | 24.09.2011 | 24.09.2011 | General Statements: Debt Crisis, Growth, Mechanisms |

*(Continued)*

**Table A3.1. Continued**

| IO | Year | Neg. | Start Date | End Date | Topic |
|---|---|---|---|---|---|
| IBRD IMF | 2011 | 3 | 16.04.2011 | 16.04.2011 | Responding to Global Food Price Volatility and its Impact on Food Security |
| IBRD IMF | 2011 | 4 | 16.04.2011 | 16.04.2011 | Global Economic Situation |
| IBRD IMF | 2012 | 1 | 12.10.2012 | 12.10.2012 | General Statements: Global Economy, Role of the IMF |
| IBRD IMF | 2012 | 2 | 13.10.2012 | 13.10.2012 | Global Economic and Financial Challenges |
| IBRD IMF | 2012 | 3 | 20.12.2012 | 20.12.2012 | Creating Jobs Good for Development |
| IBRD IMF | 2012 | 4 | 20.12.2012 | 20.12.2012 | Creating Jobs Good for Development |
| ICCAT | 2008 | 1 | 17.11.2008 | 24.11.2008 | Opening Statements: Situation of the Tuna, Challenges for the ICCAT |
| ICCAT | 2008 | 2 | 17.11.2008 | 24.11.2008 | Report of the Standing Committee on Research and Statistics (SCRS): Albacore, Bluefin Tuna |
| ICCAT | 2008 | 3 | 17.11.2008 | 24.11.2008 | Measures for the Conservation of Stocks and Criteria for the Allocation of Fishing Possibilities |
| ICCAT | 2008 | 4 | 17.11.2008 | 24.11.2008 | Research: Bluefin Tuna |
| ICCAT | 2009 | 1 | 09.11.2009 | 15.11.2009 | Opening Statements: Situation of the Tuna, Challenges for the ICCAT |
| ICCAT | 2009 | 2 | 09.11.2009 | 15.11.2009 | Examination of the Compliance Status of Contracting Parties Based on Point 6 of Rec. 08–13 |
| ICCAT | 2009 | 3 | 09.11.2009 | 15.11.2009 | Harvest Bluefin Tuna |
| ICCAT | 2009 | 4 | 09.11.2009 | 15.11.2009 | Harvest Bluefin Tuna |
| ICCAT | 2010 | 1 | 17.11.2010 | 27.11.2010 | Opening Statements: Situation of the Tuna, Challenges for the ICCAT |
| ICCAT | 2010 | 2 | 17.11.2010 | 27.11.2010 | Necessary Preparatory Actions for the Implementation of Kobe II Course of Actions |
| ICCAT | 2010 | 3 | 17.11.2010 | 27.11.2010 | Consideration and Review of Compliance with Paragraph 1 of Rec. 09–06 |
| ICCAT | 2010 | 4 | 17.11.2010 | 27.11.2010 | Consideration and Review of Compliance with Paragraph 46 of Rec. 08–05 |
| ICCAT | 2011 | 1 | 11.11.2011 | 19.11.2011 | Opening Statements: Situation of the Tuna, Challenges for the ICCAT etc. |
| ICCAT | 2011 | 2 | 09.05.2011 | 13.05.2011 | Response to Recommendation 10–09, Sea Turtle by-Catch Mitigation |

| IO | Year | Neg. | Start Date | End Date | Topic |
|----|------|------|------------|----------|-------|
| ICCAT | 2011 | 3 | 21.02.2011 | 25.02.2011 | Review and Approval of Fishing, Inspection and Capacity Reduction Plans |
| ICCAT | 2011 | 4 | 11.11.2011 | 19.11.2011 | Focus Issues for Kobe III |
| ICCAT | 2012 | 1 | 02.04.2012 | 06.04.2012 | Review and Consideration of Monitoring, Control and Surveillance Issues |
| ICCAT | 2012 | 2 | 28.05.2012 | 31.05.2012 | Discussion of Appropriate Next Steps to Address Issues Identified by CPCs |
| ICCAT | 2012 | 3 | 02.07.2012 | 06.07.2012 | Review of Information Needed to Assess the Impact of ICCAT Fisheries on Sea Turtles |
| ICCAT | 2012 | 4 | 12.11.2012 | 19.11.2012 | Opening Statements: Situation of the Tuna, Challenges for the ICCAT |
| ILO | 2008 | 1 | 10.03.2008 | 14.03.2008 | The Decent Work Agenda in Poverty Reduction Strategy Papers (PRSPs): Recent Developments |
| ILO | 2008 | 2 | 28.05.2008 | 28.05.2008 | Efforts to Reach ILO Objectives in the Context of Globalization |
| ILO | 2008 | 3 | 28.05.2008 | 28.05.2008 | Skills for Improved Productivity, Employment Growth and Development |
| ILO | 2008 | 4 | 28.05.2008 | 28.05.2008 | Rural Employment for Poverty Reduction |
| ILO | 2009 | 1 | 03.06.2009 | 03.06.2009 | Gender Equality at the Heart of Decent Work |
| ILO | 2009 | 2 | 03.06.2009 | 03.06.2009 | HIV/AIDS and the World of Work |
| ILO | 2009 | 3 | 03.06.2009 | 03.06.2009 | General Discussion on the Thematic Dialogues and Draft Outline |
| ILO | 2009 | 4 | 04.06.2009 | 04.06.2009 | Programme and Budget Proposals for 2010–2011 |
| ILO | 2010 | 1 | 02.06.2010 | 02.06.2010 | A Discussion on the Strategic Objective of Employment |
| ILO | 2010 | 2 | 02.06.2010 | 02.06.2010 | Decent Work for Domestic Workers |
| ILO | 2010 | 3 | 02.06.2010 | 02.06.2010 | HIV/AIDS and the World of Work |
| ILO | 2010 | 4 | 03.06.2010 | 03.06.2010 | Review of the Follow-Up to the 1998 ILO Declaration on Fundamental Principles and Rights at Work |
| ILO | 2011 | 1 | 01.06.2011 | 01.06.2011 | Decent Work for Domestic Workers |
| ILO | 2011 | 2 | 01.06.2011 | 01.06.2011 | Labour Administration and Labour Inspection |
| ILO | 2011 | 3 | 01.06.2011 | 01.06.2011 | Strategic Objective of Social Protection (social security) |

(Continued)

**Table A3.1.  Continued**

| IO | Year | Neg. | Start Date | End Date | Topic |
|----|------|------|-----------|----------|-------|
| ILO | 2011 | 4 | 10.06.2011 | 10.06.2011 | Review of the Follow-Up to the 1998 ILO Declaration on Fundamental Principles and Rights at Work |
| ILO | 2012 | 1 | 14.06.2012 | 14.06.2012 | Information and Reports on the Application of Conventions and Recommendations |
| ILO | 2012 | 2 | 30.05.2012 | 30.05.2012 | The Youth Employment Crisis |
| ILO | 2012 | 3 | 30.05.2012 | 30.05.2012 | Recurrent Discussion Under the ILO Declaration on Social Justice for a Fair Globalization |
| ILO | 2012 | 4 | 30.05.2012 | 30.05.2012 | Elaboration of an Autonomous Recommendation on the Social Protection Floor |
| IOM | 2008 | 1 | 02.12.2008 | 05.12.2008 | General Debate |
| IOM | 2008 | 2 | 02.12.2008 | 05.12.2008 | Return Migration: Challenges and Opportunities |
| IOM | 2008 | 3 | 02.12.2008 | 05.12.2008 | Migration Highlights |
| IOM | 2008 | 4 | 18.06.2008 | 18.06.2008 | Applications for Membership in the Organisation |
| IOM | 2009 | 1 | 22.11.2009 | 26.11.2009 | Impact of the Global Financial Crisis in Terms of Reduced Remittances, Migrational Issues |
| IOM | 2009 | 2 | 22.11.2009 | 26.11.2009 | Human Rights and Migration: Working Together for Safe, Dignified and Secure Migration |
| IOM | 2009 | 3 | 22.11.2009 | 26.11.2009 | Global Forum on Migration and Development |
| IOM | 2009 | 4 | 29.06.2009 | 29.06.2009 | Applications for Membership in the Organisation |
| IOM | 2010 | 1 | 29.11.2010 | 02.12.2010 | General Debate: Migration, Humanitarian Assistance |
| IOM | 2010 | 2 | 29.11.2010 | 02.12.2010 | Migration and Social Change |
| IOM | 2010 | 3 | 29.11.2010 | 02.12.2010 | Migration Highlights : Key Developments |
| IOM | 2011 | 1 | 05.12.2011 | 07.12.2011 | General Debate: Interdependence Migration and Development, Humanitarian Response |
| IOM | 2011 | 3 | 05.12.2011 | 07.12.2011 | Special Panes: Migrant's Voices |
| IOM | 2012 | 1 | 27.11.2012 | 30.11.2012 | Refugee Situation in Somalia |
| IOM | 2012 | 2 | 27.11.2012 | 30.11.2012 | Managing Migration in Crisis Situations |
| IOM | 2012 | 3 | 27.11.2012 | 30.11.2012 | General Debate: Budget, Institutional Reform |
| ITTO | 2008 | 1 | 03.11.2008 | 08.11.2008 | Entry into Force of ITTA |

| IO | Year | Neg. | Start Date | End Date | Topic |
|---|---|---|---|---|---|
| ITTO | 2008 | 2 | 03.11.2008 | 08.11.2008 | Conservation and Sustainable Use of Biodiversity in Tropical Timber Producing Forests |
| ITTO | 2008 | 3 | 03.11.2008 | 08.11.2008 | Role of ITTO in Climate Change Adaption and Mitigation |
| ITTO | 2008 | 4 | 03.11.2008 | 08.11.2008 | ITTO Children's Environmental Education Programme |
| ITTO | 2009 | 1 | 09.11.2009 | 14.11.2009 | Informal Advisory Group, Time Management |
| ITTO | 2009 | 2 | 09.11.2009 | 14.11.2009 | Entry into Force of ITTA |
| ITTO | 2009 | 3 | 09.11.2009 | 14.11.2009 | Biennial Work Programme 2010–2011 |
| ITTO | 2009 | 4 | 09.11.2009 | 14.11.2009 | Proposal for the Establishment of a Private Sector Consultative Board |
| ITTO | 2010 | 1 | 13.12.2010 | 18.12.2010 | Report of the Informal Advisory Group (IAG): Financial Aspects, Next Council Session |
| ITTO | 2010 | 2 | 13.12.2010 | 18.12.2010 | Entry into Force of ITTA |
| ITTO | 2010 | 3 | 13.12.2010 | 18.12.2010 | Developments in the UNFCCC on Tropical Forests & Implications for Tropical Timber Economy |
| ITTO | 2010 | 4 | 13.12.2010 | 18.12.2010 | International Year of Biodiversity and International Year of Forests |
| ITTO | 2011 | 1 | 14.11.2011 | 19.11.2011 | Implementation of the CITES Programme |
| ITTO | 2011 | 2 | 14.11.2011 | 19.11.2011 | ITTO Biennial Work Programme and Funding |
| ITTO | 2011 | 3 | 14.11.2011 | 19.11.2011 | ITTO Thematic Programmes and Funding |
| ITTO | 2011 | 4 | 14.11.2011 | 19.11.2011 | Developments in the UNFCCC on Tropical Forests & Implications for Tropical Timber Economy |
| ITTO | 2012 | 1 | 05.11.2012 | 10.11.2012 | Report of the Informal Advisory Group (IAG): Financial Aspects, Next Council Session |
| ITTO | 2012 | 2 | 05.11.2012 | 10.11.2012 | Entry into Force of ITTA |
| ITTO | 2012 | 3 | 05.11.2012 | 10.11.2012 | ITTO Biennial Work Programme 2013–2014 |
| ITTO | 2012 | 4 | 05.11.2012 | 10.11.2012 | ITTO Strategic Action Plan 2013 |
| IWC | 2008 | 1 | 23.06.2008 | 27.06.2008 | Whale Stocks |
| IWC | 2008 | 2 | 23.06.2008 | 27.06.2008 | Aboriginal Subsistence Whaling |
| IWC | 2008 | 3 | 23.06.2008 | 27.06.2008 | Sanctuaries |
| IWC | 2008 | 4 | 23.06.2008 | 27.06.2008 | Whalewatching |
| IWC | 2009 | 1 | 22.06.2009 | 25.06.2009 | Whale Killing Methods and Associated Welfare Issues |
| IWC | 2009 | 2 | 22.06.2009 | 25.06.2009 | Aboriginal Subsistence Whaling |

(Continued)

**Table A3.1. Continued**

| IO | Year | Neg. | Start Date | End Date | Topic |
|---|---|---|---|---|---|
| IWC | 2009 | 3 | 22.06.2009 | 25.06.2009 | Whalewatching |
| IWC | 2009 | 4 | 22.06.2009 | 25.06.2009 | Small Cetaceans |
| IWC | 2010 | 1 | 21.06.2010 | 25.06.2010 | The IWC in the Future |
| IWC | 2010 | 2 | 21.06.2010 | 25.06.2010 | Whale Stocks |
| IWC | 2010 | 3 | 21.06.2010 | 25.06.2010 | Whale Killing Methods and Associated Welfare Issues |
| IWC | 2010 | 4 | 21.06.2010 | 25.06.2010 | Whalewatching |
| IWC | 2011 | 1 | 11.06.2011 | 14.06.2011 | The IWC in the Future |
| IWC | 2011 | 2 | 11.06.2011 | 14.06.2011 | Whale Stocks |
| IWC | 2011 | 3 | 11.06.2011 | 14.06.2011 | Aboriginal Subsistence Whaling |
| IWC | 2011 | 4 | 11.06.2011 | 14.06.2011 | North Atlantic Fin Whales |
| IWC | 2012 | 1 | 02.07.2012 | 06.07.2012 | Sanctuaries |
| IWC | 2012 | 2 | 02.07.2012 | 06.07.2012 | The IWC in the Future |
| IWC | 2012 | 3 | 02.07.2012 | 06.07.2012 | Aboriginal Subsistence Whaling |
| IWC | 2012 | 4 | 02.07.2012 | 06.07.2012 | Whalewatching |
| NASCO | 2008 | 1 | 03.06.2008 | 06.06.2008 | Canadian and U.S. Salmon Management Measures |
| NASCO | 2008 | 2 | 03.06.2008 | 06.06.2008 | Salmon Stocks in the Commission Area |
| NASCO | 2008 | 3 | 03.06.2008 | 06.06.2008 | Salmon Stocks in the Commission Area |
| NASCO | 2008 | 4 | 03.06.2008 | 06.06.2008 | Management of Atlantic Salmon under the Precautionary Approach |
| NASCO | 2009 | 1 | 02.06.2009 | 05.06.2009 | Canadian and U.S. Salmon Management Measures |
| NASCO | 2009 | 2 | 02.06.2009 | 05.06.2009 | Salmon Stocks in the Commission Area |
| NASCO | 2009 | 3 | 02.06.2009 | 05.06.2009 | Salmon Stocks in the Commission Area |
| NASCO | 2009 | 4 | 02.06.2009 | 05.06.2009 | Management of Atlantic Salmon under the Precautionary Approach |
| NASCO | 2010 | 1 | 01.06.2010 | 04.06.2010 | Salmon Stocks in the Commission Area |
| NASCO | 2010 | 2 | 01.06.2010 | 04.06.2010 | Salmon Stocks in the Commission Area |
| NASCO | 2010 | 3 | 01.06.2010 | 04.06.2010 | Salmon Stocks in the Commission Area |
| NASCO | 2010 | 4 | 01.06.2010 | 04.06.2010 | Management of Atlantic Salmon under the Precautionary Approach |
| NASCO | 2011 | 1 | 04.06.2011 | 06.06.2011 | Salmon Stocks in the Commission Area |
| NASCO | 2011 | 2 | 04.06.2011 | 06.06.2011 | Salmon Stocks in the Commission Area |

| IO | Year | Neg. | Start Date | End Date | Topic |
|----|------|------|------------|----------|-------|
| NASCO | 2011 | 3 | 04.06.2011 | 06.06.2011 | Salmon Stocks in the Commission Area |
| NASCO | 2011 | 4 | 04.06.2011 | 06.06.2011 | Management of Atlantic Salmon under the Precautionary Approach |
| NASCO | 2012 | 1 | 05.06.2012 | 08.06.2012 | Salmon Stocks in the Commission Area |
| NASCO | 2012 | 2 | 05.06.2012 | 08.06.2012 | Salmon Stocks in the Commission Area |
| NASCO | 2012 | 3 | 05.06.2012 | 08.06.2012 | Salmon Stocks in the Commission Area |
| NASCO | 2012 | 4 | 05.06.2012 | 08.06.2012 | Management of Atlantic Salmon under the Precautionary Approach |
| OPCW | 2008 | 1 | 02.12.2008 | 05.12.2008 | General Debate |
| OPCW | 2008 | 2 | 07.04.2008 | 18.04.2008 | General Debate |
| OPCW | 2008 | 3 | 02.12.2008 | 05.12.2008 | Universality of the Convention, National Implementation |
| OPCW | 2009 | 1 | 30.11.2009 | 04.12.2009 | General Debate |
| OPCW | 2009 | 2 | 13.10.2009 | 16.10.2009 | General Debate |
| OPCW | 2009 | 3 | 14.06.2009 | 17.06.2009 | General Debate |
| OPCW | 2009 | 4 | 21.04.2009 | 24.04.2009 | General Debate |
| OPCW | 2010 | 1 | 29.11.2010 | 03.12.2010 | General Debate |
| OPCW | 2010 | 2 | 29.06.2010 | 02.07.2010 | Destruction of Stockpiles, Support of Technical Secretariat |
| OPCW | 2010 | 3 | 20.04.2010 | 23.04.2010 | Terrorism, Destruction Deadline |
| OPCW | 2010 | 4 | 29.11.2010 | 03.12.2010 | Programme and Budget 2011, Destruction Deadline |
| OPCW | 2011 | 1 | 28.11.2011 | 02.12.2011 | General Debate |
| OPCW | 2011 | 2 | 28.11.2011 | 02.12.2011 | Status of Implementation of the Convention |
| OPCW | 2011 | 3 | 03.06.2011 | 06.06.2011 | General and Complete Disarmament |
| OPCW | 2011 | 4 | 15.02.2011 | 18.02.2011 | Universal Adherence to the Convention, Article X |
| OPCW | 2012 | 1 | 26.11.2012 | 29.11.2012 | Progress of Destruction, Guidelines |
| OPCW | 2012 | 2 | 25.09.2012 | 28.09.2012 | General Debate |
| OPCW | 2012 | 3 | 10.07.2012 | 13.07.2012 | General Debate |
| OPCW | 2012 | 4 | 01.05.2012 | 04.05.2012 | General Debate |
| SC | 2008 | 1 | 21.01.2008 | 21.01.2008 | Iraq: Structural, Political and Security Challenges |
| SC | 2008 | 2 | 22.01.2008 | 22.01.2008 | Humanitarian Situation in the Gaza Strip |
| SC | 2008 | 3 | 30.01.2008 | 30.01.2008 | Middle East Peace Process |
| SC | 2008 | 4 | 08.02.2008 | 08.02.2008 | African Union-United Nations Hybrid Operation in Darfur (UNAMID) |

(Continued)

**Table A3.1.  Continued**

| IO | Year | Neg. | Start Date | End Date | Topic |
|---|---|---|---|---|---|
| SC | 2009 | 1 | 07.01.2009 | 07.01.2009 | Conflict between Israel and Hamas Militants in the Gaza Strip |
| SC | 2009 | 2 | 08.01.2009 | 08.01.2009 | Refugee Situation Worldwide |
| SC | 2009 | 3 | 23.01.2009 | 23.01.2009 | The Challenges of Modern Peacekeeping |
| SC | 2009 | 4 | 09.02.2009 | 09.02.2009 | Situation in Sierra Leone |
| SC | 2010 | 1 | 27.09.2010 | 27.09.2010 | Threats to International Peace and Security Caused by Terrorist Acts |
| SC | 2010 | 2 | 22.11.2010 | 22.11.2010 | Protection of Civilians in Armed Conflict |
| SC | 2010 | 3 | 13.01.2010 | 13.01.2010 | Cooperation Between the United Nations and Regional and Subregional Organisations |
| SC | 2010 | 4 | 15.06.2010 | 15.06.2010 | Extended the Mandate of the United Nations Peacekeeping Force in Cyprus |
| SC | 2011 | 1 | 05.12.2011 | 05.12.2011 | Reinforcing Sanctions Regime Against Eritrea |
| SC | 2011 | 2 | 09.06.2011 | 09.06.2011 | Monitoring Sanctions against Iran |
| SC | 2011 | 3 | 17.03.2011 | 17.03.2011 | No-Fly Zone Over Libya |
| SC | 2011 | 4 | 18.02.2011 | 18.02.2011 | Fails to Adopt Text Demanding Israel to Halt Settlements |
| SC | 2012 | 1 | 26.09.2012 | 26.09.2012 | Collective Efforts for the Peaceful Settlement of Conflicts in the Middle East |
| SC | 2012 | 2 | 20.09.2012 | 20.09.2012 | Long Term Partnership between Afghanistan and the World Community |
| SC | 2012 | 3 | 30.08.2012 | 30.08.2012 | Situation in Syria |
| SC | 2012 | 4 | 03.10.2012 | 03.10.2012 | Haiti and Peacekeeping Mandate |
| UNCTAD | 2008 | 1 | 16.09.2008 | 16.09.2008 | Evolution of the International Trading System and of International Trade |
| UNCTAD | 2008 | 2 | 24.09.2008 | 24.09.2008 | Investment for Development: Transnational Corporations, Infrastructure and Development |
| UNCTAD | 2008 | 3 | 17.09.2008 | 17.09.2008 | Interdependence: Mobilizing Resources for Development |
| UNCTAD | 2008 | 4 | 22.09.2008 | 22.09.2008 | Development Strategies in a Globalized World |
| UNCTAD | 2009 | 1 | 15.09.2009 | 15.09.2009 | Development Strategies in a Globalized World: Challenge of Climate Change |
| UNCTAD | 2009 | 2 | 23.09.2009 | 23.09.2009 | UNCTAD's Communication Strategy and Publication Policy |

| IO | Year | Neg. | Start Date | End Date | Topic |
|---|---|---|---|---|---|
| UNCTAD | 2009 | 3 | 22.09.2009 | 22.09.2009 | Investment for Development and Technical Cooperation Activities |
| UNCTAD | 2009 | 4 | 18.09.2009 | 18.09.2009 | Implementation of the Programme of Action for the LDCs for the Decade |
| UNCTAD | 2010 | 1 | 08.06.2010 | 09.06.2010 | Discussion on the MDGs |
| UNCTAD | 2010 | 2 | 15.09.2010 | 28.09.2010 | President' Summary: Opening Statements |
| UNCTAD | 2010 | 3 | 09.06.2010 | 09.06.2010 | Discussion on the MDGs |
| UNCTAD | 2010 | 4 | 09.06.2010 | 09.06.2010 | Discussion on the MDGs |
| UNCTAD | 2011 | 1 | 12.09.2011 | 23.09.2011 | President' Summary: Opening Statements |
| UNCTAD | 2011 | 2 | 16.09.2011 | 16.09.2011 | Implementation of the Outcome from LDC-IV: UNCTAD's Contribution |
| UNCTAD | 2011 | 3 | 14.09.2011 | 14.09.2011 | Evolution of the International Trading System and of International Trade |
| UNCTAD | 2011 | 4 | 16.09.2011 | 16.09.2011 | Implications of Non-Equity Forms of Transnational Corporations' Operations |
| UNCTAD | 2012 | 1 | 17.09.2012 | 28.09.2012 | President' Summary: Opening Statements |
| UNCTAD | 2012 | 2 | 17.09.2012 | 28.09.2012 | UNCTAD Assistance to the Palestinian People |
| UNCTAD | 2012 | 3 | 20.09.2012 | 20.09.2012 | Economic Development in Africa: Structural Transformation and Sustainable Development |
| UNCTAD | 2012 | 4 | 22.04.2012 | 22.04.2012 | General Debate |
| UNEP | 2008 | 1 | 26.12.2008 | 26.12.2008 | Bali Plan; Issue of Mercury |
| UNEP | 2008 | 2 | 15.12.2008 | 15.12.2008 | Bali Plan; Issue of Mercury |
| UNEP | 2008 | 3 | 20.12.2008 | 20.12.2008 | Report of the Executive Director to the Committee |
| UNEP | 2008 | 4 | 15.12.2008 | 15.12.2008 | Report of the Work of the Subcommittees |
| UNEP | 2009 | 1 | 16.02.2009 | 20.02.2009 | Green Economy Initiative |
| UNEP | 2009 | 2 | 15.07.2009 | 18.07.2009 | Substances that Deplete the Ozone Layer |
| UNEP | 2009 | 3 | 16.02.2009 | 20.02.2009 | Mercury |
| UNEP | 2009 | 4 | 16.02.2009 | 20.02.2009 | Global Crises: national chaos?' – Towards a 'Green Economy |
| UNEP | 2010 | 1 | 15.06.2010 | 18.06.2010 | Substances that Deplete the Ozone Layer |
| UNEP | 2010 | 2 | 15.06.2010 | 15.06.2010 | Enhancing Cooperation with UN Organisations and Civil Society |
| UNEP | 2010 | 3 | 16.03.2010 | 16.03.2010 | Funding; Status of EU |

(Continued)

**Table A3.1. Continued**

| IO | Year | Neg. | Start Date | End Date | Topic |
|---|---|---|---|---|---|
| UNEP | 2010 | 4 | 16.03.2010 | 16.03.2010 | Climate Change; Chemicals |
| UNEP | 2011 | 1 | 21.02.2011 | 21.02.2011 | Preparations for the UN Conference on Sustainable Development |
| UNEP | 2011 | 2 | 21.02.2011 | 21.02.2011 | Green Economy Initiative |
| UNEP | 2011 | 4 | 19.12.2011 | 19.12.2011 | Capacity Building |
| UNEP | 2012 | 1 | 20.02.2012 | 22.02.2012 | Preparations United Nations Conference on Sustainable Development |
| UNEP | 2012 | 2 | 20.02.2012 | 20.02.2012 | Preparations United Nations Conference on Sustainable Development |
| UNEP | 2012 | 3 | 20.02.2012 | 22.02.2012 | Preparations United Nations Conference on Sustainable Development |
| UNESCO | 2008 | 1 | 03.07.2008 | 03.07.2008 | Sustainability of the World Heritage Fund |
| UNESCO | 2008 | 2 | 03.07.2008 | 03.07.2008 | Progress of the African World Heritage Fund |
| UNESCO | 2008 | 3 | 26.03.2008 | 28.03.2008 | Debate on Media Development Indicators |
| UNESCO | 2008 | 4 | 03.07.2008 | 03.07.2008 | Budget and Funding |
| UNESCO | 2009 | 1 | 22.06.2009 | 22.06.2009 | World Heritage Centre Activities and Implementation of World Heritage Committee Decisions |
| UNESCO | 2009 | 2 | 07.10.2009 | 07.10.2009 | General Policy Debate |
| UNESCO | 2009 | 3 | 11.09.2009 | 05.10.2009 | Consideration of the Draft Programme and Budget for 2010–2011 |
| UNESCO | 2009 | 4 | 11.09.2009 | 05.10.2009 | Rapport et Projet de Décision Recommandé au Conseil Exécutif |
| UNESCO | 2010 | 1 | 11.01.2010 | 11.01.2010 | Discussion of the Draft Operational Guidelines |
| UNESCO | 2010 | 2 | 26.07.2010 | 26.07.2010 | Implementation of the Decisions |
| UNESCO | 2010 | 3 | 24.03.2010 | 26.03.2010 | Debate on the Safety of Journalists and the Danger of Impunity: What Can IPDC Do? |
| UNESCO | 2010 | 4 | 24.03.2010 | 26.03.2010 | Free, Independent and Pluralistic Media: The Enabling Role of the State |
| UNESCO | 2011 | 1 | 09.11.2011 | 09.11.2011 | Working Capital Fund: Level and Administration |
| UNESCO | 2011 | 2 | 28.10.2011 | 28.10.2011 | Future Strategic and Programmatic Orientations of UNESCO |
| UNESCO | 2011 | 3 | 31.10.2011 | 31.10.2011 | Request for the Admission of Palestine to UNESCO |

| IO | Year | Neg. | Start Date | End Date | Topic |
|---|---|---|---|---|---|
| UNESCO | 2011 | 4 | 02.11.2011 | 02.11.2011 | Tenth Anniversary of the UNESCO Universal Declaration of Cultural Diversity |
| UNESCO | 2012 | 1 | 22.03.2012 | 23.03.2012 | Debate on the Safety of Journalists and the Issue of Impunity |
| UNESCO | 2012 | 2 | 22.03.2012 | 23.03.2012 | Debate on Gender and Media |
| UNESCO | 2012 | 3 | 15.10.2012 | 15.10.2012 | Buildings |
| UNESCO | 2012 | 4 | 01.03.2012 | 01.03.2012 | Financial Situation and its Implications for the Implementation of the Programme |
| UNFCCC | 2008 | 1 | 01.12.2008 | 12.12.2008 | High-Level Segment |
| UNFCCC | 2008 | 2 | 01.12.2008 | 12.12.2008 | Other Matters |
| UNFCCC | 2008 | 3 | 21.08.2008 | 27.08.2008 | Organisational Matters |
| UNFCCC | 2008 | 4 | 31.03.2008 | 04.04.2008 | Mission Reduction Targets and Identification of Ways to Enhance their Effectiveness |
| UNFCCC | 2009 | 1 | 07.12.2009 | 19.12.2009 | High-Level Segment |
| UNFCCC | 2009 | 2 | 07.12.2009 | 19.12.2009 | Organisational Matters |
| UNFCCC | 2009 | 3 | 01.06.2009 | 12.06.2009 | Organisation of the Work of the Session |
| UNFCCC | 2009 | 4 | 29.03.2009 | 08.04.2009 | Opening Statements |
| UNFCCC | 2010 | 1 | 29.11.2010 | 10.12.2010 | Agenda Items Related to the Kyoto Protocol |
| UNFCCC | 2010 | 2 | 29.11.2010 | 10.12.2010 | Organisational Matters |
| UNFCCC | 2010 | 3 | 04.10.2010 | 09.10.2010 | Organisation of the Work of the Session |
| UNFCCC | 2010 | 4 | 09.04.2010 | 11.04.2010 | Organisation and Methods of Work in 2010 |
| UNFCCC | 2011 | 1 | 28.11.2011 | 11.12.2011 | Amendments to the Convention under Articles 15 and 16 |
| UNFCCC | 2011 | 2 | 28.11.2011 | 11.12.2011 | Green Climate Fund – Report of the Transitional Committee |
| UNFCCC | 2011 | 3 | 05.04.2011 | 08.04.2011 | Opening Statements |
| UNFCCC | 2011 | 4 | 28.11.2011 | 11.12.2011 | Agenda Items 12 and 19 of the Conference of the Parties Related to the Kyoto Protocol |
| UNFCCC | 2012 | 1 | 26.11.2012 | 08.12.2012 | Organisational Matters |
| UNFCCC | 2012 | 2 | 26.11.2012 | 08.12.2012 | Long-Term Cooperative Action under the Convention |
| UNFCCC | 2012 | 3 | 26.11.2012 | 08.12.2012 | Agenda Items 18 and 19 of the Conference of the Parties Related to the Kyoto Protocol |
| UNFCCC | 2012 | 4 | 15.05.2012 | 24.05.2012 | Organisational Matters |
| UNGA C1 | 2008 | 1 | 14.10.2008 | 16.10.2008 | Nuclear Weapons |
| UNGA C1 | 2008 | 2 | 17.10.2008 | 20.10.2008 | Other Weapons of Mass Destruction |

(Continued)

**Table A3.1.  Continued**

| IO | Year | Neg. | Start Date | End Date | Topic |
|---|---|---|---|---|---|
| UNGA C1 | 2008 | 3 | 20.10.2008 | 22.10.2008 | Conventional Weapons |
| UNGA C1 | 2008 | 4 | 24.10.2008 | 24.10.2008 | Regional Disarmament and Security |
| UNGA C1 | 2009 | 1 | 14.10.2009 | 15.10.2009 | Nuclear Weapons |
| UNGA C1 | 2009 | 2 | 16.10.2009 | 16.10.2009 | Other Weapons of Mass Destruction |
| UNGA C1 | 2009 | 3 | 16.10.2009 | 21.10.2009 | Conventional Weapons |
| UNGA C1 | 2009 | 4 | 19.10.2009 | 19.10.2009 | Outer Space |
| UNGA C1 | 2010 | 1 | 14.10.2010 | 15.10.2010 | Nuclear Weapons |
| UNGA C1 | 2010 | 2 | 15.10.2010 | 15.10.2010 | Disarmament Machinery |
| UNGA C1 | 2010 | 3 | 18.10.2010 | 20.10.2012 | Conventional Weapons |
| UNGA C1 | 2010 | 4 | 20.10.2010 | 22.10.2010 | Regional Disarmament and Security |
| UNGA C1 | 2011 | 1 | 12.10.2011 | 14.10.2011 | Nuclear Weapons |
| UNGA C1 | 2011 | 2 | 17.10.2011 | 17.10.2011 | Other Weapons of Mass Destruction |
| UNGA C1 | 2011 | 3 | 17.10.2011 | 20.10.2011 | Conventional Weapons |
| UNGA C1 | 2011 | 4 | 20.11.2011 | 24.10.2011 | Regional Disarmament and Security |
| UNGA C1 | 2012 | 1 | 17.10.2012 | 22.10.2012 | Nuclear Weapons |
| UNGA C1 | 2012 | 2 | 22.10.2012 | 22.10.2012 | Other Weapons of Mass Destruction |
| UNGA C1 | 2012 | 3 | 23.10.2012 | 01.11.2012 | Conventional Weapons |
| UNGA C1 | 2012 | 4 | 24.10.2012 | 01.11.2012 | Regional Disarmament and Security |
| UNGA C2 | 2008 | 1 | 06.10.2008 | 06.10.2008 | Adopt Varied Responses to Avert Global Recession |
| UNGA C2 | 2008 | 2 | 07.10.2008 | 07.10.2008 | Agricultural Production and Sustainable Development |
| UNGA C2 | 2008 | 3 | 13.10.2008 | 13.10.2008 | Regulatory Overhaul and Stronger Surveillance of International Financial Institutions |
| UNGA C2 | 2008 | 4 | 28.10.2008 | 28.10.2008 | Sustainable Development |
| UNGA C2 | 2009 | 1 | 05.10.2009 | 05.10.2009 | Nine Joint Initiatives to Respond to Several Crises |
| UNGA C2 | 2009 | 2 | 06.10.2009 | 06.10.2009 | Global Food Crisis |
| UNGA C2 | 2009 | 3 | 07.10.2009 | 07.10.2009 | Measures to Stop Global Warming |
| UNGA C2 | 2009 | 4 | 12.10.2009 | 12.10.2009 | Restore Global Economic Health and Help Developing Nations |
| UNGA C2 | 2010 | 1 | 05.10.2010 | 05.10.2010 | Rich Nations Pressed to Shoulder Historic Responsibility |
| UNGA C2 | 2010 | 2 | 13.10.2010 | 13.10.2010 | Funding for United Nations Development Activities |
| UNGA C2 | 2010 | 3 | 18.10.2010 | 18.10.2010 | Programme of Action for the LDCs |
| UNGA C2 | 2010 | 4 | 21.10.2010 | 21.10.2010 | Deadline for Meeting the Millennium Development Goals |
| UNGA C2 | 2011 | 1 | 03.10.2011 | 03.10.2011 | Equitable Development Models |
| UNGA C2 | 2011 | 2 | 10.10.2011 | 10.10.2011 | External Debt Sustainability and Development |
| UNGA C2 | 2011 | 3 | 17.10.2011 | 17.10.2011 | Eradicating Poverty |
| UNGA C2 | 2011 | 4 | 25.10.2011 | 25.10.2011 | Agriculture Development and Food Security |

| IO | Year | Neg. | Start Date | End Date | Topic |
|---|---|---|---|---|---|
| UNGA C2 | 2012 | 1 | 10.10.2012 | 10.10.2012 | Eradicating Poverty |
| UNGA C2 | 2012 | 2 | 17.10.2012 | 17.10.2012 | Resources Beyond Mandate |
| UNGA C2 | 2012 | 3 | 08.11.2012 | 08.11.2012 | Desertification |
| UNGA C2 | 2012 | 4 | 12.11.2012 | 12.11.2012 | Mobil Telephony and Digital Development |
| UNGA C3 | 2008 | 1 | 10.10.2008 | 10.10.2008 | Strategies to Combat Transnational Organised Crime |
| UNGA C3 | 2008 | 2 | 16.10.2008 | 16.10.2008 | Promotion and Protection of Rights of Children |
| UNGA C3 | 2008 | 3 | 28.10.2008 | 28.10.2008 | Caution Against the 'Politicization' of Human Rights Issues |
| UNGA C3 | 2008 | 4 | 11.11.2008 | 11.11.2008 | Approves Drafts on Human Rights, Poverty, Indigenous Issues |
| UNGA C3 | 2009 | 1 | 06.10.2009 | 06.10.2009 | Well-Being of the World's Youth |
| UNGA C3 | 2009 | 2 | 08.10.2009 | 08.10.2009 | Crime Prevention, Criminal Justice and International Drug Control |
| UNGA C3 | 2009 | 3 | 12.10.2009 | 12.10.2009 | Women's Empowerment |
| UNGA C3 | 2009 | 4 | 16.10.2009 | 16.10.2009 | Children's Rights |
| UNGA C3 | 2010 | 1 | 05.10.2010 | 05.10.2010 | Social Development |
| UNGA C3 | 2010 | 2 | 07.10.2010 | 07.10.2010 | Crime Prevention, Criminal Justice and International Drug Control |
| UNGA C3 | 2010 | 3 | 12.10.2010 | 12.10.2010 | Women's Empowerment |
| UNGA C3 | 2010 | 4 | 27.10.2010 | 27.10.2010 | Promoting Human Rights |
| UNGA C3 | 2011 | 1 | 06.10.2011 | 06.10.2011 | Crime Prevention, Criminal Justice and International Drug Control |
| UNGA C3 | 2011 | 2 | 11.10.2011 | 11.10.2011 | Advancement of Women |
| UNGA C3 | 2011 | 3 | 14.10.2011 | 14.10.2011 | Promotion and Protection of the Rights of the Child |
| UNGA C3 | 2011 | 4 | 28.10.2011 | 28.10.2011 | Combat Racism, Racial Discrimination, Xenophobia and Related Intolerance |
| UNGA C3 | 2012 | 1 | 18.10.2012 | 18.10.2012 | Fight Transnational Organised Crime and Bring Justice |
| UNGA C3 | 2012 | 2 | 06.11.2012 | 06.11.2012 | Several Human Rights Issues |
| UNGA C3 | 2012 | 3 | 14.11.2012 | 14.11.2012 | Funding for Human Rights Challenges |
| UNGA C3 | 2012 | 4 | 26.11.2012 | 26.11.2012 | Ending the Practice of Female Genital Mutilation |
| UNGA C4 | 2008 | 1 | 06.10.2008 | 06.10.2008 | Decolonization Issues |
| UNGA C4 | 2008 | 2 | 15.10.2008 | 15.10.2008 | Peaceful Use of Outer Space |
| UNGA C4 | 2008 | 3 | 20.10.2008 | 20.10.2008 | General Debate in Information |
| UNGA C4 | 2008 | 4 | 27.10.2008 | 27.10.2008 | Whole Question of Peacekeeping |
| UNGA C4 | 2009 | 1 | 09.10.2009 | 09.10.2009 | Decolonization Issues |
| UNGA C4 | 2009 | 2 | 21.10.2009 | 21.10.2009 | International Cooperation in the Peaceful Uses of Outer Space |
| UNGA C4 | 2009 | 3 | 28.10.2009 | 28.10.2009 | Whole Question of Peacekeeping |

(Continued)

**Table A3.1. Continued**

| IO | Year | Neg. | Start Date | End Date | Topic |
|---|---|---|---|---|---|
| UNGA C4 | 2009 | 4 | 03.11.2009 | 03.11.2009 | Debate on the Work of UNRWA |
| UNGA C4 | 2010 | 1 | 08.10.2010 | 08.10.2010 | Decolonization Issues |
| UNGA C4 | 2010 | 2 | 14.10.2010 | 14.10.2010 | International Cooperation in the Peaceful Uses of Outer Space |
| UNGA C4 | 2010 | 3 | 26.10.2010 | 26.10.2010 | Whole Question of Peacekeeping |
| UNGA C4 | 2010 | 4 | 08.11.2010 | 08.11.2010 | General Debate on Israeli Practices Affecting the Human Rights of the Palestinian People |
| UNGA C4 | 2011 | 1 | 13.10.2011 | 13.10.2011 | Preventing an Arms Race in Space |
| UNGA C4 | 2011 | 2 | 21.10.2011 | 21.10.2011 | Effects of Atomic Radiation |
| UNGA C4 | 2011 | 3 | 28.10.2011 | 28.10.2011 | Consideration of Mine Action Assistance |
| UNGA C4 | 2011 | 4 | 04.11.2011 | 04.11.2011 | Debate on the Work of UNRWA |
| UNGA C4 | 2012 | 1 | 12.10.2012 | 12.10.2012 | Decolonization Issues |
| UNGA C4 | 2012 | 2 | 02.11.2012 | 02.11.2012 | Review of Peacekeeping and Concluded its Consideration of the Peaceful Uses of Outer Space |
| UNGA C4 | 2012 | 3 | 08.11.2012 | 08.11.2012 | Improvement in Both the Operational and Doctrinal Aspects of Peacekeeping |
| UNGA C4 | 2012 | 4 | 07.11.2012 | 07.11.2012 | Debate on the Work of UNRWA |
| UNHCR | 2008 | 1 | 09.10.2008 | 09.10.2008 | Programme Budgets, Management, Financial Control and Administrative Oversight |
| UNHCR | 2008 | 2 | 06.10.2008 | 06.10.2008 | General Debate Humanitarian Space |
| UNHCR | 2008 | 3 | 08.10.2008 | 08.10.2008 | International Protection, Asylum |
| UNHCR | 2009 | 1 | 28.09.2009 | 28.09.2009 | General Debate on Displaced Persons |
| UNHCR | 2009 | 2 | 30.09.2009 | 30.09.2009 | International Protection |
| UNHCR | 2009 | 3 | 01.10.2009 | 01.10.2009 | Programme Budgets, Management, Financial Control and Administrative Oversight |
| UNHCR | 2010 | 1 | 04.10.2010 | 04.10.2010 | General Debate on Asylum |
| UNHCR | 2010 | 2 | 06.10.2010 | 06.10.2010 | International Protection |
| UNHCR | 2010 | 3 | 07.10.2010 | 07.10.2010 | Programme Budgets, Management, Financial Control and Administrative Oversight |
| UNHCR | 2010 | 4 | 07.10.2010 | 07.10.2010 | Partnerships with NGOs |
| UNHCR | 2011 | 1 | 05.10.2011 | 05.10.2011 | International Protection |
| UNHCR | 2011 | 2 | 06.10.2011 | 06.10.2011 | Programme Budgets, Management, Financial Control and Administrative Oversight |
| UNHCR | 2011 | 3 | 06.10.2011 | 06.10.2011 | Coordination with NGOs |

| IO | Year | Neg. | Start Date | End Date | Topic |
|---|---|---|---|---|---|
| UNHCR | 2011 | 4 | 03.10.2011 | 03.10.2011 | General Debate on Asylum |
| UNHCR | 2012 | 1 | 01.10.2012 | 01.10.2012 | General Debate on International Support and Assistance |
| UNHCR | 2012 | 2 | 04.10.2012 | 04.10.2012 | HIV; New Technologies |
| UNHCR | 2012 | 3 | 04.10.2012 | 04.10.2012 | Programme Budgets, Management, Financial Control and Administrative Oversight |
| UNHCR | 2012 | 4 | 04.10.2012 | 04.10.2012 | Consideration of Reports Relating to Programme and Administrative Oversight and Evaluation |
| WHO | 2008 | 1 | 26.05.2008 | 26.05.2008 | Human Organ and Tissue Transplantation |
| WHO | 2008 | 2 | 22.01.2008 | 22.01.2008 | Climate Change and Health |
| WHO | 2008 | 3 | 21.01.2008 | 21.01.2008 | Pandemic Influenza Preparedness: Sharing of Influenza Viruses and Access to Vaccines |
| WHO | 2008 | 4 | 25.01.2008 | 25.01.2008 | Infant and Young Child Nutrition: Biennial Progress Report |
| WHO | 2009 | 1 | 23.05.2009 | 23.05.2009 | Global Elimination of Measles |
| WHO | 2009 | 2 | 23.05.2009 | 23.05.2009 | Availability, Safety and Quality of Blood Products |
| WHO | 2009 | 3 | 21.01.2009 | 21.01.2009 | Primary Health Care, Including Health System Strengthening |
| WHO | 2009 | 4 | 24.01.2009 | 24.01.2009 | Public Health, Innovation and Intellectual Property: Global Strategy and Plan of Action |
| WHO | 2010 | 1 | 17.05.2010 | 17.05.2010 | Pandemic Influenza Preparedness: Sharing of Influenza Viruses and Access to Vaccines |
| WHO | 2010 | 2 | 19.05.2010 | 19.05.2010 | Counterfeit Medical Products |
| WHO | 2010 | 3 | 18.05.2010 | 18.05.2010 | Public Health, Innovation and Intellectual Property: Global Strategy and Plan of Action |
| WHO | 2010 | 4 | 19.05.2010 | 19.05.2010 | Infant and Young Child Nutrition: Biennial Progress Report |
| WHO | 2011 | 1 | 17.01.2011 | 17.01.2011 | Public Health, Innovation and Intellectual Property |
| WHO | 2011 | 2 | 18.01.2011 | 18.01.2011 | Cholera: Mechanism for Control and Prevention |
| WHO | 2011 | 3 | 19.01.2011 | 19.01.2011 | The Future of Financing for WHO |
| WHO | 2011 | 4 | 21.01.2011 | 21.01.2011 | Prevention and Control of Noncommunicable Diseases |
| WHO | 2012 | 1 | 28.05.2012 | 28.05.2012 | Outcome of the Sixty-Fifth World Health Assembly |
| WHO | 2012 | 2 | 28.05.2012 | 28.05.2012 | WHO Reform |

(Continued)

**Table A3.1. Continued**

| IO | Year | Neg. | Start Date | End Date | Topic |
|---|---|---|---|---|---|
| WHO | 2012 | 3 | 30.05.2012 | 30.05.2012 | Membership of the Independent Expert Oversight Advisory Committee |
| WHO | 2012 | 4 | 24.05.2012 | 24.05.2012 | WHO Reform |
| WIPO | 2008 | 1 | 12.12.2008 | 12.12.2008 | General Statements |
| WIPO | 2008 | 2 | 22.09.2008 | 30.09.2008 | Proposal for a Study on the Possible Introduction of 'Filing Languages' in the Madrid System |
| WIPO | 2008 | 3 | 10.12.2008 | 11.12.2008 | Revised Program and Budget for 2008/09 |
| WIPO | 2008 | 4 | 07.07.2008 | 11.07.2008 | Consideration of Work Program for Implementation of Adopted Recommendations |
| WIPO | 2009 | 1 | 22.09.2009 | 01.10.2009 | General Statements |
| WIPO | 2009 | 2 | 22.09.2009 | 01.10.2009 | PCT Working Group |
| WIPO | 2009 | 3 | 16.11.2009 | 20.11.2009 | General Statements on Development Agenda |
| WIPO | 2009 | 4 | 22.09.2009 | 01.10.2009 | New Conference Hall Project |
| WIPO | 2010 | 1 | 22.09.2010 | 29.09.2010 | General Statements |
| WIPO | 2010 | 2 | 22.09.2010 | 29.09.2010 | A Progress Report on the Revision of the WIPO Staff Regulations and Staff Rules |
| WIPO | 2010 | 3 | 22.09.2010 | 29.09.2010 | PTC Union |
| WIPO | 2010 | 4 | 22.09.2010 | 29.09.2010 | Report of the Committee on Development and Intellectual Property |
| WIPO | 2011 | 1 | 26.09.2011 | 05.10.2011 | General Statements on Economic Development |
| WIPO | 2011 | 2 | 26.09.2011 | 05.10.2011 | Webcasting at WIPO |
| WIPO | 2011 | 3 | 26.09.2011 | 05.10.2011 | Future Development of the PCT System |
| WIPO | 2011 | 4 | 14.07.2011 | 14.07.2011 | Conclusions |
| WIPO | 2012 | 1 | 01.10.2012 | 09.10.2012 | Implementation of the Development Agenda Recommendations |
| WIPO | 2012 | 2 | 01.10.2012 | 09.10.2012 | Protection-Related Issues |
| WIPO | 2012 | 3 | 01.10.2012 | 09.10.2012 | Outcome of the Beijing Diplomatic Conference on the Protection of Audiovisual Performances |
| WIPO | 2012 | 4 | 01.10.2012 | 09.10.2012 | Implementation of the Development Agenda Recommendations |
| WTO | 2008 | 1 | 05.02.2008 | 06.02.2008 | Accession of Ukraine |
| WTO | 2008 | 2 | 31.07.2008 | 31.07.2008 | Discussion and General Statements on Agriculture and Nama |
| WTO | 2008 | 3 | 07.05.2008 | 07.05.2008 | Discussion and General Statements on Food Crisis |
| WTO | 2008 | 4 | 14.10.2008 | 14.10.2008 | Discussion and General Statements on Agriculture |

| IO | Year | Neg. | Start Date | End Date | Topic |
|---|---|---|---|---|---|
| WTO | 2009 | 1 | 10.07.2009 | 10.07.2009 | Environmental Requirements and Market Access |
| WTO | 2009 | 2 | 26.05.2009 | 27.05.2009 | Discussion and General Statements on DOHA Round negotiations |
| WTO | 2009 | 3 | 28.07.2009 | 28.07.2009 | Aid for Trade |
| WTO | 2009 | 4 | 19.02.2009 | 19.02.2009 | Surveillance of Implementation of Recommendations Adopted by the DSB |
| WTO | 2010 | 1 | 04.05.2010 | 04.05.2010 | Discussion and General Statements on Multilateral System |
| WTO | 2010 | 2 | 04.05.2010 | 04.05.2010 | The Financial and Economic Crisis and the Role of the WTO |
| WTO | 2010 | 3 | 22.02.2010 | 22.02.2010 | Accession of Developing Countries |
| WTO | 2010 | 4 | 14.12.2010 | 14.12.2010 | Transparency for Preferential Trade Arrangements – Draft Decision |
| WTO | 2011 | 1 | 22.02.2011 | 22.02.2011 | Discussion and General Statements on Developing Countries |
| WTO | 2011 | 2 | 22.02.2011 | 22.02.2011 | Review of the Exemption Provided Under Paragraph 3 of the GATT 1994 |
| WTO | 2011 | 3 | 27.07.2011 | 27.07.2011 | Aid for Trade |
| WTO | 2011 | 4 | 27.07.2011 | 27.07.2011 | Work Programme on E-Commerce |
| WTO | 2012 | 1 | 25.07.2012 | 26.06.2012 | Accession of Vanuatu |
| WTO | 2012 | 2 | 25.07.2012 | 26.06.2012 | Discussion and General Statements on Trade Facilitation |
| WTO | 2012 | 3 | 01.05.2012 | 01.05.2012 | Discussion and General Statements on Global Value Chains |
| WTO | 2012 | 4 | 01.05.2012 | 01.05.2012 | Openness and Improving of Observer Status |

**Table A3.2.  Factor analysis of policy fields**

| Policy Field | Factor1 | Factor2 | Factor3 | Factor4 | Factor5 | Factor6 | Uniqueness |
|---|---|---|---|---|---|---|---|
| Agriculture | 0.2679 | −0.144 | 0.3759 | −0.024 | −0.0673 | 0.0412 | 0.7594 |
| Development | 0.376 | 0.4007 | −0.0378 | 0.2136 | 0.0832 | 0.0178 | 0.6438 |
| Education | 0.0252 | 0.0875 | −0.015 | −0.0826 | 0.1072 | −0.1687 | 0.9447 |
| Environment/ ecology | 0.351 | −0.2054 | 0.3679 | −0.0329 | −0.1344 | −0.0695 | 0.6753 |
| Finance/ economy | 0.4119 | 0.1921 | −0.0366 | 0.2047 | −0.012 | 0.0271 | 0.7493 |
| Health | −0.06 | −0.0036 | 0.0639 | −0.1872 | 0.4078 | −0.0087 | 0.7909 |
| Human rights | −0.1995 | 0.3186 | −0.0174 | −0.3073 | −0.1831 | 0.0597 | 0.7269 |
| Internal issues | 0.2441 | −0.3865 | −0.5033 | −0.0166 | −0.06 | 0.0174 | 0.5335 |
| Technology | 0.101 | −0.1122 | 0.1189 | −0.0132 | 0.1995 | 0.1413 | 0.9031 |
| Trade | −0.0326 | 0.0855 | −0.0313 | 0.2636 | 0.047 | −0.035 | 0.9177 |
| Security | −0.6517 | 0.0045 | 0.1279 | 0.2804 | −0.0422 | 0.0133 | 0.4783 |
| Social affairs | 0.1323 | 0.4039 | −0.0498 | −0.1544 | −0.0559 | 0.0014 | 0.7899 |

# Annex (Chapter 4)

**Table A4.1.  Descriptive statistics**

| Variables | | Obs | Mean | Std. Dev. | Min | Max |
|---|---|---|---|---|---|---|
| Member state properties | Government effectiveness | 17381 | −0.052 | 0.976 | −2.239 | 2.430 |
| | Polity | 17381 | 4.102 | 6.226 | −10 | 10 |
| | GDP (billions, log); fixed part | 17381 | 76.485 | 1375.141 | −1459.913 | 14129.79 |
| | GDP (billions, log); random part | 17381 | 408.733 | 446.399 | 25.766 | 2114.809 |
| | Membership in ROs | 17381 | 3.243 | 1.610 | 0 | 6 |
| RO properties | RO size | 741 | 34.899 | 8.666 | 21.286 | 56 |
| | RO policy scope | 409 | 2.685 | 1.127 | 0 | 5.5 |
| | RO office at IO HQs (dummy) | 741 | 0.178 | 0.204 | 0 | 0.8 |
| IO properties | IO size | 27 | 159.557 | 55.203 | 7 | 198 |
| | IO majority | 27 | 0.855 | 0.352 | 0 | 1 |
| IO negotiation issues | Agriculture | 512 | 0.043 | 0.204 | 0 | 1 |
| | Development | 512 | 0.258 | 0.437 | 0 | 1 |
| | Education | 512 | 0.001 | 0.029 | 0 | 1 |
| | Environment, ecology | 512 | 0.122 | 0.327 | 0 | 1 |
| | Finance, economy | 512 | 0.166 | 0.372 | 0 | 1 |
| | Health | 512 | 0.040 | 0.197 | 0 | 1 |
| | Human rights | 512 | 0.150 | 0.357 | 0 | 1 |
| | Internal issues | 512 | 0.287 | 0.452 | 0 | 1 |
| | Technology | 512 | 0.039 | 0.193 | 0 | 1 |
| | Trade | 512 | 0.067 | 0.249 | 0 | 1 |
| | Security | 512 | 0.241 | 0.428 | 0 | 1 |
| | Social affairs | 512 | 0.156 | 0.363 | 0 | 1 |

*(Continued)*

325

**Table A4.1.  Continued**

| Variables | | Obs | Mean | Std. Dev. | Min | Max |
|---|---|---|---|---|---|---|
| Cross-level effects | RO homogeneity | 17360 | 10.003 | 7.275 | 1.098 | 28.139 |
| | RO chair position | 17360 | 0.011 | 0.105 | 0 | 1 |
| | RO policy overlap | 17360 | 0.323 | 0.337 | 0 | 2.6 |
| | Formal status of RO in IO | 17360 | 0.007 | 0.036 | 0 | 0.5 |
| | RO office at IO HQs | 17360 | 0.041 | 0.515 | 0 | 13 |

## A4.2  MODEL DIAGNOSTICS FOR COMPREHENSIVE MULTILEVEL MODELS

## A4.2.1. Model 1

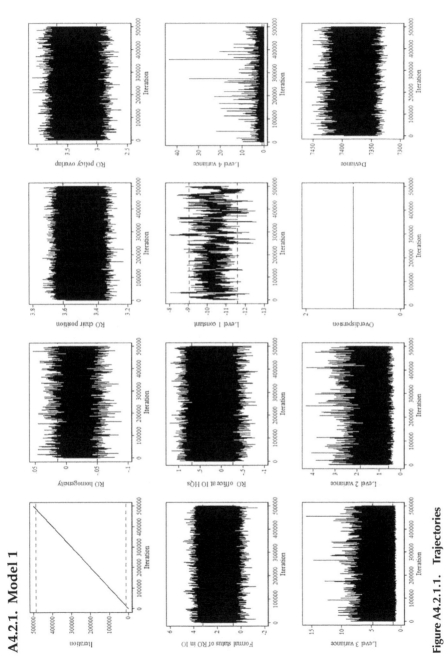

**Figure A4.2.1.1.    Trajectories**

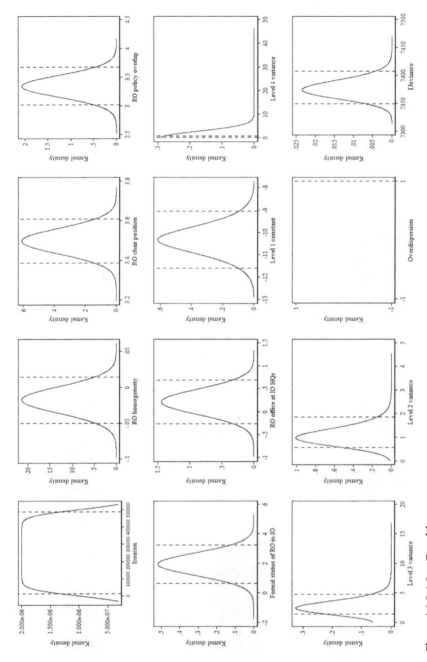

**Figure A4.2.1.2.    Densities**

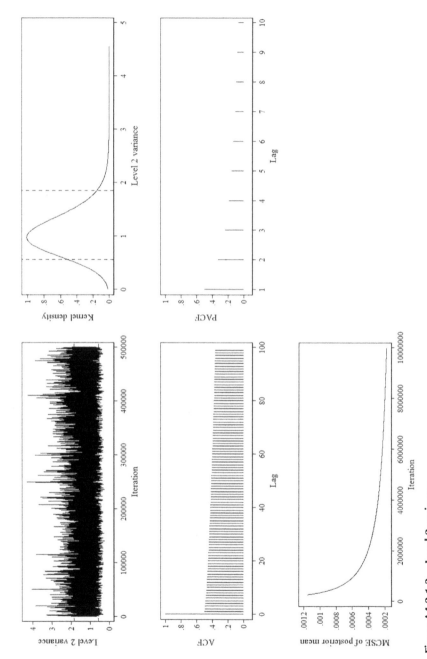

**Figure A4.2.1.3.    Level 2 variance**

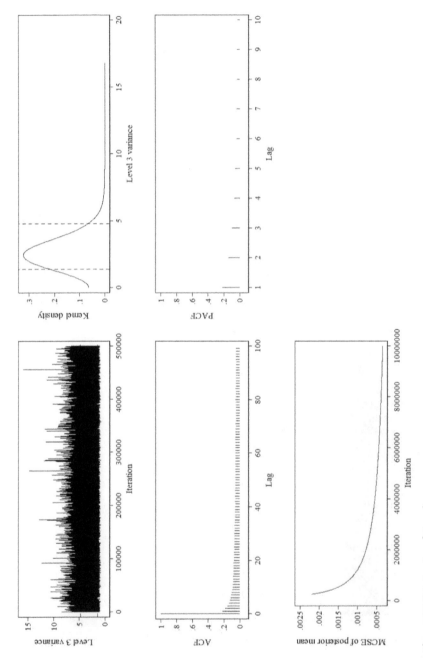

**Figure A4.2.1.4.** Level 3 variance

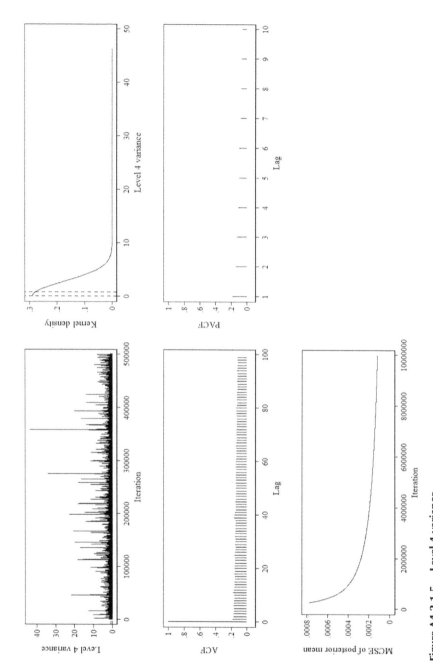

**Figure A4.2.1.5. Level 4 variance**

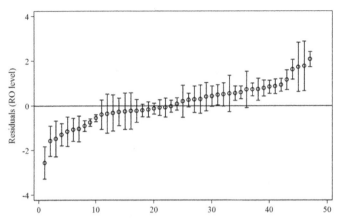

**Figure A4.2.1.6.    Residuals (RO level)**

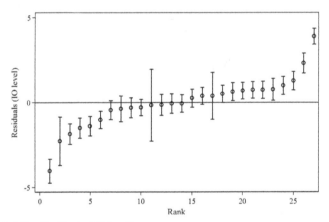

**Figure A4.2.1.7.    Residuals (IO level)**

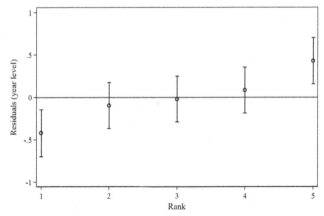

**Figure A4.2.1.8.    Residuals (year level)**

## A4.2.2. Model 2

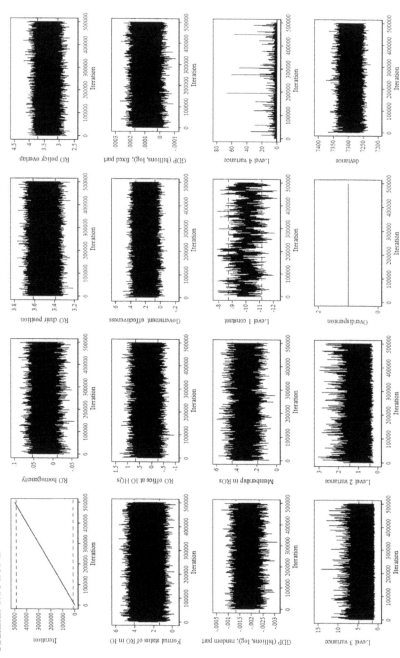

**Figure A4.2.2.1.   Trajectories**

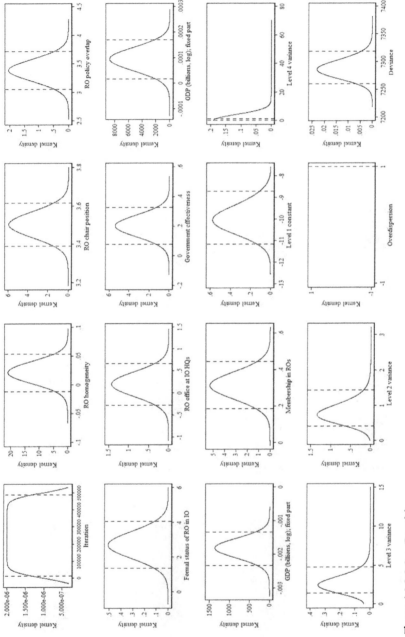

**Figure A4.2.2.2. Densities**

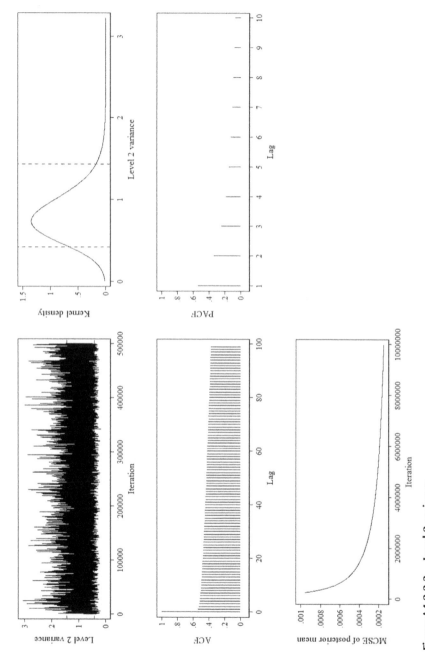

**Figure A4.2.2.3.  Level 2 variance**

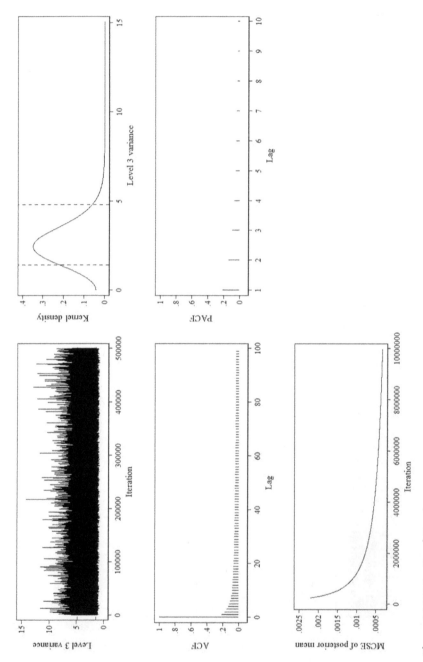

**Figure A4.2.2.4. Level 3 variance**

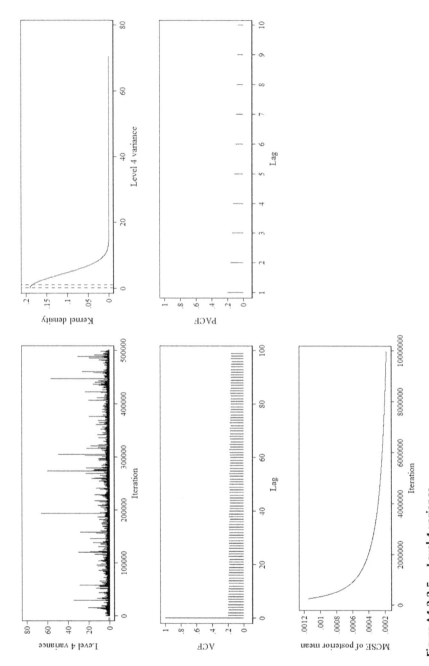

**Figure A4.2.2.5.    Level 4 variance**

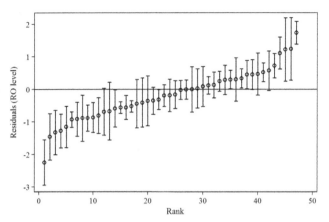

**Figure A4.2.2.6.   Residuals (RO level)**

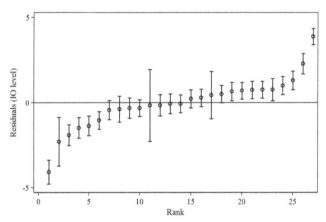

**Figure A4.2.2.7.   Residuals (IO level)**

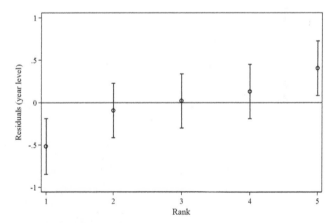

**Figure A4.2.2.8.   Residuals (year level)**

## A4.2.3. Model 3

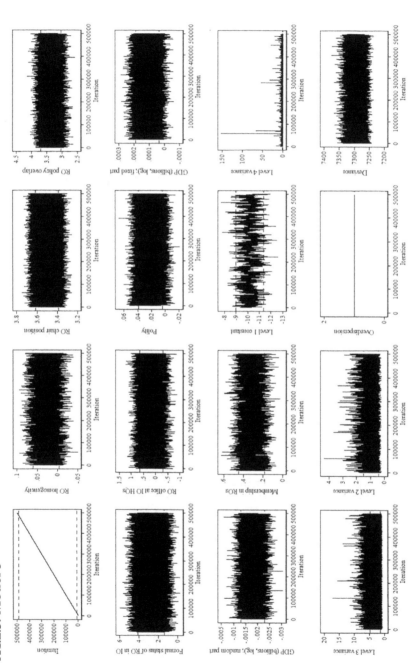

**Figure A4.2.3.1. Trajectories**

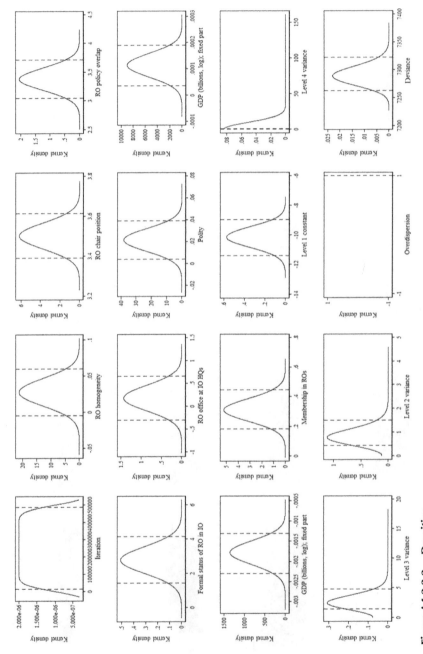

**Figure A4.2.3.2.  Densities**

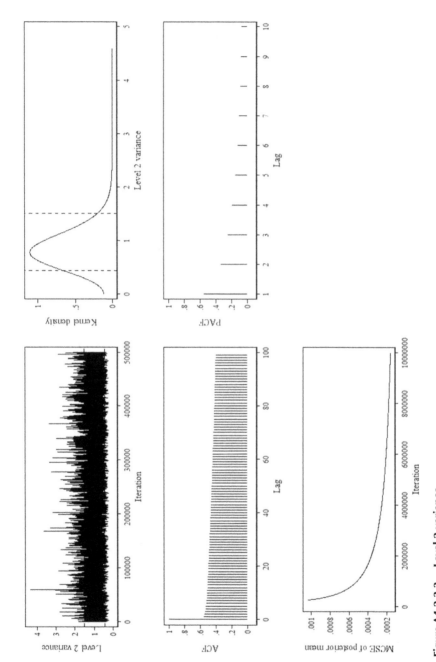

**Figure A4.2.3.3. Level 2 variance**

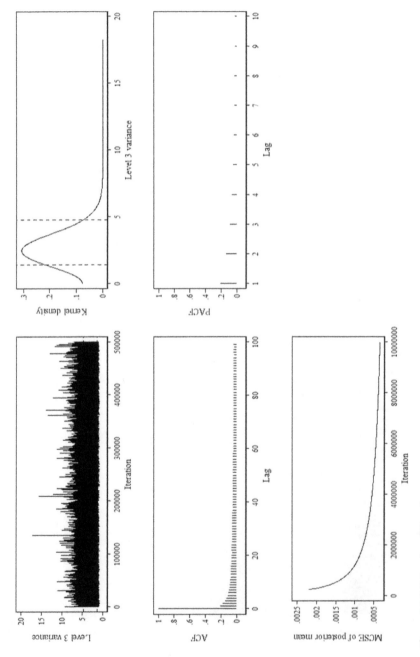

**Figure A4.2.3.4.    Level 3 variance**

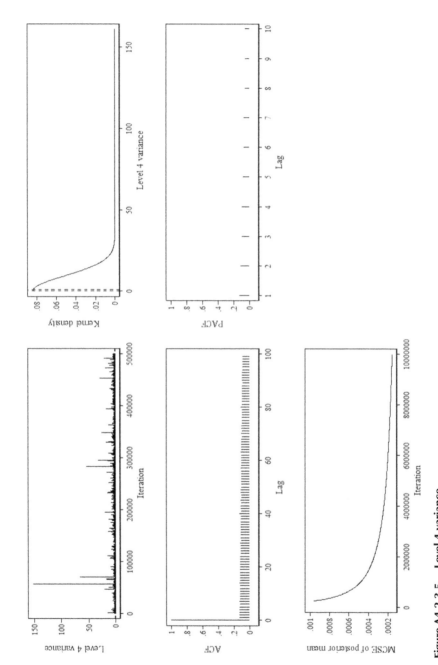

**Figure A4.2.3.5.   Level 4 variance**

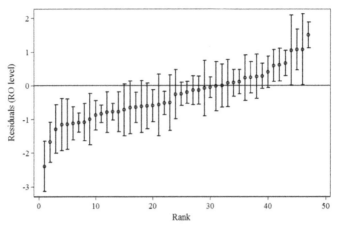

**Figure A4.2.3.6.  Residuals (RO level) 299**

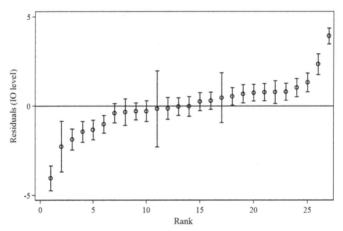

**Figure A4.2.3.7.  Residuals (IO level)**

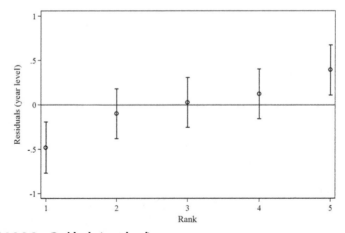

**Figure A4.2.3.8.  Residuals (year level)**

## A4.2.4. Model 4

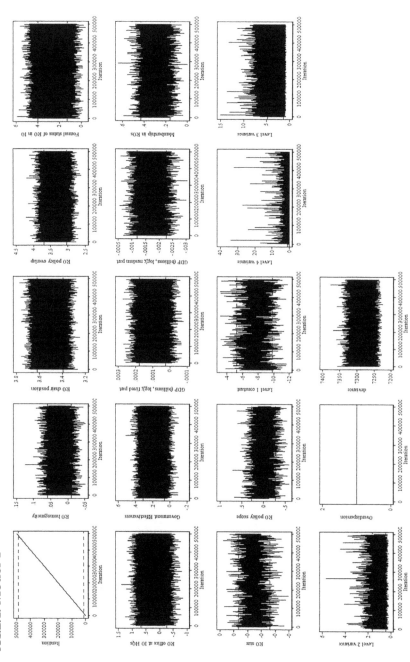

**Figure A4.2.4.1.  Trajectories**

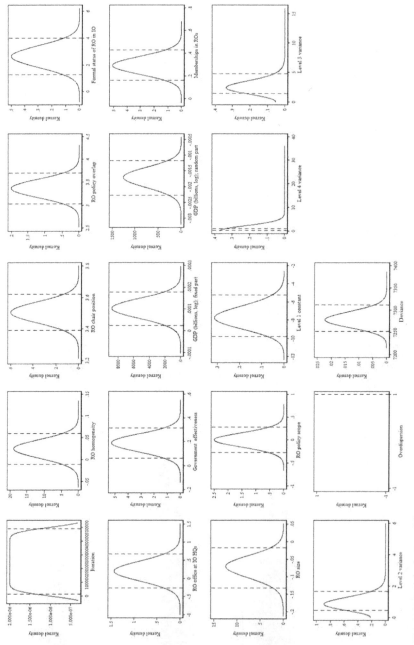

**Figure A4.2.4.2.** Densities

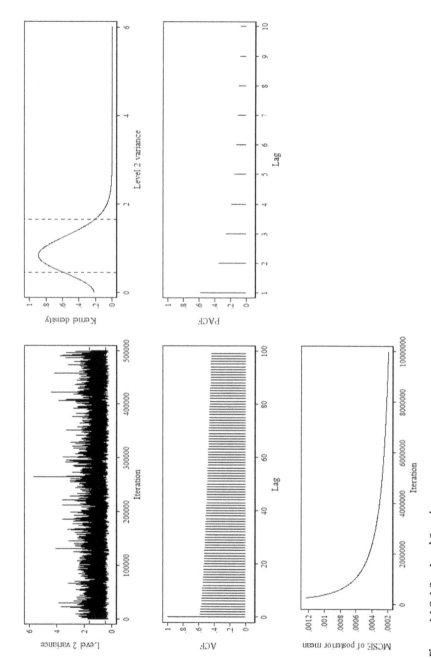

**Figure A4.2.4.3.   Level 2 variance**

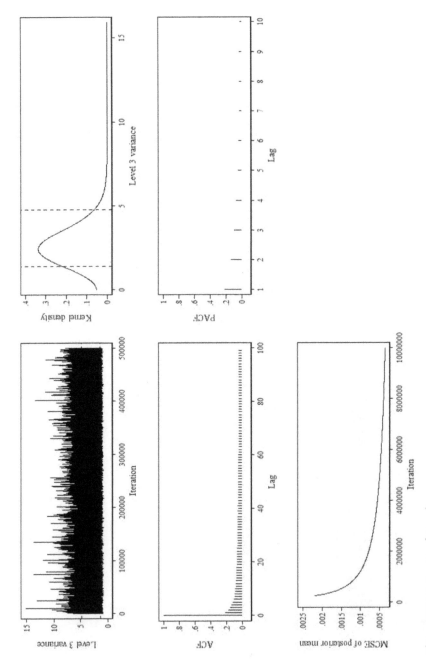

**Figure A4.2.4.4.** Level 3 variance

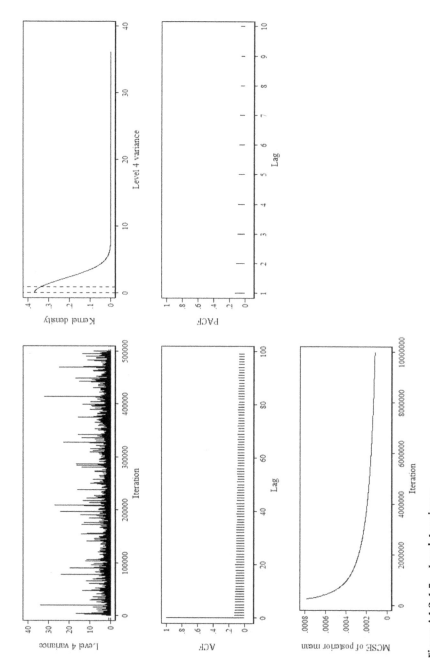

**Figure A4.2.4.5. Level 4 variance**

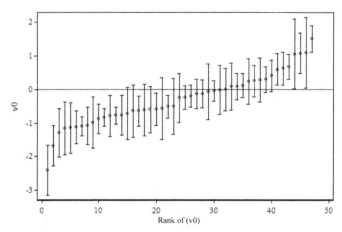

**Figure A4.2.4.6.** **Residuals (RO level)**

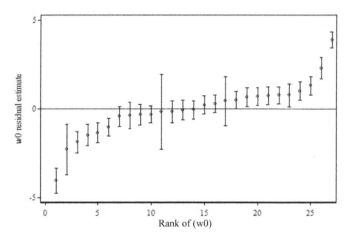

**Figure A4.2.4.7.** **Residuals (IO level)**

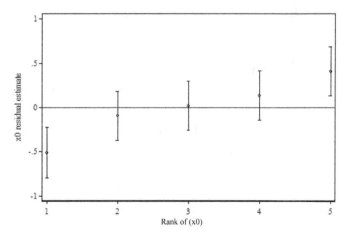

**Figure A4.2.4.8.** **Residuals (year level)**

## A4.2.5. Model 5

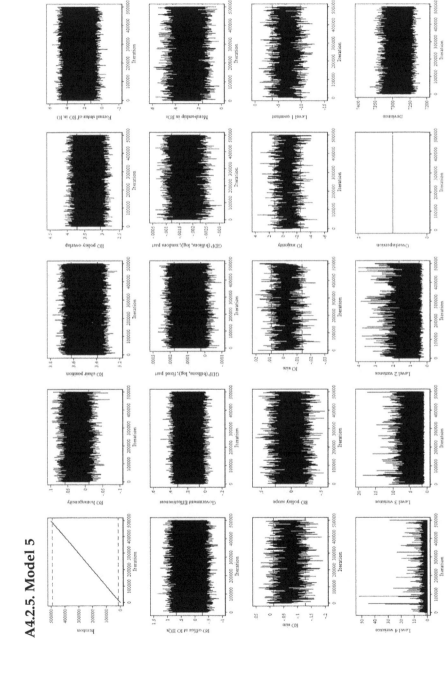

**Figure A4.2.5.1. Trajectories**

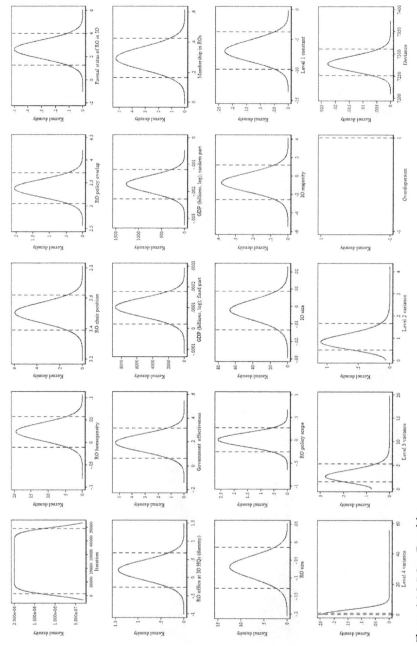

**Figure A4.2.5.2.    Densities**

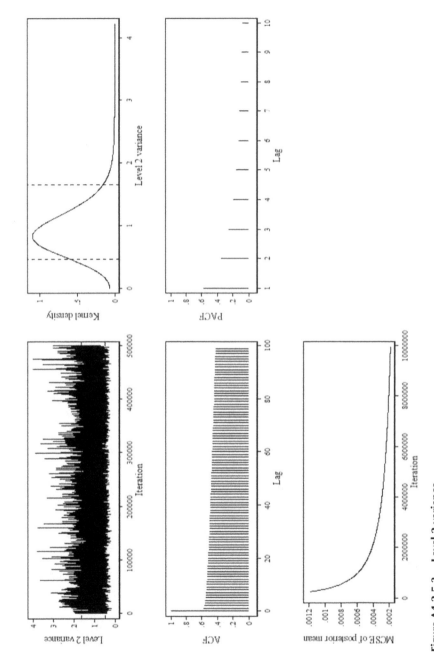

**Figure A4.2.5.3.    Level 2 variance**

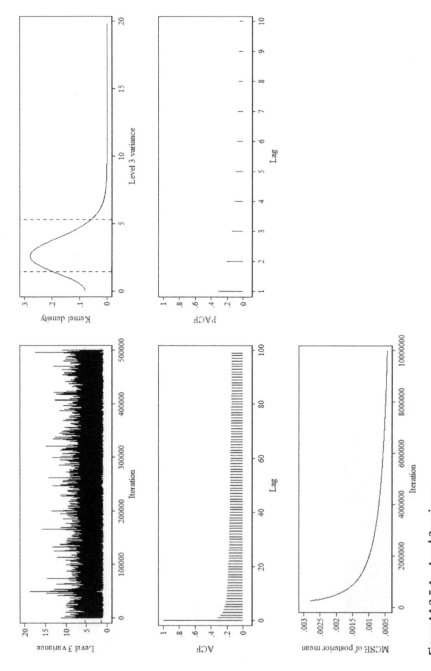

**Figure A4.2.5.4.** Level 3 variance

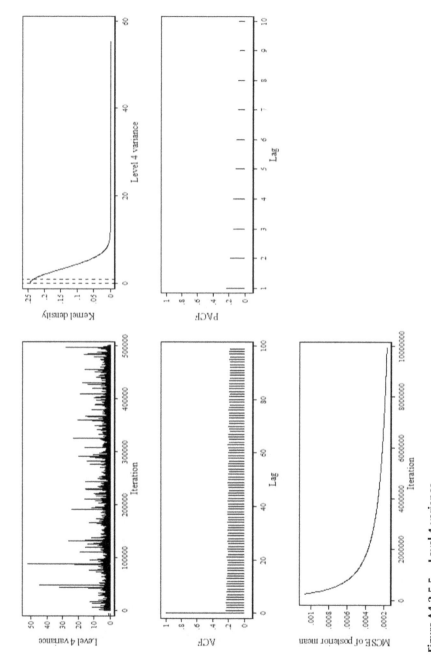

**Figure A4.2.5.5.   Level 4 variance**

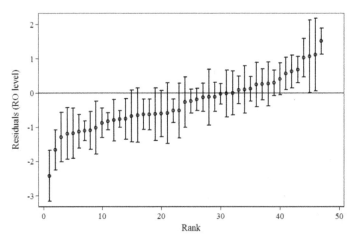

**Figure A4.2.5.6.** **Residuals (RO level)**

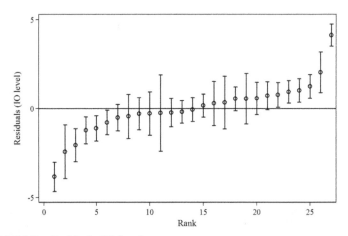

**Figure A4.2.5.7.** **Residuals (IO level)**

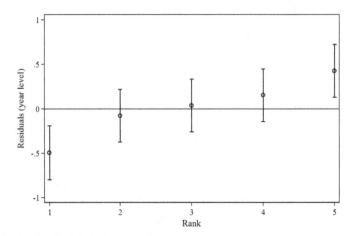

**Figure A4.2.5.8.** **Residuals (year level)**

## A4.2.6. Model 6

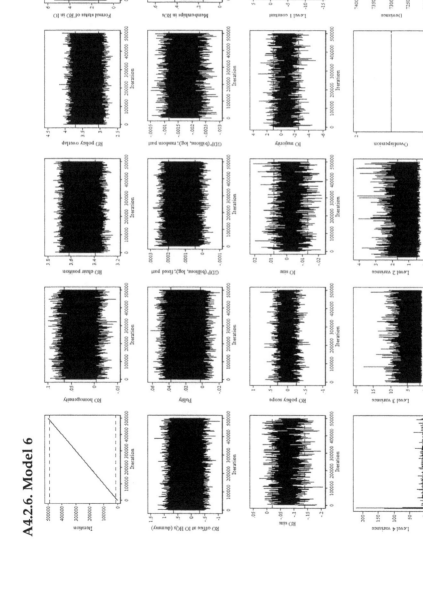

**Figure A4.2.6.1. Trajectories**

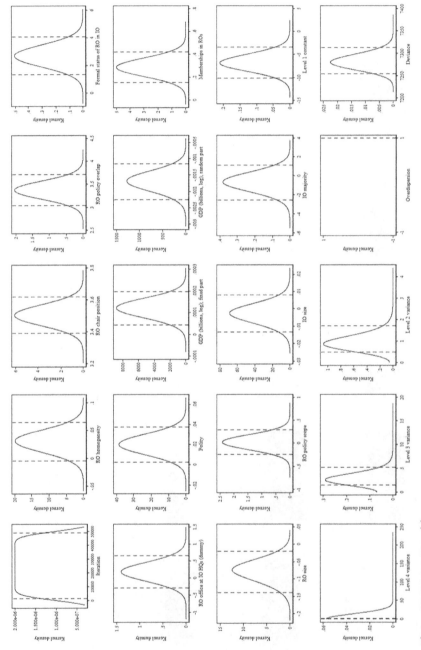

**Figure A4.2.6.2. Densities**

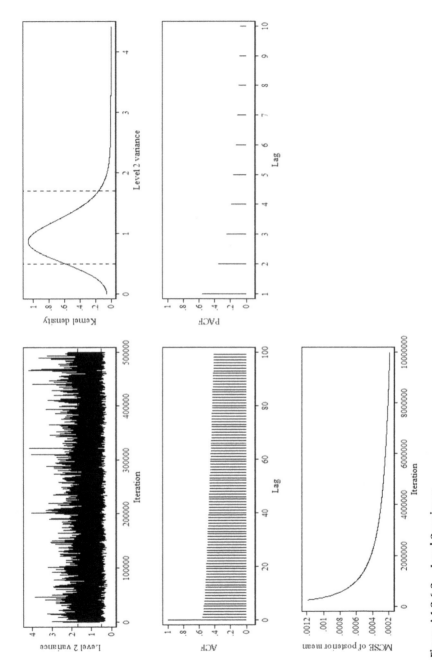

**Figure A4.2.6.3.** Level 2 variance

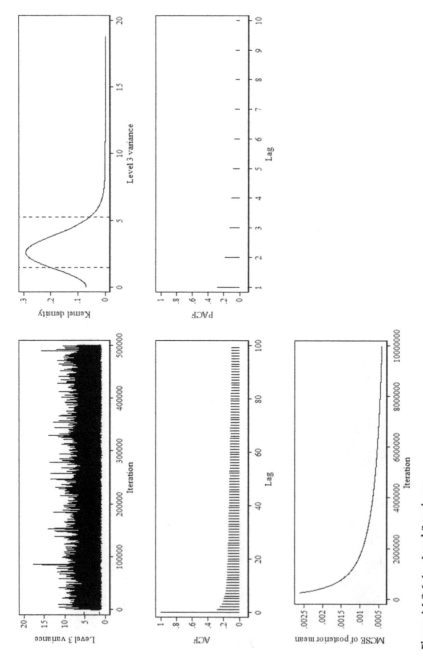

**Figure A4.2.6.4.** Level 3 variance

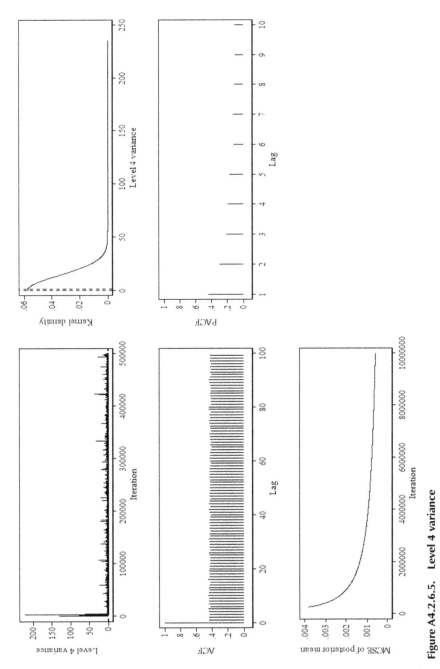

**Figure A4.2.6.5.    Level 4 variance**

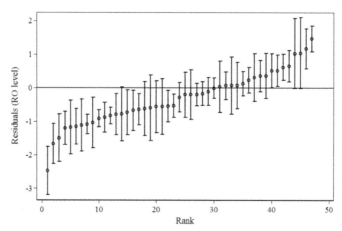

**Figure A4.2.6.6.    Residuals (RO level)**

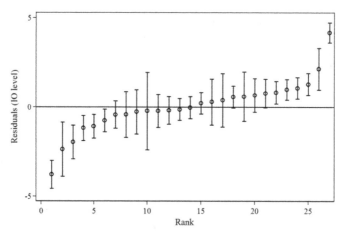

**Figure A4.2.6.7.    Residuals (IO level)**

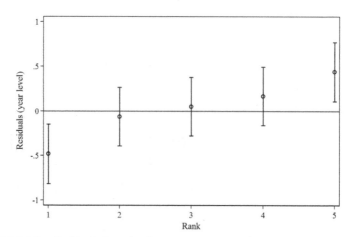

**Figure A4.2.6.8.    Residuals (year level)**

# A4.3 OUTLIER ANALYSIS FOR COMPREHENSIVE MULTILEVEL MODELS

**Table A4.3.1.** Multilevel regression results (outlier)

| | Model 1 | Model 2 | Model 3 | Model 4 | Model 5 | Model 6 |
|---|---|---|---|---|---|---|
| Government effectiveness | | 0.228** | | 0.222** | 0.216* | |
| | | (0.086) | | (0.084) | (0.0842) | |
| Polity | | | 0.028* | | | 0.028* |
| | | | (0.012) | | | (0.012) |
| GDP (billions, log); fixed part | –0.000 | –0.000 | –0.000 | –0.000 | –0.000 | |
| | (0.000) | (0.000) | (0.000) | (0.000) | (0.000) | |
| GDP (billions, log); random part | –0.002*** | –0.002*** | –0.001*** | –0.001*** | –0.002*** | |
| | (0.000) | (0.000) | (0.000) | (0.000) | (0.000) | |
| Membership in ROs | –0.157 | –0.185 | –0.198* | –0.195* | –0.211* | |
| | (0.087) | (0.098) | (0.097) | (0.099) | (0.095) | |
| RO size | | | –0.016 | –0.018 | –0.02 | |
| | | | (0.024) | (0.024) | (0.024) | |
| RO policy scope | | | 0.03 | 0.029 | 0.063 | |
| | | | (0.114) | (0.115) | (0.12) | |
| IO size | | | | –0.005 | –0.004 | |
| | | | | (0.004) | (0.00416) | |
| IO majority | | | | –0.812 | –0.852 | |
| | | | | (0.693) | (0.640) | |
| Homogeneity of ROs | 0.036* | 0.069** | 0.086*** | 0.074** | 0.076** | 0.088*** |
| | (0.018) | (0.022) | (0.021) | (0.024) | (0.024) | (0.023) |
| RO chair position | 3.52*** | 3.538*** | 3.532*** | 3.534*** | 3.536*** | 3.528*** |
| | (0.102) | (0.103) | (0.103) | (0.101) | (0.101) | (0.101) |
| RO policy overlap | 2.765*** | 2.843*** | 2.872*** | 2.842*** | 2.858*** | 2.876*** |
| | (0.198) | (0.196) | (0.197) | (0.196) | (0.198) | (0.205) |
| Formal status of RO in IO | –2.559* | –2.400 | –2.473* | –2.425* | –2.397 | –2.442* |
| | (1.21) | (1.228) | (1.244) | (1.226) | (1.249) | (1.244) |
| RO office at IO headquarters | –0.968** | –0.968** | –0.944** | –0.947** | –0.944** | –0.927** |
| | (0.325) | (0.330) | (0.329) | (0.327) | (0.329) | (0.332) |
| Intercept | –10.21*** | –9.816*** | –9.896*** | –8.965*** | –6.460* | –7.913*** |
| | (0.475) | (0.506) | (0.482) | (1.775) | (2.664) | (1.422) |

*(Continued)*

**Table A4.3.1. Continued**

|  | Model 1 | Model 2 | Model 3 | Model 4 | Model 5 | Model 6 |
|---|---|---|---|---|---|---|
| Level 2 variance | 0.271* | 0.329** | 0.370** | 0.379* | 0.388** | 0.409** |
|  | (0.107) | (0.126) | (0.140) | (0.149) | (0.146) | (0.155) |
| Level 3 variance | 1.579** | 1.648** | 1.651** | 1.659** | 1.580** | 1.595** |
|  | (0.570) | (0.596) | (0.592) | (0.609) | (0.599) | (0.611) |
| Level 4 variance | 0.0481 | 0.0176 | 0.0194 | 3.421 | 12.45 | 0.717 |
|  | (0.371) | (0.043) | (0.041) | (15.42) | (38.71) | (3.512) |
| Overdispersion | 2.054 | 1.911*** | 1.876*** | 1.887*** | 1.907*** | 1.858 |
|  | (.) | (0.000) | (0.000) | (0.000) | (0.000) | (.) |
| N | 16467 | 16467 | 16467 | 16467 | 16467 | 16467 |
| DIC | 4035.1 | 4000.4 | 3999.1 | 3999.4 | 3999.4 | 3998.7 |

Negative binomial regression coefficients; standard errors in parentheses; DIC, Deviance Information Criterion; significance levels are: $^*p < 0.05$, $^{**}p < 0.01$, $^{***}p < 0.001$.

## A4.4 MODEL DIAGNOSTICS FOR OUTLIER ANALYSIS OF COMPREHENSIVE MULTILEVEL MODELS

## A4.4.1. Model 1

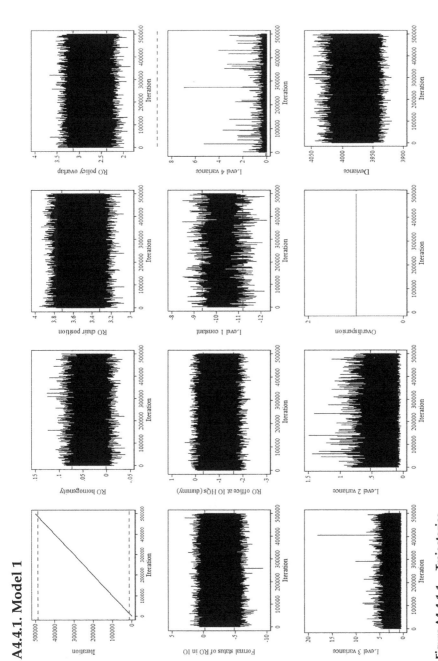

**Figure A4.4.1.1. Trajectories**

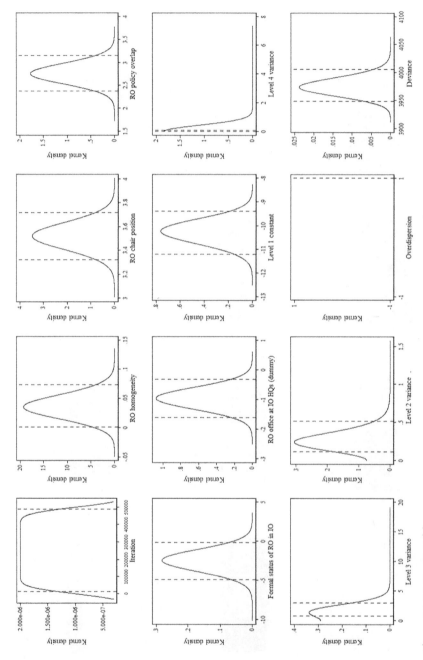

**Figure A4.4.1.2. Densities**

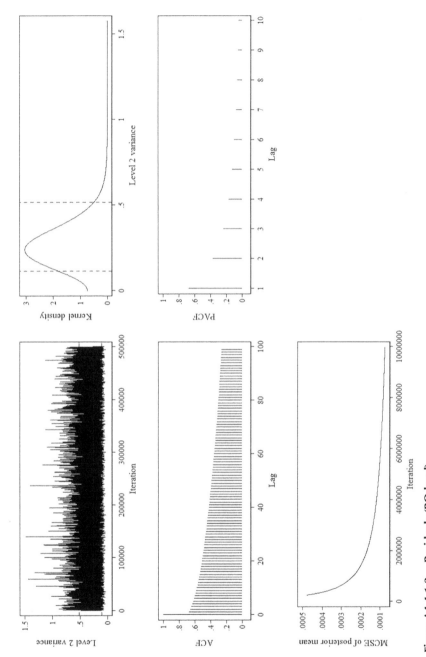

**Figure A4.4.1.3.   Residuals (RO level)**

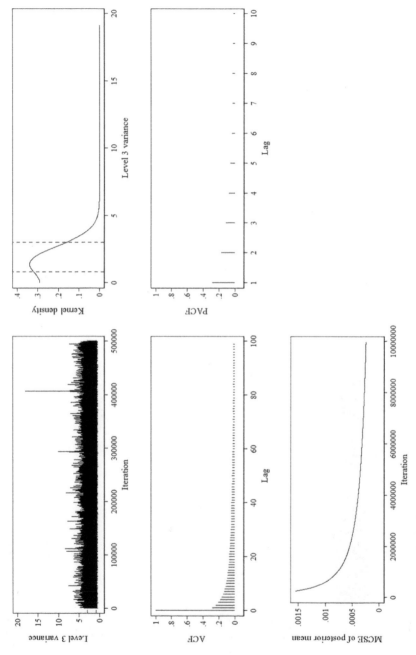

**Figure A4.4.1.4.** Residuals (IO level)

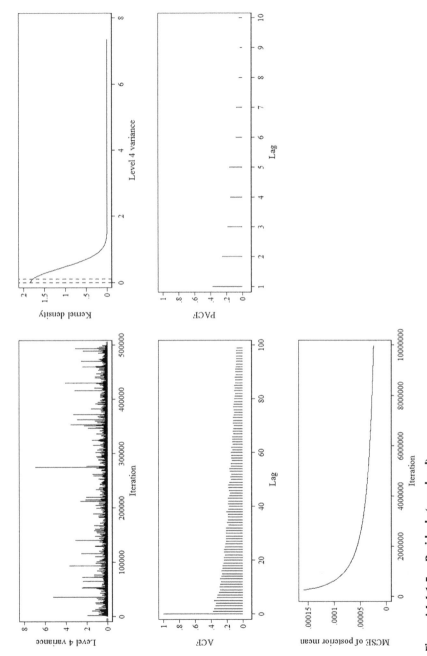

**Figure A4.4.1.5. Residuals (year level)**

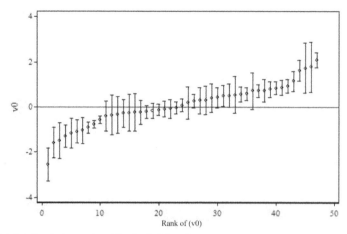

**Figure A4.4.1.6.   Intercept residuals (RO level)**

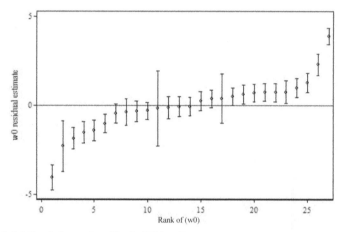

**Figure A4.4.1.7.   Intercept residuals (IO level)**

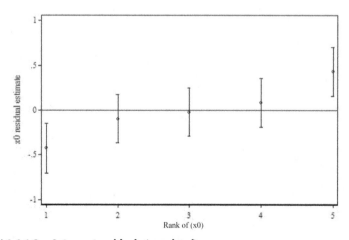

**Figure A4.4.1.8.   Intercept residuals (year level)**

## A4.4.2. Model 2

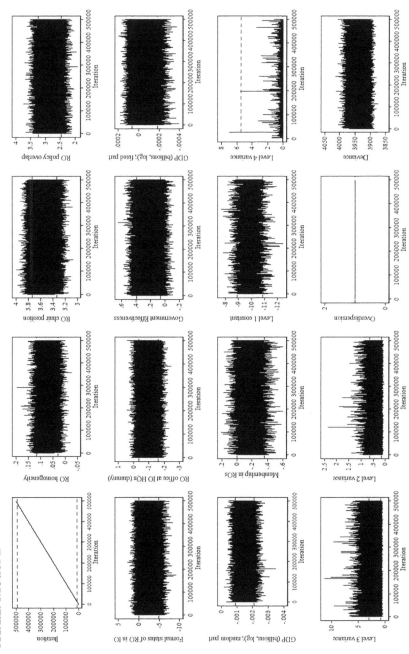

**Figure A4.2.1.  Trajectories**

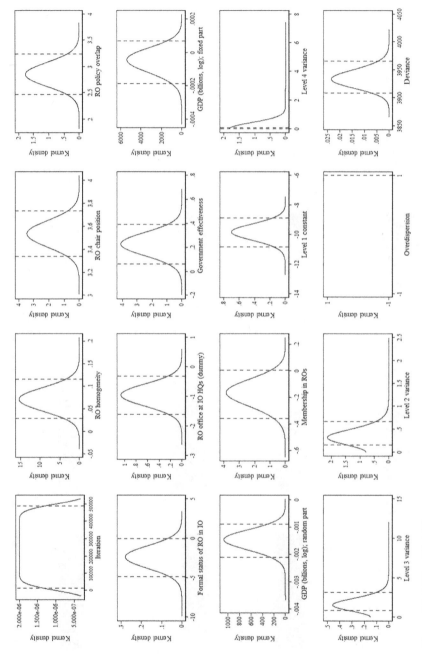

**Figure A4.4.2.2.   Densities**

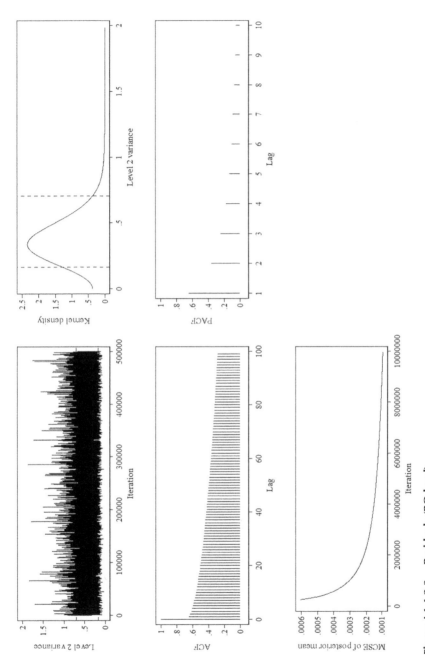

**Figure A4.4.2.3.    Residuals (RO level)**

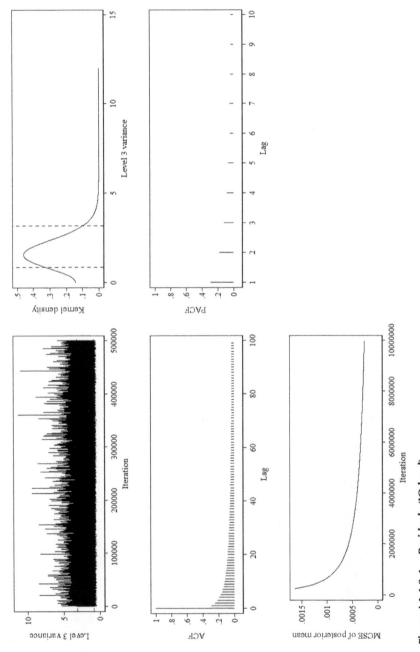

**Figure A4.4.2.4.   Residuals (IO level)**

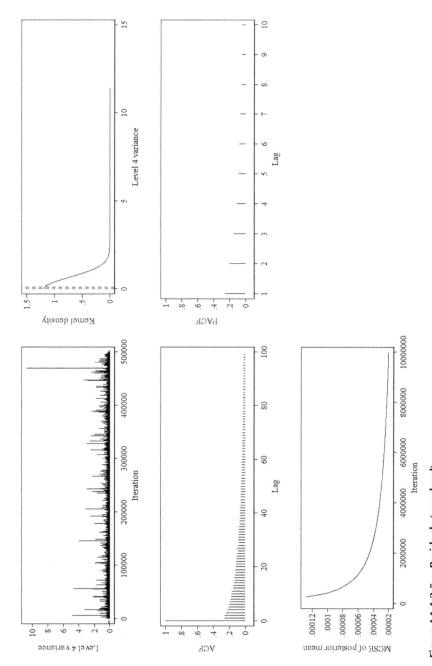

**Figure A4.4.2.5.    Residuals (year level)**

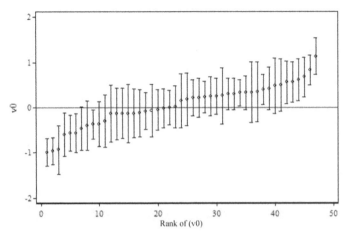

**Figure A4.4.2.6.** Intercept residuals (RO level)

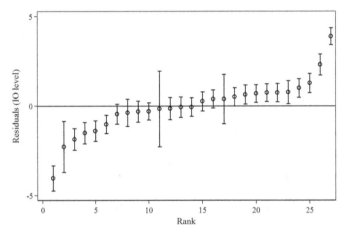

**Figure A4.4.2.7.** Intercept residuals (IO level)

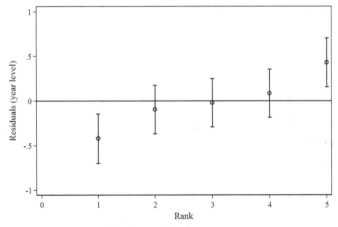

**Figure A4.4.2.8.** Intercept residuals (year level)

# A4.4.3. Model 3

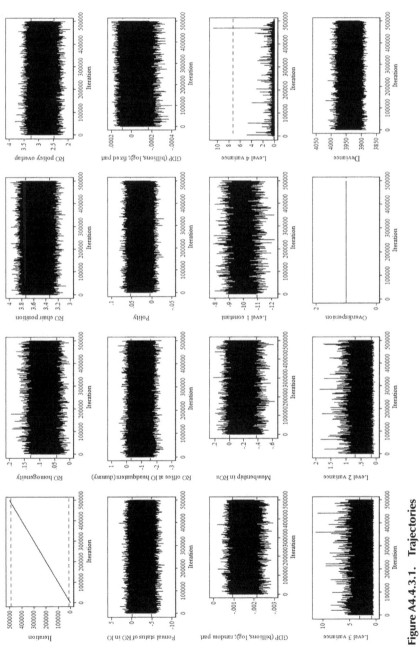

**Figure A4.4.3.1.   Trajectories**

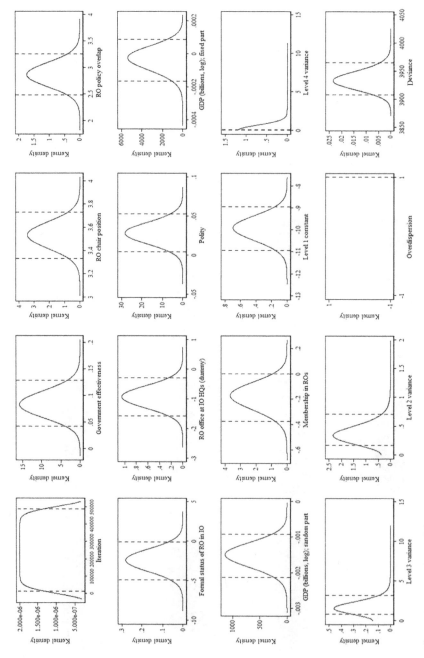

**Figure A4.4.3.2.   Densities**

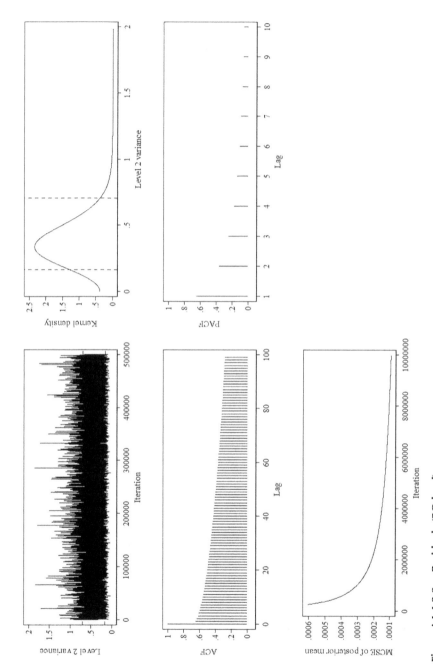

**Figure A4.4.3.3.  Residuals (RO level)**

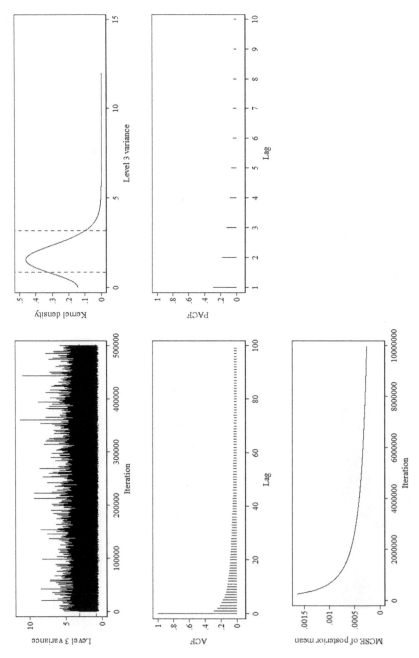

**Figure A4.4.3.4.** Residuals (IO level)

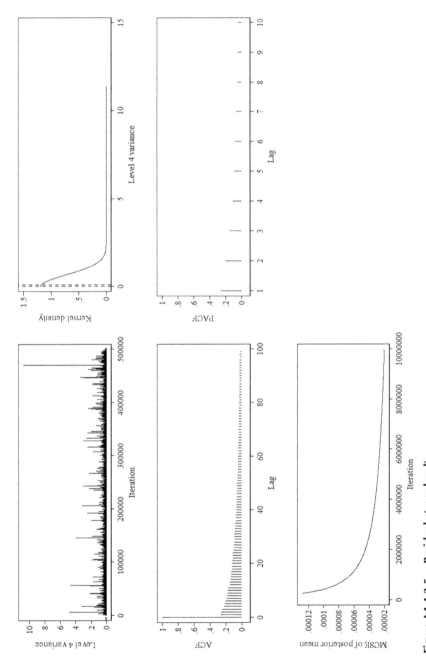

**Figure A4.4.3.5. Residuals (year level)**

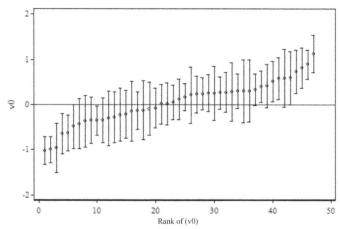

**Figure A4.4.3.6.** Intercept residuals (RO level)

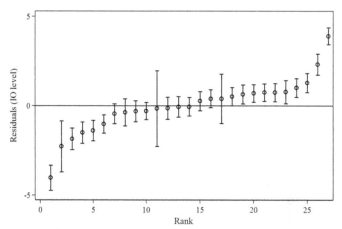

**Figure A4.4.3.7.** Intercept residuals (IO level)

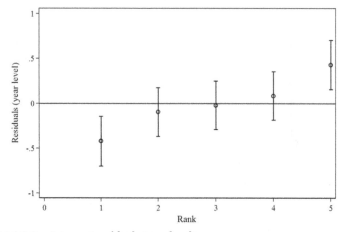

**Figure A4.4.3.8.** Intercept residuals (year level)

## A4.4.4. Model 4

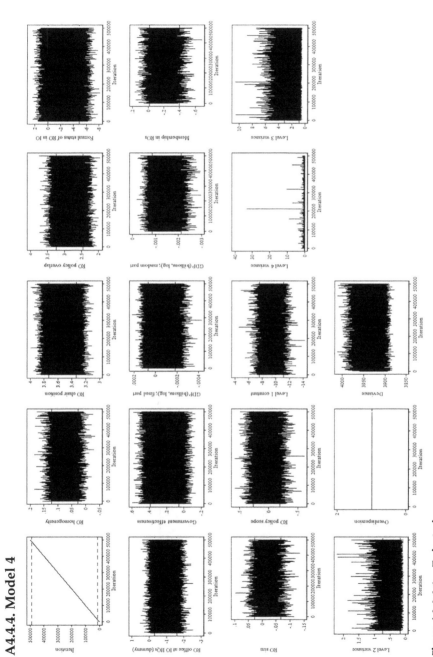

**Figure A4.4.4.1. Trajectories**

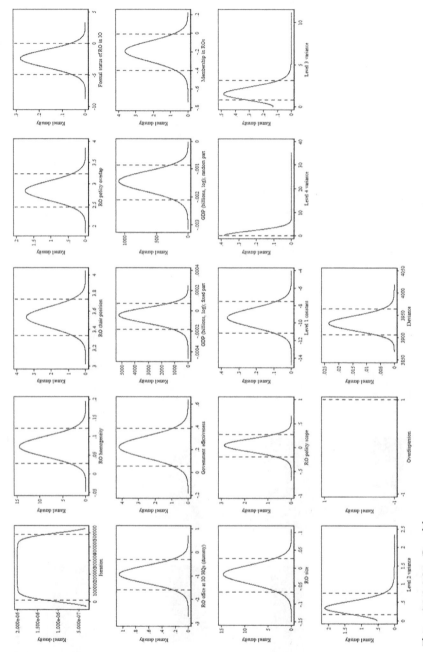

**Figure A4.4.2.** Densities

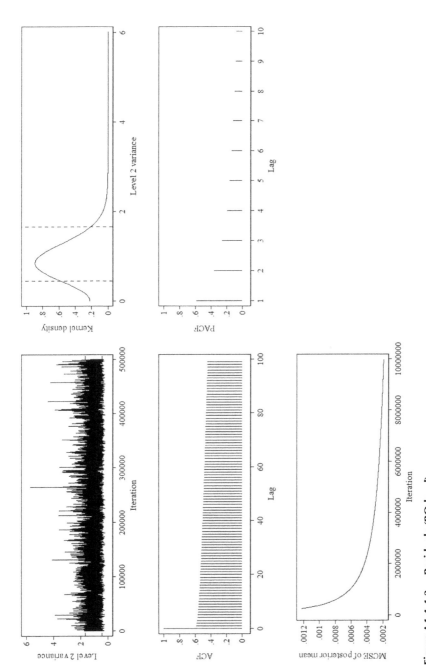

**Figure A4.4.3.** Residuals (RO level)

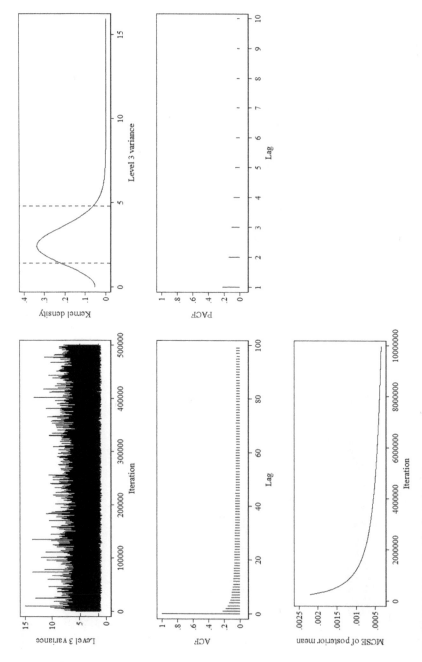

**Figure A4.4.4.4.    Residuals (IO level)**

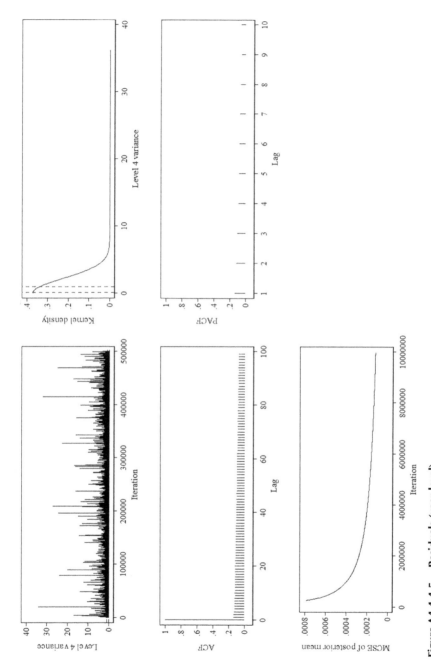

**Figure A4.4.5. Residuals (year level)**

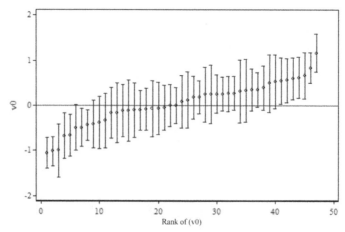

**Figure A4.4.4.6.   Intercept residuals (RO level)**

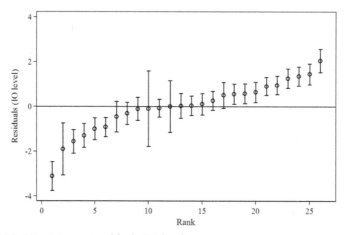

**Figure A4.4.4.7.   Intercept residuals (IO level)**

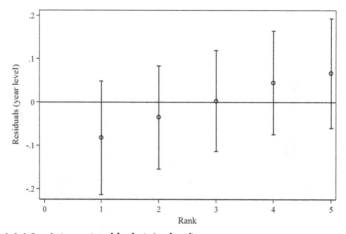

**Figure A4.4.4.8.   Intercept residuals (year level)**

## A4.4.5. Model 5

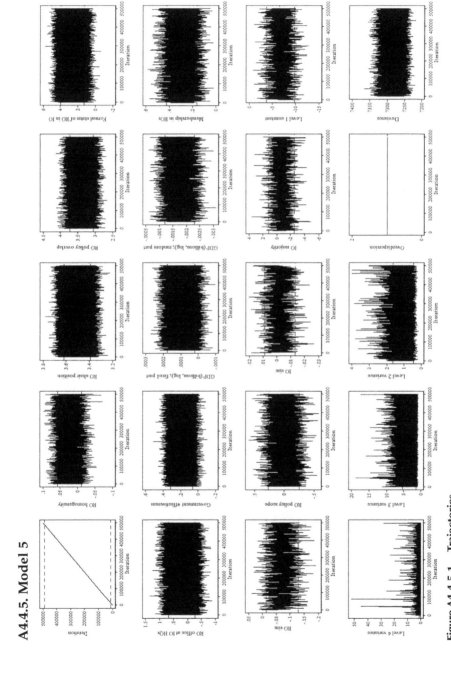

**Figure A4.4.5.1. Trajectories**

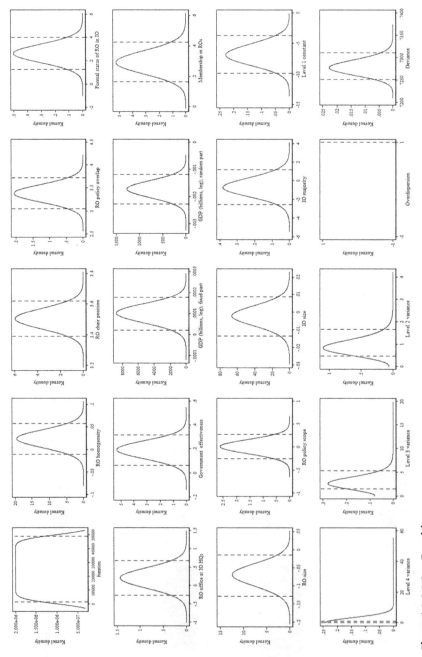

**Figure A4.4.5.2.   Densities**

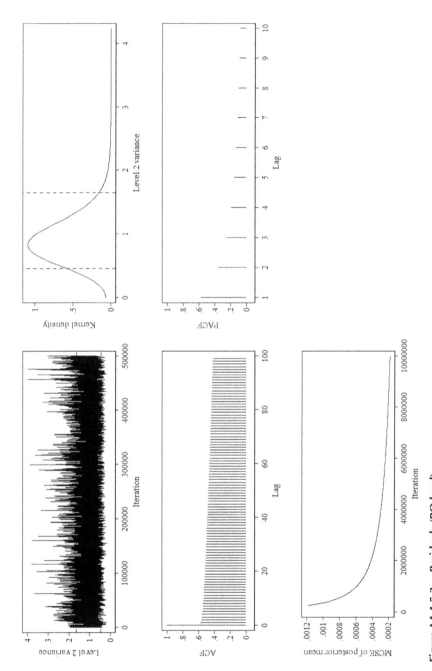

**Figure A4.4.5.3.    Residuals (RO level)**

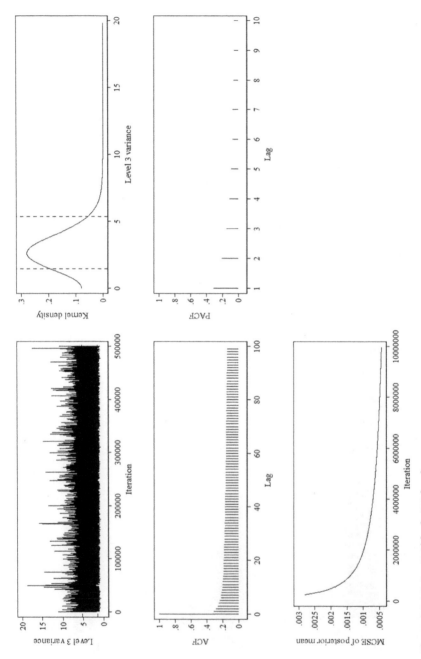

**Figure A4.4.5.4. Residuals (IO level)**

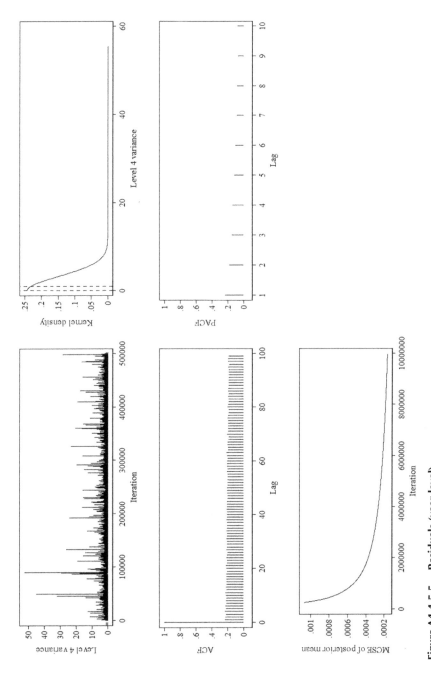

**Figure A4.4.5.5.   Residuals (year level)**

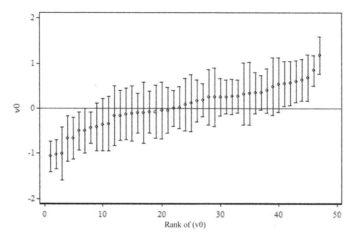

**Figure A4.4.5.6.   Intercept residuals (RO level)**

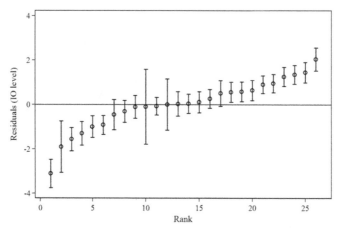

**Figure A4.4.5.7.   Intercept residuals (IO level)**

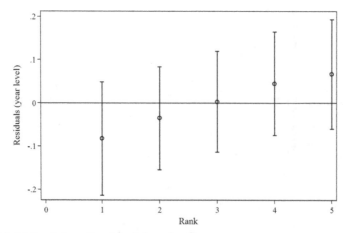

**Figure A4.4.5.8.   Intercept residuals (year level)**

## A4.4.6. Model 6

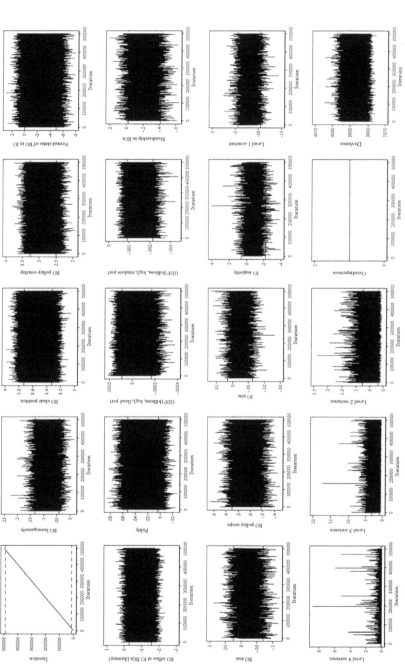

**Figure A4.4.6.1.** Trajectories

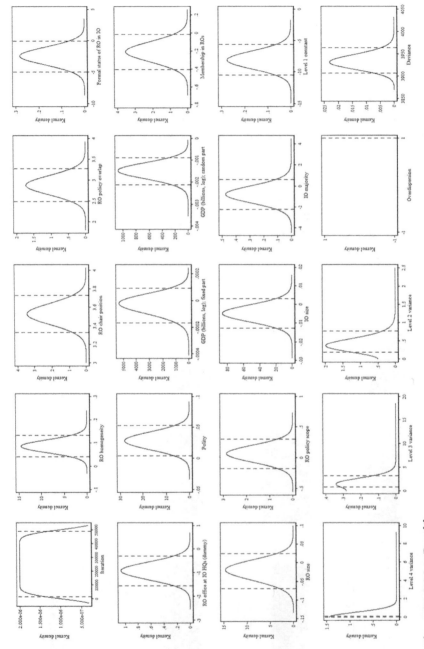

**Figure A4.4.6.2.  Densities**

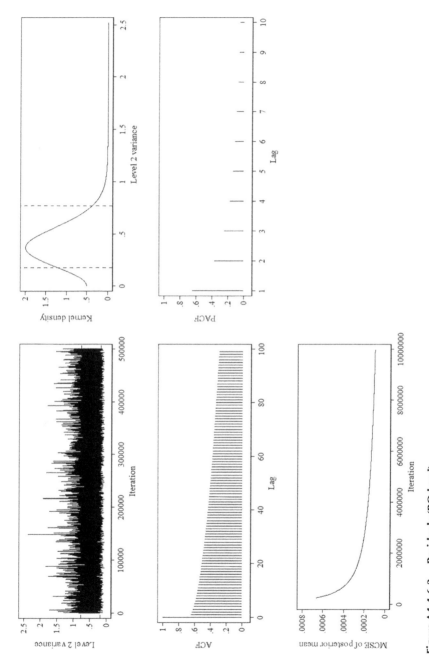

**Figure A4.4.6.3.  Residuals (RO level)**

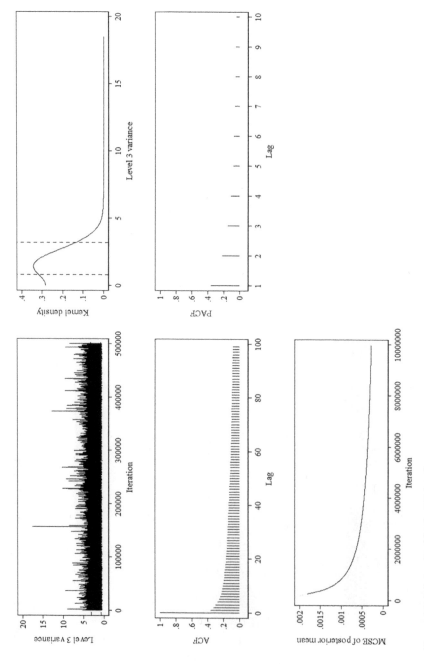

**Figure A4.4.6.4. Residuals (IO level)**

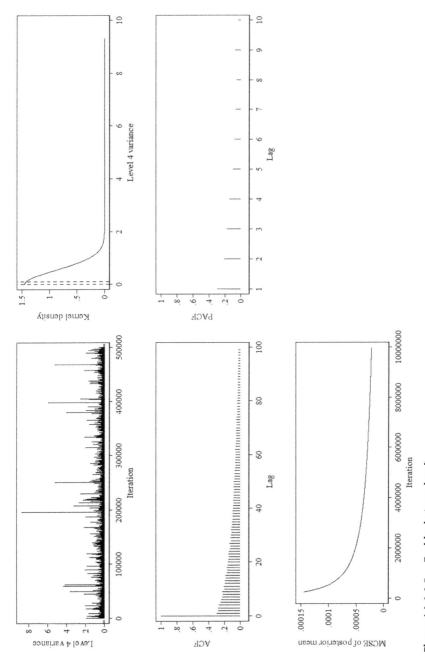

**Figure A4.4.6.5. Residuals (year level)**

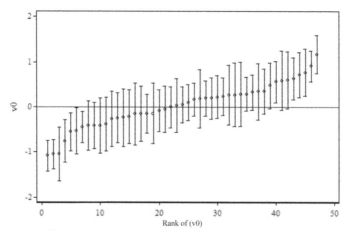

**Figure A4.4.6.6.   Intercept residuals (RO level)**

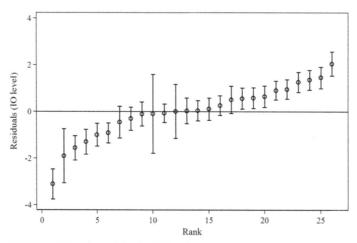

**Figure A4.4.6.7.   Intercept residuals (IO level)**

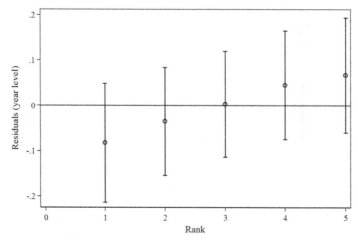

**Figure A4.4.6.8.   Intercept residuals (year level)**

# Annex (Chapter 7)

**Table A7.1.   FAO and WHO regional groups**

| Food and Agriculture Organization (FAO) | |
|---|---|
| *Regional Group* | *Member States* |
| African regional group (AFRICA) | Algeria, Angola, Benin, Botswana, Burkina Faso, Burundi, Cabo Verde, Cameroon, Central African Republic, Chad, Comoros, Congo, Côte d'Ivoire, Democratic Republic of the Congo, Equatorial Guinea, Eritrea, Ethiopia, Gabon, Gambia, Ghana, Guinea, Guinea-Bissau, Kenya, Lesotho, Liberia, Madagascar, Malawi, Mali, Mauritania, Mauritius, Morocco, Mozambique, Namibia, Niger, Nigeria, Rwanda, Sao Tome and Principe, Senegal, Seychelles, Sierra Leone, South Africa, South Sudan, Swaziland, Togo, Tunisia, Uganda, United Republic of Tanzania, Zambia and Zimbabwe |
| European regional group (ERG) | Albania, Andorra, Armenia, Austria, Azerbaijan, Belarus, Belgium, Bosnia and Herzegovina, Bulgaria, Croatia, Cyprus, Czech Republic, Denmark, Estonia, Finland, France, Georgia, Germany, Greece, Hungary, Iceland, Ireland, Israel, Italy, Latvia, Lithuania, Luxembourg, Malta, Monaco, Montenegro, Netherlands, Norway, Poland, Portugal, Republic of Moldova, Romania, Russian Federation, San Marino, Serbia, Slovakia, Slovenia, Spain, Sweden, Switzerland, The former Yugoslav Republic of Macedonia, Turkey, Ukraine and the United Kingdom |

*(Continued)*

**Table A7.1.    Continued**

| Food and Agriculture Organization (FAO) | |
|---|---|
| *Regional Group* | *Member States* |
| Latin America and Caribbean group (GRULAC) | Antigua and Barbuda, Argentina, Bahamas, Barbados, Belize, Bolivia, Brazil, Chile, Colombia, Costa Rica, Cuba, Dominica, Dominican Republic, Ecuador, El Salvador, Grenada, Guatemala, Guyana, Haiti, Honduras, Jamaica, Mexico, Nicaragua, Panama, Paraguay, Peru, Saint Kitts and Nevis, Saint Lucia, Saint Vincent and the Grenadines, Suriname, Trinidad and Tobago, Uruguay and Venezuela (Bolivarian Republic of) |
| Near East regional group (NEEA) | Afghanistan, Bahrain, Djibouti, Egypt, Iran (Islamic Republic of), Iraq, Jordan, Kuwait, Kyrgyzstan, Lebanon, Libya, Oman, Qatar, Saudi Arabia, Somalia, Sudan, Syrian Arab Republic, Tajikistan, Turkmenistan, United Arab Emirates and Yemen |
| Southwest Pacific group (SWP) | Australia, Cook Islands, Fiji, Kiribati, Marshall Islands, Micronesia (Federated States of), Nauru, New Zealand, Niue, Palau, Papua New Guinea, Samoa, Solomon Islands, Tonga, Tuvalu and Vanuatu |
| North America group (NOAM) | Canada, United States of America |
| **World Health Organization (WHO)** | |
| **Regional Group** | **Member States** |
| European Region (EUR) | Albania, Andorra, Armenia, Austria, Azerbaijan, Belarus, Belgium, Bosnia and Herzegovina, Bulgaria, Croatia, Cyprus, Czech Republic, Denmark, Estonia, Finland, France, Georgia, Germany, Greece, Hungary, Iceland, Ireland, Israel, Italy, Kazakhstan, Kyrgyzstan, Latvia, Lithuania, Luxembourg, Malta, Monaco, Montenegro, Netherlands, Norway, Poland, Portugal, Republic of Moldova, Romania, Russian Federation, San Marino, Serbia, Slovakia, Slovenia, Spain, Sweden, Switzerland, Tajikistan, The former Yugoslav Republic of Macedonia, Turkey, Turkmenistan, Ukraine, United Kingdom and Uzbekistan |
| African Region group (AFR) | Algeria, Angola, Benin, Botswana, Burkina Faso, Burundi, Cameroon, Cabo Verde, Central African Republic, Chad, Comoros, Congo, Côte d'Ivoire, Democratic Republic of the Congo, Equatorial Guinea, Eritrea, Ethiopia, Gabon, Gambia, Ghana, Guinea, Guinea-Bissau, Kenya, Lesotho, Liberia, Madagascar, Malawi, Mali, Mauritania, Mauritius, Mozambique, Namibia, Niger, Nigeria, Rwanda, Sao Tome and Principe, Senegal, Seychelles, Sierra Leone, South Africa, South Sudan, Swaziland, Togo, Uganda, United Republic of Tanzania, Zambia and Zimbabwe |

| Food and Agriculture Organization (FAO) | |
|---|---|
| *Regional Group* | *Member States* |
| Region of the Americas (AMR) | Antigua and Barbuda, Argentina, Bahamas, Barbados, Belize, Bolivia, Brazil, Canada, Chile, Colombia, Costa Rica, Cuba, Dominica, Dominican Republic, Ecuador, El Salvador, Grenada, Guatemala, Guyana, Haiti, Honduras, Jamaica, Mexico, Nicaragua, Panama, Paraguay, Peru, Saint Kitts and Nevis, Saint Lucia, Saint Vincent and the Grenadines, Suriname, Trinidad and Tobago, United States of America, Uruguay and Venezuela (Bolivarian Republic of) |
| Western Pacific Region group (WPR) | Australia, Brunei Darussalam, Cambodia, China, Cook Islands, Fiji, Japan, Kiribati, Lao People's Democratic Republic, Malaysia, Marshall Islands, Micronesia (Federated States of), Mongolia, Nauru, New Zealand, Niue, Palau, Papua New Guinea, Philippines, Republic of Korea, Samoa, Singapore, Solomon Islands, Tonga, Tuvalu, Vanuatu, Vietnam |
| Eastern Mediterranean Region group (EMR) | Afghanistan, Bahrain, Djibouti, Egypt, Iran (Islamic Republic of), Iraq, Jordan, Kuwait, Lebanon, Libya, Morocco, Oman, Pakistan, Qatar, Saudi Arabia, Somalia, Sudan, Syrian Arab Republic, Tunisia, United Arab Emirates and Yemen |
| South-East Asia Region (SEAR) | Bangladesh, Bhutan, Democratic People's Republic of Korea, India, Indonesia, Maldives, Myanmar, Nepal, Sri Lanka, Thailand and Timor-Leste |

# Index

*Note:* Page references for figures are italicized.

405

# About the Authors

**Diana Panke** holds the Chair in 'Multi-Level Governance' at University of Freiburg and is the PI of the research project 'Nested Games. Regional Organizations in International Organizations'. Her research interests include international negotiations, comparative regionalism, small states in international affairs, multilateral diplomacy, international norms, institutional design, European Union politics as well as compliance and legalization. In these fields, she has published several monographs and journal articles in outlets such as the *Review of International Organizations, International Political Science Review, European Journal of International Relations, British Journal of Politics and International Relations, Comparative Political Studies, Cooperation and Conflict, Journal of Common Market Studies, Journal of European Public Policy, Journal of European Integration* and ECPR Press.

**Stefan Lang** is a PhD candidate at the University of Freiburg. His research interests include international negotiations, regionalism as well as domestic conflicts and interventions. He specialized in quantitative methods. Since November 2013 Lang works a research associate in the project 'Nested Games. Regional Organizations in International Organizations'. His publications have appeared in the *British Journal of Politics and International Relations, Journal of International Relations and Development* and *Global Affairs*.

**Anke Wiedemann** is a PhD candidate at the University of Freiburg. Her research interests include comparative regionalism, interregionalism and international negotiations. She specialized in qualitative methods. Wiedemann

411

works as a research associate in the project 'Nested Games. Regional Organizations in International Organizations' since October 2013. Her publications have appeared in the *British Journal of Politics and International Relations*, *Journal of International Relations and Development* and *Global Affairs*.

Lightning Source UK Ltd.
Milton Keynes UK
UKHW03n1952260418
321712UK00001B/24/P